Regional Aviation Safety Organisations

Aviation Law and Policy Series

Volume 10

Series Editor

Pablo Mendes de Leon

International Institute of Air and Space Law, Leiden University

The global liberalization regime of the past two decades has fundamentally affected the operation of international air transport services.

This process calls for reflection and analysis across a wide range of legal and policy areas, including but not limited to public international air law and policy, with special reference to safety, security and environmental concerns, liability, competition law regimes, company law, and the complex relationship between European Community law and public international law.

The *Aviation Law and Policy Series* critically examines developments around liberalization of air services internationally resulting in the establishment of Open Aviation Areas; institutional questions such as the external powers of the European Community and the relationship between international organizations such as ICAO and EUROCONTROL; the coming into force of unlimited liability regimes and related case law; the granting of antitrust immunity to international airline alliances; and cooperation between competition authorities. Attention will also be paid to topical safety and security issues, and the growing impact of aviation in relation to the environment, dictating the design of emission trade systems. Last but not least, commercially oriented subjects such as aircraft financing and leasing will be addressed, both from the perspective of national and international legal regimes, taking into account practical cases and case law.

The objective of the *series* is to make a contribution to legal thinking on the multifaceted aspects of this important field of law. The publications are designed to document and anticipate the evolution of aviation law and policy in the twenty-first century.

The titles published in this series are listed in the back of this volume.

Regional Aviation Safety Organisations

Enhancing Air Transport Safety through Regional Cooperation

Mikołaj Ratajczyk

Wolters Kluwer
Law & Business

Published by:
Kluwer Law International
PO Box 316
2400 AH Alphen aan den Rijn
The Netherlands
Website: www.kluwerlaw.com

Sold and distributed in North, Central and South America by:
Aspen Publishers, Inc.
7201 McKinney Circle
Frederick, MD 21704
United States of America
Email: customer.service@aspenpublishers.com

Sold and distributed in all other countries by:
Turpin Distribution Services Ltd
Stratton Business Park
Pegasus Drive, Biggleswade
Bedfordshire SG18 8TQ
United Kingdom
Email: kluwerlaw@turpin-distribution.com

Printed on acid-free paper.

ISBN 978-90-411-5861-1

Printed and Bound by CPI Group (UK) Ltd, Croydon, CR0 4YY.

With love, to Sarah and Martha

About the Author

Mikołaj Ratajczyk (Ph.D.) was born on 6 September 1978 in Warsaw, Poland. He graduated from the Warsaw University as a Master of Law and Administration in 2002, and subsequently completed postgraduate studies in civil aviation management at the National Academy of Defense in Warsaw. He obtained his doctorate degree in 2014 from the International Institute of Air and Space Law of the Leiden University.

In 2003, he joined the Polish Civil Aviation Authority where he worked in positions of increasing responsibility until 2006, when he was seconded to the Air Transport Directorate of the European Commission and where he dealt with development of policy and legislation related to air accident investigations, occurrence reporting and international safety information exchange programmes.

In 2011, he worked for the Polish Presidency of the European Union, and was involved in chairing the Aviation Working Group of the EU Council. In 2012 he joined the European Aviation Safety Agency, and is currently involved in supporting the European Commission in developing a new aviation safety policy for the EU.

Mikołaj is a member of the European Air Law Association (EALA), and periodically lectures on aviation safety law at the International Institute of Air and Space Law of the Leiden University. He has published articles on aviation related topics in Polish and international aviation law periodicals, and presented papers on aviation safety at international conferences.

Table of Contents

Foreword

In 2014, the international aviation community celebrated the 70th anniversary of the signing of the Chicago Convention. During this time, safety has been, and remains, the primary objective for ICAO, regulators and industry in the development of civil aviation. The current safety record of the air transport sector is the result of concerted and tireless efforts of aviation safety professionals all over the world. With global aviation traffic predicted to double in the next twenty years, increased efforts are needed today in order to maintain and further improve the safety performance of civil aviation, especially in regions with higher than average accident rates.

While the concept of Regional Aviation Safety Organisations, which is the subject matter of this book, was not foreseen in 1944, the Chicago Convention has proven to be flexible enough to accommodate their development. ICAO has played an instrumental role in actively promoting regional cooperation in civil aviation for many years now, including, with respect to safety, and has always seen such cooperation as a valuable tool for achieving effective and harmonised implementation of the International Standards and Recommended Practices contained in the 19 Annexes to the Chicago Convention.

The last five years in particular have seen a number of important developments related to the promotion of regional cooperation, where ICAO has taken a leadership role. Perhaps foremost among these, and indeed a turning point for global aviation, was the 2010 ICAO Council endorsement of the new Policy and Framework for Regional Cooperation. It formalised the collaborative basis between ICAO and regional aviation safety bodies, both in the technical and policy aspects of international civil aviation. This new policy is currently being implemented by ICAO through arrangements with regional organisations and regional civil aviation bodies, many of which have established specialised regional safety agencies dealing with regulatory oversight or aircraft accident investigations.

In 2011, ICAO further hosted its first Symposium on Regional Aviation Safety Organisations, which reconfirmed the value of this approach for States and industry alike. ICAO has also been supporting States at a very practical level, for example by publishing manuals on the functioning of Regional Aviation Safety Organisations, as well as disseminating best practices. I am confident that ICAO will continue to play an active role in promoting these organisations, which can be seen as an alternative solution to nationally-based safety oversight and play a strategic role in aviation's ever more global safety planning.

All of the above considerations make this work by Dr Mikołaj Ratajczyk a very timely contribution to discussions on the value of regional cooperation in civil aviation safety, not to mention the challenges that States and Regional Aviation Safety Organisations encounter in the design and functioning of such bodies. This study, which is the first comprehensive book available on this topic, not only provides an overview of the current state of play with regard to regional cooperation on civil aviation safety, but also analyses the place of Regional Aviation Safety Organisations in the international legal framework. In doing so, the work of Dr Ratajczyk provides valuable food for thought on the future role of such organisations, and the concepts which underpin them, in the global governance of air transport. This study also reflects on the basic principles of the Chicago Convention, which remain the basis for the safe and orderly development of air transport.

Mr Ratajczyk's *Regional Aviation Safety Organisations* is comprehensive in scope and greatly benefits from the practical experience of the author, who has worked in national as well as EU aviation administrations – including the European Aviation Safety Agency and the European Commission. It will doubtlessly be of considerable interest to safety management professionals, officials of aviation authorities, legal practitioners and scholars of international aviation law.

Raymond Benjamin
Secretary General
International Civil Aviation Organization
May 2015

List of Figures

List of Tables

List of Abbreviations

AAMAC	Civil Aviation Authorities of Africa and Madagascar (Autorités Africaines et Malgache de l'Aviation Civile)
AASL	Annals of Air and Space Law
ACAAC	Association of Civil Aviation Authorities of the Caribbean
ACAC	Arab Civil Aviation Commission
ACSA	Central American Aviation Safety Agency (Agencia Centroamérica para la Seguridad Aeronáutica)
AD	Airworthiness Directive
AFCAC	African Civil Aviation Commission
AFI-CIS	AFI – Cooperative Inspector Scheme
AIP	Aeronautical Information Publication
AMC	Acceptable Means of Compliance
AMO	Approved Maintenance Organisation
ANC	Air Navigation Commission
ANS	Air Navigation Services
ANSP	Air Navigation Service Provider
AOC	Air Operator's Certificate
ASA	Air Services Agreement
ASECNA	Agency for Aerial Navigation Safety in Africa and Madagascar (l'Agence pour la Sécurité de la Navigation Aérienne en Afrique et à Madagascar)
ASL	Air and Space Law
ASSA-AC	Central African Aviation Safety Oversight Agency (Agence de Supervision de la Sécurité Aérienne en Afrique Centrale)
ATM	Air Traffic Management
AU	African Union
BAGAIA	Banjul Accord Group Accident Investigation Agency
BAGASOO	Banjul Accord Group Aviation Safety Oversight Organisation
BASA	Bilateral Aviation Safety Agreement
CAA	Civil Aviation Authority

CARICOM	Caribbean Community
CASA	Civil Aviation Safety Authority of Australia
CASSOA	Civil Aviation Safety and Security Oversight Agency
CASSOS	Caribbean Aviation Safety and Security Oversight System
CE	Critical Element of State Safety Oversight
CEMAC	Economic Community of Central African States (Communauté Economique et Monétaire de l' Afrique Centrale)
CEPS	Centre for European Policy Studies
CFR	Code of Federal Regulations
CIS	Commonwealth of Independent States
CJEU	Court of Justice of the European Union
CMA	Continuous Monitoring Approach
CMLR	Common Market Law Review
COSCAP	Cooperative Development of Operational Safety and Continuing Airworthiness Programme
CS	Certification Specification
CSA	Comprehensive Systems Approach
DARIO	Draft Articles on Responsibility of International Organizations
DASR	Draft Articles on State Responsibility
DOA	Design Organisation Approval
EAA	European Aviation Authority
EAC	East African Community
EASA	European Aviation Safety Agency
ECAC	European Civil Aviation Conference
ECCAA	Eastern Caribbean Civil Aviation Authority
ECR	European Court Reports
EFOD	Electronic Filing of Differences
EFTA	European Free Trade Association
EJIL	European Journal of International Law
ELR	European Law Review
ENCASIA	European Network of Civil Aviation Safety Investigation Authorities
ENP	European Neighbourhood Policy
EP	European Parliament
EU	European Union
EUROCONTROL	European Organisation for the Safety of Air Navigation
FAA	US Federal Aviation Administration
GASON	Global Aviation Safety Oversight Network
GASP	Global Aviation Safety Plan
HLSC (2010)	ICAO High Level Safety Conference (2010)
IAC	Interstate Aviation Committee
IAEA	International Atomic Energy Agency
IASA	International Aviation Safety Assessment
ICAN	International Commission for Air Navigation
ICAO	International Civil Aviation Organization
ICJ	International Court of Justice

ICVM	ICAO Coordinated Validation Missions
IDISIR	Safety Ramp Inspections Data Exchange Programme
IIL	Institute of International Law
ILC	International Law Commission of the United Nations
ILM	International Legal Materials
IMO	International Maritime Organization
IOLR	International Organizations Law Review
ISASI	International Society of Air Safety Investigators
JAA	Joint Aviation Authorities
JALC	Journal of Air Law and Commerce
JAR(s)	Joint Aviation Requirements
JEPP	Journal of European Public Policy
LACAC	Latin American Civil Aviation Commission
LAR	Latin American Aviation Regulation
LNTS	League of Nations Treaty Series
MARB	Monitoring and Assistance Review Board
MoC	Memorandum of Cooperation
MoU	Memorandum of Understanding
NAA	National Aviation Authority of an EU Member State
NPA	Notice of Proposed Amendment
OCLJ	Ocean and Coastal Law Journal
OECS	Organisation of the Eastern Caribbean States
OJ	Official Journal of the European Union
PANS	Procedures for Air Navigation Services
PASO	Pacific Aviation Safety Office
PCIJ	Permanent Court of International Justice
PICASST	Pacific Islands Civil Aviation Safety and Security Treaty
PSC	Port State Control
RAIO	Regional Accident Investigation Organisation
RANP	Regional Air Navigation Plan
RASG	Regional Aviation Safety Group
RASO	Regional Aviation Safety Organisation
RCAA	Regional Civil Aviation Authority
REC	Regional Economic Community
REIO	Regional Economic Integration Organisation
RIAA	Reports of International Arbitral Awards
RSOO	Regional Safety Oversight Organisation
RTK	Revenue Tonne Kilometre
SADC	Southern African Development Community
SAFA	Safety Assessment of Foreign Aircraft
SARP(s)	Standards and Recommended Practices
SAS	Scandinavian Airline System
SASO	Southern African Development Community Aviation Safety Organisation
SES	Single European Sky
SMS	Safety Management System

SRVSOP	Regional Cooperation System on Safety Oversight in Latin America (Sistema Regional de Cooperación para la Vigilancia de la Seguridad Operacional)
SSC	Significant Safety Concern
STK	Scandinavian Flight Safety Office
TEU	Treaty on the European Union
TFEU	Treaty on the Functioning of the European Union
UAE	United Arab Emirates
UEMOA	West African Economic and Monetary Union
UKTS	United Kingdom Treaty Series
UN	United Nations
UNTS	United Nations Treaty Series
US	United States
USC	United States Code
USD	United States Dollars
USOAP	Universal Safety Oversight Audit Programme
WA	Working Arrangement
WTO	World Trade Organization

Acknowledgements

This book is a commercial edition of a doctorate thesis which was defended at the Leiden University in the Netherlands in November 2014. It is the result of five years of research on legal aspects of regional cooperation in civil aviation safety. While writing a doctorate thesis is at the end of the day a very personal experience, I have been fortunate to be supported in this endeavour by a number of extraordinary people, colleagues and friends, without whom - and of that I am absolutely sure - this work would have never been completed.

First of all, I would like to express my deepest gratitude to my supervisor Prof. Dr Pablo Mendes de Leon, Director of the International Institute of Air and Space Law of the Leiden University, whose professional mentoring, clear guidance and encouragement, which were also provided in moments of doubt, were absolutely invaluable for me in accomplishing this study.

My sincere thanks go also to Prof. Dr Niels Blokker, Prof. Dr Vincent Correia and Messrs Frank Manuhutu, Grégory Lièvre, Krzysztof Kędzierski and Guillermo Iovino for making suggestions for improvement, discussing ideas and reviewing parts of the text.

Likewise I would like to thank numerous officers, present and past, of the Regional Aviation Safety Organisations which are addressed in this study, for kindly providing information about the functioning of their organisations, sharing with me views on the value of regional cooperation in improving aviation safety and reviewing relevant parts of the manuscript.

A special acknowledgment is also given to ICAO for granting me permission to use some of its copyrighted data and materials.

I should also not forget to thank Ms Paula van der Wulp from Leiden University for all the administrative support.

I owe a special indebtedness to my parents and parents-in-law, for supporting me during all those holiday weeks which I spent in their houses researching and writing.

My greatest thanks and love go to my wife Sarah and our daughter Martha, to whom this work is dedicated. Sarah believed so strongly in me over these past five years, and without her support and patience this work would not have been possible.

Finally, I would like to underline that I wrote this work in my private capacity and take full responsibility for the views expressed therein, as well as for any errors, omissions or inaccuracies which may have occurred. All those who helped me in the research or agreed to be interviewed have done so in their private capacity and not as officers of their organisations.

Mikołaj Ratajczyk
Brussels, March 2015

CHAPTER 1

Research Questions, Methodology and Structure of the Study

> When we look at the future of aviation,
> we must ... look at the future of safety.[1]

Roberto Kobeh González
President of the ICAO Council (2006-2013)

§1.01 OBJECTIVE OF THE STUDY

This study is a first comprehensive attempt to analyse, from a legal and institutional point of view, how regional cooperation and more specifically the so called Regional Aviation Safety Organisations (RASOs) can contribute to the improvement of civil aviation safety and the achievement of the objective of 'uniformity in regulations, standards, procedures, and organization' as formulated in Article 37 of the Convention on International Civil Aviation (hereinafter 'Chicago Convention').[2]

So far the bulk of analysis related to RASOs has been performed by the International Civil Aviation Organization (ICAO).[3] With the exception of a few articles published in air law journals (see section §1.06), there has so far been no attempt in the academic world to address this phenomenon.

There is also at present no internationally agreed definition of a RASO, and ICAO and its Member States tend to treat this concept as a broad category encompassing different forms of regional cooperation. For the purpose of this study a specific definition and typology of regional aviation safety bodies is proposed in Chapter 3.

1. ICAO, 'Journal', 1 (2012), p. 4.
2. 'Convention on International Civil Aviation', Chicago, 7.12.1944, 15 UNTS 295.
3. ICAO, 'Safety Oversight Manual, Part B: The Establishment and Management of a Regional Safety Oversight Organization', Doc. 9734, (2011). See also: ICAO, 'Manual on Regional Accident and Incident Investigation Organization', Doc. 9946, (2011).

The scope of this study is limited to civil aviation and primarily focuses on commercial air transport. It addresses regulation of civil aviation safety understood in broad terms. This includes functions of: rulemaking, including the development and promulgation of civil aviation safety laws and operating regulations; certification and continuous oversight, including the issuance of approvals and continuous assurance that the certificate holder meets the applicable safety requirements; and enforcement designed to ensure compliance. In addition, this study also analyses regional accident investigation organisations.

With a view to reaching the study's primary objective of verifying the extent to which RASOs meet the expectations vested in them by the international aviation community, seven specific research questions have been formulated:

(1) What should be the role of RASOs in global governance of civil aviation safety?
(2) Can the optimal RASO model be identified from a legal point of view? If yes, how can it best be defined and structured?
(3) In which domains can RASOs yield maximum safety benefits, and under which legal conditions?
(4) For which States are RASOs most relevant?
(5) What is the expected future evolution of RASO type bodies?
(6) Are there any shortcomings in the current international legal framework that pose an obstacle to further development of RASOs?
(7) What are the international responsibility and civil liability implications resulting from RASOs establishment and functioning?

In addition to addressing the above research questions, this study will also propose, in Chapter 5, a practical methodology or a 'tool-box' for the setting up of RASOs. The author made a preliminary presentation of this concept at the ICAO Symposium on Regional Safety Oversight Organisations (Montréal, 26-28 October 2011), which was positively received by the participants, and is reflected in the final conclusions of the Symposium.[4]

§1.02 CIVIL AVIATION SAFETY AS A GLOBAL CONCERN

Civil aviation is a global industry that directly and indirectly supports the employment of 56.6 million people, contributes over USD 2 trillion to global gross domestic product, and carries over 2.5 billion passengers and USD 5.3 trillion worth of cargo annually.[5]

4. ICAO, 'Outcomes of the Symposium on Regional Safety Oversight Organisations', Oral report by the ICAO Secretary General, (194th session of the ICAO Council, 2011). See also: ICAO, 'Review of the outcomes of the Symposium on Regional Safety Oversight Organizations', C-WP/13810, (195th session of the ICAO Council, 2011).
5. ICAO, 'Global Aviation Safety Plan', Doc. 10004, (2013), p. 2.

Commercial civil aviation is also a very safe mode of transportation. Worldwide the number of passenger fatalities per 100 million passenger-kilometres flown in commercial air transport has fallen from 0.8 in 1960 to 0.08 in 1980, 0.03 in 1990, and has ranged between 0.05 and 0.01 since then.[6]

Between 2009 and 2013 there were on average 3.7 accidents each year per one million aircraft departures, involving both fatalities and non-fatal outcomes, in worldwide commercial scheduled air transport.[7] Taking into account that the average annual volume of commercial traffic in those years was nearly 30 million flights, this is a very good safety record.[8]

However, when looked at in detail, the picture is more complex. First of all, as Figure 1.1 demonstrates actual safety levels are far from being uniform across the world and there are concerns that as the air traffic and complexity of the global air transport market grow, the rate of accidents may also start to increase.[9]

6. ICAO, 'Outlook for Air Transport to the Year 2025', Circular 313, AT/134, (2007), p. 15.
7. ICAO, 'Safety Report', (2014), www.icao.int [accessed 17 July 2014], p. 8.
8. ICAO, 'Annual Reports of the Council (2009-2013)'.
9. 'Global Aviation Safety Plan', *supra* note 5, at p. 2.

Figure 1.1 Scheduled Commercial Air Transport Fatal Accident Rate per 10 Million Flights by World Region, 2004-2013

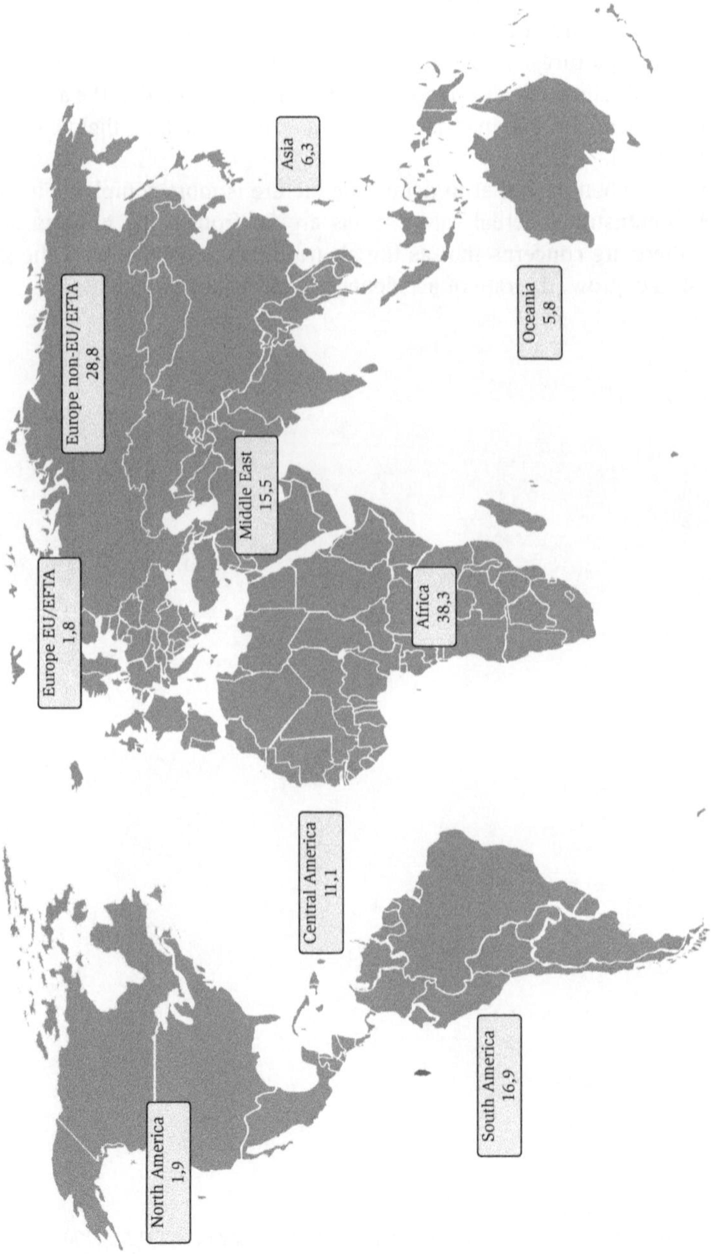

Source: European Aviation Safety Agency, Annual Safety Review (2013).

It is predicted that in Europe alone the volume of flights in the European Organisation for the Safety of Air Navigation (EUROCONTROL) area is likely to increase to 14.4 million flights per annum by 2035, or 50% more than in 2012.[10] Even more growth is expected in other parts of the world, with ICAO predicting a doubling of global aviation traffic in the next fifteen years.[11]

Secondly, the level of implementation of international civil aviation safety requirements mandated by the Chicago Convention and its Annexes,[12] although improving (see Chapter 2), is still not satisfactory. In August 2014, the global average level of implementation of the eight Critical Elements (CE)[13] of State safety oversight, as measured by ICAO under its Universal Safety Oversight Audit Programme (USOAP),[14] was standing at 62%.[15] In addition, there are significant differences in implementation of CEs between the ICAO regions, as well as within these regions. As Figure 1.2 demonstrates, in 2014 this spread ranged from 4% to 99% depending on the region. In August 2014, 43% or 79 of ICAO Member States were lacking basic safety oversight capabilities to certify their aviation service providers.[16]

10. EUROCONTROL, 'Challenges of Growth 2013: Task 4: European Air Traffic in 2013', (2013).
11. ICAO, 'ICAO Journal', *supra* note 1, at p. 5.
12. There are over ten thousand International Standards and Recommended Practices (SARPs) promulgated by ICAO in nineteen Annexes to the Chicago Convention. The vast majority of these SARPs concern civil aviation safety; see: ICAO, 'Notification and publication of differences: Summary of Decisions', C-DEC 177/14, (177th session of the ICAO Council, 2006).
13. The eight CEs of safety oversight system encompass the whole spectrum of civil aviation activities. They are the building blocks upon which an effective safety oversight system is based. The level of effective implementation of the CEs is an indication of a State's capability for safety oversight; see: ICAO, 'Universal Safety Oversight Audit Programme Continuous Monitoring Manual', Doc. 9735, (2011). See Table 1.1 below for an overview of the eight CEs and their correlation with actual accident rates.
14. A more detailed presentation of the USOAP is given in Chapter 2.
15. ICAO, 'Regional Performance Dashboards' http://www.icao.int/safety/Pages/Regional-Targets.aspx [accessed 4 August 2014].
16. *Ibid.*

Figure 1.2 USOAP Effective Implementation Level by UN Region

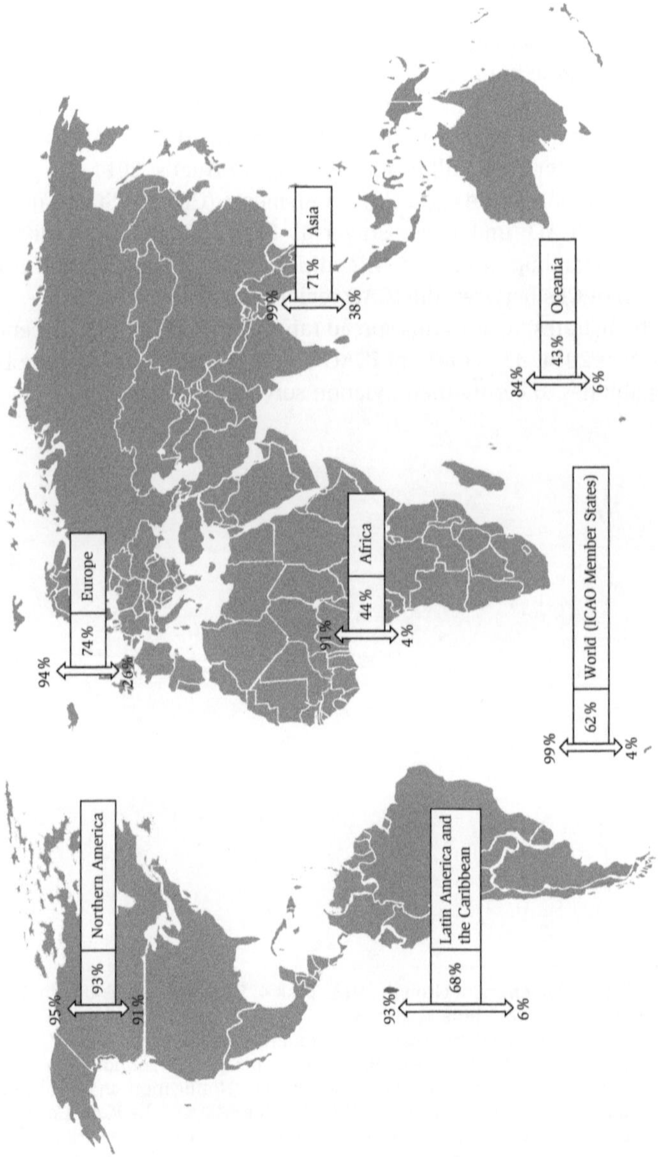

Source: ICAO, Regional Performance Dashboards (2014).[17]

17. ICAO, 'Regional Performance Dashboards' http://www.icao.int/safety/Pages/Regional-Targets.aspx [accessed 4 August 2014]. This data is the copyrighted property of the ICAO and is

The wide spread between the ICAO regions in respect to actual safety levels measured by accident rates and fatalities, as well as levels of effectiveness of States' oversight systems measured by USOAP, is a concern because aviation safety is significantly influenced by the inherently international nature of this sector – the main consequence of this being that civil aviation is only as safe as the weakest link in the system. International cooperation is thus essential to ensure network safety and implementation of coordinated policies and globally agreed standards as mandated by the Chicago Convention.[18]

What can also be observed (see Figure 1.3) is that two of the three United Nations (UN) regions which between 2005 and 2012 experienced the highest rate of traffic growth (Latin America and the Caribbean: 17%; Africa: 20%; Asia: 38%), also demonstrate the lowest level of effective implementation of the USOAP protocols (Latin America and the Caribbean: 68%; Africa: 44%; Asia: 71%). In these regions implementation efforts should be increased to ensure that this capacity expansion can be safely accommodated in the years to come.[19]

---

reproduced here with its expressed knowledge and permission. It may not be cited by or reproduced in any other publication without subsequent approval being granted by ICAO.

18. 'Chicago Convention', Article 37.
19. Each of the ICAO regions covers a large number of States, with the resulting aggregation of USOAP results at a relatively high level. As Figure 1.2 demonstrates there are large variations within each of the regions as regards the effectiveness of State safety oversight. Within each region there will therefore be States with very good safety records, as well as poor performers. For example the African region, which has today the lowest level of effective implementation of the eight ICAO CEs, aggregates information regarding both Democratic Republic of Congo which, based on the latest ICAO data, has a level of effective implementation of eight CEs significantly below the world average, and Kenya which, also based on the latest ICAO data, has a level of effective implementation above average for most of the domains. Similarly, the European ICAO region will cover the European Union Member States, as well as some of the former USSR republics; see: ICAO, 'Safety Audit Information' http://www.icao.int/safety/Pages/USOAP-Results.aspx [accessed 14 March 2014].

Figure 1.3 Departures in Scheduled Commercial Air Transport per UN Region

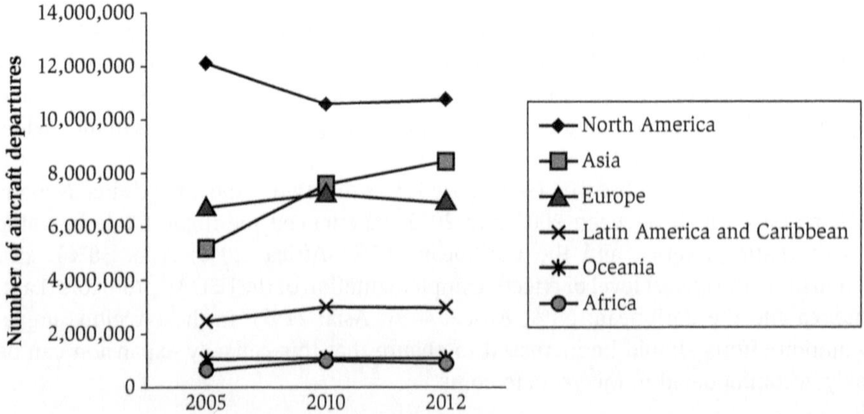

Source: ICAO, State of Global Aviation Safety (2013).[20]

The monitoring of the level of effective implementation of the eight CEs of State safety oversight is important because it was demonstrated by ICAO that a correlation exists between accident rates and USOAP results at individual State level.[21] As Table 1.1 demonstrates, this correlation is the strongest for those CEs which are directly related to the capacity of a State to ensure effective initial approval and continuing oversight of its operators, aircraft and aviation personnel and to resolve the identified safety deficiencies.

Table 1.1 Critical Elements of State Safety Oversight System and Their Correlation with Accident Rates

Critical Element	*Correlation with Accident Rates*
CE-6: Licensing, certification, authorisation and/or approval obligations	Very strong
CE-7: Surveillance obligations	Very strong
CE-3: State civil aviation system and safety oversight functions	Strong
CE-4: Technical personnel qualifications and training	Strong
CE-8: Resolution of safety concerns	Strong

20. This data is the copyrighted property of ICAO and is reproduced here with its expressed knowledge and permission. It may not be cited by or reproduced in any other publication without subsequent approval being granted by ICAO.
21. Nancy Graham, 'Briefing on the State of global aviation safety', ICAO High Level Safety Conference (Montréal, Canada, 2010), http://www.icao.int/Meetings/AMC/HLSC/Pages/default.aspx [accessed 5 August 2014].

Critical Element	*Correlation with Accident Rates*
CE-1: Primary aviation legislation	Medium
CE-2: Specific operating regulations	Medium
CE-5: Technical guidance, tools and provision of safety critical information	Medium

Source: ICAO, Report on the USOAP Comprehensive System Approach, Analysis of Audit Results, Reporting Period April 2005 to December 2008, Second Edition.[22]

The correlation identified by ICAO means that improving the level of implementation of Standards and Recommended Practices (SARPs), especially in States or regions which are expected to experience significant traffic growth in the years to come, should effectively contribute to further reduction of global accident rates, or at least to maintaining the absolute number of accidents at the current levels, while taking into account the ongoing traffic increases.

In line with the ICAO findings, a study conducted by the International Air Transport Association on accidents which occurred between 1 January 2001 and 31 December 2008 and involving commercial air transport operators located in sub-Saharan African States, showed that 'deficient regulatory oversight by the States of the operators' was one of the top contributing factors in the accidents analysed.[23]

Last but not least, in addition to challenges related to continuous improvement of safety performance, States as regulators of civil aviation face an ongoing challenge of optimising their working methods. In financially challenging times, the regulators have to accept as the '*new normal*' that budgets for safety oversight are not necessarily going to increase and that to safely accommodate the traffic growth, new methods of oversight, closer international cooperation and exchange of information across national borders is no longer nice to have, but has become an essential element of doing business.[24] The need for close international cooperation and exchange of information in order to foster aviation safety has most recently been brought to the forefront of the public debate in the aftermath of the tragic downing of the Malaysian Flight MH17 in July 2014 and the ensuing discussions about assessing risks affecting aircraft operations over conflict zones.

22. This data is the copyrighted property of ICAO and is reproduced here with its expressed knowledge and permission. It may not be cited by or reproduced in any other publication without subsequent approval being granted by ICAO.
23. Gaoussou Konate, 'Air Safety Situation in Africa, Current Problems: need for innovation', Symposium on Regional Aviation Safety Agencies (Livingstone, Zambia, 2009), http://easa.europa.eu/newsroom-and-events/events/symposium-regional-aviation-safety-agencies-rasa [accessed 21 July 2014].
24. 'Session 10 – panel report', EASA/FAA International Aviation Safety Conference (Paris, France, 2013), https://www.easa.europa.eu/events/events.php?startdate=12-06-2013&page=EASA-FAA_International_Aviation_Safety_Conference_2013#tabPresentations [accessed 11 March 2014].

§1.03 THE ICAO GLOBAL AVIATION SAFETY PLAN

The latest edition of the ICAO Global Aviation Safety Plan (GASP), adopted at the 38th ICAO Assembly, 'sets out a continuous improvement strategy for States to implement over the next 15 years through the establishment of core, and then more advanced, aviation safety systems.'[25]

The GASP framework is organised around three high level objectives and associated timeframes:

(1) Near-Term (by 2017): Implementation of an effective safety oversight system
(2) Mid-Term (by 2022): Full implementation of the ICAO State safety programme framework
(3) Long-Term (by 2027): Advanced safety oversight system including predictive risk management.

The logic of the GASP objectives is strongly anchored in the correlation that was mentioned in section §1.02 above between the effectiveness and sophistication of States' safety oversight systems and the actual levels of safety. The GASP objectives envisage that over the next fifteen years, States will gradually be moving towards more advanced methods of safety oversight and that this evolution should bring further reductions in the number of accidents and associated fatalities.

The GASP objectives are supported by a number of safety performance enablers, which include: more uniform implementation of ICAO SARPs; closer collaboration between States, industry and regional initiatives such as Regional Aviation Safety Oversight Organisations; continuing investment by States in maintaining, upgrading and replacing aviation infrastructure and investment in technical and human resources; and finally exchange of safety information.[26]

The implementation challenges faced by States under the GASP will not necessarily be smaller than those of implementing the more traditional approaches pursued by ICAO so far. Implementation of the GASP targets will necessitate the use of sophisticated tools and expertise which is not yet available in all the States, as the USOAP results show. It is questionable whether all of the States will be able to deliver. As pointed out by the Director of ICAO Air Navigation Bureau, during the 2010 High Level Safety Conference (2010 HLSC):

> States that have not yet implemented the eight critical elements of a safety oversight system effectively must first resolve these deficiencies and develop a sound foundation upon which to build their State Safety Programmes. Only those States having mature safety oversight systems will be able to realize the benefits associated with safety management principles, and achieve further reductions in their accident rates.[27]

25. 'Global Aviation Safety Plan', *supra* note 5, at p. 3.
26. *Ibid.*, at p. 4.
27. Graham, *supra* note 21.

Thus, a further question which needs to be asked is whether States which today face difficulties in establishing reasonably functioning safety oversight systems will be able to overcome these difficulties in the future, as the focus is switching more and more towards sophisticated safety management techniques.[28] If not, there is a danger that the gap between States with good and poor safety performance could widen even more.

It is in this context that ICAO and the international aviation community are exploring not only new approaches to managing aviation safety, but also looking for more efficient and sustainable means of ensuring adequate administrative capacity of States which is required for overseeing and regulating aviation activities. Regional cooperation, such as regional safety oversight programmes and RASOs, is one potentially promising approach, and is the subject matter of this legal study.

§1.04 TOWARDS REGIONAL COOPERATION ON CIVIL AVIATION SAFETY

The global regulatory framework for civil aviation safety is set out in the Chicago Convention and Annexes thereto. Originally this framework was designed chiefly to ensure the development of uniform standards and procedures for international civil aviation, while the implementation of these requirements has been left to individual States.[29]

With the establishment of the USOAP, which was launched in 1992,[30] ICAO and its Member States came to a realisation that not only does the level of implementation of SARPs vary across the world, but that there are also States which lack the administrative capacity to administer these requirements in an effective manner. Over the last fifteen years, all but one of ICAO Assemblies[31] expressed concern about the level of implementation of SARPs and safety oversight capabilities of some of the ICAO Member States.[32]

USOAP results demonstrate that States whose level of effective implementation of ICAO requirements has been judged as not sufficient often do not have enough resources or expertise to overcome the safety concerns identified by the ICAO audits:

28. ICAO, 'Safety Management Manual ', Doc. 9859, (2013).
29. Jiefang Huang, Aviation Safety through the Rule of Law: ICAO's mechanism and practices, (2009), pp. 24-42.
30. ICAO, 'Assembly Resolution A32-11: Establishment of an ICAO universal safety oversight audit programme', (32nd ICAO Assembly, 1998).
31. With the exception of the 34th, extraordinary session of the ICAO Assembly, which dealt with limited matters related to elections to the ICAO Council and financing of aviation security.
32. ICAO, 'Assembly Resolution A33-9: Resolving Deficiencies and Encouraging Quality Assurance', (33rd ICAO Assembly, 2001). ICAO, 'Assembly Resolution A35-7: Unified strategy to resolve safety related deficiencies', (35th ICAO Assembly, 2004). ICAO, 'Assembly Resolution A36-5: International Financial Facility for Aviation Safety (IFFAS)', (36th ICAO Assembly, 2007). ICAO, 'Assembly Resolution A37-8: Regional cooperation and assistance to resolve safety-related deficiencies', (37th ICAO Assembly, 2010). ICAO, 'Assembly Resolution A38-5: Regional cooperation and assistance to resolve safety deficiencies, establishing priorities and setting measurable targets', (38th ICAO Assembly, 2013).

> The most common reason a State fails to establish an effective safety oversight capability is its inability to provide the required financial and human resources. There is often an insufficient number of qualified personnel available for States to fulfil their safety oversight responsibilities. In addition, due to a lack of financial resources, training may not be adequate to ensure the currency and competency of technical personnel.[33]

For some States this problem could be a vicious circle, as even though the primary and secondary aviation legislation have been promulgated *on paper*, the State still requires appropriate organisation, qualified personnel and the tools for effective implementation of the legislation. Similarly, surveillance obligations and resolution of identified safety concerns, two elements for which a strong correlation exists with the actual accident rates (see Table 1.1), will need adequate technical and legal tools to ensure effective and efficient implementation.

With national budgets under pressure, States may find it difficult to secure adequate funding for their national civil aviation administrations.[34] Even when they are able to secure the funds, it is not uncommon that the newly recruited inspectors and specialists, once trained and qualified, leave the national administrations to take up better paid employment opportunities in the private sector.[35]

In the African region in particular, the situation is made additionally complicated by the fact that the still low levels of aviation traffic (see Figure 1.3 above) cannot generate the funds required to support effective national safety oversight systems.[36] In some African States, aviation was heavily subsidised in the past, but cannot continue to depend on subsidy any more due to other pressing needs in sectors such as health or education.[37]

It has also been proved that:

> Poor safety oversight results in more expensive insurance premiums and the inability to develop code sharing and other business arrangements, and that it also scares away potentially high-yield international customers and potential private sector investors.[38]

The problems associated with effective implementation of ICAO safety requirements can also lead to international tensions. This is because States with a good safety record, such as the United States (US), or Member States of the European Union (EU) have developed programmes to protect their citizens from unsafe operators, which in practice lead to operating bans or restrictions on operators or States which have been

33. ICAO Doc. 9734 Part B, *supra* note 3, at paragraph 2.1.3.
34. *Ibid.*, at paragraph 1.1.2.
35. ICAO, 'Report of ARRB – Report of the Audit Results Review Board (ARRB): Summary of Decisions', C-DEC 191/2, (191st session of the ICAO Council, 2010).
36. Haile Belai, 'Air Transport Safety: Africa', Symposium on Regional Aviation Safety Agencies (Livingstone, Zambia, 2009), http://easa.europa.eu/newsroom-and-events/events/symposium-regional-aviation-safety-agencies-rasa [accessed 10 August 2014].
37. Charles Schlumberger, Open Skies for Africa: Implementing the Yamoussoukro Decision, (2010), p. 165.
38. *Ibid.*, at p. 174.

found, under these programmes, not to be compliant with the minimum ICAO requirements.[39]

The above considerations have led ICAO and the international aviation community to look for new ways to assist States, especially those in regions with higher than average accident rates, in resolving the identified safety deficiencies. USOAP is obviously at the centre of this strategy, as a main diagnosis tool. This strategy also involves technical assistance and safety promotion initiatives that ICAO coordinates through a Safety Collaborative Assistance Network which was established following the 2010 HLSC.[40]

Most importantly however, ICAO has in recent years been carefully following the development of regional organisations dealing with civil aviation safety matters. The Secretary General of ICAO observed during the 2010 HLSC that these organisations are seen by ICAO as an 'alternative solution' to national based safety oversight, and one which can play a 'strategic role' in the new global safety approach.[41]

The concept of regional cooperation in civil aviation is not new. The International Civil Aviation Conference in 1944 discussed a number of principles with a view to making regional cooperation an integral part of the post-war aviation institutional and regulatory order.[42] Organisations such as the European Civil Aviation Conference (ECAC), African Civil Aviation Commission (AFCAC) or Latin American Civil Aviation Commission (LACAC) today constitute well established landmarks on the worldwide aviation horizon. The Chicago Convention makes reference to regional cooperation in its Articles 55, 77 and 78.

Similarly, the regional civil aviation safety bodies have already established a certain tradition. The history of some of the organisations functioning today can be traced back to as early as the 1970s, as Chapter 3 will demonstrate.

The current renaissance and renewed attention to these bodies can however be attributed to a number of new factors. First of all, the general trend towards regionalisation of governance, which has particularly accelerated in the second half of the twentieth century,[43] secondly the increased visibility and success of some of these organisations such as the European Aviation Safety Agency (EASA) in the EU (see

39. Aviassist, 'Insight into the EU Blacklist', Safety Focus: Quarterly Journal on African aviation safety, (2010), http://www.aviassist.org/ [accessed 5 August 2014].
40. ICAO, 'State of Global Aviation Safety', (2013), www.icao.int [accessed 6 March 2014], p. 22.
41. Raymond Benjamin, 'Closing remarks, Final Report of the Conference', ICAO High Level Safety Conference (Montreal, 2010), http://www.icao.int/Meetings/AMC/HLSC/Pages/default.aspx [accessed 5 August 2014].
42. 'Canadian Revised Preliminary Draft of an International Air Convention', proposing to establish Regional Councils of the International Air Authority, which were to be responsible for regional aviation matters and certification of international air operators established in States of a given region; see: 'Canadian Revised Preliminary Draft of an International Air Convention', Volume I, Part II - Work of the Committees, Committee I - Multilateral Aviation Convention and International Aeronautical Body, International Civil Aviation Conference (Chicago, USA, 1944), http://www.icao.int/ChicagoConference/Pages/vI_pII_ctteeI.djvu [accessed 17 July 2014].
43. For a general overview of the relationship between the universal and regional international organisations and the role of regionalism in global governance see: Laurence Boisson de Chazournes, 'Les relations entre organisations régionales et organisations universelles', in: L'Académie de droit international de la Haye: Recueil des Cours, (2010), pp. 79-406. For an overview of regionalisation trends in civil aviation governance see: 'EC-ICAO Symposium on

Chapter 4), thirdly the increasing pressure on the budgets of many authorities which necessitate sharing and optimisation in the use of resources, and finally the increased awareness of the international aviation community of the global safety picture as a result of the implementation of the USOAP.

ICAO has been encouraging the development of regional aviation safety bodies for some time, but it has really been since 2010 that its policy on this subject gained additional momentum with the adoption of the new ICAO 'Policy on Regional Cooperation'. This new policy aims at integrating the 'regional dimension' more closely with the overall ICAO strategic objectives, in particular in the area of aviation safety.[44]

The current ICAO position with regard to regional aviation safety cooperation was reconfirmed by the 2013 Assembly, which recognised that:

> Establishment of subregional and regional aviation safety and safety oversight bodies, including regional safety oversight organizations (RSOOs), has great potential to assist States in complying with their obligations under the Chicago Convention through economies of scale and harmonization on a larger scale resulting from the collaboration among Member States in establishing and operating a common safety oversight system.[45]

By mid-2014 a number of more or less successful examples of regional cooperation in civil aviation safety matters existed in many regions of the world. As will be demonstrated in this study, these regional initiatives take many different legal forms and have different scopes of activity and objectives. They also attract increasing attention, as expectations concerning their added value have been raised by ICAO and the international community.

At the same time, the legal conditions under which such regional schemes or bodies are able to provide optimal benefits for States and regions concerned, and thus to lead to the actual enhancement of aviation safety, have not yet been subject to comprehensive research.

§1.05 RESEARCH METHODOLOGY AND MAIN SOURCES USED

The methodology used in this study is in the first place based on analysing case studies of existing RASOs. In this respect, a *core sample* of fourteen organisations was selected, the list of which is attached as Appendix. Where a RASO functioning today had a predecessor or an *institutional forerunner*, this has also been studied to the extent necessary. For this purpose, the founding documents of all RASOs from the core sample were obtained and studied, as well as other available documents relevant to the organisations in the sample.

Regional Organisations', (Montréal, Canada, 2008), http://ec.europa.eu/transport/air/international_aviation/european_community_icao/ec-icao_symposium_en.htm [accessed 5 August 2014].

44. ICAO, 'Assembly Resolution A37-21: Cooperation with regional organizations and regional civil aviation bodies', (37th ICAO Assembly, 2010).
45. Assembly Resolution A38-5, *supra* note 32.

References to other RASOs, that are not included in the core sample, or their institutional forerunners, are also made in the study when needed to extrapolate the findings or illustrate a certain observation.

A more detailed case study has been performed on the EASA and the EU aviation safety system in general, as it can be considered at present as the most comprehensive regional civil aviation safety system in operation. In this respect, the archives of the EU Council in Brussels have been consulted. A selection of materials has also been obtained from the archives of ECAC in Paris for the purpose of the analysis of EASA's predecessor – the Joint Aviation Authorities (JAA).

Primary material to supplement the case studies was also derived from the 2010 HLSC which took place in Montréal, 29 March – 1 April 2010, and in which the author participated, and the following symposia and conferences on regional aviation cooperation:

(1) Symposium on Regional Organisations organised jointly by ICAO and the European Commission, Montréal, 10-11 April 2008
(2) Symposium on Regional Aviation Safety Agencies organised by EASA, AFCAC and the Civil Aviation Authority of Zambia, Livingstone, 13-15 July 2009 (author participated)
(3) ICAO Symposium on Regional Safety Oversight Organisations (RSOOs), Montréal, 26-28 October 2011 (author participated)
(4) ACAC/ICAO Seminar/Workshop on Regional Safety Oversight Programmes, Rabat/Morocco, 10-12 December 2012.

In addition ICAO documentation related to regional cooperation and RASOs, including the relevant ICAO Assembly and ICAO Council documentation, has been analysed, as well as the new ICAO manuals on the 'Establishment and Management of a Regional Safety Oversight System',[46] and 'Regional Accident and Incident Investigation Organization'.[47] Reports on the implementation of the USOAP programme and other ICAO as well as EASA safety reports have been used to support the study with up to date and reliable aviation safety data and statistics.

A number of interviews were conducted with people involved in the establishment and running of RASOs in Europe and other parts of the world. The list of interviews conducted is included in the bibliography of the study. All the interviewees contributed in their private capacity.

A review of relevant international, EU and national case law and legislation was conducted to support the discussion on international responsibility and civil liability of States and RASOs for safety regulation and negligent safety oversight.

A review of the literature was conducted focusing mainly on previous writings concerning legal and institutional aspects of civil aviation safety regulation, Chicago Convention and ICAO. The main aviation law journals, including Air and Space Law

46. ICAO Doc. 9734 Part B, *supra* note 3.
47. ICAO Doc. 9946, *supra* note 3.

Journal (ASL), Annals of Air and Space Law (AASL), Journal of Air Law and Commerce (JALC), and ICAO Journal, were reviewed.

In addition, university theses on aviation safety regulation were consulted in the libraries of the Law Schools of Leiden University in the Netherlands, and of McGill University in Montreal, Canada. A summary of the main literature concerning the subject of international law and aviation safety is presented in section §1.06 below.

A review of the main contemporary writings was undertaken concerning the theory of international organisations, State and international organisations' responsibility, delegation of powers under international law, and enforcement of international law, mainly for the purpose of Chapter 6.

Available reports on the effectiveness of the functioning of EU agencies have been also consulted for the purpose of the case study of EASA and the EU system.

Last but not least, the author draws on personal experience of over eleven years of work as a civil servant in both national and regional civil aviation safety administrations in Europe, including in the Civil Aviation Administration of Poland, the Air Safety Unit of the Directorate General for Mobility and Transport of the European Commission, and in the International Cooperation Department of EASA.

The research was finalised in mid-2014, and unless indicated otherwise, the study reflects the situation which existed at that time.

§1.06 REVIEW OF THE PRINCIPAL LITERATURE ON INTERNATIONAL LAW AND AVIATION SAFETY REGULATION

In the existing literature, the regulation of international civil aviation safety is usually addressed as part of the broader discussion of the general ICAO framework. These studies focus on the presentation of the ICAO regulatory functions, especially the development of the SARPs, and the oversight of their implementation through the USOAP.[48]

As part of the discussion on the effectiveness of ICAO in ensuring 'the highest practicable degree of implementation of SARPs', there are also studies dedicated to the subject of transparency mechanisms, which are used by ICAO as a *quasi-enforcement* tool, and which together with technical cooperation and assistance have contributed to the improvement of civil aviation safety.[49]

One of the most comprehensive works to date addressing the international legal framework for civil aviation safety is the dissertation of Dr Jiefang Huang, focusing on the notion of aviation safety as an obligation *erga omnes* under international law, and which also advocates closer regional collaboration between States, in order to counterbalance the dominance of the main powers in the ICAO decision making machinery.[50]

48. Michael Milde, International Air Law and ICAO, (2012); Ludwig Weber, International Civil Aviation Organization: An Introduction, (2007).
49. Jimena Blumenkron, Transparency and the International Civil Aviation Organisation: Implications of increased transparency in safety audit information, (2011).
50. Huang, *supra* note 29.

In the European context, the question of the regulation of Air Traffic Management (ATM) and, more generally, the implementation of the Single European Sky (SES) has also been addressed in recent studies.[51]

In addition, from the perspective of this study, of particular importance is the work undertaken by Dr Niels van Antwerpen related to the delegation of tasks and responsibilities in the area of Air Navigation Services (ANS), and the need for safeguarding transparent lines of State responsibility in case of delegation.[52]

As far as the specific issue of RASOs is concerned, some work has been undertaken on describing the process of establishing EASA in the EU and the relationship between this agency and its predecessor – the JAA.[53] A very limited number of articles have been published on the RASO concept and their relationship with ICAO.[54]

§1.07 STRUCTURE OF THE STUDY

This study is composed of seven chapters, including this Chapter 1 with introductory remarks, five chapters describing the research findings and their analysis, as well as the final Chapter 7 with general conclusions and recommendations.

Chapter 2, which follows, summarises the main principles of the Chicago Convention and assesses their impact on safety regulation at national level. It evaluates the strengths and weaknesses of the ICAO regime and offers explanations on how they influence the effectiveness of the global aviation safety system. Chapter 2 then presents the regional aviation policy of ICAO, including on aviation safety. It argues that regional cooperation should not only be seen as a tool for helping States to raise their level of compliance with SARPs and increase the effectiveness of their safety oversight systems, but also as a way to change the architecture of the current – predominantly national based and largely inefficient – system, into a more efficient Global Aviation Safety Oversight Network (GASON).

Chapter 3 is based on case studies of RASOs and pre-RASOs from different parts of the world, including Africa, South America, the Pacific Region, and the Commonwealth of Independent States. It introduces the notion of a RASO and pre-RASO, presents different types of such organisations and categorises them on the basis of the

51. Daniel Calleja Crespo and Pablo Mendes de Leon, 'Achieving the Single European Sky: Goals and challenges', (2011).
52. Niels van Antwerpen, Cross-Border Provision of Air Navigation Services with Specific Reference to Europe: Safeguarding Transparent Lines of Responsibility and Liability, (2008).
53. Frank Manuhutu, 'Aviation Safety Regulation in Europe: Towards a European Aviation Safety Authority', ASL, 25 (2000), pp 264-272; Thaddée Sulocki and Axelle Cartier, 'Continuing Airworthiness in the framework of the transition from the Joint Aviation Authorities to the European Aviation Safety Agency', ASL, 28 (2003), pp. 311-330.
54. Michael Jennison, 'Regional safety oversight bodies deliver economies of scale and greater uniformity', ICAO Journal, 61 (2006), pp. 9-12; Ruwantissa Abeyratne, 'Ensuring regional safety in air transport', ASL, 35 (2010), pp. 249-262;. Mikołaj Ratajczyk, 'Regional Safety Oversight Organisations: an overview', The Aviation and Space Journal, X (2011), pp.2-7;. Charles E. Schlumberger and Shruti Vijayakumar, 'Regional Safety Oversight Organisation: Service provider or more? The case of the Pacific Aviation Safety Office', AASL, XXXIX (2014), pp. 213-245.

specific features of their legal and organisational set-ups. Chapter 3 also proposes a RASO definition, taking into account the elements which would stimulate the introduction of the most efficient forms of such organisations.

Chapter 4 is a detailed case study of EASA providing a specific example of a RASO which is part of and relies for its functioning on a Regional Economic Integration Organisation (REIO). This chapter demonstrates how EASA, which is currently the RASO of reference for many other similar organisations, contributes to the improvement of aviation safety and efficiency of regulatory processes, notably by taking advantage of the EU's legally binding and directly applicable legal framework. It demonstrates, from the Chicago Convention point of view, the consequences of the far reaching delegation of safety functions from EU Member States to EASA, and considers the feasibility of transforming this agency into a single civil aviation authority for Europe.

Chapter 5 offers more general observations and conclusions on the extent to which the various functions of RASOs and the continuing evolution of these organisations contribute to the improvement of global aviation safety and achievement of the objectives of uniformity in regulations, procedures and operations in civil aviation. This chapter in particular offers a classification of the different levels of delegation arrangements that States use when creating RASOs. It also presents the different types of safety functions that RASOs may exercise, and analyses key trends that can be observed around the world regarding the setting up and functioning of these organisations. It also addresses the functioning of RASOs as international actors.

Chapter 6 examines the consequences that the establishment of RASOs may have in terms of international responsibility and civil liability for wrongful acts in relation to the Member States of the RASO, and third countries, as well as the regional body itself. It clarifies and systematises the general principles and concepts concerning the attribution and delegation of State safety functions to aviation authorities from the perspective of domestic and international law. Chapter 6 also examines whether there are any provisions in the Chicago Convention or its Annexes which could limit the possibility of delegating State safety functions to RASOs, or more generally to exercising these functions on a non-national basis. On this basis, it considers the conditions which would have to be met in order to trigger international responsibility of the RASO or its Member States. Chapter 6 also conducts a review of case law and principles related to tort law liability of civil aviation authorities and extrapolates the findings of this review to RASOs functioning. Finally, it assesses the need for amending the Chicago Convention in view of the emergence of RASOs.

Chapter 7 formulates general conclusions of the study, makes recommendations based on its findings, and suggests further areas of research.

CHAPTER 2

Towards a Global Aviation Safety Oversight Network: Regional Cooperation on Aviation Safety in the Context of the Chicago Convention

Greater regional cooperation can improve the efficiency of air transport operations and simultaneously generate economic growth for States and Regions alike.[1]

Roberto Kobeh González,
President of the ICAO Council (2006-2013)

§2.01 INTRODUCTION

Regional cooperation on aviation safety has visibly intensified since the beginning of the twentieth first century, as evidenced in particular by the new ICAO policy on regional cooperation, which is presented in section §2.04 of this chapter, and the establishment of a significant number of new RASOs.[2]

This intensification of regional cooperation has been to a large extent stimulated by the conviction of the international aviation community that, by focusing efforts at regional levels, States will be better able to meet their obligations stemming from the Chicago Convention and to overcome certain of its alleged weaknesses, such as lack of a legally binding nature of ICAO Annexes or weak enforcement competences of ICAO. For some regions, such as Africa, regional cooperation has emerged as an indispensable element of ICAO strategy for addressing aviation safety problems that they face.[3]

1. ICAO, 'Agreements on Regional Cooperation to Promote Efficiency and Sustainability of Air Transport', Press Release No. 09/10, (2010).
2. See Chapters 3 and 5 for detailed statistics.
3. ICAO, 'Assembly Resolution A38-7: Comprehensive Regional Implementation Plan for Aviation Safety in Africa', (38th ICAO Assembly, 2013). See also: ICAO, 'Comprehensive Regional

Before presenting and analysing selected cases of regional cooperation on civil aviation safety in different parts of the world, it is therefore necessary to put regional cooperation in the broader context of the Chicago Convention and global jurisdiction of ICAO.

This chapter will firstly summarise the main principles of the Chicago Convention and its impact on safety regulation at national level. The strengths and weaknesses of the ICAO regime will be reviewed and explanations offered on how they influence the effectiveness of the global aviation safety system (section §2.02). This will include a demonstration of how States have traditionally dealt with inefficiencies stemming from the system of the Chicago Convention, including in particular through Bilateral Aviation Safety Agreements (BASAs).

Following on from that, the oversight and enforcement mechanisms used by ICAO will be concisely compared with the mechanisms used in the international maritime sector, in which States and the International Maritime Organization (IMO) faced similar problems with effective implementation and enforcement of maritime safety requirements and ultimately reached a conclusion that regional cooperation can be a good way of addressing some of these problems (section §2.03).

This chapter will also present the regional aviation policy of ICAO. Against this backdrop it will be argued that regional cooperation should be seen not only as a tool for helping States in raising their level of compliance with ICAO SARPs and increasing the effectiveness of their safety oversight systems, but also as a way to change the architecture of the current – predominantly national based and arguably largely inefficient – system (section §2.04).

Finally, this chapter will propose the concept of a 'Global Aviation Safety Oversight Network' or GASON, and will demonstrate that by working more closely with and relying on robust and appropriately empowered RASOs, ICAO could not only help individual States to increase their compliance with international requirements, but also to ensure more uniformity in their implementation and to better harmonise actual safety levels in regions across the world (section §2.05).

§2.02 STRENGTHS AND WEAKNESSES OF THE CHICAGO CONVENTION FROM AN AVIATION SAFETY PERSPECTIVE

The Chicago Convention is a very successful treaty if looked at from the perspective of its global acceptance. In 2014, 191 States were parties to this instrument.[4]

Yet views on the effectiveness of the Chicago Convention in addressing contemporary problems of international civil aviation are divided. Leaving aside the economic aspects of aviation regulation, which are not the subject matter of this study, the arguments used by practitioners and academic writers usually point out that while

Implementation Plan for Aviation Safety in Africa, 12th meeting of the steering committee: report', AFI SC/2013/12, (2013), http://www.icao.int/safety/afiplan/Documents/AFI-SC12-Report%202013.pdf [accessed 15 March 2014], at paragraph 2.1.

4. ICAO, 'Member States' http://www.icao.int/about-icao/Pages/member-States.aspx [accessed 5 August 2014].

ICAO has been quite successful in developing SARPs concerning civil aviation safety and security, it has somewhat failed in ensuring global uniformity in their implementation and especially enforcement.[5]

It is further pointed out in the literature that the alleged deficiencies of ICAO and the Chicago Convention in ensuring effective implementation of international requirements, particularly in the domain of aviation safety, led to the development of unilateral oversight and enforcement schemes[6] such as the US International Aviation Safety Assessment (IASA) programme,[7] or the EU's regulation on the list of air carriers subject to an operating ban.[8]

While not wanting to repeat the discussion on the above issues, the alleged weaknesses of the system of the Chicago Convention do appear paradoxically to have also contributed to its success in terms of global acceptance and endurance. This is because the authors of the Chicago Convention have managed to strike a relatively good balance between, on the one hand, the desire to secure 'the highest practicable degree of uniformity in regulations, standards, procedures, and organization in relation to aircraft, personnel, airways and auxiliary services',[9] which is necessary for aviation as a global industry, and on the other hand, the principle that 'each State has complete and exclusive sovereignty over the airspace above its territory',[10] which at the time of the adoption of the Chicago Convention was of fundamental importance to States in the aftermath of the second world war.

The predecessor of the Chicago Convention, the 1919 Convention Relating to the Regulation of Aerial Navigation (hereinafter the 'Paris Convention'),[11] was much more ambitious, if looked at from the objective of achieving harmonisation of aviation standards, yet it failed to achieve universal acceptance.[12] The novel elements of the

5. Olivier Onidi, 'A critical perspective on ICAO', ASL, 33 (2008), pp. 38-45. Gilbert Guillaume, 'ICAO at the beginning of the 21st century', ASL, 33 (2008), pp. 313–317.
6. Milde, *supra* note 48 in Ch. 1, at pp. 177-178.
7. For an overview of IASA see: Anthony J. Broderick and James Loos, 'Government Aviation Safety Oversight: trust but verify ', JALC, 67 (2002), pp. 1039-1044, 1053-1055. Paul S. Dempsey, 'Compliance and enforcement in international law: achieving global uniformity in aviation safety', North Carolina Journal of International Law and Commercial Regulation, 30 (2004), pp. 27-33. FAA, 'IASA website' www.faa.gov/about/initiatives/iasa/ [accessed 5 August 2014].
8. EU, 'Regulation (EC) No 2111/2005 of the European Parliament and of the Council of 14 December 2005 on the establishment of a Community list of air carriers subject to an operating ban within the Community and on informing air transport passengers of the identity of the operating air carrier, and repealing Article 9 of Directive 2004/36/EC', (OJ L 344, 27.12.2005). EC, 'List of airlines banned within the EU' http://ec.europa.eu/transport/modes/air/safety/air-ban/index_en.htm [accessed 5 August 2014]. See also: Alan D. Reitzfeld and Cheryl S. Mpande, 'EU Regulation on Banning of Airlines for Safety Concerns', ASL, 33 (2008), pp. 132-154. Paul S. Dempsey, 'Blacklisting: Banning the unfit from the heavens', AASL, XXXII (2007), pp. 29-63.
9. 'Chicago Convention', Article 37.
10. *Ibid.*, Article 1.
11. 'Convention Relating to International Air Navigation Agreed to by the Allied and Associated Parties', Paris, 13 October 1919, LNTS (1922) No. 297.
12. Duane W. Freer, 'Regionalism is asserted: ICAN's global prospects fade (1926 to 1943)', ICAO Bulletin, Special Series 4 (1986), pp. 66-68.

Paris Convention, such as the legally binding nature of its technical annexes,[13] qualified majority voting used for their adoption,[14] and inequality of States in the International Commission for Air Navigation (ICAN) in terms of their voting power,[15] combined with the post first world war politics, led to a situation where a number of important States, including the Soviet Union and the US, declined to become parties to it, while other States started to explore alternative courses.[16] This in practice put a halt, until 1944, to all serious attempts to develop a global legal regime for civil aviation.

The subsequent parts of this section will therefore critically analyse selected elements of the system of the Chicago Convention in order to verify if, at the beginning of the twenty-first century, it is still fit for purpose, as far as aviation safety is concerned. The elements selected for this analysis include:

(1) the principle of State sovereignty under the Chicago Convention (section §2.02[A]);
(2) implementation of SARPs and notification of differences (section §2.02[B]);
(3) recognition of certificates and licences, including of those not envisaged under the Chicago Convention (section §2.02[C]);
(4) role of ICAO in global safety oversight (section §2.02[D]);
(5) ICAO enforcement efforts and competences (section §2.02[E]).

[A] The Principle of State Sovereignty under the Chicago Convention

The Chicago Convention is based on the principle of complete and exclusive sovereignty of a State over the airspace above its territory,[17] and where this territory is defined as 'land areas and territorial waters adjacent thereto under the sovereignty, suzerainty, protection or mandate of such State.'[18]

Although the meaning and scope of the concept of State sovereignty is highly contested in modern studies of international law,[19] for the purpose of this study a simple meaning of this notion, as proposed by Steinberger, has been adopted:

13. 'Paris Convention', Article 39: 'The provisions of the present Convention are completed by the Annexes A to H, which, subject to Article 34 (c), shall have the same effect and shall come into force at the same time as the Convention itself.'
14. *Ibid.*, Article 34: 'Any modification of the provisions of any one of the Annexes may be made by the International Commission for Air Navigation when such modification shall have been approved by three-fourths of the total possible votes which could be cast if all the States were represented and shall become effective from the time when it shall have been notified by the International Commission for Air Navigation to all the contracting States.'
15. *Ibid.*, Article 35.
16. Such as the development of the competing Ibero-American Aviation Convention and the Pan-American Convention on Commercial Aviation; see: Freer, 'Regionalism is asserted: ICAN's global prospects fade (1926 to 1943)', *supra* note 12, at p. 67.
17. 'Chicago Convention', Article 1.
18. *Ibid.*, Article 2.
19. Dan Sarooshi, International organizations and their exercise of sovereign powers, (2005), pp. 3-14.

> Sovereignty in the sense of contemporary international law denotes the basic international legal status of a State that is not subject, within its territorial jurisdiction, to the governmental, executive, legislative, or judicial jurisdiction of a foreign State or to foreign law other than public international law.[20]

From a general perspective it is important to distinguish between State sovereignty as a principle of international law, and the exercise of this sovereignty. This distinction has been present in legal discourse from the beginning of constitutional theory. For example, Hobbes in *De Cive* observes:

> We must then distinguish between the Right, and the exercise of supreme authority, for they can be divided; as for example, when he who hath the Right, either cannot, or will not be present in judging trespasses, or deliberating of affaires: For Kings sometimes by reason of their age cannot order their affaires, sometimes also though they can doe it themselves, yet they judge it fitter, being satisfied in the choyce of their Officers and Counsellors, to exercise their power by them.[21]

The practical significance of the above distinction is that, although it is generally recognised that, from the perspective of international law, State sovereignty as such cannot be transferred, the exercise of sovereign powers by States can be subject to limitations, conditions or delegations.[22] As observed by Wassenbergh, State sovereignty as the principle of customary international law recalled by Article 1 of the Chicago Convention 'applies only in so far as it is not expressly restricted by other provisions of the Convention or by engagements entered into elsewhere.'[23]

From the perspective of this study, the above means that although under the Chicago Convention a State has the overall responsibility for regulating civil aviation safety, the actual exercise of this responsibility, in whole or in part, can be delegated to other entities, including to RASOs, as will be demonstrated in Chapters 3-6.

[B] Implementation of SARPs and Notification of Differences

One of the key objectives of the Chicago Convention is to secure 'the highest practicable degree of uniformity in regulations, standards, procedures and organization in relation to aircraft, personnel, airways and auxiliary services in all matters in which such uniformity will facilitate and improve air navigation.'[24] Such uniformity is essential given the global nature of international aviation.

The provisions of the Chicago Convention have a mandatory character, which, as demonstrated by Milde, stems from its very text, as well as State practice.[25] This

20. Helmut Steinberger, 'Sovereignty', in Encyclopedia of Public International Law, ed. by Rudolf Bernhardt (2000), p. 501.
21. Thomas Hobbes, 'De Cive', (1651).
22. Sarooshi, *supra* note 19, at p. 18.
23. Henri A. Wassenbergh, Post-War International Civil Aviation Policy and the Law of the Air, (1962), p. 100.
24. 'Chicago Convention', Article 37.
25. Milde, *supra* note 48 in Ch. 1, at p. 18.

ensures uniformity in relation to basic aviation safety requirements contained in the Convention such as an obligation to issue or validate airworthiness certificates and pilot licences,[26] or to investigate aviation accidents.[27]

On the other hand, States have been given flexibility, under Article 38 of the Chicago Convention, to file *differences* with *Standards* adopted by the ICAO Council and designated *for convenience* as Annexes to the Convention.[28] Whilst it could be argued that this flexibility opened the gates to the erosion of the system in terms of its uniform implementation, it also undoubtedly contributed, as the example of the earlier Paris Convention shows, to worldwide acceptance of the Chicago Convention, and success of ICAO in developing a comprehensive set of SARPs contained all together in nineteen Annexes.

The reality is that ICAO is not a supranational organisation like the EU, empowered to adopt by qualified majority legally binding and directly applicable legislation for its Member States and it is not likely that it will ever be given such supranational competences. It is an intergovernmental organisation largely subordinate to the will of its Member States. With only 19% of the contracting States to the Chicago Convention represented at the ICAO Council and 10% of them represented at the Air Navigation Commission (ANC) which prepares the proposals for SARPs,[29] the right to file a difference, is intended to safeguard the interests of those States which may not wish, for whatever reasons, the minority to impose its views on them.

In addition to the right of filing differences under Article 38, there is also a provision for any Annex to the Chicago Convention or amendment thereto to be rejected by a majority of ICAO Member States during the adoption process.[30] Yet in practice, at least by the end of 2013, there has not been a single case of the majority of States blocking adoption of new SARPs in the ICAO Council.[31] This proves that the process of adopting ICAO SARPs is overall well balanced and that its preparatory steps ensure that major controversies are eliminated before a proposal reaches the level of the ICAO Council.

As far as the legal status of SARPs is concerned, one important aspect has to be underlined. Upon their entry into force, *Standards*[32] are binding upon ICAO Member States, unless a difference has been filed. ICAO underlines this principle it its 'State Letters' which announce adoption of new SARPs by repeatedly stating that 'international Standards in Annexes have a conditional binding force, to the extent that the

26. 'Chicago Convention', Articles 31-32.
27. *Ibid.*, Article 26.
28. For a detailed overview of Article 38 of the Chicago Convention see: Huang, *supra* note 29 in Ch. 1, at pp. 58-65.
29. *Ibid.*, p. 58.
30. 'Chicago Convention', Article 90.
31. Based on a review of voting results in the ICAO Council (2009- 2013). For an overview of the situation prior to 2009 see: Huang, *supra* note 29 in Ch. 1, at p. 55.
32. Only 'Standards' have a mandatory character, unless a difference is filed under Article 38 of the Chicago Convention. For a definition of 'Standards' and 'Recommended Practices' see 'Forward' to any of the ICAO Annexes.

State or States concerned have not notified any difference thereto under Article 38 of the Convention.'[33]

Following on from the above, if a notification under Article 38 has not been made, other ICAO Member States are entitled to presume that full compliance with a Standard has been achieved. As pointed out by Van Antwerpen, 'failure by the State to comply with the notification obligation should be considered as a breach of treaty obligations.'[34] Therefore, if as a result of non-notification, a safety incident occurs this could arguably lead to State responsibility under international law, although this study did not identify any case law in this respect.[35]

Another important aspect related to notification of differences is the fact that although by filing a difference a State releases itself from the obligation of compliance with an ICAO Standard, this does not mean that other States are obliged to respect that non-compliance. For example, if a State has filed differences related to airworthiness standards of aircraft on its register, then other ICAO Member States would have a right to consider such aircraft as not complying with minimum requirements set for the purpose of recognition of airworthiness certificates under Article 33 of the Chicago Convention.

The practical consequence of the above could be a denial of over-flight or landing rights for the aircraft of the notifying State in accordance with the applicable provisions of bilateral Air Services Agreements' (ASA) clauses dealing with the issuance of operating authorisations and technical permissions.[36] Such situations have for example occurred in the past in Europe following adoption by ICAO of SARPs concerning the maximum age of pilots, and where France, which was strictly adhering to the ICAO set limit of sixty years, on certain occasions did not allow British operators to fly in French airspace if one of the pilots was older than sixty years.[37] This particular aspect of the SARPs' status has led commentators to argue that in practice at least some of the ICAO Standards have a value of law or 'law of gravity' with which compliance is simply unavoidable in practice,[38] or that some of the Standards 'are of such fundamental importance that the departure from them may not be tolerated.'[39]

The main objective of notification of differences however is transparency, especially towards operational personnel, such as pilots, who need to be aware if national rules and practices in a given State differ in any respect from those prescribed by ICAO. This function of SARPs can be illustrated by the following example: if State 'A' does not follow the ICAO standards concerning markings of runways and taxiways of international airports, it should notify other States accordingly, as otherwise aircrews from other parts of the world may be confused when using airports located in

33. See for example: ICAO, 'State letter concerning the adoption of Amendment 16 to Annex 6, Part III, Attachement D: Note on the notification of differences', AN 11/32.3.8-11/46, (2011).
34. Van Antwerpen, *supra* note 52 in Ch. 1, at p. 31.
35. See Chapter 6 for further discussion about State responsibility for breaches of obligations stemming from international law, including the Chicago Convention.
36. See Article 3 of a Template Bilateral Air Services Agreement in: ICAO, 'Policy and Guidance Material on the Economic Regulation of International Air Transport', ICAO Doc. 9587, (2008).
37. Former President of the ICAO Air Navigation Commission, 'Interview No 1', (2013).
38. Milde, *supra* note 48 in Ch. 1, at p. 164.
39. Huang, *supra* note 29 in Ch. 1, at p. 61.

State 'A'. Because of that inherent safety link, ICAO, in addition to differences notified by States under Article 38, also gathers information on differences under the USOAP.[40]

Looking at practical aspects related to application of Article 38 of the Chicago Convention, the main deficiencies in this respect have so far been largely associated with the lack of mechanisms in the ICAO Member States for systematic identification of differences as new SARPs and national legislation are promulgated. By the end of 2013, over 70% of the ICAO Member States had not established or implemented a mechanism for the identification and notification of differences to ICAO.[41]

In addition, ICAO methods used so far for the management of the differences have not been very efficient. Originally, the process of reporting differences was handled entirely by correspondence between States and ICAO. This was a 'laborious and time-consuming activity' which required substantial resources from both ICAO and its Member States.[42] In addition, the dissemination of differences, which is an obligation of ICAO under Article 38, was fulfilled by appending them as Supplements to the latest edition of each Annex. This procedure created delays and could not always ensure that the situation described in a given Annex corresponded to reality in the ICAO Member States.[43] In 2013, ICAO admitted that this is still largely the case today.[44]

Similar problems with identification of differences were revealed under the USOAP. In the course of audits conducted by ICAO between April 2005 and August 2010, only 49% of the USOAP compliance checklists had been duly completed by the 165 States audited. The remaining 51% were either left blank or not appropriately completed, as Figure 2.1 demonstrates.

40. Under the individual Memoranda of Understanding (MoU) signed between ICAO and its Member States for the conduct of the USOAP-CMA activities, States undertake to supply information on their compliance with SARPs in the form of the 'Safety Oversight Compliance Checklists'. Copy of a generic MoU is attached as Appendix B to: ICAO Doc. 9735, *supra* note 13 in Ch. 1.
41. Official of the European Aviation Safety Agency, 'Interview No 4', (2014). This situation remains largely unchanged since 2011, see: ICAO Secretariat, 'Known Issues and Difficulties', 1st Meeting of Filing of Differences Task Force (Montreal, Canada, 2011), slide 3.
42. ICAO, 'Notification and publication of differences: Report to Council by the President of the Air Navigation Commission', C-WP/12412, (177th session of the ICAO Council, 2006), at paragraph 2.3.
43. *Ibid.*
44. ICAO, 'Formulation and implementation of Standards and Recommended Practices (SARPS) and Procedures for Air Navigation Services (PANS) and notification of differences', A38-WP/48, (38th ICAO Assembly, 2013), at paragraph 2.8.

Figure 2.1 Differences Identified through USOAP Compliance Checklists (April 2005 to August 2010)

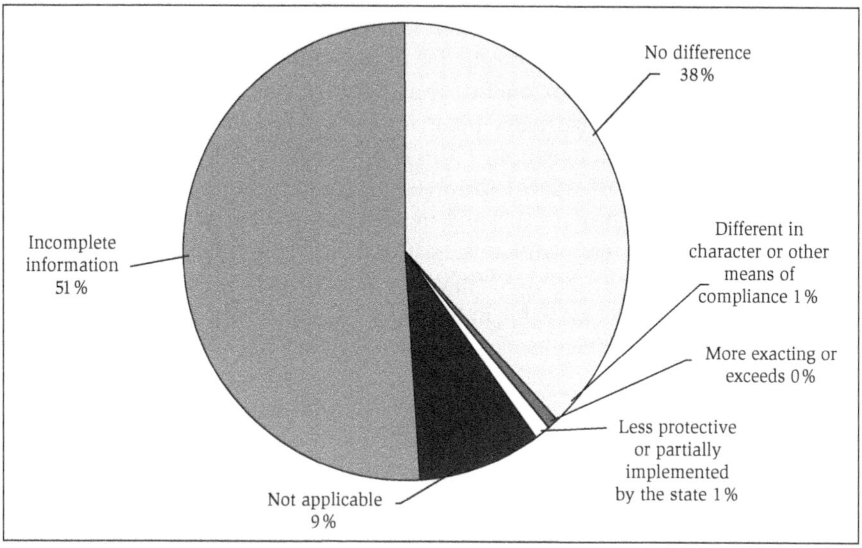

Source: ICAO, 'USOAP-CSA: Reporting of audit results – April 2005 to August 2010' (2010).[45]

Even more importantly, the differences are largely invisible to operational personnel as the Aeronautical Information Publications (AIPs) of ICAO Member States do not include material relating to all Annexes and approximately 76% of States did not publish significant differences in their AIPs, as required under Annex 15.[46]

Overall, ICAO admitted in 2013 that the 'status of the notification and publication of differences is far from satisfactory.'[47]

In order to remedy the above deficiencies, in 2011 ICAO embarked on a reform program. At its core lies a new system for Electronic Filing of Differences (EFOD).[48] The objective of EFOD is to create a single process through which States could satisfy the obligation of filing differences under Article 38 of the Chicago Convention, as well as to provide information on the level of implementation of SARPs for the purpose of USOAP.[49] ICAO expects all States to complete EFOD as an essential part of the new

45. This data is the copyrighted property of ICAO and is reproduced here with its expressed knowledge and permission. It may not be cited by or reproduced in any other publication without subsequent approval being granted by ICAO.
46. 'Known Issues and Difficulties', *supra* note 41.
47. ICAO, 'Progress Report on Comprehensive Study on Known Issues in Respect of the Notification and Publication of Differences', C-WP/13954, (198th session of the ICAO Council, 2013), paragraph 3.
48. ICAO, 'State Letter', Ref. AN 1/1 – 11/28, (2011).
49. ICAO, 'Progress report on the implementation of the electronic filing of differences (EFOD) system ', C-WP/13803, (195th session of the ICAO Council, 2012).

USOAP Continuous Monitoring Approach (CMA), which commenced in January 2013.[50]

Although implementation of EFOD is a big step forward, States will still need to have internal processes and necessary technical expertise for the identification of differences and to dedicate resources to this activity. In addition, ICAO Member States are not obliged to use EFOD as a means for formal notification of differences under Article 38 of the Chicago Convention. By the end of 2013, only 38 ICAO Member States declared that they will be using EFOD for formal notification of differences under Article 38 of the Chicago Convention.[51] The effectiveness of EFOD in remedying the current problems remains therefore to be assessed as experience with its use is gained.

More importantly however, beyond new technical tools for the reporting and dissemination of information on differences, ICAO should provide States with a clearer policy, including guidelines, on the application of Article 38 in order to ensure that standardised information is available in EFOD. At the time of writing this study ICAO has been in the course of reviewing its guidance material on the notification of differences.[52]

Some consideration also needs to be given as to the exact need for collecting significant amount of information from 191 States about all their differences with SARPs, which today, in safety and environment related Annexes alone, amount to over ten thousand.[53] Although under Article 38 of the Chicago Convention States are only required to notify the differences with Standards, in practice the ICAO Assembly has been urging States to also notify differences with Recommended Practices.[54] Recommended Practices are also covered by the USOAP compliance checklists.[55]

Finally ICAO requires States to notify a difference not only when a national standard is less demanding but also when it is more demanding or even when it is simply achieving the same objective by other means than required by ICAO.[56] In practice therefore the scope of obligation to notify differences under Article 38 has been significantly extended by ICAO.

Similar to regulations adopted at national level, the safety relevance of each SARP is not the same, and some of them establish administrative requirements only.[57] It can be argued that focusing on differences with those SARPs which contain requirements most relevant from the safety perspective of international air navigation would be more

---

50. ICAO, 'Policy and Principles on the Use of the Electronic Filing of Differences (EFOD) System', C-WP/13803, (195th session of the ICAO Council, 2012), Appendix C.
51. Source: 'Interview No 4', (2014), *supra* note 41.
52. A38-WP/48, *supra* note 44, at paragraph 2.2.
53. C-DEC 177/14, *supra* note 12 in Ch. 1.
54. ICAO, 'Assembly Resolution A38-11: Formulation and implementation of Standards and Recommended Practices (SARPs) and Procedures for Air Navigation Services (PANS) and notification of differences', (38th ICAO Assembly, 2013), Associated Practice n. 7.
55. ICAO Doc. 9735, *supra* note 13 in Ch. 1, at paragraph 1.3.
56. C-WP/12412, *supra* note 42, at Appendix A (as approved by ICAO Council by C-DEC 177/14).
57. For example, the layout of certificates, see: ICAO, 'Annex 6 to the Chicago Convention: Operation of Aircraft, Part I – International Commercial Air Transport with Aeroplanes', (2010), Appendix 6.

efficient and in line with a risk based approach to safety management.[58] This would also be more manageable for States with limited resources.

Whether narrowing the scope of the obligation to notify differences would be feasible *de lege lata*, is however not clear. The language of Article 38 does not seem to leave much space for such interpretations. It speaks about the need to comply 'in all respects', and to bring domestic regulations and practices 'into full accord' with ICAO requirements, and to notify a difference if such domestic regulations and practices were to differ 'in any particular respect', from those set by ICAO. This broad formulation can be a source of various interpretations by ICAO Member States.[59]

This straight jacket is made even more restrictive by the fact that ICAO is encouraging its Member States to use in their own national regulations, as far as practicable, the precise language of Standards that are of a regulatory character.[60] As ICAO is moving towards *performance based standards* – where only *what* is defined by the requirements, while the *how* is left to States, assisted by appropriate guidance material – this inflexible approach to Article 38 of the Chicago Convention may prove difficult to be maintained in the future.[61]

The ICAO Assembly recognised in its resolutions a need for a more focused approach to notification of differences and mandated the ICAO Council to encourage 'the elimination of those differences that are important for the safety and regularity of international air navigation or are inconsistent with the objectives of the international Standards.'[62] It is not certain whether such resolutions could be a way to narrow the scope of application of Article 38, in particular by constituting a 'subsequent agreement between the parties regarding the interpretation of the treaty or the application of its provisions', as envisaged under Article 31(3)(a) of the Vienna Convention on the Law of the Treaties[63] – the practice of ICAO so far seems to indicate that this is not the case.

In view of the above, beyond an amendment of the Chicago Convention with a view to updating Article 38, which is currently not on the table and unlikely in the foreseeable future, ICAO, when adopting Standards, could explicitly indicate which of them are of particular importance for the 'safety and regularity of international air navigation'. Although this would not change the obligation to notify the differences, it would give more visibility to those requirements which are safety critical.

The second issue on which additional work is needed is clarity as to what exactly constitutes a difference and especially a 'significant difference' which States are obliged to publish in their AIPs under paragraph 4.1.2 (c) of Annex 15 to the Chicago

58. ICAO Doc. 9859, *supra* note 28 in Ch. 1.
59. 'Interview No 1', (2013), *supra* note 37. In this interview, an example was given of Spain, France and United Kingdom, three EU Member States, which have assessed the same provision of 'EU OPS' – a regulation of the European Commission dealing with safety of air operations – which was different from an ICAO Standard contained in Annex 6 to the Chicago Convention, and each of them came to a different conclusion (i.e., that the EU requirement is more demanding, less demanding and finally different in character from the ICAO Standard).
60. ICAO, 'Assembly Resolution A29-3: Global Rule Harmonization', (29th ICAO Assembly, 1992). Similar encouragement is included in all the Annexes to the Chicago Convention.
61. A38-WP/48, *supra* note 44, at paragraph 2.6.
62. Assembly Resolution A38-11, *supra* note 54, at paragraph 13.
63. 'Vienna Convention on the Law of the Treaties', Vienna, 23 May 1969, 1155 UNTS 33.

Convention. ICAO has been trying to address this issue through provision of guidance material, which however is still quite generic and does not address the 'significant difference' issue. [64]

To summarise, and as pointed out by a former president of the ICAO ANC,[65] Article 38 is at the same time both a strength and a weakness of the Chicago Convention. Although this study does not question the need to have a mechanism for filing of differences, it nevertheless argues that States and ICAO need to change the way this provision is used in practice.

Beyond the migration from paper-based notifications to EFOD, which in itself is a big step forward, ICAO should in the first place *do less but better* when it comes to implementation of Article 38. Today ICAO finds it difficult even to find the resources necessary to translate the differences received into all ICAO working languages.[66] It would be unrealistic then to expect that ICAO will be able to dedicate the necessary time and resources to analyse the details of the language used and possible ways of implementation of over ten thousand SARPs in 191 States. ICAO should, instead of expanding, be in practical terms narrowing the scope of the obligation to notify the differences and focusing especially on differences with those SARPs which are of particular relevance for the safety and regularity of air navigation.

ICAO should also, rather than expecting States to use the precise language of Standards that are of a regulatory character, be primarily focusing on whether the objective of a Standard is met while leaving to States flexibility as to the means to achieve compliance - this would be more in line with the shift towards performance based regulation. ICAO should also be providing more standardisation as to what constitutes a difference, and especially a *significant* one. Such standardisation should be promoted not only through provision of guidance material to States but also at a practical level through the USOAP and provision of technical training to State specialists dealing with identification and notification of differences.

Finally RASOs have great potential to help ICAO and States in achieving more harmonisation and efficiencies in the way Article 38 is applied in practice. This will be demonstrated in detail using the example of EASA in Chapter 4.

[C] Recognition of Certificates and Licences

[1] Certificates and Licences Envisaged under the Chicago Convention

The drafters of the Chicago Convention were aiming at maximum possible facilitation of international air navigation from a technical point of view. This was supposed, *inter alia*, to be achieved through Article 33 of the Convention which provides that:

> Certificates of airworthiness and certificates of competency and licenses issued or rendered valid by the contracting State in which the aircraft is registered, shall be

64. C-WP/12412, *supra* note 42, at Appendix A (as approved by ICAO Council by C-DEC 177/14).
65. 'Interview No 1', (2013), *supra* note 37.
66. A38-WP/48, *supra* note 44, at paragraph 2.10.

> recognized as valid by the other contracting States, provided that the requirements under which such certificates or licenses were issued or rendered valid are equal to or above the minimum standards which may be established from time to time pursuant to this Convention.

The above provision is the only exception in the Chicago Convention from the principle that:

> The laws and regulations of a Contracting State relating to the admission to or departure from its territory of aircraft engaged in international air navigation, or to the operation and navigation of such aircraft while within its territory, shall be applied to the aircraft of all Contracting States without distinction as to nationality, and shall be complied with by such aircraft upon entering or departing from or while within the territory of that State.[67]

Obviously as aircraft cross multiple jurisdictions in international operations, it would be impracticable to expect that with each crossing of the border aircraft and crew would have to comply with the different rules of the overflow or served countries.

The multilateral recognition regime of Article 33 has two dimensions. Firstly, it gives a right to the 'State of Registry' to demand recognition of its certificates if they have been issued in accordance with the minimum standards established by ICAO.[68] Secondly, with this right comes an obligation of other ICAO Member States to grant the recognition if the conditions envisaged in this article are met by the 'State of Registry'.

ICAO has clarified in Annex 8[69] and Annex 1[70] to the Chicago Convention that, as far as the certificates of airworthiness and pilot licences are concerned, the minimum standards to which Article 33 makes reference will be the ones contained in those Annexes. In addition, Articles 39 and 40 of the Chicago Convention stipulate that an aircraft or a pilot which has failed to meet in any respect these international standards should have this clearly indicated on the certificate or license and that in such case other contracting States are entitled to restrict the operations of such aircraft or personnel in their territories. This, similar to the procedure of filing of differences, underlines the importance of the principle of transparency which, although not directly articulated in the Chicago Convention, is nevertheless present in a number of its provisions, as well as numerous Assembly resolutions.[71]

---

67. 'Chicago Convention', Article 11.
68. Where a 'State of Registry' has transferred some of its responsibilities under Article 83bis of the Chicago Convention, these rights apply also to the 'State of Operator'.
69. ICAO, 'Annex 8 to the Chicago Convention: Airworthiness of Aircraft', (2010). Paragraph 3.2.2 states: 'A Contracting State shall not issue or render valid a Certificate of Airworthiness for which it intends to claim recognition pursuant to Article 33 of the Convention on International Civil Aviation unless it has satisfactory evidence that the aircraft complies with the applicable Standards of this Annex through compliance with appropriate airworthiness requirements'.
70. ICAO, 'Annex 1 to the Chicago Convention: Personnel Licensing', (2011). See 'Forward', which states: 'Annex 1 contains Standards and Recommended Practices adopted by the International Civil Aviation Organization as the minimum standards for personnel licensing'.
71. ICAO, 'Assembly Resolution A37-5: The Universal Safety Oversight Audit Programme (USOAP) continuous monitoring approach', (37th ICAO Assembly, 2010); ICAO, 'Assembly Resolution A37-1: Principles for a code of conduct on the sharing and use of safety information', (37th ICAO Assembly, 2010); Assembly Resolution A32-11, *supra* note 30 in Ch. 1.

[2] Recognition of an Air Operator's Certificate

What can be quickly noticed is that Article 33 does not address the Air Operator's Certificate (AOC), which, in addition to the certificate of airworthiness and licenses of the aircrew, is an essential prerequisite for international air navigation in commercial air transport according to Annex 6 to the Chicago Convention.[72] This is because amongst the first twelve annexes that were developed during the Chicago Conference in 1944, there was no separate Annex concerning safety of aircraft operations.[73]

ICAO has clarified the link between Article 33 and AOC through interpretative Assembly Resolutions,[74] and provisions in Annex 6, which require:

> Contracting States to recognize as valid an air operator certificate issued by another Contracting State, provided that the requirements under which the certificate was issued are at least equal to the applicable Standards specified in Annex 6.[75]

However, given the fact that this requirement is set out in an Annex and not in the Chicago Convention, its legal value is not as strong as that of Article 33, and notification of differences is, at least theoretically, possible.

In order to safeguard the recognition of certificates in the context of commercial air transport operations, States also incorporate appropriate provisions dealing with this issue in bilateral ASA. Such provisions usually reproduce in the ASA the text of Article 33 of the Chicago Convention, and make the issuance of operating authorisations and technical permissions, which are necessary to utilise the traffic rights, conditional upon the maintenance of minimum safety standards, established under the Chicago Convention, by the State designating the airline. ASA clauses also allow the State which has issued the operating authorisations and technical permissions to withhold, revoke or limit them if the other party does not have or does not maintain safety oversight programmes in compliance with ICAO standards or if the designated airline is no longer compliant with the minimum ICAO safety requirements.[76]

The question of recognition of AOCs is a somewhat controversial subject, as States such as the US, Australia, Canada, China and the Member States of the EU, require under their legislation that foreign operators obtain a prior safety authorisation in order to be able to fly to and from their territories.[77] Such schemes have been developed largely because the results of the USOAP have shown in the past that States 'cannot reasonably assume without verification that the condition for recognition

72. Annex 6, Part I to the Chicago Convention, at paragraph 4.2.1.1 which states: 'An operator shall not engage in commercial air transport operations unless in possession of a valid air operator certificate issued by the State of the Operator'.
73. The notion of AOC was introduced only in 1990; see: Annex 6 to the Chicago Convention, at 'Forward'.
74. ICAO, 'Assembly Resolution A36-6: State Recognition of the Air Operator Certificate of Foreign Operators and Surveillance of their Operations', (36th ICAO Assembly, 2007).
75. Annex 6, Part I to the Chicago Convention, at paragraph 4.2.2.1.
76. For standard clauses concerning designation, authorisation, safety and recognition of certificates see ICAO Template Bilateral Air Services Agreement in: ICAO Doc. 9587, *supra* note 36, at Appendix 5.
77. These are sometimes referred to as Foreign Aircraft Air Operator's Certificates.

Stated in Article 33 is actually being met by another State.'[78] Because of this reason, ICAO encouraged States to put in place mechanisms to verify that the conditions for such recognition are met, before recognising AOCs as valid.[79] Requirements and guidance material concerning surveillance of foreign aircraft operations have also been adopted by ICAO.[80]

Although the existence of AOC authorisation schemes can be justified from the perspective of ICAO requirements, they should be seen as a tool to be used by States exclusively for assessing if the rules under which AOC was issued were at least equal to the applicable Standards specified in Annex 6 to the Chicago Convention. Following on from that, it should not be the purpose of authorisation schemes to dilute the responsibilities of the 'State of the Operator', who should remain the primary authority responsible for the AOC, or to impose on operators additional requirements which go beyond the minimum standards provided for in Annex 6.

In the EU, for example, the regulation establishing EASA stipulates that third country operators flying to the EU may have to comply with EU requirements to the extent that there are no applicable ICAO standards.[81] Although initially EASA proposed including requirements over and above ICAO SARPs in implementing rules on third country operator authorisations,[82] it finally decided not to do so, as it faced criticism from operators for not respecting the Chicago Convention.[83] It is important that ICAO remains vigilant to such initiatives which risk eroding the consistency of the international framework for aircraft operations. If there are deficiencies which would justify development of additional minimum requirements for international aircraft operations, this should be done through the ICAO rulemaking machinery.

The above does not mean that any requirement imposed unilaterally on aircraft operators would be in contradiction with the Chicago Convention and its Annexes. Certain requirements, especially airspace related, may have to be imposed on a country or region specific basis. For example, if a State has introduced reduced separation minima in order to increase airspace capacity, all aircraft may have to be required, in order to use that airspace, to carry equipment which is not necessarily envisaged under minimum ICAO requirements. This would be fully in line with Article 11 of the Chicago

---

78. ICAO, 'Mutual Recognition', DGCA/06-WP/8, Directors General of Civil Aviation Conference on Global Strategy for Aviation Safety (Montréal, Canada, 2006), at paragraph 1.2.
79. *Ibid.*, at paragraph 3.
80. Annex 6, Part I to the Chicago Convention, at paragraphs 2.2.2.2 and 4.2.2.2 which require States to establish programmes with procedures for the surveillance of operations in their territory by a foreign operator and for taking appropriate action when necessary to preserve safety. Guidance on the surveillance of foreign operators can be found in: ICAO, 'Manual of Procedures for Operations Inspection, Certification and Continued Surveillance', Doc. 8335, (2010). See also: Assembly Resolution A36-6, *supra* note 74.
81. EU, 'Regulation (EU) No 216/2008 of 20 February 2008 on common rules in the field of civil aviation and establishing a European Aviation Safety Agency, and repealing Council Directive 91/670/EEC, Regulation (EC) No 1592/2002 and Directive 2004/36/EC', (OJ L 79, 19.3.2008), Article 9(1).
82. EASA, 'Notice of Proposed Amendment relating to rules on third country operators for commercial air transport', (NPA No 2011-05), at paragraph 21.
83. EASA, 'Comment Response Document to NPA No 2011-05', at paragraph 15.

Convention, however in such a case a difference should be notified with ICAO indicating a requirement which is more demanding than the minimum ICAO SARPs.[84]

[3] *Other Certificates Not Envisaged under the Chicago Convention*

Limiting the analysis related to recognition of certificates to AOCs, pilot licences and certificates of airworthiness only - however important these three categories of certificates are - would however not be sufficient. Today the concept of 'State of Registry' or even 'State of the Operator' introduced through Article 83bis of the Chicago Convention, is no longer at the centre of the aviation regulatory world.

In addition to certificates of airworthiness, licenses of the aircrews, and even the AOC, aviation has seen a real proliferation of certificates and approvals. Certificates are issued for the design of aircraft and its components, organisations responsible for aircraft manufacture, aircraft maintenance, training of aircrew, international aerodromes, and other activities and organisations.[85] Some of those certificates, such as the design organisation approval,[86] are not even envisaged in ICAO Annexes. Such certifications are considered as 'safety barriers' erected by States to maintain safety levels which are expected from aviation activities by the general public.[87]

The problem is that international standards governing the conditions for issuance of some of those other certificates are not always precise or comprehensive. This is, for example, the case for production organisation approvals which are subject to only three general standards set out in Annex 8 to the Chicago Convention.[88] Similarly guidance for the issuance of an approval to maintenance or training organisations is not as detailed as that available for an AOC.[89] This leaves States with little option but to develop the detailed requirements on their own. In addition, as the Chicago Convention is limited to recognition of airworthiness certificates and pilot licences, and through Annex 6 also the recognition of AOCs, there are no internationally agreed conditions under which such other certificates should be recognised between States.

84. For example the EU mandated the carriage of Aircraft Collision Avoidance System (ACAS) II version 7.1 within the EU airspace earlier than the dates stipulated by ICAO in Annex 10 to the Chicago Convention; see: EU, 'Commission Regulation (EU) No 1332/2011 of 16 December 2011 laying down common airspace usage requirements and operating procedures for airborne collision avoidance', (OJ L 336, 20.12.2011).

85. Annex 1 to the Chicago Convention, at paragraph 1.2.8.2 for Approved Training Organisations; Annex 6, Part I to the Chicago Convention, at paragraph 8.7.1.1 for Approved Maintenance Organisations; Annex 8 to the Chicago Convention, at paragraph 2.4.1 for Approved Production Organisations; ICAO, 'Annex 14 to the Chicago Convention: Aerodromes, Volume I – Aerodrome Design and Operations', (2013), paragraph 1.4.1 for certified aerodromes.

86. The concept of a design organisation approval (DOA) is, for example, envisaged under the EU regulatory framework, see: EU, 'Commission Regulation (EU) No 748/2012 of 3 August 2012 laying down implementing rules for the airworthiness and environmental certification of aircraft and related products, parts and appliances, as well as for the certification of design and production organisations', (OJ L 224, 21.8.2012).

87. ICAO Doc. 9859, *supra* note 28 in Ch. 1, at paragraph 2.3.4.

88. Annex 8 to the Chicago Convention, at Chapter 2.

89. ICAO, 'Recognition and validation of approvals and certificates issued by other States', HLSC 2010-WP/9, ICAO High Level Safety Conference (Montréal, 2010), paragraph 2.4.2.

This results in differences between jurisdictions and duplication of oversight and approval schemes for industry and regulators.

The paradox of this situation is the fact that proliferation of certificates and associated audits and inspections, although having as its objective the safeguarding of civil aviation safety, at the same time goes directly in opposition to the main objective of the Chicago Convention, namely promotion of uniformity and efficiency in international air navigation. It also disperses the precious resources of the aviation community which could be used in a more efficient manner.

A very striking example of this situation can be observed in the domain of aircraft maintenance organisations (AMOs). Many States, including for example Singapore, Canada, Japan, Brazil, US or the EU Member States, require foreign AMOs working on aircraft registered in their registries to hold an approval issued by these states in addition to an approval from a local authority.[90] This means that an AMO which has clients from different parts of the world, may have to hold several approvals for performing exactly the same business only because the aircraft it maintains are registered in different countries. It is not rare that an AMO holds up to twenty approvals from different States.[91]

The consequence of the above is that AMOs may be subject to repetitive audits from many different States, in addition to internal quality audits and audits by customers, and may have to comply with different sets of requirements. This is not only costly, but also means that AMO personnel is required to use different procedures depending upon the 'State of Registry' of the aircraft, which adds an element of safety risk.[92] The justification for such schemes is that each 'State of Registry' wants to be sure that the same standard is being achieved as if the aircraft was maintained by an AMO which is under its domestic jurisdiction.

Another example of inefficiencies comes from the domain of product certification. Article 33 of the Chicago Convention covers recognition of certificates of airworthiness for the purpose of day-to-day operations only, that is when an aircraft registered in one State temporarily enters the airspace of another State.[93] However, when an aircraft changes registry, it is up to the new 'State of Registry' to determine its airworthiness and issue appropriate certificate.[94] In such cases, ICAO, through Annex

90. For examples of AMO certificates issued by various authorities see certificates held by the Airbus company at: Airbus, 'Airbus policy and certificates' http://www.airbus.com/tools/policy/ [accessed 15 March 2014].

91. Singapore, 'Recognition and validation of foreign AMO approvals', HLSC 2010-WP/73, ICAO High Level Safety Conference (Montréal, 2010), paragraph 1.1.

92. ICAO, Recognition and validation of approvals and certificates issued by other States, *supra* note 89, at paragraph 1.1.

93. Annex 8 to the Chicago Convention, at 'Forward' which states that: 'The requirements governing the issuance of Type Certificates in accordance with applicable provisions of Annex 8 are not part of the minimum standards which govern the issuance or validation of Certificates of Airworthiness, and lead to the recognition of their validity pursuant to Article 33 of the Convention'.

94. *Ibid.*, at paragraph 3.2.1 which states that: 'A Certificate of Airworthiness shall be issued by a Contracting State on the basis of satisfactory evidence that the aircraft complies with the design aspects of the appropriate airworthiness requirements.'

8 to the Chicago Convention, promotes acceptance of a previous certificate of airworthiness as satisfactory evidence that the aircraft complies with applicable ICAO standards.[95] This is, however, theory.

In practice, because Annex 8 sets only broad airworthiness performance objectives for different categories of aircraft, States still have to adopt detailed codes of airworthiness at the national level. This means that the conditions to be met before a certificate of airworthiness is issued vary between States. States with important manufacturing industries, such as the US, Russia through the Interstate Aviation Committee (IAC), or the EU Member States through EASA, adopt detailed airworthiness codes which, despite harmonisation efforts, may contain dissimilar requirements. For example, the US Federal Aviation Administration (FAA) has identified forty significant and twenty-three non-significant standards differences between the US and EU certification requirements for transport category aeroplanes.[96]

Multiple sets of similar but differing certification requirements may lead to repetitive certifications of the same product, resulting in additional administrative burden and cost for authorities and industry in import and export. Large manufacturing States, including the US, Brazil, Canada or the EU Member States acting through EASA, would use a specific method of certification called *validation*, to determine compliance with their airworthiness requirements. Validations are supposed to limit the involvement of the importing State to checking compliance with their unique import requirements only, while in other respects to rely on the determinations already made by the primary certificating authority.[97] Other States, for example Australia, would not perform validation of a foreign type certificate but simply accept it following familiarisation with the product, if they have confidence in the foreign authority which issued the original certificate.[98]

Although validation contributes to the reduction of unnecessary repetitive checks and determinations in export and import of aeronautical products, it has not been able to eliminate the duplication of work and dissimilar regulatory requirements which represent a burden and cost for the authorities and the manufacturers. Major manufacturing States like the US recognise that 'multiple sets of similar yet differing certification requirements among Civil Aviation Authorities can lead to a significant burden when certifying and validating aeronautical products and parts for import and

95. *Ibid.*, at paragraph 3.2.4 which states that: 'The new State of Registry, when issuing its Certificate of Airworthiness may consider the previous Certificate of Airworthiness as satisfactory evidence, in whole or in part, that the aircraft complies with the applicable Standards of this Annex through compliance with the appropriate airworthiness requirements'.
96. FAA, 'List of FAA Significant and Non-Significant Standards Differences' http://www.faa.gov/aircraft/air_cert/design_approvals/transport/transport_intl/sd_list/ssd_nonssd_list [accessed 5 August 2014].
97. See for example: Type Validation Principles under the Technical Implementation Procedures (TIP) to 'Agreement between the United States of America and the European Community on cooperation in the regulation of civil aviation safety', 30 June 2008, (OJ L 291, 9.11.2011). At: EASA, 'Bilateral Agreements' http://easa.europa.eu/document-library/bilateral-agreements [accessed 5 August 2014].
98. CASA, 'Civil Aviation Safety Regulations (as amended)', (Statutory Rules No. 237), Part 21.029A.

export.'[99] A study conducted by the Aviation Working Group in 2011 estimates that dissimilar technical requirements affecting transfers of aircraft between various jurisdictions cost the aviation industry up to 369 million USD per annum, and that the projected cost over the next twenty years of such dissimilar requirements may be as much as 7.286 billion USD.[100]

In the past, efforts were undertaken by the US, European countries, and other major 'States of Design' to harmonise their airworthiness codes.[101] ICAO has also tried to take up this work at the global level, but today an old and in practice never implemented Assembly resolution on a 'globally harmonized design code' is the only remainder of that ambitious initiative.[102]

The duplication of certifications and associated audits and inspections necessary for their recognition is currently one of the greatest inefficiencies in the ICAO system and the source of a significant waste of resources of the international aviation community. This 'death by audit' situation, as it was referred to at the 2013 FAA/EASA International Aviation Safety Conference, needs to be addressed, as in the longer term it is simply unsustainable.[103]

RASOs have a great potential for reducing redundant audits and certifications by allowing large scale, multilateral programmes for acceptance of certification findings or even the certificates themselves, as will be demonstrated in detail on the example of EASA in Chapter 4.

[4] International Aviation Safety Agreements

The discussion about recognition of aviation safety certificates under international law would not be complete without also addressing the international aviation safety agreements. These agreements, which are usually of a bilateral nature, constitute a traditional tool through which States address limitations of the Chicago Convention in terms of acceptance of certificates. International aviation safety agreements were used

99. United States of America, 'Improving international cooperation in certification and validation of products and parts', HLSC 2010-WP/33, ICAO High Level Safety Conference (Montréal, 2010), Summary.
100. Aviation Working Group, 'Economic impact assessment and select recommendations: dissimilar technical regulatory requirements impacting cross border transfer of aircraft', (2011), www.awg.aero/assets/docs/Report%20v%201.02.pdf [accessed 5 August 2014], p. 2.
101. For many years the US FAA and the European Joint Aviation Authorities (JAA) have been implementing a Harmonization Work Program which was launched as a result of the commitment made by the FAA and the JAA at the 9th FAA/JAA Harmonization Meeting (1992). The harmonisation programme has been stopped following the dissolution of the JAA in 2009, and recently taken up again by EASA and FAA in the framework of the EU - US Agreement on Cooperation in the Regulation of Civil Aviation Safety.
102. ICAO, 'Assembly Resolution A33-11: A global design code for aircraft', (33rd ICAO Assembly, 2001).
103. Author's notes from the 2013 EASA/FAA International Aviation Safety Conference; In addition see: '2013 EASA/FAA International Aviation Safety Conference', http://easa.europa.eu/newsroom-and-events/events/easa-faa-international-aviation-safety-conference-2013 [accessed 5 August 2014].

as early as the 1930s to approve aeronautical products in export and import.[104] In Europe, a rare example of a multilateral aviation safety agreement was signed in 1960, but is no longer applicable.[105]

Bilateral aviation safety agreements or BASAs aim at reducing redundant certifications and oversight. Such agreements require a high degree of mutual confidence, as their provisions usually do not relieve parties from finding compliance with their own requirements, but allow reliance on the equivalency of the other party's regulatory system in order to find such compliance.[106]

Compliance with at least the minimum ICAO requirements, in addition to more specific confidence building exercises and regulatory special conditions, will therefore be a necessary pre-requisite for concluding a BASA.[107]

Aviation safety agreements can cover various domains of aviation safety, such as initial and continuing airworthiness, pilot licensing, or qualification of flight simulation training devices.[108] In the area of initial aircraft certification, for example, they allow for more efficient aircraft design approval processes, sometimes even relieving the parties altogether from an obligation to issue an additional approval. In areas such as production, maintenance, pilot licensing or qualification of flight simulation training devices, they allow reliance on each other's monitoring of facilities and devices, and thereby limit the technical work to those regulatory areas which are significantly different.

The benefits of BASA agreements can be very well illustrated with the example of the maintenance annex to the EU-US BASA.[109] In 2014, there were over 1400 EASA

104. Mary Cheston, 'U.S. Perspective on Bilateral Safety Agreements: where we've been and where we're going', Europe/U.S. International Aviation Safety Conference http://www.easa.europa.eu/conferences/conference2005/presentations/day1/Bilaterals/us_bilaterals_cheston.pdf [accessed 5 August 2014].

105. 'Multilateral Agreement Relating to Certificates of Airworthiness for Imported Aircraft', 22 April 1960, ICAO Doc. 8056.

106. See for example the FAA's policy on the bilateral air safety agreements at: FAA, 'Bilateral agreements: purpose' http://www.faa.gov/aircraft/air_cert/international/bilateral_agreements/purpose/ [accessed 5 August 2014]. See also: 'Preamble' to EU – Canada BASA which states that: 'Reciprocal acceptance needs to offer an assurance of conformity with applicable technical regulations or standards equivalent to the assurance offered by a Party's own procedures', 'Agreement on civil aviation safety between the European Community and Canada', 6 May 2009, (OJ L 153, 17.06.2009). Similarly 'Preamble' to EU – Brazil BASA states that: 'Each Party has determined that the standards and systems of the other Party for the airworthiness and environmental certification or acceptance of Civil Aeronautical Products are sufficiently equivalent to its own to make an agreement practicable', 'Agreement between the European Union and the Government of the Federative Republic of Brazil on civil aviation safety', 14 July 2010, (OJ L 273, 19.10.2011).

107. See the US process and requirements for concluding a bilateral air safety agreement at: FAA, 'Generic Steps for Obtaining a Bilateral Aviation Safety Agreement' http://www.faa.gov/aircraft/air_cert/international/bilateral_agreements/media/BASAProcess.pdf [accessed 5 August 2014]. The policy of the US FAA is also to require that a potential BASA partner country has been positively assessed under the FAA IASA program.

108. For examples of BASA agreements concluded by the EU and US see: EASA, 'Bilateral Agreements' http://easa.europa.eu/document-library/bilateral-agreements [accessed 5 August 2014]; FAA, 'List of BASA agreements' http://www.faa.gov/aircraft/air_cert/international/bilateral_agreements/baa_basa_listing/ [accessed 5 August 2014].

109. 'EU-US BASA', *supra* note 97.

approved AMOs located in the US,[110] which is a significant number of organisations. It would be impossible for EASA to ensure oversight of all of them with the resources available without relying on the help of the FAA. Under the 'Maintenance Annex' to the EU-US BASA, the bilateral partners have agreed that EASA's involvement will be limited only to those aspects of AMO monitoring which are significantly different in the US compared with the EU. In addition, even for areas identified as significantly different, the EU has delegated compliance verification to the US, where the FAA makes recommendations to EASA for the issuance and continuation of AMO approvals. Therefore, instead of inspecting every single AMO, EASA monitors only the overall quality of the inspection work done by the FAA through a system of sampling inspections.[111] The result is a significant leveraging of EASA's resources and less cost for the industry. The same procedure is applied to AMOs located in the EU and seeking FAA certification.

As indicated above, BASAs are concluded on the premise of equivalency of regulatory systems of the bilateral partners. This means that although the requirements do not have to be exactly the same, they have to produce equivalent results.[112] Therefore, although full harmonisation of requirements between the BASA partners is not absolutely necessary, the benefits of a BASA will be larger where differences are smaller. Under a BASA, once the significant differences are identified, they are addressed through, so-called 'special conditions'.[113] The ICAO objective of achieving 'the highest practicable degree of uniformity in regulations, standards, procedures'[114] is therefore also very relevant for such agreements.

BASAs however also have limitations. Traditionally, they address acceptance of technical findings only, with limited possibility of certificate acceptance. Even under the EU-US BASA, which is based on many years of regulatory harmonisation between Europe and US, the scope of certificate acceptance is very limited. In 2014, only certain design (minor changes, repairs, design organisations) and production (production organisations) approvals were being accepted by the parties without re-issuance of a separate approval. Beyond technical differences, there are also legal reasons for such limitations. The EU-US BASA is considered by the US government as an 'executive agreement' concluded without the 'advice and consent' of the US Senate.[115] This

110. EASA, 'Maintenance organisations located in the USA: Part-145 US Approvals (MOA)' http://easa.europa.eu/system/files/dfu/USA_EASA_145.pdf [accessed 5 August 2014].

111. EASA-FAA Maintenance Annex Guidance (MAG Change 4 – 29 January, 2014) , http://easa.europa.eu/document-library/bilateral-agreements [accessed 5 August 2014].

112. EASA, 'Aviation Safety Agreement between the United States and the European Community' 2011) www.faa.gov/aircraft/repair/media/EASA_US_roadshows.pdf [accessed 5 August 2014].

113. In the EU-US BASA, *supra* note 97, special conditions are defined as: 'those requirements in the EU and US regulations that have been found, based on a regulatory comparison, not to be common to both systems and which are significant enough that they must be addressed.'

114. 'Chicago Convention', Article 37.

115. Under US law, a treaty is an agreement negotiated and signed by the executive branch that enters into force if it is approved by a two-thirds majority of the Senate and is subsequently ratified by the President. However, the great majority of international agreements that the US enters into are not treaties but executive agreements, meaning agreements entered into by the executive branch, that are not submitted to the Senate for its advice and consent. Congress

means that it cannot derogate from domestic US law. From the EU perspective, an international agreement that has been ratified by the European Parliament and the Council has status above EU regulations.[116] A practical consequence of that difference is that although the EU could directly accept FAA issued certificates, this is not possible for the US.[117]

Development of BASAs also takes time and resources, as they involve detailed regulatory comparisons and confidence building exercises. For example, it took seven years for the EU and US to develop and conclude their BASA.[118] The effort involved will therefore only make their conclusion worthwhile between States exchanging high volumes of aeronautical products, personnel and services. Finally, because they are bilateral in nature, BASA do not necessarily contribute to unification of the international regime, and sometimes may even contribute to its further fragmentation. This is because the requirements for acceptance of products, services or personnel may be different in each bilateral case.

Beyond the BASAs, other methods used by States to reduce redundant regulatory oversight and accepting certifications made by other authorities is through multilateral harmonisation and cooperation initiatives, including at regional levels. Such cooperation can take various forms, such as joint inspection schemes, development of common regulatory requirements, or establishing a RASO type body.

[D] Role of ICAO in Global Safety Oversight

The role of ICAO in overseeing implementation of international civil aviation safety standards has already been subject to analyses by many authors.[119] Today consensus seems to exist that the most successful instrument that ICAO has at its disposal in this

---

generally requires only notification upon the entry into force of an executive agreement. For further information see: Congressional Research Service, 'International Law and Agreements: Their Effect Upon U.S. Law', RL32528, (2010).

116. Herwig C.H. Hofmann, Gerard C. Rowe, and Alexander H. Türk, Administrative Law and Policy of the European Union, (2011), pp. 78-79. For an overview of the legal status of international agreements in the internal EU legal order see also: 'Case C-366/10, Air Transport Association of America v. Secretary of State for Energy and Climate Change', in: [2011] ECR I-13755, (CJEU, 2011) (paragraph 50).

117. Michael Jennison, 'The Future of Aviation Safety Regulation: New US-EU Agreement Harmonizes and Consolidates the Transatlantic Regime, but What is the Potential for Genuine Regulatory Reform', ASL, 38 (2013), p. 344.

118. The negotiating mandate was granted to the European Commission on 9 March 2004, the Agreement entered into force on 1 May 2011; see: EASA, 'Information Note: Agreement between the United States of America and the European Union on cooperation in the regulation of civil aviation safety' http://easa.europa.eu/document-library/bilateral-agreements/eu-usa [accessed 5 August 2014].

119. Blumenkron, *supra* note 49 in Ch. 1, at pp. 12-24; Huang, *supra* note 29 in Ch. 1, at pp. 68-81; Weber, *supra* note 48 in Ch. 1, at pp. 90-92; Meglena Boteva, 'A new century and a new attitude towards safety oversight in air transportation', in Master Thesis, (McGill University: Institute of Air and Space Law, 2000), pp. 64-85; Zachary D. Detra, 'The legitimacy of the International Civil Aviation Organization's Universal Safety Oversight Audit Programme', in Master Thesis, (McGill University: Institute of Air and Space Law, 2006); Broderick and Loos, 'Government Aviation Safety Oversight: trust but verify ', *supra* note 7 in Ch. 2, at pp. 1047-1054; Michael Milde, 'Aviation Safety Oversight: Audits and the Law', AASL, XXVI (2001), pp. 173-176.

respect is its USOAP, and the associated transparency mechanisms, which have even been referred to as ICAO's 'quasi-enforcement' tool.[120]

The main strength of the USOAP comes from the fact that it is a mandatory programme with a standardised methodology applicable to all ICAO Member States. It is used by ICAO for assessing the level of implementation of ICAO SARPs, and more generally States' overall capability for ensuring effective safety oversight. In practice USOAP has proved to be a powerful diagnosis tool for global aviation safety.

The worldwide level of effective implementation of USOAP protocols can justifiably be criticised as still too low, as Figure 2.2 demonstrates. However, USOAP reports show that generally ICAO Member States make consistent progress in the level of effective implementation of SARPs and in increasing their overall safety oversight capabilities.

Figure 2.2 Level of Effective Implementation of the Eight ICAO CEs of State Safety Oversight (ICAO Member States, August 2014)

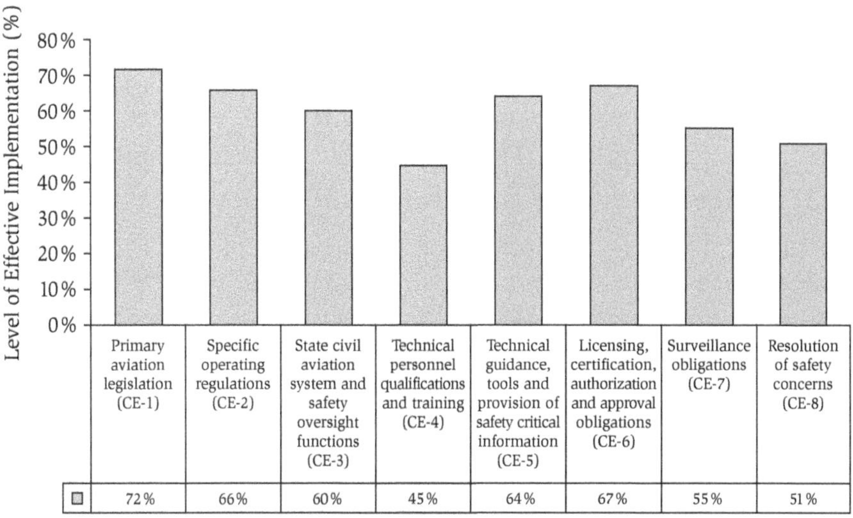

Source: ICAO, Regional Performance Dashboards (2014).[121]

In order to verify the progress that States make in improving their level of effective implementation of the eight CEs, the ICAO USOAP information related to a sample of 35 States was analysed (see Table 2.1). The States in the analysed sample were audited by ICAO in the years 2005-2010, and their corrective action plans were

120. The most comprehensive overview of transparency as ICAO's enforcement tool has been given Blumenkron, *supra* note 49 in Ch. 1, at p. 87; see also Milde, *supra* note 48 in Ch. 1, at p. 180.
121. ICAO, 'Regional Performance Dashboards' http://www.icao.int/safety/Pages/Regional-Targets.aspx [accessed 4 August 2014]. This data is the copyrighted property of the ICAO and is reproduced here with its expressed knowledge and permission. It may not be cited by or reproduced in any other publication without subsequent approval being granted by ICAO.

subsequently verified by ICAO during the ICAO Coordinated Validation Missions (ICVM) in the years 2011–2013.[122] This analysis has shown that all States in the sample have improved the level of effective implementation of USOAP protocols. On average the improvement has been almost 15%. The highest improvements were observed for CEs 1-5 (between 16.3% and 17.5%), followed by CEs 6-7 (12.8% – 10.4%), and finally CE 8 (9.8%).

The above analysis shows that States, at least those in the sample, were able to achieve the highest improvement for those CEs which are related to development of legislation and procedures, while it has been most difficult for them to achieve improvements in CEs related to safety oversight and enforcement obligations. In other words, the greatest improvement has been achieved for CEs which are related to the *establishment of a State's safety oversight system*, while the lowest improvement is for CEs related to its *implementation*, including with respect to enforcement obligations.

Table 2.1 Improvement in the Level of Effective Implementation of the Eight ICAO CEs of State Safety Oversight (Sample of 35 ICAO Member States)

Critical Elements of Safety Oversight System (Correlation with Actual Safety Performance)	*Lack of Effective Implementation during the USOAP CSA Cycle (2005-2010)*	*Lack of Effective Implementation during the USOAP ICVM Cycle (2011-2013)*	*Improvement in the Level of Effective Implementation*
CE-1 (medium)	39.4%	22.6%	16.8%
CE-2 (medium)	48.9%	32.3%	16.6%
CE-3 (strong)	61.1%	44.8%	16.3%
CE-4 (strong)	80.4%	63.0%	17.4%
CE-5 (medium)	54.5%	37.0%	17.5%
CE-6 (very strong)	45.3%	32.5%	12.8%
CE-7 (very strong)	56.1%	45.7%	10.4%
CE-8 (strong)	65.8%	56.0%	9.8%

Source: ICAO, Regional Performance Dashboards and USOAP reports.[123]

The conclusions of the above analysis are important in view of the existing correlation between effective implementation of USOAP protocols and actual accident rates, which is the highest for CEs 6 and 7 (very strong correlation) and CEs 3,4,8 (strong correlation).

122. The purpose of the ICAO ICVM is to ascertain whether previously identified safety deficiencies have been satisfactorily resolved by assessing the status of corrective actions or mitigating measures taken by ICAO Member States to address findings and recommendations, including Significant Safety Concerns (SSC); see ICAO Doc. 9735, *supra* note 13 in Ch. 1, at paragraph 3.5.6.

123. ICAO, 'Regional Performance Dashboards' http://www.icao.int/safety/Pages/Regional-Targets.aspx [accessed 4 August 2014]. This data is the copyrighted property of the ICAO and is reproduced here with its expressed knowledge and permission. It may not be cited by or reproduced in any other publication without subsequent approval being granted by ICAO.

In addition, as has already been demonstrated in Chapter 1 (Figure 1.2), review of the USOAP data shows that levels of implementation of CEs differ across the ICAO regions, as well as within the regions, which means that the Chicago Convention's objective of 'the highest practicable degree of uniformity in regulations, standards, procedures, and organization in relation to aircraft, personnel, airways and auxiliary services' is still far from being met.[124]

Finally, it is clear that the implementation of USOAP has not yet resulted in elimination or significant decrease in the practice of additional safety assessment schemes. The US continues with its IASA programme, while the EU maintains its list of unsafe operators. There are also reciprocal inspections conducted within the framework of BASAs,[125] special purpose assessments conducted on the basis of national or regional requirements,[126] or technical cooperation and assistance programmes assessments.[127]

Although each of such audits or assessments has its own distinct objective and merits, there are overlaps between them which result in duplication of auditing effort and inefficiencies in the use of resources. The objective of some of them, such as the US IASA, or the EU 'safety list' is the same as of USOAP – namely to verify compliance of States with ICAO requirements.

One of the major steps towards improving and optimising the auditing effort at the global level is the ICAO transition towards the CMA. Endorsed by the ICAO Assembly in 2010,[128] the CMA is the most recent step in the development of USOAP and, as of January 2013, is being used to monitor safety oversight capabilities and safety performance of ICAO Member States on a continuous basis, using a risk based approach.[129]

The main reason behind the transition to CMA has been the fact that performance of full scale USOAP audits for all 191 ICAO Member States has become a very expensive and burdensome exercise. At the same time, it provided only a 'snap-shot' reflecting the situation at the moment of the audit. Given that under the traditional approach each State was audited only every five or six years, USOAP was not able to provide up-to-date information regarding global safety oversight performance.[130] Under USOAP CMA, ICAO should be able to provide more reliable, *real time* information about safety oversight performance of States. This, in turn, should offer more possibilities for using

124. 'Chicago Convention', Article 37.
125. Such as the Sampling Inspection Scheme (SIS) under Annex 2 of the 'Agreement between the United States of America and the European Community on cooperation in the regulation of civil aviation safety' (*supra* note 97).
126. For example when EASA in the EU validates a type certificate issued by a third country, it will normally conduct an assessment of its regulatory system concerning aircraft design and continuing airworthiness.
127. It is standard practice to commence a technical assessment project by conducting a gap analysis, which takes ICAO or regional standards as a point of reference.
128. Assembly Resolution A37-5, *supra* note 71.
129. For an overview of the USOAP-CMA see: ICAO Doc. 9735, *supra* note 13 in Ch. 1.
130. ICAO, 'Evolution of the ICAO Universal Safety Oversight Audit Programme (USOAP) beyond 2010', C-WP/13356, (187th session of the ICAO Council), paragraph 5.2.

this information for the purpose of defining corrective actions, taking enforcement actions and certificates acceptance.

In addition to gathering information through remote means, on-site audits will continue to be used under the CMA approach as they provide the possibility to verify, on the ground, information provided by States. They will however be deployed on a more selective basis, essentially in those cases where information provided by States or obtained from other sources by ICAO would indicate a deteriorating safety situation.[131]

From the perspective of this study, the transition to CMA, and the flexibility that it offers in terms of the use of different sources of information to verify compliance with ICAO requirements is of major importance. Of particular relevance, is the fact that when authorising the transition to the CMA, the ICAO Assembly directed the Council to:

> Foster coordination and cooperation between USOAP and audit programmes of other organizations related to aviation safety ... in order to reduce the burden on States caused by repetitive audits or inspections and to decrease the duplication of monitoring activities.[132]

Chapter 4 will demonstrate, using the EU and EASA as examples, how elimination of monitoring activities can be achieved in practice by relying on a regional aviation safety system. Increasing reliance on RASOs by ICAO for monitoring States' compliance with the Chicago Convention and its Annexes is one of the key elements of the GASON concept as proposed in section §2.05 of this chapter.

[E] ICAO Enforcement Efforts and Competences

In addition to being a monitoring tool, USOAP has also become ICAO's main enforcement instrument. Although the evolution towards full transparency of USOAP results has been slow,[133] overall the progress made by ICAO in this respect over the years is encouraging. Today, not only are the USOAP audits shared between all the ICAO Member States, but even the levels of implementation of USOAP protocols per domain of aviation safety are available to the general public.[134]

In addition, at the end of 2012, ICAO Council took a decision to share with the general public, as of January 2014, so-called 'Significant Safety Concerns' (SSC).[135] This decision in practice means the establishment of a global list of States which allow their certificate holders to exercise the privileges attached to the certificate 'although

131. ICAO Doc. 9735, *supra* note 13 in Ch. 1, at paragraphs 3.4-3.5.
132. Assembly Resolution A37-5, *supra* note 71.
133. Blumenkron, *supra* note 49 in Ch. 1, at pp. 26-49.
134. ICAO, 'Safety Audit Information' http://www.icao.int/safety/Pages/USOAP-Results.aspx [accessed 14 March 2014].
135. ICAO, 'Significant Safety Concerns (SSCs) – A mechanism for the sharing of SSCs with the public: Summary of decisions', C-DEC 197/4, (197th session of the ICAO Council, 2012).

the minimum requirements established by the State and by the Standards set forth in the ICAO Annexes are not met, resulting in an immediate safety risk to international civil aviation.'[136]

The decision of ICAO to publish SSCs has important practical and legal consequences. So far the SSCs had been available to States only through a secure ICAO website. This meant that SSCs constituted confidential information which States normally should not disclose to the general public. In practice, States did take this information into account when deciding whether to authorise operators from States with SSCs to perform operations to and from their territories, and even disclosed such information to the general public.[137]

With the SSCs made officially public, it is now possible for States to make direct references to them without any risk of violating ICAO confidentiality arrangements, and even automatically ban affected operators, by refusing to recognise their certificates on the basis of Article 33 and Annex 6. Such automatic bans would be an efficiency gain, as resources would not have to be spent on investigating cases where clear evidence of non-compliance exists and had been made public by ICAO. Passengers and charterers are now also able to directly consult the SSC list when taking travel or business decisions.

In practical terms, although a number of SSCs have been successfully resolved over the past years,[138] overall the number of States affected by them has remained stable since 2010. At the end of 2014, there were fourteen SSCs attributed by ICAO to twelve States, as Table 2.2 demonstrates, half of them from Africa.[139] This shows that there seems to be a group of between eleven and thirteen States which find it very difficult to maintain compliance with even the minimum safety standards of the Chicago Convention. In 2012, the airlines of these States carried in total 1.4 billion of revenue tonne kilometres (RTK) in international scheduled air navigation, which represents only around 0.3 % of worldwide traffic registered by ICAO.[140] This can be considered as a marginal risk to global aviation safety.

136. Definition of 'SSC' can be found in: ICAO Doc. 9735, *supra* note 13 in Ch. 1, at paragraph 1.3.
137. This is for example the case with the EU, which makes reference to the SSCs in decisions banning operators from operating in the airspace of EU Member States, see: EU, 'Commission implementing Regulation (EU) No 659/2013 of 10 July 2013 amending Regulation (EC) No 474/2006 establishing the Community list of air carriers which are subject to an operating ban within the Community', (OJ L 190, 11.7.2013), at paragraph 16.
138. ICAO, 'Universal Safety Oversight Audit Programme - Continuous Monitoring Approach (USOAP CMA)', A38-WP/50, (38th ICAO Assembly, 2013), paragraph 3.3.
139. ICAO, 'Safety Audit Information' http://www.icao.int/safety/Pages/USOAP-Results.aspx [accessed 14 March 2014].
140. ICAO, 'Civil Aviation: 2012 International RTK by State of Air Operator Certificate (AOC)' 2013) http://www.icao.int/Meetings/a38/Pages/documentation-reference-documents.aspx [accessed 14 March 2014].

Table 2.2 ICAO Member States with Significant Safety Concerns (SSC)

End of the Year	*Number of SSC and ICAO Member States with SSC*
2014	14 unresolved SSCs attributed to 12 States
2013	17 unresolved SSCs attributed to 13 States
2012	16 unresolved SSCs attributed to 11 States
2011	16 unresolved SSCs attributed to 12 States
2010	19 unresolved SSCs attributed to 13 States

Source: ICAO, Electronic Bulletins (2010-2014). [141]

In addition to using transparency, ICAO has tried to secure operational enforcement competences, but so far with mixed success. During the 2010 HLSC the ICAO Secretariat proposed that the attribution of three letter designator codes used for radiotelephony purposes could be denied by ICAO to aircraft operators registered in States with SSC.[142] Such competence would effectively allow ICAO to freeze the number of AOC holders in affected States. The 2010 HLSC rejected this proposal on the grounds that granting such competences to ICAO could constitute an undesirable precedent for the future in terms of enforcement powers.[143] The ICAO Secretariat has only been able to convince the ICAO Council to agree to a recommendation that 'States with OPS-related SSCs postpone any request for a new three-letter designator for use in international operations as long as the SSCs remain unresolved.'[144] This demonstrates that possibilities for stronger enforcement measures exist, but in the first place depend on political will rather than legal limitations.

There are also other potential enforcement instruments available, such as the competence of the ICAO Council under Articles 86-87 of the Chicago Convention to determine if an 'international airline is operating in conformity with the provisions of this Convention.' In practice, the banning by ICAO of an international airline under these provisions seems to be a theoretical possibility only, and has so far never been used.[145] This procedure is part of the dispute settlement mechanism and involves the ICAO Council. Past experiences show that ICAO Council is generally reluctant to take formal decisions in the case of disputes between Member States and prefers consultations and negotiations as a tool for resolution of differences.[146] This is scarcely

141. This data is the copyrighted property of the ICAO and is reproduced here with its expressed knowledge and permission. It may not be cited by or reproduced in any other publication without subsequent approval being granted by ICAO.
142. ICAO, 'Improving ICAO Transparency Policy: Sharing and Using Information in a Transparent, Consistent and Fair Manner', HLSC 2010-WP/12, ICAO High Level Safety Conference (Montréal, 2010), paragraph 4.4.
143. 'Personal notes of the author', (ICAO High Level Safety Conference, 2010). Author participated in the conference as the European Commission's coordinator for the EU delegation.
144. ICAO, 'Encouraging the improvement of safety oversight in States with significant safety concerns (SSCs): Summary of decisions', C-DEC 195/6, (195th session of the ICAO Council, 2012).
145. Huang, *supra* note 29 in Ch. 1, at p. 203.
146. Weber, *supra* note 48 in Ch. 1, at pp. 41-44.

acceptable in cases involving aviation safety, which should be kept as a strictly technical matter and acted upon rapidly.

Past criticism concerning ICAO's lack of enforcement competences in the domain of aviation safety is not entirely justified, especially given ICAO's intergovernmental status. As pointed out by Milde, currently none of the UN specialised organisations actually have the competence to take real enforcement measures.[147] Discussions in other UN specialised agencies show that even very serious incidents do not change the general principle of supremacy of State sovereignty in traditional inter-governmental organisations.[148] In terms of achieving improvements ICAO stands out in a relatively positive way.

ICAO will never become a true global enforcer of aviation safety requirements, but also does not have to be. It is in the first place the responsibility of States, individually or jointly, where individually they are too weak, to ensure effective safety oversight and act decisively to address identified deficiencies. ICAO's role should be to monitor States' compliance and to step in with determination if they fail to discharge their responsibilities. In this respect, transparency is likely to remain the main enforcement tool of ICAO at the global level, and States should demonstrate the political will to continue providing it with a clear mandate to further develop and enhance this tool.

The main problem today when it comes to safety oversight and enforcement is the fact that with 191 Member States ICAO does not have the resources and capacity to devote equal attention to all of them. The transition to the CMA is supposed to address this issue by allowing ICAO to focus on those States which present the greatest risk to the international aviation safety system. It remains to be seen, however, if all States will have sufficiently reliable information to support the CMA. One way of addressing this issue is for ICAO to rely more on regional organisations, which could *feed* USOAP-CMA with information about the safety performance of their Member States and ultimately allow ICAO to better prioritise the use of its resources. Relying more on regional organisations could also help ICAO in addressing the enforcement issue. Here a useful analogy with the international maritime sector can be made.

§2.03 LESSONS LEARNED FROM THE INTERNATIONAL MARITIME SECTOR

ICAO is not the only universal organisation responsible for regulating transport matters. In the maritime sector, a similar organisation was established – the IMO.

147. Milde, *supra* note 48 in Ch. 1, at p. 180.
148. See in particular the largely non-conclusive discussions on the extension of inspection and enforcement competences of the International Atomic Energy Agency (IAEA) in the aftermath of the nuclear incidents in the Fukushima nuclear plant in Japan in 2011, at: The Associated Press, 'IAEA's nuclear-disaster measures stay voluntary' http://www.cbc.ca/news/world/iaea-s-nuclear-disaster-measures-stay-voluntary-1.1078542 [accessed 13 March 2014]. For more general discussion about IAEA enforcement competences see also: Jack I. Garvey, Nuclear Weapons Counterproliferation: A new grand bargain, (2013), p. 103.

Created in 1948 as a specialised agency of the UN, IMO has global membership and is responsible for the safety and security of international shipping and the prevention of marine pollution by ships.[149] IMO has been facing problems similar to ICAO in terms of ensuring uniform implementation and enforcement of its safety standards. The approach of the maritime sector to tackling these problems has been by setting standards at the global level and relying on regional cooperation to ensure their correct implementation and enforcement.

In contrast to ICAO, IMO regulates maritime safety by means of international conventions which are legally binding. In practice, however, it also experienced problems with their implementation. Maritime conventions, although ratified by the majority of the world tonnage States, still need implementation into national legal orders and proper enforcement.[150] Given that not all States have the same expertise, experience and resources to do this properly, the 'origination of an IMO convention does not always translate into its implementation and effective enforcement'[151] by the 'Flag States'. These experiences suggest that even if ICAO Annexes had a legally binding nature – meaning without the possibility of filing differences – it is not likely that this would actually translate into their better implementation at national levels.

The problem with implementation of IMO safety standards became very acute in the 1950s, with the emergence of the so-called 'open registries' or 'flags of convenience', which offered ship-owners much more favourable registration conditions than those in traditional national 'Flag States', including tax incentives and the ability to hire non-national, usually cheaper, crews.[152] Such 'open registries', by focusing on maximising the number of registrations and associated registration fees, attracted significant criticism from both inside and outside the maritime industry for not being able to exercise sufficient oversight over the safety standards of ships carrying their flags.[153] This in turn put into question the legitimacy of the exclusivity of 'Flag State' jurisdiction – which has been a traditional principle of IMO, similar to the 'State of Registry' jurisdiction under the Chicago Convention. The situation thus called for 'supplementary jurisdiction over ships by port and coastal States.'[154]

A turning point in the attitude of the international community to enforcement of international maritime safety standards was when a massive oil spill occurred off the coast of Brittany, France, as a result of the grounding of the 'MV Amoco Cadiz', which flew the Liberian flag.[155] This incident caused 'a strong political and public outcry in Europe for far more stringent regulations with regard to the safety of shipping.'[156]

149. IMO, 'IMO website' http://www.imo.org [accessed 14 March 2014].
150. Oya Z. Özçayır, 'The use of port State control in maritime industry and the application of the Paris MoU', OCLJ, 14 (2009), pp. 201-204.
151. *Ibid.* See also: IMO, 'Implementation, Control and Coordination' http://www.imo.org/OurWork/Safety/Implementation/Pages/Default.aspx [accessed 14 March 2014].
152. Allianz, 'Safety and Shipping 1912-2012: From Titanic to Costa Concordia', (2012), p. 38.
153. *Ibid.*
154. Henrik Ringbom, The EU maritime safety policy and international law, (2008), p. 167.
155. 'History's 10 Most Famous Oil Spills', http://www.gcaptain.com/historys-10-most-famous-oil-spills/ [accessed 5 August 2014].
156. 'Paris Memorandum of Understanding on Port State Control', https://www.parismou.org/about-us/history [accessed 5 August 2014].

Following these developments, a number of European countries together with the European Commission, the IMO, and the International Labour Organization agreed that 'the elimination of substandard shipping would be best achieved by coordination of port States.'[157] This resulted in the signing in 1982, of the first regional memorandum of understanding on Port State Control (PSC) – the 'Paris MoU'.[158]

PSC involves the inspection of foreign ships in national ports to verify that the condition of the ship and its equipment comply with the requirements of international regulations and that the ship is manned and operated in compliance with these rules.[159] At the time of the signing of the Paris MoU, the concept of PSC was not new – many of the IMO conventions already contained provisions for ships to be inspected when they visit foreign ports to ensure that they met requirements prescribed by these instruments.[160] It was however the regional approach to port control that gave this traditional instrument a completely new, 'extremely effective' dimension.[161] As observed by a commentator:

> The wide-scale adoption of port State control is an attempt to develop an exception to the competitive relationship of ports within the same region. Where the ports cooperate by agreeing to apply the same rules in a similar manner, then no single port seeks or acquires competitive advantage by offering to overlook sub-standard vessels.[162]

Following the Paris MoU other regions followed suit. At present, nine regional MoUs on PSC are in place in different parts of the world, all based on the Paris MoU model.[163] The Paris MoU is considered the most stringent one, as in addition to the

157. Özçayır, 'The use of port State control in maritime industry and the application of the Paris MoU', *supra* note 150, at p. 209.
158. 'Memorandum of Understanding on Port State Control', Paris, 26 January 1982.
159. IMO, 'Port State Control' http://www.imo.org/OurWork/Safety/Implementation/Pages/PortStateControl.aspx [accessed 5 August 2014].
160. 'International Convention for the Safety of Life at Sea (SOLAS)', London, 1 November 1974, 1184 UNTS 3; 'International Convention on Load Lines', London, 5 April 1966, 640 UNTS 133; 'International Convention on Standards of Training, Certification and Watchkeeping for Seafarers', London, 7 July 1978, 1361 UNTS 2; 'International Convention for the Prevention of Pollution from Ships (MARPOL 1973) as modified by the Protocol 1978 relating thereto (MARPOL 73/78)', London, 17 February 1978, 1340 UNTS 61.
161. IMO, 'Port State Control' http://www.imo.org/OurWork/Safety/Implementation/Pages/PortStateControl.aspx [accessed 5 August 2014].
162. Ted L. McDorman, 'Regional port State control agreements: some issues of international law', OCLJ, 5 (2000), p. 209.
163. 'The Acuerdo De Vina del Mar Agreement on Port State Control of Vessels', 5 November 1992; 'The Memorandum of Understanding on Port State Control in the Asia-Pacific Region', 2 December 1993; 'The Memorandum of Understanding on Port State Control in the Mediterranean Region', 11 July 1997; 'The Memorandum of Understanding on Port State Control for the Indian Ocean Region', 5 June 1998; 'The Memorandum of Understanding on Port State Control for the West and Central Africa Region', 22 October 1999; 'The Memorandum of Understanding on Port State Control in the Black Sea Region', 1 April 2000; 'Paris MoU', *supra* note 158; 'The Memorandum of Understanding on Port State Control in the Caribbean Region ', 9 February 1996; 'The Riyadh Memorandum of Understanding on Port State Control in the Gulf Region', 30 June 2004.

detention of sub-standard vessels – which is a feature of all PSC MoUs – it also envisages banning those ships persistently found not to be in compliance with IMO standards from the ports of the participating States.[164] All regional MoUs also publish *white*, *gray* and *black* lists of States, according to the safety performance of the vessels carrying their flag.[165]

Although originally intended to be a back up to 'Flag State' implementation, PSC has become an indispensable instrument in enforcing international maritime conventions, and a reaction of the international community against the weaknesses in the enforcement of IMO rules.[166]

However, the emergence of regional MoUs on PSC has been a *bottom-up* process.[167] Although IMO encouraged and promoted this system, notably through the adoption of common requirements for PSC,[168] it was not directly involved in coordinating such schemes or taking measures on the basis of the results of the inspections conducted by the 'Port States'. The largest 'Flag States' have in fact been sceptical about a more active role for IMO in PSC.[169]

The PSC system is not an ideal solution. First of all, it is not a substitute for the proper exercise of 'Flag State' responsibility. As in the aviation sector, ramp inspections cannot be a substitute for proper oversight by the 'State of Registry' of an aircraft. Also, as observed by another commentator, PSC do not have uniform application in all regions and sometimes not even within the same region, which may result in varied standards of inspectors and inspections.[170]

Despite the above, the data available as well as the opinions of the commentators indicate that PSC is overall an effective instrument. A study conducted in Sweden on the PSC data collected by the Swedish Maritime Administration in the years 1996-2001 indicates a high percentage of vessels exhibiting a reduction in the total number of reported deficiencies between earlier and subsequent inspections.[171] Similarly at the level of Paris[172] and Tokyo MoUs,[173] and in the US (US Coast Guard's Port State Control)[174] the ratio of ship detentions in the years 2001-2010 has decreased, although

164. 'Paris MoU', *supra* note 158, at section 4.
165. See for example: Tokyo MoU Secretariat, 'Annual Report on Port State Control in the Asia-Pacific Region', (2012), http://www.tokyo-mou.org/doc/ANN12-r.pdf [accessed 14 March 2014].
166. Former official of the European Maritime Safety Agency (EMSA), 'Interview No 5', (2014).
167. Official of the European Maritime Safety Agency (EMSA), 'Interview No 2', (2012).
168. IMO, 'Assembly Resolution A.1052(27): Procedures for Port State Control', (2011).
169. 'Interview No 5', (2014), *supra* note 166.
170. Özçayır, 'The use of port State control in maritime industry and the application of the Paris MoU', *supra* note 150, at p. 238.
171. Pierre Cariou, Maximo Q. Jr. Mejia, and Francois-Charles Wolff, 'On the effectiveness of port State control inspections', Transportation Research Part E (2008), pp. 491–503.
172. Paris MoU Secretariat, 'Annual Report, Statistical Annex', (2012).
173. Annual Report on Port State Control in the Asia-Pacific Region, (2012), *supra* note 165, at pp. 2019-2020.
174. US Coast Guard, 'Port State Control in the United States: Annual Report', (2011), p. 4.

the overall number of inspections in these three regions has increased during that period. It is believed that the PSC, despite some of its shortcomings, will 'remain as the most effective control systems for shipping in a progressing world.'[175]

The PSC system, and in particular the Paris MoU, are important for this study because they inspired the EU rules concerning the banning of unsafe aircraft.[176] Similar to the Paris MoU region, in the EU, the ratio of findings[177] under the Safety Assessment of Foreign Aircraft (SAFA) programme[178] has been decreasing over time, suggesting that the overall safety compliance of aircraft landing at European airports has improved (Figure 2.3).[179]

The SAFA data has however to be interpreted with caution, as it does not necessarily mean that all sub-standard aircraft affected by the SAFA inspections have improved their performance. The observed improvement can in part be attributed to the fact that some of the aircraft stopped operating to the EU because of operating restrictions imposed on them as a result of identified deficiencies. If however SAFA, like PSC, had global or nearly global coverage, the sub-standard aircraft would find it more difficult to relocate their operations to regions more tolerant to safety deficiencies. The EU is leading in this respect with its SAFA programme, covering by the end of 2013 not only the 28 EU Member States but also most ECAC States and a number of non-European countries including Morocco, Singapore, Canada, Israel and United Arab Emirates (UAE). [180] Another example of a regional aircraft ramp inspection programme is the Safety Ramp Inspection Data Exchange Programme – IDISR operated by the Regional System on Safety Oversight in Latin America (SRVSOP), and which is very similar to the EU SAFA programme.[181]

175. Özçayır, 'The use of port State control in maritime industry and the application of the Paris MoU', *supra* note 150, at p. 239.
176. The Head of Unit of the European Commission, who was leading the development of this legislation, had previously been responsible for maritime safety in the European Commission.
177. Ratio of findings stands here for number of findings per inspection.
178. For an overview of the SAFA programme see: EC, 'The EC SAFA Programme: Past, Present and Future' http://ec.europa.eu/transport/modes/air/safety/doc/2009_12_04_info_fiche_safa_programme.pdf [accessed 5 August 2014].
179. EC, 'European Union SAFA Program', COM (2012) 91 final, p. 12.
180. See: EASA, 'Safety Assessment Of Foreign Aircraft (EC SAFA Programme)' http://easa.europa.eu/easa-and-you/aviation-domain/commercial-aviation/safety-assessment-foreign-aircraft-ec-safa-programme [accessed 5 August 2014]. Negotiations with other non-European States on their participation in the EU SAFA programme were ongoing at the time of writing this study.
181. Official of the Regional System on Safety Oversight in Latin America (SRVSOP), 'Interview No 8', (2014).

Figure 2.3 Evolution of the SAFA Inspections Ratio on a Regional Basis

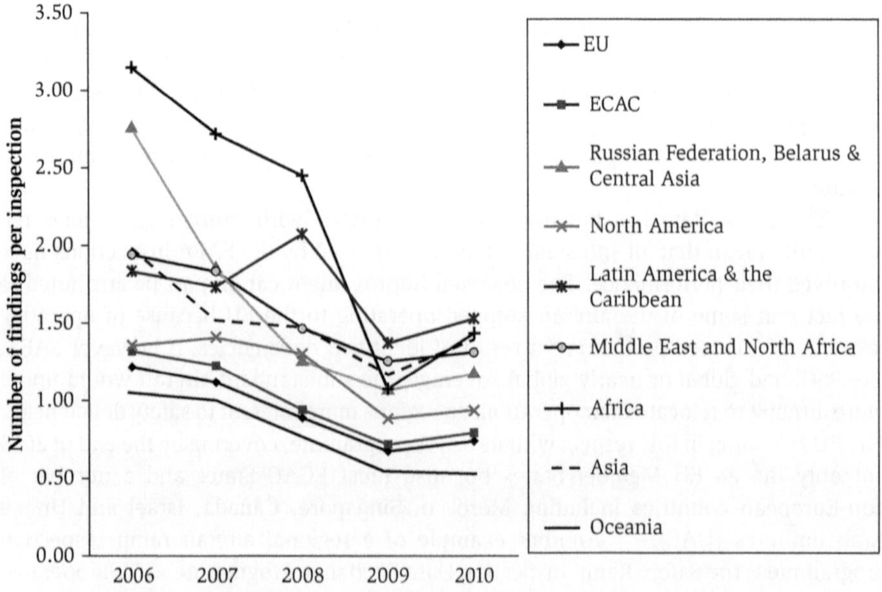

Source: European Commission, Annual EU SAFA programme reports (2006-2010).

The legal basis for such a global ramp inspection safety network is set out in Article 16 of the Chicago Convention, which gives States the right to search, without unreasonable delay, aircraft of the other contracting States on landing or departure, and to inspect the certificates and other documents prescribed by the Chicago Convention. This provision could be used by ICAO to promote the development of regional ramp inspection schemes similar to PSC MoUs. The practical implementation of such schemes at regional levels could be coordinated by RASOs, as is the case in Europe or in Latin America.

This is just one example of how regional cooperation can contribute to better implementation and enforcement of international safety requirements and help ICAO to achieve a more uniform application in different parts of the world. The subsequent chapters of this study will demonstrate how RASOs, and regional cooperation initiatives more generally, can be used to develop and promote these and other safety initiatives, or even to exercise safety functions on behalf of States or national aviation authorities. Before that, it is however necessary to briefly analyse the role of ICAO in promoting regional cooperation on aviation safety in general.

§2.04 ICAO AND THE REGIONAL GOVERNANCE OF CIVIL AVIATION SAFETY

[A] Development of ICAO Regional Policy

The idea of regional collaboration in international civil aviation has a long tradition. The Chicago Conference in 1944 discussed the concept of 'Regional Councils of the International Air Authority', which were supposed to be 'responsible for regional aviation matters and certification of international air operators established in States of a given region.'[182]

From the perspective of the Chicago Convention, the main provision addressing the issue of regional cooperation is Article 55(a), which gives the ICAO Council the possibility of:

> Establishing subordinate air transport commissions on a regional or other basis and define groups of States or airlines with or through which it may deal to facilitate the carrying out of the aims of this Convention.

In practice the above article has not been used much, as ICAO prefers instead to rely on Assembly resolutions to cooperate with regional civil aviation bodies.[183] This is the traditional way which ICAO uses to develop policy and programmes in areas which are not explicitly addressed in the Chicago Convention.[184]

In 1956, the ICAO Assembly adopted a policy framework to govern relations with ECAC - the oldest regional aviation body in existence today.[185] This cooperation was subsequently extended to other regional aviation organisations or bodies such as the AFCAC, LACAC and the Arab Civil Aviation Commission (ACAC).[186]

These very first arrangements between ICAO and regional civil aviation bodies were largely of an administrative nature, and covered issues such as provision of secretarial services, coordination of meeting agendas or exchange of documentation and studies on technical subjects.[187] Under these arrangements, regional offices of ICAO were also used to provide assistance, especially in the initial phase of setting up a regional body.[188]

182. In particular see: 'Canadian Revised Preliminary Draft of an International Air Convention' (Proceedings of the International Civil Aviation Conference), *supra* note 42 in Ch. 1.
183. Weber, *supra* note 48 in Ch. 1, at pp. 119-123.
184. Other examples of ICAO using Assembly Resolutions to develop policies in areas not covered by the Chicago Convention include the setting up of USOAP, or dealing with environmental protection issues.
185. ICAO, 'Assembly Resolution A10-5: Relationship of ICAO with the European Civil Aviation Conference', (10th ICAO Assembly, 1956).
186. Weber, *supra* note 48 in Ch. 1, at pp. 119-123.
187. For an overview of the early cooperation between ICAO and regional civil aviation bodies see: ICAO, 'Relationship of ICAO with regional civil aviation bodies', A21-WP/35, (21st ICAO Assembly, 1974).
188. *Ibid.*

This initial ICAO policy was consolidated in 1989 following adoption of the ICAO Assembly Resolution on general principles of cooperation with regional civil aviation bodies. The objective of this policy was to:

> Support the work and activities of any existing or future regional civil aviation bodies wherever such support is requested by the regional body concerned and duly approved, taking into account the resources of ICAO and the implementation of its Work Programme.[189]

The 1989 policy helped to give more predictability and stability to the planning of financial support to regional bodies, whilst at the same time providing a generic, formal basis for cooperation in the shape of working arrangements to be concluded by the Council on behalf of ICAO.

At present much of the ICAO work is organised on a regional basis, with the Headquarters responsible for defining the overall policy, and relying on regional meetings and offices for implementation and feedback:

(1) From the air navigation perspective ICAO divided the world into nine air navigation regions, with their boundaries corresponding more or less with the geography of major continental/sub-continental and oceanic masses.[190] Each of the regions has its corresponding Regional Air Navigation Meeting, responsible for planning of air navigation services and facilities which are then set out in Regional Air Navigation Plans (RANP). The monitoring of the implementation of RANPs is conducted through Planning and Implementation Regional Groups, established by the ICAO Council.[191]

(2) Going beyond air navigation matters, the implementation of ICAO policies in the regions is the responsibility of the seven regional offices located in Bangkok, Cairo, Dakar, Lima, Mexico, Nairobi, and Paris. Regional offices are the *eyes and ears* of ICAO in the regions and the main tool through which support is provided 'on the ground' to ICAO Member States. Their activities involve, in particular:
   (a) developing plans of actions to assist States with significant safety concerns, or facing difficulties in resolving safety-related deficiencies, as well as following them up through dedicated USOAP activities;
   (b) organisation of regional symposia, workshops and training activities;
   (c) support to implementation of air navigation plans and programmes such as performance based navigation;

189. ICAO, 'Assembly Resolution A27-17: Relationship between ICAO and Regional Civil Aviation Bodies', (27th ICAO Assembly, 1989).

190. Asia (ASIA), Pacific (PAC), Middle East (MID), African Ocean (AFI), North America (NAM), Caribbean (CAR), South America (SAM), Europe (EUR) and North Atlantic (NAT); see: ICAO, 'Directives to Regional Air Navigation Meetings and Rules of Procedure for their Conduct', ICAO Doc. 8144-AN/874, (1991).

191. For a more detailed overview of the ICAO regional air navigation planning mechanisms see: Van Antwerpen, *supra* note 52 in Ch. 1, at pp. 25-27.

(d) helping States to develop action plans for mitigating impact of aviation on environment;
(e) providing technical support with a view to enhancing the capacity of States to effectively implement SARPs.[192]

Most recently, in the area of aviation safety a dedicated regional framework with global coverage has been also put in place – the Regional Aviation Safety Groups (RASGs), which will be addressed in more detail in section §2.04[C] below.

To conclude, although the Chicago Convention only very scarcely addresses the issue of regional cooperation, this has in practice not prevented ICAO from basing its operations largely on a regional basis, and developing active cooperation with a number of regional civil aviation bodies. This policy however has been built incrementally and largely on an ad hoc basis. With the increasing role of regional organisations such as the EU and the African Union (AU) in regulating civil aviation, ICAO felt that there was a need to review its policy and to make its cooperation with regional civil aviation organisations and bodies more operational and much deeper. This was a trigger for the development of a completely new comprehensive policy and framework for regional cooperation which is presented in the following section.

[B] The 2010 ICAO Policy and Framework for Regional Cooperation

In 2009, ICAO started reviewing its policy on cooperation with regional aviation bodies. There were two main drivers behind that development. Firstly, the growing significance of regional cooperation in different parts of the world meant that there was a need for closer coordination between ICAO and these bodies, with a view to avoiding duplication of work or even conflicting developments. Secondly, the emergence of specialised regional aviation bodies with regulatory, oversight and even enforcement competences was being increasingly seen by ICAO and the international aviation community as a way to address some of the pressing problems especially in the area of aviation safety.

The trigger for the commencement of this review work was a Symposium on regional organisations organised in 2008 by ICAO and the European Commission.[193] The objective of the Symposium was to discuss the experiences of regional aviation bodies, their contributions to international civil aviation, and how to strengthen their relationship with ICAO.[194]

The Symposium concluded that 'Regional Organisations in civil aviation are already a positive reality and that a clear trend towards more regional governance can be observed.'[195] It also underlined that, 'while ICAO has historically always been positively inclined to the role of regional organisations, more should be done in

192. For an overview of ICAO regional offices' activities see: ICAO, 'Annual Report to Council on Regional Offices' activities during 2012 and Work Programmes for 2013', C-WP/13919, (2013).
193. EC-ICAO Symposium on Regional Organisations, *supra* note 43 in Ch. 1.
194. *Ibid.*, at 'Summary of Conclusions', paragraph 1.
195. *Ibid.*, at 'Summary of Conclusions', paragraph 5.

strengthening the cooperation and relationship of regional civil aviation bodies with ICAO.'[196] The Symposium made a number of recommendations, which were in particular related to:

- the need for ICAO to continue to use cooperative arrangements with regional organisations such as Memoranda of Understanding (MoU) or Memoranda of Cooperation (MoC);
- the contribution of regional safety organisations to a more effective implementation of ICAO's SARPs; and
- the development of a regular dialogue between ICAO and regional organisations.

The recommendations of the 2008 Symposium were further developed by a multidisciplinary group comprised of members of the ICAO Secretariat, representatives of the ICAO Council and interested representatives of international organisations.[197] The multidisciplinary group delivered its final report for the 188th session of the ICAO Council.[198]

The work of the multidisciplinary group resulted in a far reaching overhaul of the ICAO policy on regional cooperation, including a recommendation that more involvement of ICAO and States at a high level was necessary to implement the policy of regional cooperation.[199] The multidisciplinary group developed three documents, which were subsequently endorsed by the ICAO Council,[200] and the Assembly:[201]

- ICAO's policy on regional cooperation;
- ICAO Framework of Regional Cooperation, and a Strategic Plan of Action for ICAO Headquarters and Regional Offices;
- Template Agreement for Regional Cooperation.

Analysis of the above documents, and the discussions held by the multidisciplinary group, show that the key concern of ICAO has been to avoid, or at least to minimise, the duplication between its activities, at the headquarters' and regional offices' levels, and those of the regional organisations competent in civil aviation, as well as to ensure better harmonisation in all regions of implementation of SARPs and related policies.[202]

196. *Ibid.*, at 'Summary of Conclusions', paragraph 11.
197. ICAO, 'Proposed Terms of Reference of the Secretariat/Council Group on Regional Bodies: Summary of Decisions', C-DEC 186/2, (186th session of the ICAO Council, 2009).
198. ICAO, 'Report of the Secretariat/Council Group on Regional Bodies', C-WP/13404, (188th session of the ICAO Council, 2009).
199. *Ibid.*, at paragraph 2.2.
200. ICAO, 'Report of the Secretariat/Council Group on Regional Bodies: Summary of Decisions', C-Dec 188/3, (2009).
201. Assembly Resolution A37-21, *supra* note 44 in Ch. 1.
202. ICAO, 'Cooperation with Regional Organizations and Regional Civil Aviation Bodies', A37-WP/28, (37th ICAO Assembly, 2010). See in particular: Appendix, Point 3 'Objectives of the Policy'.

In order to achieve the objectives of the new policy, and to make sure that all areas of regional cooperation are covered, the above mentioned 'ICAO Framework of Regional Cooperation' proposes 'eight strategic thrusts':

(1) common efforts at harmonizing, between States, operational regulations requirements and procedures based on ICAO SARPs implementation;
(2) understanding each other's roles and responsibilities;
(3) establishment of improved mechanisms for consultation and cooperation, including electronic information sharing;
(4) coordinated programme planning and implementation between ICAO and the regional civil aviation bodies;
(5) periodic review of regional issues;
(6) maximising the effective use of resources at ICAO;
(7) benefiting from each other's competence and expertise; and
(8) joint training and capacity building.

Following its endorsement by the Assembly, the policy is being implemented by ICAO through regional operational plans, consistent with the overall ICAO Business Plan.[203] As indicated above, one of the key objectives of the new policy is to better define the roles and responsibilities of ICAO and regional civil aviation bodies and organisations in the various ICAO regions with a view to avoiding overlap and optimising the use of resources. This is being achieved by formalising the cooperation through MoUs.

Although ICAO in the past used different instruments to formalise cooperation with regional bodies, the new regional policy envisages a more systematic and standardised approach. Based on a 'Template Agreement for Regional Cooperation', by the end of 2013 ICAO had signed MoUs with all the main regional civil aviation bodies and organisations, including: AU, EU, ACAC, AFCAC, ECAC and LACAC.[204]

The MoUs address issues such as improved mechanisms for consultation and cooperation, including electronic information sharing; coordinated programme planning and implementation by ICAO and the regional civil aviation bodies; and joint training and capacity building.

The MoUs provide a general framework of cooperation between ICAO and regional organisations and regional civil aviation bodies, including in respect of safety matters, where the RASOs play an increasingly important role.

203. ICAO, 'Cooperation with Regional Organizations and Regional Civil Aviation Bodies', A38-WP/9, (38th ICAO Assembly, 2013).
204. ICAO, Press Release No. 09/10, *supra* note 1.

[C] ICAO Views on Regional Aviation Safety Organisations

The global picture of regional cooperation on aviation safety matters is currently quite complex and involves a number of layers and forms of cooperation.

Following the establishment of USOAP in the 1990s, ICAO realised that SARPs are far from being applied in a uniform manner across the world, and that in addition some of the States do not have the necessary expertise or resources to establish effective safety oversight systems. In response to these problems it started setting up technical assistance programmes on a regional basis known as COSCAPs (Cooperative Development of Operational Safety and Continuing Airworthiness Programme).[205]

The main objective of COSCAPs is to assist States in the development of a harmonised regulatory framework and effective implementation of the CEs of safety oversight as identified by ICAO.[206] Their scope was originally limited to pilot licensing, flight operations and airworthiness matters, that is Annexes 1, 6 and 8 to the Chicago Convention, but over time extended to other areas of aviation safety, including ATM, aerodromes, and accident investigation, in line with the CSA of USOAP.[207] At the end of 2014, seven COSCAP projects were still in operation.[208]

Finally, in 2010 ICAO decided to create another structure – the RASGs – 'to address and harmonize all flight operations safety issues on an ICAO region-wide basis.'[209] When establishing the RASGs ICAO argued that both COSCAPs and RASOs created by States are established on a sub-regional basis only and focus mainly on oversight issues. The main objective behind ICAO creating RASGs is to have a system with world-wide coverage (see Figure 2.4) to monitor and coordinate the implementation of the GASP.

205. The first COSCAP projects were set up at the end of the 1990s when ICAO has been transitioning to USOAP as a mandatory programme.
206. ICAO Doc. 9734 Part B, *supra* note 3 in Ch. 1, at paragraph 3.2.2.
207. ICAO, 'COSCAPs in Five Regions ', World Bank/ICAO Air Transport Development Forum (Kuala Lumpur, 2008), http://www.icao.int/Meetings/wrdss2011/Documents/Development Forum2008/Sander-Fischer.pdf [accessed 18 March 2014].
208. ICAO, 'RSOOs and COSCAPs' 2014) http://www.icao.int/safety/Implementation/Lists/COS CAP_RSOO/AllItems.aspx [accessed 14 October 2014].
209. ICAO, 'Report of ANC — Establishment of Regional Aviation Safety Groups (RASGs): Summary of Decisions', C-Dec 190/4, (190th session of the ICAO Council 2010).

Figure 2.4 ICAO Regional Aviation Safety Groups

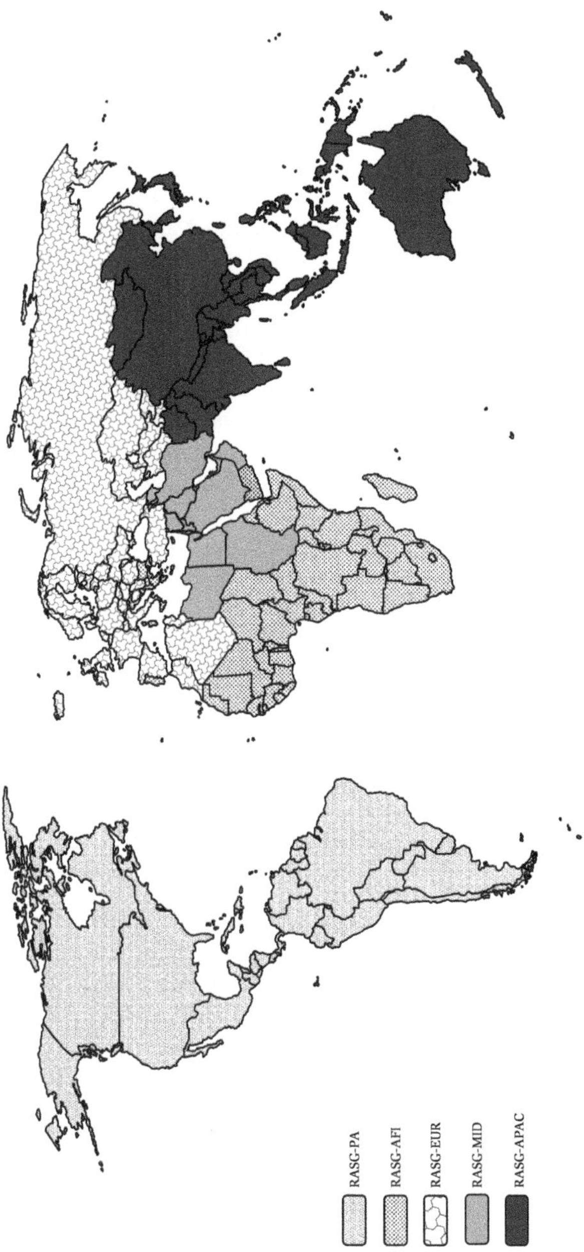

Source: ICAO, State of Global Aviation Safety (2013).[210]

210. This map is the copyrighted property of the ICAO and is reproduced here with its expressed knowledge and permission. It may not be cited by or reproduced in any other publication without subsequent approval being granted by ICAO.

What we can therefore see is that, although the Chicago Convention is almost silent about regional cooperation, the concept itself is very much supported by ICAO as far as aviation safety matters are concerned. This is especially visible when it comes to RASOs – which in the ICAO jargon are referred to as Regional Safety Oversight Organisations (RSOO) or Regional Accident Investigation Organisations (RAIO) depending on the type of activity they undertake.[211]

RASOs are specialised bodies tasked with assisting States in regulating and overseeing civil aviation activities, or even taking over some or all of such functions from the national governments. A limited number of such bodies evolved from COSCAP projects as Chapter 3 will demonstrate. Although some of these organisations have history dating back as far as the 1970s, a significant number of them have only been set up in the last twelve years.

The concept of establishing RASOs was endorsed by ICAO Assembly in 2004[212] and since then has become an official part of ICAO policy, currently reflected in a number of Assembly resolutions,[213] ICAO Annexes[214] and manuals, two of which are dedicated entirely to the establishment of RSOOs and RAIOs.[215] One of the Assembly resolutions even puts RSOOs almost on an equal footing with States, when it comes to the USOAP.[216]

Under the current policy established by the Assembly, the ICAO Council is directed to 'promote the concept of regional cooperation for the purpose of enhancing safety and safety oversight, including the establishment of regional safety oversight organizations.'[217] Similarly, ICAO Member States are encouraged 'to participate in, or provide tangible support for, the strengthening and furtherance of sub-regional and regional aviation safety and safety oversight bodies, including regional safety oversight organizations.'[218] In general, ICAO believes that:

> Establishment of sub-regional and regional aviation safety and safety oversight bodies, including regional safety oversight organizations, has great potential to assist States in complying with their obligations under the Chicago Convention through economies of scale and harmonization on a larger scale.[219]

In particular, RASOs are believed to be an important element of ICAO's response to safety oversight problems faced by Africa, which is currently the least performing ICAO region in terms of aviation safety. As highlighted by AFCAC:

211. Definition and typology of RASOs will be provided in Chapter 3.
212. Assembly Resolution A35-7, *supra* note 32 in Ch. 1, at paragraph 6.
213. See in particular: Assembly Resolution A37-5, *supra* note 71; Assembly Resolution A38-7, *supra* note 3; ICAO, 'Assembly Resolution A38-2: ICAO global planning for safety and air navigation', (38th ICAO Assembly 2013); Assembly Resolution A38-5, *supra* note 32 in Ch. 1.
214. The concept of RSOO and RAIO is referred to in: ICAO, 'Annex 19 to the Chicago Convention: Safety Management', (2013), Forward; ICAO, 'Annex 13 to the Chicago Convention: Aircraft Accident and Incident Investigation', (2010), paragraph 5.1 and paragraph 5.1.2.
215. ICAO Doc. 9734 Part B, *supra* note 3 in Ch. 1; ICAO Doc. 9946, *supra* note 3 in Ch. 1.
216. Assembly Resolution A37-5, *supra* note 71.
217. Assembly Resolution A38-5, *supra* note 32 in Ch. 1.
218. *Ibid.*
219. *Ibid.*

> Many African States do not have adequate aviation activities that could generate the necessary resources. This low volume of activity is not enough to run a workable safety oversight system. To overcome this problem a Regional Safety Oversight Organization (RSOO) can provide access to the necessary expertise through the sharing and pooling of resources.[220]

The limited available research by aviation experts on RASO type bodies suggests that, under certain conditions, they can provide economies of scale to 'conserve precious human and fiscal resources', and 'promote harmonisation of safety requirements, reducing the burden...on struggling airlines.'[221]

In addition to providing policy and guidance material on RASOs, ICAO is also involved, hands-on, in the development and management of some of these organisations, especially in the initial phase of their operations. Such support includes: drafting of RASO constituent documents, assistance in their management and technical operations, consultation services, training of personnel, provision of information and documents that a RASO may need, and even financial assistance.[222] Finally ICAO also promotes transition of COSCAP projects to RASO type bodies, but in 2014 this process was still ongoing, as Chapter 3 will demonstrate.

Overall, the picture which emerges from a review of ICAO documents and programmes is that of a well-established policy favouring regional cooperation and in particular RASO type bodies as one of the key answers to global safety oversight problems. On the other hand the implementation of this policy is not yet complete, as for example the transition of COSCAPs to RASO is still ongoing. In addition, the parallel existence of RASGs, COSCAPs and RASOs creates a risk of duplication of activities and resulting waste of resources.

The biggest test case for RASOs will be in Africa. Only if RASOs manage to achieve tangible results in helping African States to resolve SSCs and raise the level of implementation of their safety oversight systems to world-average levels, will the real value of these bodies be demonstrated. So far this is not yet the case. As Chapter 5 will demonstrate, the benefits of establishing RASOs cannot always be taken for granted.

Finally, from the perspective of global governance of civil aviation, the ICAO new policy on regional cooperation, and the emergence of RASOs can be seen as exemplification of the phenomenon which is referred to by Boisson de Chazournes as 'dualisme fonctionnel'.[223] This concept, characterises the regional trends which have been taking place since the middle of the twentieth century, and where the regional organisations are seen as vehicles not only to address issues of regional concern but also to tackle global problems, and thus to contribute to better implementation of international law in general.

220. AFCAC, 'Establishment of Regional Safety Oversight Organizations in Africa', A37-WP/166, (37th ICAO Assembly, 2010), paragraph 2.2.
221. Jennison, 'Regional safety oversight bodies deliver economies of scale and greater uniformity', *supra* note 54 in Ch. 1, at pp. 9-12, 34-35.
222. ICAO Doc. 9734 Part B, *supra* note 3 in Ch. 1, at paragraph 6.2.
223. Boisson de Chazournes, *supra* note 43 in Ch. 1, at p. 145-146.

§2.05 PROPOSAL FOR A GLOBAL AVIATION SAFETY OVERSIGHT NETWORK

ICAO needs to reflect on what the ultimate role should be of the RASOs or more generally of regional aviation safety systems, in global safety governance. So far their role has mainly been seen as a way to address deficiencies in safety oversight systems of States which are unable to deal with these deficiencies on their own.

This study argues that, looking from a global perspective, in the short term the most important function of RASOs should continue to be to assist States in resolving their safety oversight deficiencies and setting up sustainable safety oversight systems where this is not yet the case. In the mid- to long term[224] however they should be looked at as potential building blocks for a GASON, as presented by Figure 2.5.

Figure 2.5 Global Aviation Safety Oversight Network[225]

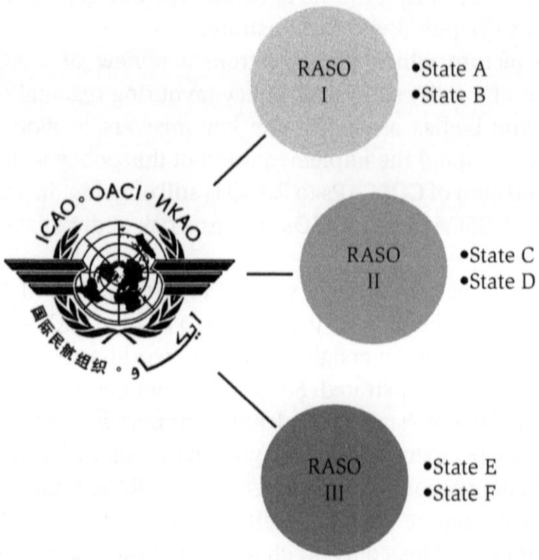

The proposal for a GASON in the first place stems from the fact that, even if individual States are able to ensure implementation of the eight CEs of safety oversight at a satisfactory level, this is by no means a guarantee of the 'highest practicable degree of uniformity in regulations, standards, procedures, and organization', as called for by the Chicago Convention. Implementation can be uneven in terms of uniformity of the legal and procedural frameworks, as well as actual safety levels. States will always

224. As defined in the ICAO Global Aviation Safety Plan (*supra* note 5 in Ch. 1, at p. 4), which means a time horizon between 2022 and 2027.

225. The ICAO logo is the copyrighted property of ICAO and is reproduced here with its expressed knowledge and permission. It may not be cited by or reproduced in any other publication without subsequent approval being granted by ICAO.

retain the right to file differences with SARPs, and thus to make their national systems less or more demanding than the minimum requirements set by ICAO. Also, with the move towards performance based regulation and safety management approaches, as referred to in Chapter 1, standardisation by ICAO of regulatory frameworks between States may become more and more difficult.

From the perspective of ICAO, with its 191 Member States and its current resources, even with the introduction of the USOAP-CMA, it is going to be difficult for it to continue providing support to implementation and oversight at a level required to maintain and hopefully further improve the current safety levels, taking into account the increases in the volume of aviation traffic and in complexity of aviation businesses. Also, as already pointed out in this chapter, although ICAO has good tools for global safety oversight, it is unlikely that it will ever become a true global enforcer of SARPs.

The architecture of the proposed GASON should be based on ICAO relying on and working closely with a number of strong RASOs, which could ensure harmonised implementation of SARPs at regional levels and organise regional enforcement mechanisms, such as ramp inspection schemes.

In a GASON, the RASOs would be an intermediary between the ICAO and States, feeding USOAP-CMA with information about the level of implementation of SARPs and eight CEs in the regions, without prejudice to the right of ICAO to reach out directly to a State if it deemed it necessary.

Such a system would not only allow ICAO to be more efficient in the use of its resources, but would also contribute to more uniform implementation of SARPs as, instead of a multitude of national regimes, the system could ultimately provide for just a few dozen regional schemes which would be much easier for ICAO to standardise. The regions could also conclude multilateral aviation safety agreements enabling large scale recognition of audit results and certifications and thus greatly contributing to the facilitation of aviation business.

As part of the GASON, the regions, through regional safety plans and programmes to be coordinated by ICAO RASGs, could also move in a more concerted manner towards harmonising their actual safety performance, thus contributing to more uniform implementation of safety targets agreed at the global level, in particular in the GASP. From the perspective of an air passenger, the aviation sector should offer not only high but also as uniform as possible level of safety regardless of the points of departure and destination.

The concept of a GASON would of course require a high level of confidence by ICAO in the robustness of the regional systems which it would be monitoring and relying on. This in turn requires the RASOs to be strong and appropriately empowered. This is not yet the case because, as will be demonstrated in subsequent chapters, the vast majority of RASOs currently have only advisory or support functions, with only a few of them having competence to take legally binding decisions or to enforce aviation standards.

Based on the above considerations, this study proposes the following definition of the GASON:

> A worldwide system for the standardisation and monitoring of ICAO Member States' level of effective implementation of eight Critical Elements of State safety oversight, relying on information generated by Regional Aviation Safety Organisations; which are empowered, through international agreements or supranational law, to ensure uniform compliance of their Member States with the Chicago Convention and Standards and Recommended Practices laid down in the Annexes to this Convention.

The first enablers of the GASON are already coming into place. The Assembly Resolution introducing the USOAP-CMA[226] envisages the possibility of ICAO relying on information provided by RASOs. In Europe, the EU has already concluded a special arrangement with ICAO which will allow for an interaction between the ICAO USOAP-CMA and EASA standardisation inspections with a view to ultimately relieving EU States of ICAO audits, and for ICAO to rely on standardisation inspections to verify the level of implementation of the eight CEs and ICAO SARPs in the EU Member States.[227] Other regional organisations, such as the IAC, which will be presented in the next chapter, have entered into arrangements with ICAO to share safety oversight information.[228] Although, still very preliminary, these developments could be seen as small building blocks for the future GASON.

As will be demonstrated in Chapter 5, there is also a clearly visible trend for RASOs to evolve over time into more formalised structures with legal personality and stronger oversight and enforcement competences, which should allow them over time to be able to demonstrate to ICAO that they are able to effectively ensure oversight and discharge other safety functions required by the Chicago Conventions and its Annexes on behalf of States, and thus hopefully to prove effective components of the GASON.

§2.06 GENERAL CONCLUSIONS

The Chicago Convention is a very successful international treaty, if looked at from the perspective of its global acceptance, and predominantly focuses on the regulation of technical aspects of international civil aviation. Yet, in the past it had been subject to some criticism with regard to the effectiveness of global implementation of aviation safety standards, and the enforcement competences of ICAO.

In reality, the very fact that the Chicago Convention achieved such a broad degree of acceptance can be largely attributed to the fact that its drafters managed to strike a good balance between, on the one hand a desire to achieve 'the highest practicable degree of uniformity in regulations, standards, procedures, and organization in relation to aircraft, personnel, airways and auxiliary services', which is necessary for aviation

226. Assembly Resolution A37-5, *supra* note 71.
227. See paragraph 7 of: 'Annex on aviation safety to the Memorandum of Cooperation between the European Union and the International Civil Aviation Organization providing a framework for enhanced cooperation', (OJ L 232, 9 September 2011).
228. A38-WP/50, *supra* note 138, at Appendix, paragraph 5.1.

as a global industry, and on the other hand, the principle that 'each State has complete and exclusive sovereignty over the airspace above its territory.'

The greatest paradox of the system of the Chicago Convention is that over time it has become the victim of the original compromise which allowed the system to be born in the first place. With ICAO's membership increasing steadily to 191 participating States, and based on the principle of individual State responsibility for safety oversight, it has become virtually unavoidable that the level of implementation of SARPs and eight CEs will be variable across the world.

With the differences - sometimes significant - in safety oversight between individual national jurisdictions revealed thanks to USOAP transparency, States, especially those with a good safety record, started to increasingly ring-fence their airspaces and territories with requirements for additional certifications, authorisations, audits and checks. Unilateral inspection schemes started to emerge duplicating the USOAP efforts. Today even the recognition of very basic certificates necessary for day-to-day cross border operations of airlines, such as AOCs, and certificates of airworthiness is being increasingly made conditional upon additional authorisations and surveillance programmes.

It is really hard not to criticise a system which requires, for example, a repair station to obtain up to twenty different certificates to perform exactly the same work, only because the aircraft it works on are registered in twenty different States and which, at least in theory, should follow the same set of minimum international requirements. This '*death by audit*' and, one could also add, '*death by re-certification*', has today become a major source of inefficiency in the global system, in addition to problems that some States experience in setting up effective safety oversight arrangements.

States are of course aware of these inefficiencies and try to address them, in particular through the BASAs, in the hope that this will bring them back to achieving the objective of 'the highest practicable degree of uniformity in regulations, standards, procedures'. However, because they are only bilateral in nature, BASAs, whilst giving benefits to a specific pair of States, from a more general perspective actually contribute to the fragmentation of the global regulatory system.

At the same time, it cannot be denied that ICAO has drawn lessons from the past and is making good progress in helping States to improve their compliance with international requirements, within the scope of its mandate and taking into account the legal and political limitations that it has as an intergovernmental organisation. Differences in safety oversight performance between and within ICAO regions persist, but the review of ICAO audit results show that States are consistently managing to improve the level of effective implementation of USAOP protocols. The overall trend is therefore positive.

At the end of 2013, States with SSCs represented overall only 0.3% of the worldwide international air traffic and ICAO is very committed to further reducing this figure. ICAO is also working on improving the implementation of Article 38 on filing of difference, and has managed to secure a competence to publish, as of 2014, a publicly available list of States with the most serious safety deficiencies. This is not a bad result compared to other intergovernmental organisations, such as the IAEA which is still struggling to convince its Member States to agree to a mandatory system of inspections, even after accidents as terrible as the one at the nuclear plant in Fukushima, Japan in 2011.

There are of course elements which can be further improved, such as more standardisation and uniformity in application of Article 38 on the filing of differences, where ICAO should, in addition to offering an EFOD system, conduct a more general review as to the scope and purpose of notifying the differences.

What is however certainly clear today, is that ICAO, with its 191 Member States, will not be able to continue working as it did in the past with the resources available. The recent shift to the USOAP-CMA methodology is a telling example of that new reality.

ICAO therefore needs to find a way which would allow it, in addition to monitoring State safety performance and helping States in addressing the detected deficiencies and enforcing global standards, to also address more decisively the ongoing erosion of the aviation safety system in terms of redundant regulatory oversight and waste of resources deriving from duplicate certifications. Regional cooperation can be seen as one of the principal answers to these challenges.

Regional cooperation, although only scarcely addressed in the Chicago Convention, is not a new subject for ICAO, who in 2010 adopted a comprehensive 'Policy and Framework for Regional Cooperation'. An integral part of this policy is recognition of the value and support that regional aviation safety organisations or RASOs can provide. Today there is a strong conviction amongst the international aviation community that:

> Establishment of subregional and regional aviation safety and safety oversight bodies, including regional safety oversight organizations, has great potential to assist States in complying with their obligations under the Chicago Convention through economies of scale and harmonization on a larger scale.[229]

The main test case for the effectiveness of RASOs will be in Africa, where many States do not individually have the necessary resources 'to run a workable safety oversight system', and where the overall safety levels – despite improvement – remain the lowest in the world. ICAO should also finalise the transition of COSCAPs into RASO type bodies where it is possible, as the parallel existence of RASGs, COSCAPs and RASOs creates the risk of duplication of effort and waste of resources. This duplication will be further demonstrated in Chapter 3.

Experiences from the international maritime sector and the European SAFA programme demonstrate that regional cooperation can be an effective way to ensure more uniform implementation and enforcement of international safety standards. It can be argued however that ICAO should not be looking at RASOs merely from the perspective of tools to be deployed to address deficiencies in safety oversight systems of States which are unable to deal with such problems on their own. Instead RASOs should be fully integrated into the way ICAO manages safety and used as building blocks for a future GASON.

229. Assembly Resolution A38-5, *supra* note 32 in Ch. 1.

The architecture of the GASON should be based on ICAO relying on and working closely with a number of strong RASOs, which could ensure harmonised implementation of SARPs at regional levels and organise regional enforcement mechanisms. Such a system would not only allow ICAO to be more efficient in the use of resources, but would also contribute to more uniform implementation of SARPs, as instead of a multitude of national regimes, the system could ultimately provide for a more limited number of regional schemes which would be much easier to standardise and control. The regional approach would also contribute to harmonisation of actual safety performance through regional safety performance planning at RASG level and consistent with globally agreed GASP targets.

The concept of the GASON would however require a high level of confidence by ICAO in the robustness of the regional systems which it would be monitoring and relying on. This, in turn, would necessitate strong and appropriately empowered RASOs which is not yet always the case, as the following chapters - presenting and analysing these organisations in detail - will show.

CHAPTER 3
Definition and Typology of Regional Aviation Safety Organisations

> The establishment of regional civil aviation bodies with regulatory and/or executive tasks and responsibilities should not be seen as a threat to the global framework for civil aviation, but as an opportunity to reinforce it and to make it work better.
>
> Daniel Calleja Crespo
> Director for Air Transport at the European Commission (2004-2011)[1]

§3.01 INTRODUCTION

Following a presentation and analysis of the international aviation safety framework as established by the Chicago Convention, as well as of the regional aviation safety policy of ICAO, this chapter will introduce the notion of a RASO (section §3.02) and propose a definition of this kind of organisation (section §3.03). It will also propose a typology of regional aviation safety bodies based on specific features of their legal and organisational set-ups, and illustrate this typology with examples of RASOs and pre-RASOs from different parts of the world (sections §3.04 and §3.05). Finally it will introduce the notion of a Regional Civil Aviation Authority (RCAA), and present and analyse the only existing example of such organisation, the Eastern Caribbean Civil Aviation Authority (ECCAA, section §3.06).

§3.02 THE RASO CONCEPT IN STATE AND ICAO PRACTICE

At present, there is no internationally agreed definition of a RASO as understood in the ICAO context. As was explained in the previous chapters, in practice each of these

1. Former Director of the Air Transport Directorate of the European Commission speaking on the occasion of the EC-ICAO Symposium on Regional Organisations, *supra* note 43 in Ch. 1.

organisations falls into one of the two basic categories, that is RSOO and RAIOs, depending on whether its function is safety regulation and oversight, or investigation of aviation accidents and incidents.

The present approach of ICAO and of the international aviation community is to treat RSOOs and RAIOs as broad concepts covering different forms of cooperation, even including technical cooperation projects. The common denominator which is used by ICAO and States to define an organisation or form of cooperation as a RSOO or a RAIO is its general objective of strengthening safety oversight and investigation capabilities of States located in the same geographical region, rather than being defined by the particular institutional or legal setup.[2]

The above understanding is confirmed by ICAO manuals, which in the case of RSOOs explain that this term:

> Covers, in a general sense, a number of legal forms and institutional structures that range from highly formalized international intergovernmental organizations...to less institutionalized projects established under the ICAO Cooperative Development of Operational Safety and Continuing Airworthiness Programme.[3]

ICAO further explains in its RSOO manual that:

> Assembly resolutions essentially leave it up to each group of States that wishes to establish an RSOO to determine the legal form and institutional structure that best fits the needs and characteristics of their specific region.[4]

In the case of a RAIO, the ICAO manual on this subject simply describes the different functions that such organisations may undertake without offering any specific definition.[5]

There are at least two reasons for this current broad approach of ICAO. Firstly, from a policy point of view, ICAO does not want to exclude from its regional safety framework any initiative, even if institutionally not very formalised, which contributes to the improvement of aviation safety. Most importantly however, as will be demonstrated in Chapter 5, regional aviation safety bodies have a general tendency to evolve over time into more institutionalised forms. Therefore, an organisation which today is only a loose association of national aviation safety authorities could tomorrow be a fully-fledged regional aviation safety agency with legal personality and executive competences. ICAO wants to follow and support such evolutions.

The practical result of the current broad approach is that RASOs differ a lot in the tasks they undertake, their legal status and organisational set ups. At the same time the notion of a RASO, and especially of a RSOO, is being used increasingly in ICAO documentation, including Assembly resolutions and Annexes to the Chicago Convention. In recent years, a tendency can be observed to include in ICAO documents provisions which address specific requests directly to RASOs, or even envisage a

2. See: ICAO, Symposium on regional safety oversight organizations (Montreal, Canada, 2011), http://www.icao.int/Meetings/RSOOSYMPO/Pages/default.aspx [accessed 18 March 2014].
3. ICAO Doc. 9734 Part B, *supra* note 3 in Ch. 1, at Forward.
4. *Ibid.*
5. ICAO Doc. 9946, *supra* note 3 in Ch. 1, at Chapters 2-3.

possibility of attributing to them functions which traditionally, under the Chicago Convention and its Annexes, have been the exclusive domain of States. Two examples can be given to illustrate this trend:

- Under the 2010 Assembly resolution on the USOAP-CMA, RSOOs are considered as States where applicable.[6] This is the first instance of an ICAO Assembly resolution which explicitly places RSOOs on equal footing with States.
- Under Amendment 13 to ICAO Annex 13 adopted in 2010, States now have a possibility to 'delegate the whole or any part of the conducting of ... investigation to...a regional accident investigation organization by mutual arrangement and consent.'[7]

In situations like the two examples cited above, lack of a definition makes it difficult to understand to whom exactly such documents are addressed. In the future, more references to RASOs are expected to find their way into ICAO documentation. It would thus be desirable to eliminate any ambiguity as to who is the addressee of the provisions contained in ICAO documents, especially where such documents grant to a RSOO or a RAIO a right to carry out functions so far normally exercised only by States.

§3.03 PROPOSAL FOR THE DEFINITION OF A RASO

In view of the above, it would be advisable for ICAO to develop a definition, or at least basic criteria, to classify RASOs from the perspective of regulatory, oversight or investigative functions they can carry out.

A desire for a definition and classification criteria for RASOs was also expressed in 2011 by the ICAO RSOO symposium, which felt that such a definition would allow all stakeholders, including ICAO and technical cooperation partners, to 'better adapt their activities to the different types of RASOs.'[8] By mid-2014 such a definition has not been developed.

The purpose of a RASO definition should not only be to codify the current ICAO and State practice, but also to stimulate the most efficient forms of such organisations. In this respect, from a legal point of view, the most significant criteria that should be highlighted in such a definition would be a possession by a RASO of a competence to carry out, on behalf of States, safety related functions and duties set out by the Chicago Convention, in a legally binding manner. Such competence 'provides the best dividend in terms of efficiency and the effective use of resources',[9] which strengthens the RASO mandate and makes it more suitable to be an effective part of the GASON, as was proposed in the preceding chapter. From an international law point of view, and as will be demonstrated in Chapters 4 and 6, the granting of such powers means that a

6. See: Assembly Resolution A37-5, *supra* note 71 in Ch. 2, which provides that because RSOOs 'have an important role in the USOAP CMA', wherever applicable, the word 'States' as used in that Resolution 'should be read to include RSOOs.'
7. Annex 13 to the Chicago Convention, at paragraph 5.1 and paragraph 5.1.2.
8. Outcomes of 2011 RSOO Symposium (C-WP/13810), *supra* note 4 in Ch. 1, at paragraph 2.1.1.
9. ICAO Doc. 9734 Part B, *supra* note 3 in Ch. 1, at paragraph 3.1.1.

relationship of an international agency is established between a RASO and the States on behalf of which it carries out the subject matter functions and duties. The research done for the purpose of this study (see section §4.03[B] of Chapter 4) shows that such a relationship presupposes that the RASO either possesses a separate international legal personality, or is established in a form of an organ of an international legal person.

The building of a RASO definition is, however, not an easy task due to the much diversified nature of RASOs' legal basis and institutional set ups. Nevertheless, for the purpose of this study the following definition is proposed:

> A Regional Aviation Safety Organisation is: An organisation established by States from the same geographical region, which has legal personality under international law or is established in a form of an organ of an international legal person, and whose principal purpose is the provision of support for the carrying out of safety-related functions and duties set out by the Chicago Convention and its Annexes, and preferably the actual carrying out of some or all of such functions and duties on behalf of its participating States.

The main elements of the proposed definition requiring additional comments are as follows:

- *Participants:* Although the majority of RASOs have *members,* some of them, such as the EASA which is a specialised agency of the EU, do not have State membership (see Chapter 4). The proposed definition covers the different types of relationships that may exist in this respect. The proposed definition also does not differentiate between RSOOs and RAIOs but it is understood that a RASO can have either regulatory and oversight functions or accident investigation competences.
- *International legal personality*: As Chapter 5 will demonstrate, there is a general trend for RASOs to evolve into organisations with legal personality under domestic or international law. This is because possession of a legal personality gives to a RASO the possibility to hire and fire staff and to contract services and facilities, which in turn makes the functioning of a RASO more efficient. In addition, where a RASO implements, on behalf of States, the provisions of the Chicago Convention and its Annexes this presupposes that the RASO has a separate international legal personality, or is established in a form of an organ of an international legal person, as Chapters 4 and 6 will demonstrate. The inclusion of the requirement of international legal personality or of a link with an international legal person intends therefore to promote those forms of RASOs which are able to accept the most advanced forms of delegations. On the other hand, this requirement excludes from the definition COSCAPs and similar bodies, which should not be treated as RASOs given the ICAO policy of transforming COSCAPs into RSOOs (see section §3.04[A][1]), as well as associations of aviation authorities (see section §3.04[B]), which are not capable of changing the rights and obligations of their member authorities under international law.
- *Delegation of safety functions and duties:* From the point of view of the Chicago Convention and as will be demonstrated in Chapter 6, States can

> delegate to RASOs the carrying out of safety *functions and duties* only, while the ultimate legal *responsibility* for these functions and duties remains with the States. This is also in line with the division between State sovereignty and the practical exercise of this sovereignty as was demonstrated in section §2.02[A] of Chapter 2. The proposed definition remains consistent with these principles by underlining that, when delegation takes place, this concerns only the *functions and duties* and must be done at the *State* level.[10]

Having analysed the notion of a RASO and provided a definition of this kind of organisations, a typology and classification of regional aviation safety bodies will now be proposed.

§3.04 TYPOLOGY OF REGIONAL AVIATION SAFETY BODIES

States do not follow a universal template when establishing regional aviation safety bodies. In practice such initiatives differ a lot in terms of their legal basis, functions, funding principles, scope of work and relationship with the Member States or member authorities.

In 2014, over twenty initiatives in almost all parts of the world could be considered as RASOs if looked at from the perspective of the broad approach followed at present by ICAO. This includes initiatives ranging from projects of a merely technical cooperation nature, to fully fledged regional aviation safety agencies with legal personality and competences to create legally binding effects for the aviation industry. In addition, a number of projects aiming at establishing additional RASOs were ongoing at the time of the finalisation of this study. In total, by mid-2014, over 100 ICAO Member States have been members of such organisations, and this not counting the COSCAP projects and RASO initiatives under consideration.

The typology proposed in the following sections distinguishes between two main categories of regional aviation safety bodies: (i) RASOs and (ii) pre-RASOs. While pre-RASOs do not, strictly speaking, fall within the scope of the RASO definition proposed in the preceding section because of their lack of international legal personality or formal link with an international legal person, they have however been included in this typology for the sake of completeness, and because such pre-RASOs have a tendency to evolve into RASOs proper, as Chapter 5 will demonstrate.

The below typology (Figure 3.1) is primarily focused on RSOOs, which are the dominant types of RASOs today, and uses the legal form and institutional status of the regional body as main distinguishing factors.

---

10. This is without prejudice to the fact that in practical terms there are also numerous pre-RASOs (see section §3.04), which are composed of the national authorities, and which perform technical tasks, such as aircraft certification, centrally to the benefit of those *authorities*. International law treats such situations 'as if the States were acting themselves' and not the RASO. This has been confirmed by the ICJ in: 'Certain Phosphate Lands in Nauru (Nauru v. Australia), Preliminary Objections', in: [1992] ICJ Reports 240, (ICJ,1992), (p. 258). See also: Sarooshi, *supra* note 19 in Ch. 2, at p. 34.

The typology of RAIOs is briefly addressed in section §3.05. RAIOs are differentiated by ICAO into *basic* and *complex*, depending on whether they carry out accident investigation functions and duties on behalf of their Member States, or have only advisory and coordination functions. This ICAO distinction between basic and complex RAIOs broadly corresponds to the pre-RASO and RASO dichotomy proposed by this study. In 2014, RAIOs were still very rare.

The typology proposed in this chapter was developed for the purpose of this study and is by no means the only one possible. Although every type of a pre-RASO and RASO has its *pros* and *cons*, the purpose of the proposed classification is not to present *better* or *worse* types, but rather to systematise the knowledge about these organisations.

Figure 3.1 Typology of Regional Aviation Safety Bodies

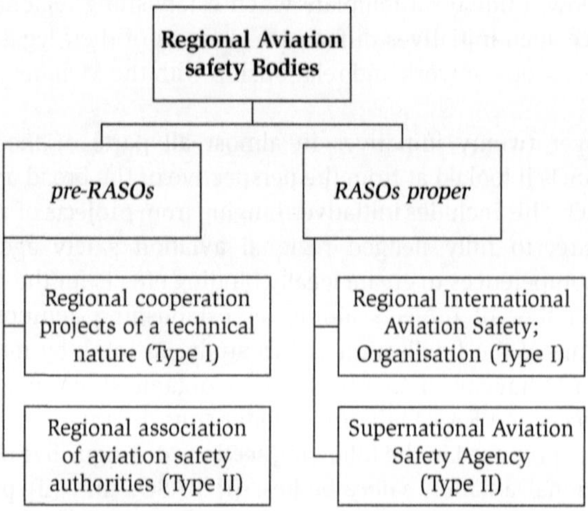

[A] Pre-RASO (Type I): Regional Cooperation Projects of a Technical Nature

A regional aviation safety body can start as a simple technical cooperation initiative and evolve over time into a more formal structure with a legal personality. A regional technical cooperation project can also from the start be based on the premise that over time it will be transformed into an organisation with legal personality. The three most prominent examples that can be given in this respect are presented below.

[1] COSCAPs and Their Transition into RASOs

COSCAPs are cooperative regional projects established under ICAO auspices with the objective of enhancing the safety oversight capabilities of participating States. In 2014, seven such initiatives were still ongoing.[11]

From a legal point of view COSCAPs depend chiefly on ICAO for managerial and administrative services.[12] They do not have separate legal personality and therefore cannot conclude, in their own name, agreements with other entities.[13] COSCAPs are usually set-up by a project document signed between ICAO and the participating States, and containing details of the objectives of the project, its governance, sources of funding, and duties and responsibilities of all the parties.[14]

From a practical point of view, COSCAPs support participating States in the harmonisation of legislation and procedures, training of inspectors, and can also provide safety oversight services for the benefit of the national aviation authorities. Given however that a COSCAP does not possess separate legal personality, the certification and surveillance services provided by the inspectors recruited through the project are considered as performed by the beneficiary national aviation authorities, that is, COSCAP inspectors are considered as members of the staff of the national authorities when performing their assistance functions.[15]

The above also means that COSCAPs do not have own enforcement competences, and COSCAP inspectors can only propose enforcement actions to participating authorities based on the technical work performed on behalf of these authorities.[16] Similarly

11. COSCAP-CIS (Azerbaijan; Armenia; Belarus; Georgia; Kazakhstan; Kyrgyzstan; Moldova; Russian Federation; Tajikistan; Turkmenistan; Uzbekistan; Ukraine), COSCAP-Gulf States (Bahrain; Kuwait; United Arab Emirates), COSCAP-North Asia (China; Democratic People's Republic of Korea; Mongolia; Republic of Korea), COSCAP-SADC (Angola; Botswana; Democratic Republic of the Congo; Lesotho; Madagascar; Malawi; Mauritius; Mozambique; Namibia; Seychelles; South Africa; Swaziland; Tanzania; Zambia; Zimbabwe), COSCAP-SEA (Cambodia; Hong Kong, China; Indonesia; Lao People's Democratic Republic; Macao, China; Malaysia; Myanmar; Philippines; Singapore; Thailand; Viet Nam), COSCAP-South Asia (Bangladesh; Bhutan; India; Maldives; Nepal; Pakistan; Sri Lanka), and COSCAP-UEMOA (Benin; Burkina Faso; Côte d'Ivoire; Guinea-Bissau; Mali; Mauritania; Niger; Senegal; Togo); Source: ICAO, 'RSOOs and COSCAPs') http://www.icao.int/safety/Implementation/Lists/COSCAP_RSOO/AllItems.aspx [accessed 14 March 2014].
12. ICAO Doc. 9734 Part B, *supra* note 3 in Ch. 1, at paragraph 3.2.5.
13. *Ibid.*
14. *Ibid.*at paragraph 3.2.3.
15. See for example: COSCAP-SA, 'Model bilateral agreement between COSCAP South Asia and States for obtaining Services of Technical Experts from COSCAP South Asia to perform Safety Oversight functions' 2009) http://www.coscapsa.org/Manuals/ifapmanual.pdf [accessed 6 August 2014]. Under paragraph 2(i) of the this model agreement COSCAP-SA Member States take full responsibility for the work, tasks or activities performed by the COSCAP-SA technical experts at their behest or on their behalf and undertake to hold the COSCAP-SA and any of its staff or ICAO harmless, not-liable and/or not responsible against potential third party action arising out of such work, tasks or activities. COSCAP-SA Member States also undertake, under paragraph 2(c) of the model agreement, to treat the COSCAP-SA technical experts as part of their technical staff when performing safety oversight activities and accord to such technical experts due respect, status and protection as provided to its own staff.
16. *Ibid.*

the regulations developed under COSCAP projects only have the status of recommendations and need to be considered and adopted by States in accordance with their domestic procedures.[17]

Although not possessing legal personality, COSCAPs can play a role in establishing fully-fledged RSOOs, and it is the policy of ICAO to promote the transitioning of COSCAPs into RSOO type bodies, where appropriate.[18] By mid-2014 this process was most advanced in Africa, where two COSCAP projects had already transitioned into a RSOO,[19] and where two additional COSCAPs were in the process of doing so.[20] In respect to other regions, this *launching pad* function of COSCAPs has so far been very limited, as Table 3.1 demonstrates.

Table 3.1 Transition of ICAO COSCAPs into RSOOs (2014)

COSCAP (Start of Operations)[21]	*RSOO Transition Arrangements*
COSCAP – BAG (2005)	Transition completed into: Banjul Accord Group Safety Oversight Organisation (BAGASOO)
COSCAP – CIS (2001)	No transition planned
COSCAP Latin America (2001)	Today known as 'SRVSOP', but operating still as an ICAO programme
COSCAP – North Asia (2003)	No transition planned
COSCAP – SADC (2008)	Transition on-going into: Southern African Development Community Aviation Safety Organisation (SASO)
COSCAP – SEA (2001)	No transition planned
COSCAP – UEMOA (2005)	In the course of transition into a RSOO

17. See for example: ICAO, 'Cooperative Development of Operational Safety and Continuing Airworthiness Programme – South Asia (COSCAP-SA) Phase III' http://www.coscapsa.org/maindocuments.php [accessed 6 August 2014]. This programme document (paragraph 4.3(e)) envisages 'Assisting Member States in the development of rules, regulations and procedures for harmonization of civil aviation regulatory affairs in the region.'
18. ICAO Doc. 9734 Part B, *supra* note 3 in Ch. 1, at Foreword.
19. This is the case for the COSCAP-BAG, which transitioned into 'Banjul Accord Group Safety Oversight Organisation (BAGASOO)', which is presented in section §3.04[C][4] of this Chapter, and the COSCAP–CEMAC, which evolved into 'Central African Aviation Safety Oversight Agency (ASSA-AC)' (see: CEMAC, 'Reunion des ministres des transports des etats membres de la cemac et sao tome et principe – communique final' http://www.cemac.int/communique-presse/reunion-des-ministres-des-transports-des-etats-membres-de-la-cemac-et-sao-tome-et' [accessed 7 August 2014].
20. AFI Plan Steering Committee Report, AFI SC/2013/12, *supra* note 3 in Ch. 2, at paragraph 1.4.
21. Len Cormier, 'Cooperative Arrangements Under ICAO Modalities – Safety', ICAO Symposium on Regional Safety Oversight Organizations (Montréal, Canada, 2011), http://www.icao.int/Meetings/RSOOSYMPO/Pages/default.aspx [accessed 18 March 2014].

COSCAP (Start of Operations)	*RSOO Transition Arrangements*
COSCAP - Gulf States (2006)	Transition into a RSOO considered
COSCAP - South Asia (1998)	No transition planned
COSCAP - CEMAC (2008)	Transition completed into: Central African Aviation Safety Oversight Agency (ASSA-AC)

Although the transitioning of COSCAPs into RSOOs is most advanced in Africa, the situation there is also most complex, as some of the States are members of multiple organisations, as Figure 3.2 demonstrates.

For example, the Republic of Tanzania is a member of COSCAP-SADC, which in 2014 was being transitioned into SASO - a RSOO of the Southern African Development Community.[22] At the same time, it is a member of the East African Community Civil Aviation Safety and Security Oversight Agency (CASSOA), by virtue of Tanzania's membership of the East African Community (EAC).

Similarly Benin, Burkina Faso, Ivory Coast, Guinea-Bissau, Mali, Niger, Senegal and Togo are members of the West African Economic and Monetary Union (UEMOA), which is currently in the process of setting up a RSOO,[23] and in parallel members of the Civil Aviation Authorities of Africa and Madagascar (AAMAC), which is a RSOO set up in 2012 (see section §3.04[C][1]). Madagascar is a member of AAMAC and at the same time one of the future members of SASO. Finally, there is an overlap in membership between AAMAC and Central African Aviation Safety Oversight Agency (ASSA-AC), although these two RSOOs have different areas of competence.[24]

22. AFI Plan Steering Committee Report, AFI SC/2013/12, *supra* note 3 in Ch. 2, at paragraph 1.4.
23. *Ibid.*
24. This concerns Cameroon, Central African Republic, Chad, Congo, Equatorial Guinea and Gabon. While AAMAC is responsible for ATM/ANS matters, ASSA-AC covers the matters dealt with by the former COSCAP-CEMAC project, namely airworthiness, licensing and flight operations.

Figure 3.2 Existing and Planned RASOs in Africa (2014)

In addition, some of the African States have also delegated regulatory competences to Regional Economic Communities (RECs), which may regulate aviation safety matters at supranational level. This is the case, for example, with UEMOA, which adopted a number of aviation safety regulations.[25]

The multiple membership of some of the African States in regional organisations and projects dealing with aviation safety makes it more difficult to achieve - or even goes against - the objectives of regional cooperation which is intended to streamline the use of resources and achieve economies of scale. ICAO and AFCAC have been repeatedly urging African States to avoid membership in multiple organisations, but

25. Schlumberger, *supra* note 37 in Ch. 1, at Appendix D.

the problem persists.[26] It is not easy to find an optimal solution to this issue, as some of the African RASO projects are linked to supranational RECs, and thus have to be seen in the context of the general political aim of regional integration in Africa.

In addition to the issue of the transition of COSCAPs into RASO type bodies in Africa, consideration should also be given in the longer term to consolidation of RASO type bodies on the African continent. According to the ICAO AFI Plan, it is ultimately envisaged to have between eleven and thirteen RASO type bodies (half of them RSOOs and half RAIO),[27] in addition to the AFCAC regional cooperative inspector scheme (see section §3.04[A][3]). Most of these RASOs will have no more than ten Member States,[28] and none of them is designed to replace the national authorities, which means that they will be functioning in parallel with national aviation administrations. Whether this will be sustainable in the long term remains to be seen, but experience so far demonstrates that achieving sustainability in safety oversight cannot be guaranteed by simply setting up a regional safety body (see Chapter 5, section §5.04[C]).

Duplication of membership in regional aviation organisations is not only characteristic of Africa. In Europe, for historic reasons, a number of organisations with overlapping mandates and membership exist which creates inefficiencies. The closure of the JAA in 2009 and the taking over of its functions by EASA has eliminated some of such inefficiencies, but in 2014 overlaps still existed between EASA, EUROCONTROL and ECAC. The recent independent evaluation of EASA conducted on the tenth anniversary of its functioning suggests that such a situation may not be sustainable in the long term, and recommends the establishment of a single European body responsible for all technical aspects of aviation, similar to the FAA.[29] The feasibility of such a proposal will be analysed in more detail in Chapter 4.

The least duplication exists today in Latin and Central America, where only two organisations encompass the vast majority of the States without any overlaps, as Figure 3.3 demonstrates.

26. ICAO, 'Progress in Africa – report on the Comprehensive Regional Implementation Plan for Aviation Safety in Africa (AFI PLAN)', A38-WP/67, (38th ICAO Assembly, 2013), at paragraph 2.7.
27. AFI Plan Steering Committee Report, AFI SC/2013/12, *supra* note 3 in Ch. 2, at Appendix B.
28. *Ibid.*
29. EASA, 'Article 62 Panel Evalutation: final report', (2013), p. 29.

Figure 3.3 RASOs in Latin and Central America

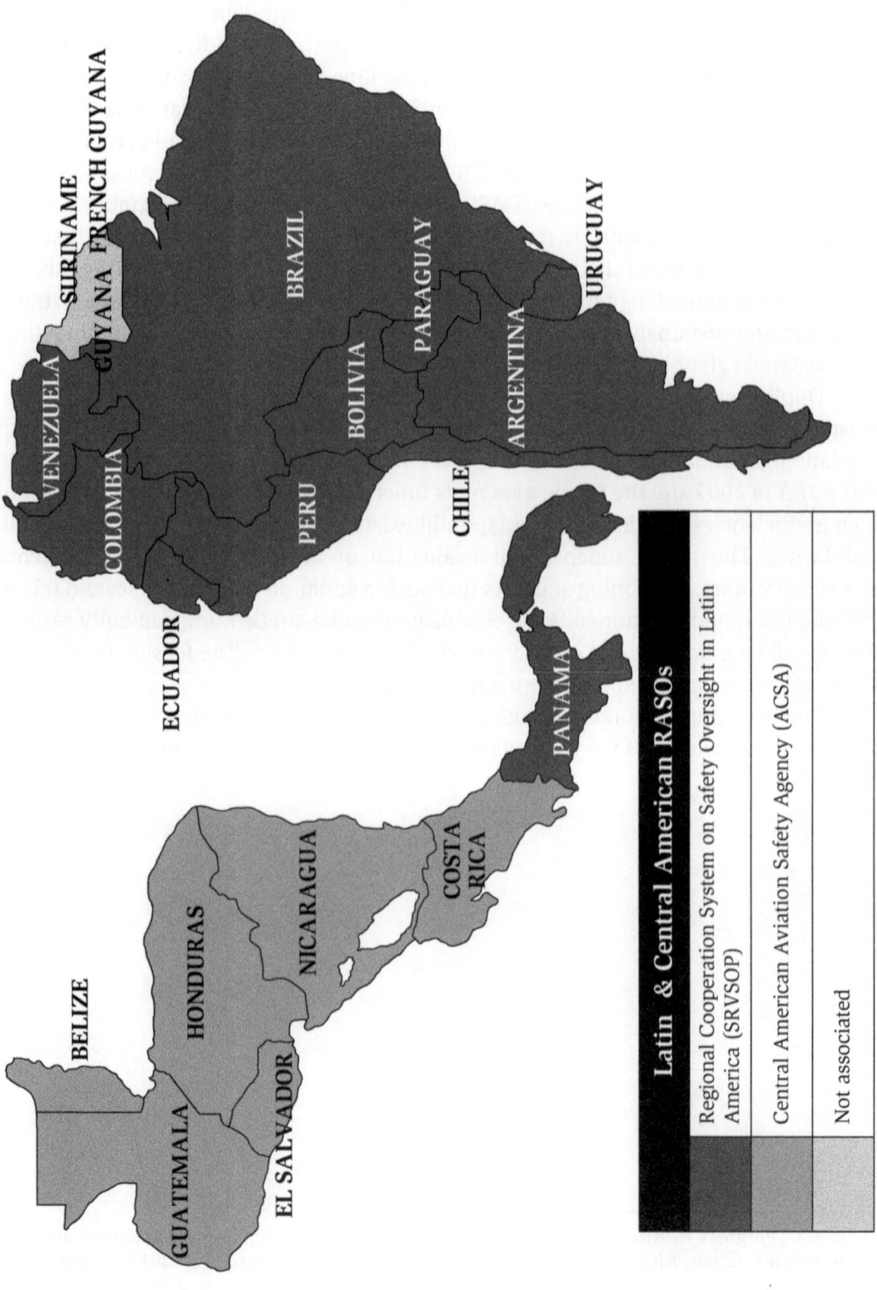

[2] Regional Cooperation System on Safety Oversight in Latin America

[a] Legal Basis and Organisational Set-Up

SRVSOP, as a TYPE I pre-RASO, is from a legal and organisational points of view similar to a COSCAP-type project, as it relies for its functioning on ICAO and does not have own legal personality.[30] Its participating States are Argentina, Bolivia, Brazil, Chile, Colombia, Cuba, Ecuador, Panama, Paraguay, Peru, Uruguay and Venezuela (see Figure 3.3).

The legal basis for the establishment of the SRVSOP is a Memorandum of Understanding signed on 1 October 1998 between ICAO and the LACAC (SRVSOP MoU),[31] which was subsequently approved by the SRVSOP participating States.[32] A Trust Fund Agreement has been also signed between ICAO and the SRVSOP participating States, which defines the conditions of ICAO support to the SRVSOP, together with the associated financial conditions.[33] The SRVSOP began operations in 2002. Its Headquarters is in ICAO Regional Office in Lima, Peru.

[b] Main Safety Functions

The SRVSOP works in five main areas: harmonisation of regulations, multinational certification activities,technical assistance to participating States, training activities and organisation of meetings.[34] In addition SRVSOP coordinates a Safety Ramp Inspection Data Exchange Programme (IDISIR), similar to the EU SAFA programme which was briefly addressed in Chapter 2.[35]

As far as rulemaking is concerned, the primary task of the SRVSOP is to develop standardised requirements, Latin American Aviation Regulations (LARs) and related guidance material, which are based on ICAO SARPs.[36] The LARs do not have a directly

30. SRVSOP evolved from a previous COSCAP-Latin America project.
31. 'Memorandum of Understanding between the Latin American Civil Aviation Commission and the International Civil Aviation Organization on the establishment of Regional Safety Oversight Cooperation System of Latin America', (1998), <http://www1.lima.icao.int/srvsop/> [accessed 25 August 2014].
32. 'Letter of agreement for the implementation of the Regional Safety Oversight Cooperation System of Latin America', <http://www1.lima.icao.int/srvsop/archivos/Acuerdo.pdf> [accessed 25 August 2014].
33. 'ICAO Technical Cooperation Project Document RLA/99/901', <http://www1.lima.icao.int/srvsop/archivos/DOC_RLA99901esp.pdf> [accessed 25 August 2014].
34. 'Interview No 8', (2014), *supra* note 181, in Ch. 2.
35. The information collected through ramp inspections by SRVSOP participating States is stored on a centralised database at the ICAOs Regional Office server in Lima. Every SRVSOP State has protected access to the information on the database for data intelligence, operator surveillance and analysis purposes.
36. LACAC, 'Recognition and validation of approvals and certifications within the Latin American safety oversight regional system', HLSC 2010-WP/65, (ICAO High Level Safety Conference, 2010).

binding effect, and must be transposed into the national legal systems of SRVSOP participating States.[37]

When an SRVSOP participating State has finalised the process of transposition and implementation of LARs, it notifies the SRVSOP accordingly and a standardisation inspection in a State is carried out to verify the effectiveness of the LAR implementation.[38] However, given the fact that SRVSOP is not based on a legally binding international agreement, the harmonisation process is of voluntary nature.[39]

SRVSOP does not have own enforcement competences and the taking of corrective measures to ensure compliance with the aviation safety regulations is the responsibility of SRVSOP participating States.[40]

In addition to rulemaking, one of the flag-ship initiatives of the SRVSOP is coordination of multinational certification projects. These initiatives are developed on the basis of multilateral arrangements signed by the aviation authorities of the SRVSOP participating States. By 2014, three such arrangements have been developed, namely for the certification of Approved Maintenance Organisations, Aeronautical Training Centres and Aeromedical Examination Centres.[41] These arrangements foresee that once the satisfactory result of the multinational certification is achieved,[42] the civil aviation authorities of the States which have signed the arrangement will issue the corresponding certificate to the organisation.[43] This process allows to achieve economies of scale and reduces time and administrative burden for the industry.

[c] Practical Aspects of Implementation

SRVSOP has achieved quite good results when it comes to harmonising the legislation of its participating States. Until mid-2013, 31 LARs have been drafted together with respective guidance manuals for safety inspectors. It has been reported in an interview conducted for the purpose of this study that some of the SRVSOP participating States have already reached a 100% status of LAR implementation.[44]

Although SRVSOP does not exclude in the future transition into an organisation institutionally independent from ICAO, in 2014 its priority was to finalise the 'process

37. Brazil on behalf of the Member States of the Latin American Civil Aviation Commission, 'The role of regional cooperation in Latin America', A38-WP/231, (38th ICAO Assembly, 2013), at paragraph 1.3.
38. 'Interview No 8', (2014), *supra* note 181, in Ch. 2.
39. *Ibid.*
40. *Ibid.*
41. *Ibid.*
42. Certification is performed by inspectors from the SRVSOP Member States which comply with the competences requirements set by the SRVSOP document 'LAR Multinational Certification Inspector' and who have been trained specifically for the SRVSOP multinational certification activities. When an inspector meets the competence requirements set forth by the SRVSOP, a credential is issued for him/her by the SRVSOP General Coordinator (Source: *Ibid*).
43. *Ibid.*
44. *Ibid.*

of harmonization of the Latin-American Aviation Regulations by States, as well as the associated documents'.[45]

The main challenge faced by the SRVSOP is to ensure that all its participating States reach by 2019, an effective average of implementation of minimum 90% in the 8CEs of a safety oversight system.[46]

At the ICAO Sixth World Air Transport Conference (ATConf/6) in 2013, LACAC presented a working paper describing the findings of a study on the financial impact of SRVSOP.[47] The paper demonstrated that, in addition to the qualitative benefits of the regional system, SRVSOP work has allowed to save its participating States over 13 million USD. As the LACAC paper explains, this value is created by SRVSOP activities such as training, assistance to States, LAR development and multinational AMO certification activities.[48]

[3] Regional Cooperative Safety Inspector Schemes

The availability of technically competent aviation inspectors is currently one of the biggest challenges for aviation authorities in ensuring effective safety oversight. The USOAP results indicate that out of the eight CEs of safety oversight, CE number four, that is 'Technical Personnel Qualification and Training', has the lowest level of effective implementation and in mid-2014 stood at only 45%.[49]

This problem is true not only for regions like Africa – where aviation does not yet generate revenues large enough to ensure appropriate staffing of the aviation authorities, and where aviation has to compete for resources with other sectors with equally pressing or even greater needs, such as health or education[50] – but also in Europe, where the public administrations also find it increasingly difficult to finance aviation safety oversight.[51]

One of the most difficult problems to resolve in this respect is the fact that, as pointed out by ICAO, 'although many donor States provide valuable financial support for training, recipient States had difficulty keeping staff once they had been trained'.[52] With the overall economic situation bleak in many regions of the world, the problem of availability of resources starts to affect even the strongest aviation authorities.[53]

45. *Ibid.*
46. *Ibid.*
47. Members of the Latin American Civil Aviation Commission, 'Cost-effectiveness of the safety oversight cooperation system (SRVSOP)', ATConf/6-WP/58, (6th ICAO Worldwide Air Transport Conference, 2013).
48. *Ibid.*
49. Regional Performance Dashboards, *supra* note 15 in Ch. 1.
50. Schlumberger, *supra* note 37 in Ch. 1, at p. 165; Belai, *supra* note 36 in Ch. 1.
51. LePoint.fr, 'Derrière le zéro accident mortel, la sécurité aérienne peut encore mieux faire en Europe' http://www.lepoint.fr/societe/derriere-le-zero-accident-mortel-la-securite-aerienne-peut-encore-mieux-faire-en-europe-27-02-2014-1796120_23.php [accessed 1 June 2014].
52. C-DEC 191/2, *supra* note 35 in Ch. 1.
53. In mid-2013 the US FAA initiated furlough of its 47,000 employees, including nearly 13,000 air traffic controllers, as part of a plan to meet 637 million USD in spending cuts required by the federal budget legislation. Even though the furloughs of air traffic control personnel were subsequently stopped by Congress at the end of April 2013, the FAA continued with spending

Although the establishment of RASOs is often put forward as a possible solution for the problem of the shortage of technical resources,[54] experience shows that establishing regional bodies does not always help in this respect, because a RASO can also compete for resources with national aviation authorities (see section §5.04[C] of Chapter 5). This is especially the case if safety tasks are carried out in parallel at national and regional levels. Another way of addressing the problem of availability of qualified staff is by creating regional pools of aviation safety inspectors.

In 2014, one of the most prominent examples of such initiatives was the Cooperative Inspectorate Scheme (AFI-CIS) developed jointly by ICAO and AFCAC within the framework of the Comprehensive Regional Implementation Plan for Aviation Safety in Africa (AFI Plan).[55] The objective of this AFI-CIS programme, which was launched in 2010,[56] is to 'assist and complement the efforts of States to resolve their safety oversight deficiencies in certification and surveillance.'[57] This is achieved by creating a pool of certified inspectors from a number of African States. The programme is managed by AFCAC with technical support from ICAO.

From a legal point of view, the AFI-CIS programme is established on the basis of a bilateral Memorandum of Understanding (hereinafter 'AFI-CIS MoU') signed between AFCAC and the civil aviation authorities of each participating State.[58] The AFI-CIS MoU is essentially a service and secondment agreement, whereby the national authority agrees to designate and to make available for the scheme its appropriately qualified national inspectors. The AFI-CIS MoU clarifies that:

> At all-time material during the performance of his duties under [the] cooperative inspectorate programme, the National Inspector shall be deemed an official of AFCAC working under the authority of the Director General of the Civil Aviation Authority of the host State.[59]

---

cuts, including in parts of the organisation responsible for safety oversight and certification activities (Source: CNN, 'FAA furloughs over, air traffic controllers back on the job' www.edition.cnn.com/2013/05/02/travel/faa-furlough/ [accessed 5 August 2014].

54. 'Main conclusions and follow-up to the Symposium', Symposium on Regional Aviation Safety Agencies (Livingstone, Zambia, 2009), http://easa.europa.eu/newsroom-and-events/events/symposium-regional-aviation-safety-agencies-rasa [accessed 10 August 2014]; Outcomes of 2011 RSOO Symposium (C-WP/13810), *supra* note 4 in Ch. 1, at paragraph 2.1.1; ICAO Doc. 9734 Part B, *supra* note 3 in Ch. 1, at paragraph 2.1.4.
55. AFI Plan was adopted in September 2007 by the ICAO Assembly; see: ICAO, 'Assemby Resolution A36-1: Comprehensive Regional Implementation Plan for Aviation Safety in Africa', (36th ICAO Assembly, 2007). To give effect to the AFI Plan, ICAO created a special programme – the AFI Comprehensive Implementation Programme (ACIP).
56. The AFI-CIS was approved by the 22nd AFCAC Extraordinary Plenary Session held in Dakar (Senegal) on 8-10 December 2010. The first pilot projects were launched in August 2011. For a detailed overview of AFI-CIS see: AFCAC, 'Report on progress made in the areas of Safety, Security, Implementation of Yamoussoukro Decision and Environment: Progress Report on the Implementation of AFI-CIS', WP/3, (22nd AFCAC Plenary Session, 2013).
57. AFCAC, 'Circular Letter No 14/10', (2010).
58. .AFCAC, 'Memorandum of Understanding (MoU) between the African Civil Aviation Commission (AFCAC) and African States for the use of national inspectors under the AFI Cooperative Inspector Scheme', (2013), http://www.afcac.org/en/documents/conferences/october2012/15 afi.pdf [accessed 5 August 2014].
59. *Ibid.*, paragraph 4.

This is a solution similar to the one used by COSCAP projects as was demonstrated under section §3.04[A][1] above.

In addition, one RSOO, namely the Banjul Accord Group Aviation Safety Oversight Organisation (BAGASOO), cooperates with the AFI-CIS and has signed the AFI-CIS MoU. As a result of this cooperation, BAGASOO makes available and receives inspectors, augmenting its own inspection potential and helping its member authorities to benefit from a broader pool of resources available in the region.[60]

From a legal point of view, the AFI-CIS inspectors enjoy delegated authority from host States, that is, States in which they perform inspection activities. The national authority - signatory of the AFI-CIS MoU - agrees to grant such authority to the programme inspectors when acting as a *host* receiving their services.[61] Formally speaking the delegated authority is granted not on the basis of the AFI-CIS MoU but on the basis of the national aviation legislation of the hosting authority. The scope of the authority is limited to inspection functions, and the AFI-CIS MoU makes it clear that the 'host State remains responsible for the issuance of any document, certificate or license issued as a result of the activities and recommendations of the AFI-CIS Inspectors.'[62]

The AFI-CIS MoU is a simple and practical tool to organise inspector exchange from a formal point of view. As of May 2014, thirty-four African States have signed the AFI-CIS MoU with AFCAC, and eighteen assistance missions have been conducted to nine States.[63] At the same time, the programme has not completely removed the problem of shortage of qualified resources for the AFCAC States. Although the AFI-CIS MoU allocates the responsibility of funding the AFI-CIS missions to the hosting States,[64] in practice very few of the recipient States have been able to fund missions, and AFCAC has had to fund all but two of the missions that were conducted up to May-2014.[65] In addition, the shortage of qualified flight operations inspectors in general and non-English speaking in particular has also held up the conduct of some of the planned missions.[66] The shortage of resources at national levels also hampers the ability of States to ensure follow-up of the AFI-CIS missions.[67]

Finally, national authorities need to allocate internal resources to coordinate the work with the AFI-CIS, and ultimately to be able to release their own inspectors for the programme missions when they are needed in other States, which is not always easy.[68] Indeed, up to September 2013, out of the 32 States which were signatories of the

60. AFI-CIS progress report (2013), *supra* note 56, at paragraph 5.1.
61. This authority is confirmed by credentials issued to an inspector by the Director General of the hosting Civil Aviation Authority. The credentials indicate that the individual was endorsed by the Secretary General of AFCAC as a member of CIS. See: AFI-CIS MoU, *supra* note 58, at Appendix 5.
62. *Ibid.*at paragraph 4.
63. AFCAC, 'AFI Cooperative Inspectorate Scheme (AFI-CIS)', Africa-Indian Ocean (AFI) Aviation Safety Symposium (Dakar, 2014), http://www.icao.int/meetings/afisymposium2014/Pages/default.aspx [accessed 5 August 2014].
64. AFI-CIS MoU, *supra* note 58, at paragraph 6.
65. AFCAC, AFI Cooperative Inspectorate Scheme (AFI-CIS), *supra* note 63.
66. AFCAC, 'Progress report on the implementation of AFI Cooperative Inspectorate Scheme (AFI-CIS)', A38-WP/214, (38th ICAO Assembly, 2013), at paragraph 6.
67. AFI-CIS progress report (2013), *supra* note 56, at paragraph 7.1.
68. *Ibid.*at paragraph 7.3.

AFI-CIS MoU at the time, only seven States actually contributed inspectors to the scheme.[69]

[B] Pre-RASO (Type II): A Regional 'Association' of Aviation Safety Authorities

A simple but practical way of organising regional cooperation on aviation safety regulation and oversight can also be through an association of national aviation safety authorities. One of the most prominent examples of this type of cooperation, although no longer existing today, was the JAA in Europe.[70]

From a legal point of view, the JAA was not an international organisation, and its constituent document, the 'Cyprus Arrangements' did not have the status of an international treaty.[71] This was a pragmatic approach which allowed the JAA to be set up and developed without affecting the rights and obligations of participating States under international law. This however meant that the JAA could not mandate any legislation, or issue regulatory documents, such as certificates or licences, on behalf of its participating States. Similarly, the Joint Aviation Requirements (JARs) developed by the JAA had to be transposed into national legal orders of the participating States, which also had a right to adopt national variants of the JARs.[72] Similarly the JAA could only make recommendations for *mutual recognition* of certificates issued by the national authorities. Such recommendations referred to different levels of JAR amendments, and were not recognised in a uniform manner by all the participating authorities. This in practice led to a patchwork of mutual recognition arrangements.[73] Finally the JAA did not have enforcement competences which remained at the national level.

Despite the weaknesses identified above, the JAA managed to build quite a successful system for aircraft certification, which allowed making use of only one set of technical findings to the benefit of all the participating authorities.[74] It also developed

69. Mam Sait Jallow, 'Progress on key activities of the comprehensive regional implementation plan for aviation safety in africa (AFI PLAN)', AFI Ministerial briefing (Montréal, 2013), http://www.icao.int/safety/afiplan/Documents/AFI%20Ministerial/AFI%20Ministerial-RDWACAF%20En.pdf [accessed 14 August 2014].
70. The JAA system was disbanded on 30 June 2009 following the extension of the competences of European Aviation Safety Agency (EASA) to flight operations and crew licensing; see: ECAC, 'Press Release No 192E', (2007).
71. . 'Arrangements concerning the development, the acceptance and the implementation of Joint Aviation Requirements', (Cyprus, 1990), http://easa.europa.eu/document-library/working-arrangements/working-arrangement-archive-jaa [accessed 8 August 2014].
72. *Ibid.*at paragraph 3(c).
73. See for example the last version of JAA mutual recognition recommendations for aircrew licensing at: EASA, 'Mutual recognition of certificates' http://easa.europa.eu/mutual-recognition [accessed 8 August 2014].
74. Because of the non-binding nature of the 'Cyprus Arrangements', the Type Certificates (TC) for products had still to be issued individually by national authorities, which could also introduce national variants; see: Filippo De Florio, Airworthiness, An Introduction to Aircraft Certification: A guide to understanding JAA, EASA and FAA standards, (2006), pp. 108-109.

a system of standardisation inspections, or audits, to verify the level of implementation of JARs in JAA States.[75]

Whilst not being an international organisation, the JAA still needed a budget and a more solid legal standing for the purposes of day to day administrative management. Thus, in parallel to the 'Cyprus Arrangements', a JAA foundation under Dutch law – 'Stichting Beheer *JAA*' – was set up to enable this organisation to have a legal personality and on this basis to contract the necessary staff, services, facilities and receive seconded personnel.[76] This was a pragmatic solution which enabled the practical problems stemming from a lack of legal personality under the 'Cyprus Arrangements' to be overcome.

A solution similar to the JAA was used in Western Africa for the establishment of the initial version of AAMAC. This organisation was set up on the basis of a Memorandum of Understanding signed in December 2001 in Dakar by the participating aviation authorities. Subsequently the AAMAC was transformed into an association under the law of the Republic of Chad, which gave it a legal personality under private law.[77] In 2012, the AAMAC association was further upgraded into a RSOO with international legal personality. This will be presented under section §3.04[C][1].

Finally, EUROCONTROL, which is an international organisation, in the period between the signature and entry into force of its constituting agreement,[78] was implemented through an association set up under the French law.[79]

To conclude, experience shows that establishing an association of national aviation safety authorities can be a practical first step to launch a RASO. The advantage of this form of cooperation is that it can be set up relatively quickly as no international agreement is necessary. It may also be easier to accept for decision makers from a political point of view, as it does not affect the rights and obligations of States under international law.

At the same time the legal form of an association gives a basic structure and legal personality under private law which in turn allows the organisation to have its own budget, conclude contracts and hire personnel. On the other hand, lack of a binding legal status does not permit an association to mandate common requirements or to deliver certificates on behalf of the Member States. This, over time, can result in a heterogeneous regulatory environment.

---

75. Manuhutu, 'Aviation Safety Regulation in Europe', *supra* note 53 in Ch. 1, at p. 267.
76. ECAC, 'Report on JAA activities, presented by the Chairman of JAA Committee', (ECAC DGCA/16, ECAC archives in Paris, 1994). See also: ECAC, 'Roadmap for JAA', (2005), at Attachement 4.
77. Guelpina Ceubah, 'Autorités Africaines et Malgaches de l'Aviation Civile', Symposium on Regional Aviation Safety Agencies (Livingstone, Zambia, 2009), http://easa.europa.eu/newsroom-and-events/events/symposium-regional-aviation-safety-agencies-rasa [accessed 6 August 2014].
78. 'Convention relating to Co-operation for the Safety of Air Navigation (EUROCONTROL) with Annexes and Protocols', 13 December 1960, UK Treaty Series No. 39 (1963).
79. L'Association pour le perfectionnement des méthodes de contrôle aérien, established on 10 December 1960. For more details see: John McInally, 'EUROCONTROL: History Book', (2010), http://www.eurocontrol.int/news/eurocontrol-history-book [accessed 12 August 2014], pp. 51-56.

[C] RASO (Type I): Regional International Aviation Safety Organisation

Having reviewed the pre-RASOs, this chapter will now present the two types of RASO forms. The first one is the Regional International Aviation Safety Organisation. This type of RASO is established on the basis of an international agreement and may exercise, in a legally binding manner, safety functions and duties on behalf of its Member States. For the purpose of this study, and as opposed to the next category described in this chapter, a Regional International Aviation Safety Organisation will also be normally established outside the institutional framework of a REIO.[80] Five examples of this type of a RASO can be given.

[1] Civil Aviation Authorities of Africa and Madagascar

[a] Legal Basis and Organisational Set-Up

AAMAC was formally established in 2012, as a successor of an association of aviation safety authorities of the same name (see section §3.04[B] above). It was established on the basis of an international agreement, signed on 20 January 2012 by seventeen States, mostly from central and western Africa but including also Madagascar.[81] Its headquarters is located in N'Djamena – the capital city of the Republic of Chad. At the beginning of 2014, the AAMAC Treaty was not yet in force, due to the lack of ratification by the signatory States.[82]

The two main purposes of the establishment of AAMAC were to strengthen the regulatory capabilities of AAMAC Member States following negative results of ICAO USOAP audits,[83] and secondly to have an independent authority for the surveillance of the Agency for Aerial Navigation Safety in Africa and Madagascar (ASECNA)[84] – a regional air navigation service provider (ANSP) originally established by seventeen AAMAC States and France in 1954[85] – in line with the ICAO recommendations for the

80. Examples of REIOs include European Union (EU), the Organisation of Eastern Caribbean States (OECS) and some Regional Economic Commissions (RECs) in Africa. REIOs have their own supranational institutions such as legislative or judiciary bodies and are authorised in certain domains to adopt legislation which is binding for its Member States and directly applicable in their domestic legal orders.
81. 'Traité relative aux Autorités Africaines et Malgache de l'Aviation Civile (AAMAC Treaty)', N'Djaména, 20 January 2012, LOI n°2012 -012 of 29 July 2012, Le Congrès de la Transition et le Conseil Supérieur de la Transition, République de Madagascar.
82. Former Rulemaking Director of EASA, 'Interview No 11', (2014).
83. *Ibid.*
84. République de Madagascar Le Congrès de la Transition et le Conseil Supérieur de la Transition, 'LOI n°2012-012: Autorisant la ratification du Traité relatif aux Autorités Africaines et Malgache de l'Aviation Civile signé à N'Djaména le 20 janvier 2012, Exposé des motifs'.
85. 'Agence pour la sécurité de la navigation aérienne en Afrique et à Madagascar (ASECNA)', originally established in 1954. Today ASECNA's legal basis is: 'Convention relative a l'Agence pour la Securite de la Navigation Aerienne en Afrique et Madagascar (ASECNA)', Ouagadougou, 28 avril 2010, Official Journal of the Republic of Senegal N° 6641, 28 January 2012.

separation of service provision and regulatory functions,[86] and following negative results of the ICAO audits in this respect.[87]

The AAMAC Treaty was inspired by the provisions of an EU regulation establishing EASA, however due to the fact that AAMAC is currently not linked to a REIO similar to the EU, AAMAC retained a number of features typical for an intergovernmental body, such as lack of competence to adopt legally binding aviation safety legislation on behalf of its Member States (see below), as well as the inability to issue certificates with a legally binding force.

AAMAC has both domestic and international legal personality, both explicitly envisaged under its founding agreement.[88]

[b] Main Safety Functions

From a legal point of view the scope of the AAMAC mandate is very broad and covers all main domains of civil aviation safety covered by ICAO Annexes, that is: airworthiness of aircraft, flight operations and crew licensing, ATM, and aerodrome safety.[89]

As far as its rulemaking competences are concerned, although AAMAC has both domestic and international legal personality, it is not entitled to issue regulatory documents with binding effect, but only prepares proposals of such regulations which need to be subsequently transposed by the AAMAC Member States into their national legal orders, either directly or through a REIO to which they may belong.[90]

Similarly, concerning implementation of regulations and oversight of regulated entities, AAMAC cannot issue certificates or licences on behalf of its Member States, but can only make recommendations for their issuance on the basis of the technical work done on behalf of its Member States.[91]

At the same time, the AAMAC Treaty imposes stricter obligations on its Member States than for example documents constituting associations of aviation safety authorities, such as the JAA. This is because the AAMAC Member States undertook to issue certificates on the basis of recommendations made by AAMAC, where it is the competent authority in a given domain,[92] and to incorporate into their national legal

86. In those States where the State is both the regulatory authority and an air traffic service provider, the requirements of the Chicago Convention will be met, and the public interest be best served, by a clear separation of authority and responsibility between the State operating agency and the State regulatory authority, Source: ICAO, 'Safety Oversight Manual, Part A: The Establishment and Management of a State's Safety Oversight System', Doc. 9734, Part A, (2006), at paragraph 2.4.9.
87. *Supra* note 84.
88. 'AAMAC Treaty', *supra* note 81, Article 7.
89. *Ibid.*, Article 5.
90. 'Interview No 11', (2014), *supra* note 82.
91. 'AAMAC Treaty', *supra* note 81, Article 6(d).
92. This is the case for organisations providing ANS, including in particular ASECNA, as well as in other domains where a Member State has decided to delegate to AAMAC the making of technical findings for the purpose of initial approval and surveillance of an organisation. The possibility of such delegation is envisaged under Article 6 (e) of the AAMAC Treaty.

systems regulations developed by this organisation without the possibility of filing regulatory differences.[93]

Similar to the JAA Cyprus Arrangements, and the regulation establishing EASA in the EU, the AAMAC Treaty provides for a system of standardisation inspections. These inspections are to be performed by AAMAC, and their main objective is to verify the level of implementation of the common AAMAC requirements in its Member States.[94] Where inspections show that the requirements are implemented correctly, Member States are under an obligation to recognise certificates issued by the compliant State without any further verification.[95]

[c] Practical Aspects of Implementation

From a legal point of view, AAMAC should be seen as an enhanced version of a regional association of aviation safety authorities, however falling short of a RSOO which could create direct and binding legal effects in the legal systems of its Member States.

At the beginning of 2014, AAMAC was not yet operational. The funding, as well as staffing issues were not resolved. Once these points are addressed, AAMAC should focus, as a first step, on ATM/ANS issues, while regional cooperation in other domains, such as airworthiness, flight operations and pilot licensing, were expected to be dealt with by ASSA-AC, which is a successor to the COSCAP-CEMAC project.[96] There is also some overlap in the membership of AAMAC and, SADC and UEMOA,[97] which are also considering establishment of RASO type bodies, as was demonstrated under section §3.04[A][1]. Clearly some rationalisation of RASOs in this part of Africa should be considered.[98]

[2] The Pacific Aviation Safety Office

[a] Legal Basis and Organisational Set-Up

PASO was established[99] on the basis of a Pacific Islands Civil Aviation Safety and Security Treaty (hereinafter 'PICASST'), an international treaty which was opened for

93. 'AAMAC Treaty', *supra* note 81, Article 10(b)-(c).
94. *Ibid.*, Article 6(f).
95. *Ibid.*, Article 10(d).
96. ICAO, 'Second meeting of the Regional Aviation Safety Group for Africa and the Indian Ocean region (RASG-AFI/2):Update on the AFI Plan and Other Safety Initiatives', RASG-AFI/2 – WP/13, (2013).
97. This concerns Benin, Burkina Faso, Ivory Coast, Guinea-Bissau, Mali, Niger, Senegal and Togo.
98. A Memorandum of Understanding was signed in June 2014 between the three parties concerned to clarify their respective roles in the region.
99. PASO was established with the help of the Asian Development Bank regional loan. See: Asian Development Bank, 'Institutional Strengthening for Aviation Regulation' http://www.adb.org/projects/43429-012/details [accessed 10 August 2014]. For further details about the history of PASO and its functioning see: Schlumberger and Vijayakumar, 'Regional Safety Oversight Organisation: Service provider or more?', *supra* note 54 in Ch.1.

signature on 7 August 2004 and entered into force on 11 June 2005.[100] It is a 'centralized technical advisory organization'[101] serving a number of small island countries of the Pacific,[102] and its main objective is to provide harmonisation of aviation regulation, training, technical advice, planning and the delivery of a wide range of surveillance oversight services to its Member States.[103] PASO has both international and domestic legal personality.[104] Its headquarters is in Vanuatu.[105]

[b] Main Safety Functions

The scope of the PASO mandate covers airworthiness, flight operations, airports, personnel licensing, as well as aviation security.[106] PASO is essentially a service provision organisation and its primary activities include routine inspection, audit and certification activity of industry within Member States and can extend to larger projects such as the technical management and certification processes associated with the introduction of new types of aircraft.[107]

The services provided by PASO are similar to those available on the market from commercial companies such as Bureau Veritas, which specialise, amongst other things, in assisting civil aviation authorities around the world in running aircraft registries, performing oversight of aviation industry, training of inspectors and even drafting of regulations and procedures.[108]

Given the fact that PASO possesses international legal personality explicitly envisaged under its founding agreement, it would be possible for its Member States to

100. 'Pacific Islands Civil Aviation Safety and Security Treaty', Apia, 7 August 2004, ICAO Registration No. 5381. PICASST was subsequently amended by a Protocol of 20 June 2006 which came into force on 20 July 2006 (ICAO Registration No. 5382). A further amendment has been developed in 2009, but in 2014 was not yet in force due to lack of sufficient number of ratifications by PASO Member States. The 2009 amendment extends the scope of PASO competence to all ICAO safety related Annexes to the Chicago Convention.
101. *Ibid.*, Article 4.
102. In 2014 PASO Member States were as follows: the Cook Islands, Kiribati, Nauru, Niue, Papua New Guinea, Samoa, Solomon Islands, Tonga, Tuvalu, and Vanuatu. In addition, Australia, Fiji and New Zealand participate in the PASO Council as non-voting observers.
103. PASO, 'Regional approach to aviation through harmonised regulatory application in the south west pacific', Working Paper WP/23, (First Meeting of the Regional Aviation Safety Group – Asia and Pacific Regions – RASG-APAC/1, 2011), at paragraph 1.1.
104. 'PICASST', *supra* note 100, at paragraph 4.3.
105. On 3 August 2007 the government of Vanuatu and PASO entered into a formal 'Host State Agreement'. PASO and its staff were accorded diplomatic privileges and immunities by order made under the 'Vanuatu Diplomatic Privileges and Immunities Act' on 24 October 2005. Vanuatu confirmed ratification of PICASST by enacting the 'Pacific Islands Civil Aviation Treaty (Ratification) Act (2005)'. See: Kimball Murray, Ron Bartsch, and Max Foon, 'Legal and Technical Review Report for the Pacific Aviation Safety Office', (AvLaw Aviation Consultants, 2007), http://www.avlaw.com.au/Legal%20and%20Technical%20Review%20_PASO.pdf [accessed 14 August 2014], p. 6.
106. 'PICASST', *supra* note 100, Article 3.
107. PASO, Regional approach to aviation (WP/23), *supra* note 103, at paragraph 2.2.
108. Bureau Veritas, 'Civil Aviation Authority ' http://www.bureauveritas.com/wps/wcm/connect/bv_com/group/home/your-industry/aerospace/civil-aviation-authority [accessed 13 August 2014].

delegate to PASO the exercise, in a legally binding manner, of safety oversight or regulatory tasks on their behalf. This is however not the case and PASO remains for the time being de facto and de lege their technical adviser only.[109] In this capacity, PASO provides technical advice, carries out inspections and submits reports to the requesting member authorities on a cost recovery basis. Once recommendations proposed by PASO are agreed with a national authority, their implementation may also be monitored by PASO.[110] The legal basis for the services provided, in addition to the PASO founding treaty, are service level agreements concluded with Member States.[111]

PASO Member States 'retain at all times full responsibility for all matters related to aviation safety and security in their respective territories.'[112] The consequence of that approach is that PASO inspectors, when carrying out their tasks on behalf of Member States, are deemed to be officers of the national civil aviation administration and have rights, privileges and responsibilities no less favourable than those granted to civil aviation officers of the State concerned.[113]

Although the technical advice and oversight services are provided by PASO using the legal environment of the requesting State,[114] the PASO Member States strive to harmonise their legislation using as a basis the law of New Zealand.[115]

[c] Practical Aspects of Implementation

Since its establishment, PASO has been experiencing serious difficulties in stabilising its budget, and at one point was almost bankrupt.[116] At the end of 2011, PASO reported to ICAO that it was experiencing financial restrictions which:

> Impact on the ability of some Member States to complete annual pre-planned activity and often results in States not completing the wider range of recommended oversight activity within their pre-planned work such as regulatory training and education programmes.[117]

---

109. 'PICASST', *supra* note 100, Article 4(2).
110. Seiuli A.W. Tuala, 'Regional cooperation for the enhancement of safety oversight', ICAO Symposium on Regional Safety Oversight Organizations (Montréal, Canada, 2011), http://www.icao.int/Meetings/RSOOSYMPO/Pages/default.aspx [accessed 12 August 2014].
111. 'PICASST', *supra* note 100, Article 1(i). See also: PASO Legal and Technical Review Report, *supra* note 105, at pp. 27-28.
112. 'PICASST', *supra* note 100, Article 5(a).
113. *Ibid.*, Article 8(2).
114. *Ibid.*, Article 7(b).
115. PASO, Regional approach to aviation (WP/23), *supra* note 103, at paragraph 2.6.
116. Radio New Zealand International, 'Pacific Aviation Safety Office in financial strife' http://www.radionz.co.nz/international/pacific-news/205665/pacific-aviation-safety-office-in-financial-strife [accessed 22 March 2014]. For a comprehensive overview of the financial, organisational and operational challenges faced by PASO see: Schlumberger and Vijayakumar, 'Regional Safety Oversight Organisation: Service provider or more?', *supra* note 54 in Ch.1, at pp. 226-229.
117. PASO, Regional approach to aviation (WP/23), *supra* note 103, at paragraph 2.3.

In addition to inefficient funding mechanisms,[118] one of the reasons for these difficulties has been, as the Asian Development Bank has identified, lack of a standardised regulatory framework in the PASO Member States, which in turn increases the costs of the inspections and technical advices provided by PASO.[119] As a result, at the end of 2013 a reform of the organisation was launched with the support of the international financial institutions.[120]

A report prepared by the World Bank in the second half of 2013 states that:

> PASO has operated at an annual financial loss since its inception. Should PASO disappear, or its operations further weaken, several Member States would confront significant challenges in meeting national and international regulatory obligations with practical and affordable service alternatives in the short to medium term.[121]

The aforementioned World Bank report further observes that PASO's business model:

> Has not proven to be sustainable since: (i) countries have not purchased the necessary safety oversight services; (ii) there is a real, or perceived, lack of qualified technical specialists in PASO to perform the technical services, affecting demand; (iii) some countries are in arrears on member subscription fees; and, (iv) salaries and cost structures for PASO exceeded income.[122]

Based on the above information concerning PASO, it can be concluded that the key problem which has created such challenges is the fact that this organisation has not in fact been set up as a RASO type body, but rather as a provider of safety oversight services. These can also be affordably contracted from the market or from some of the mature civil aviation authorities in the region which may have spare technical capacity, such as the New Zealand or Australian CAAs.[123] PASO will most probably have to reinvent itself in the future into another type of a RASO.

---

118. Seiuli A.W. Tuala, 'Establishment of a funding mechanism to ensure the sustainability of an RSOO', ICAO Symposium on Regional Safety Oversight Organizations (Montréal, Canada, 2011), http://www.icao.int/Meetings/RSOOSYMPO/Pages/default.aspx [accessed 14 August 2014].
119. Asian Development Bank PASO project, *supra* note 99.
120. World Bank, 'Pacific Aviation Safety Office Reform, project No. P145057' http://www.worldbank.org/projects/P145057/pacific-aviation-investment-program?lang=en [accessed 14 August 2014]. See also: Kim Murray and Michael Murray, 'Technical Assistance Consultant's Report, Regional: Institutional Strengthening for Aviation Regulation', Asian Development Bank, Project No 43429, (2014), www.adb.org/projects/documents/institutional-strengthening-aviation-regulation-tacr [accessed 14 October 2014].
121. World Bank, 'Pacific Aviation Safety Office Reform Project', Report No: PAD532, (2013), http://documents.worldbank.org/curated/en/2013/09/18246423/pacific-islands-pacific-aviation-safety-office-reform-project [accessed 14 August 2014], p. 2.
122. *Ibid.*
123. In 2010 the government of the Cook Islands reported that, although it recognises that the objective of PASO was to 'provide in the long-term an improvement in quality and extension of services, at a lower total cost than is currently faced by the...industry and member governments', it believed that in practice 'the contrary has occurred'. The Cook Islands government has further underlined that it intends to rely on the services provided by the Civil Aviation Authority of New Zealand. (Source: Pacific Islands Forum Secretariat, 'Pacific Plan Annual

[3] *The Interstate Aviation Committee*

[a] *Legal Basis and Organisational Set-Up*

IAC was established following the dissolution of the Union of Soviet Socialist Republics (USSR) on the basis of the Agreement on Civil Aviation and Airspace Utilization which was signed at Minsk on 30 December 1991 (hereinafter the 'Minsk Agreement') and has been in force since that date.[124] IAC has a *sui generis* legal and institutional set up which deserves a more detailed presentation, not least because in 2014 it was one of only four RASOs in the world empowered to take legally binding decisions on behalf of States.[125]

The Minsk Treaty describes IAC as an executive body of the Council for Aviation and Airspace Utilization,[126] which in turn is an organ of the Commonwealth of Independent States (CIS).[127] IAC considers itself as an international organisation.[128]

The IAC has legal personality within the domestic legal orders of the Member States, which extends to all issues which are necessary for the performance of its functions.[129] The organisational structure of the IAC comprises eight permanent commissions (Figure 3.4) which also 'possess the rights of a juridical person and independent budgets.'[130]

Progress Report Annex', (2010), http://www.forumsec.org/pages.cfm/newsroom/documents-publications/programme-project-reports/pacific-plan-progress-reports.html [accessed 14 August 2014], p. 55.

124. 'Agreement on Civil Aviation and Airspace Utilization', Minsk, 30 December 1991, ICAO Registration No. 3720. The original signatories of the Minsk Agreement were the Russian Federation, the Republic of Armenia, Republic of Azerbaijan, Republic of Belarus, Republic of Georgia, Republic of Kazakhstan, Republic of Kyrgyzstan, Republic of Moldova, Republic of Tajikistan, Republic of Uzbekistan, Turkmenistan and Ukraine.
125. The other three are EASA which is presented in Chapter 4, ECCAA which is addressed under section §3.06 of this Chapter, and ASSA-AC which is referred to in section §3.04[A][1] of this Chapter.
126. 'Statute of the Council for Aviation and Airspace Utilization and the Statute of the Interstate Aviation Committee', 19 February 1992, ICAO Registration No. 3720, p. Article I.3.
127. The Commonwealth of Independent States (CIS) is an international organisation formed in 1991 by the Russian Federation and some other republics that were formerly part of the USSR. Following the withdrawal of Georgia from the CIS in August 2009, it is now comprised of nine Member States which are the Russian Federation, the Republics of Armenia, Azerbaijan, Belarus, Kazakhstan, Kyrgyzstan, Moldova, Tajikistan and Uzbekistan. Ukraine and Turkmenistan do not consider themselves as Member States of CIS.
128. IAC, 'The Role of a Regional International Civil Aviation Organization in Ensuring Flight Safety', DGCA/06-IP/16, Directors General of Civil Aviation Conference on Global Strategy for Aviation Safety (Montréal, Canada, 2006), at paragraph 1.1.
129. 'IAC Statute', *supra* note 126, at Article II.6.
130. *Ibid.*, at Article III.13.

Figure 3.4 Organisational Structure of the Interstate Aviation Committee

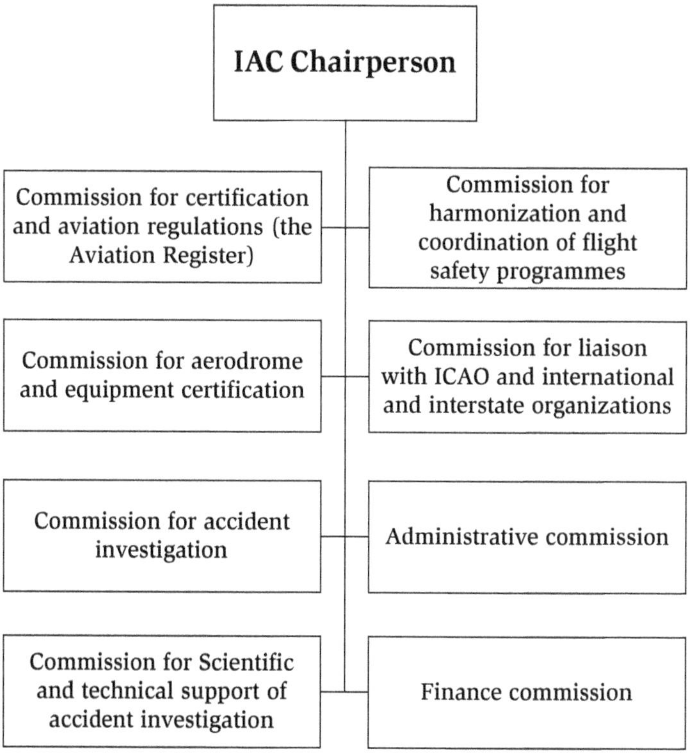

Source: Interstate Aviation Committee.[131]

[b] Main Safety Functions

The Minsk Agreement sets out the general mandate of the IAC and its possible functions and responsibilities, however the precise competences of the IAC in the territories of the contracting parties, including the delegation of the exercise of safety functions and duties, are defined in specific agreements, or protocols, concluded between the IAC and the States concerned.

For example, in the case of the Russian Federation this relationship is defined in a protocol signed between the IAC and the Ministry of Transport in 2006.[132] Under this protocol, IAC is responsible for developing rules for the Russian Federation in the areas of airworthiness of civil aircraft, certification of international aerodromes and their equipment, impact of aircraft on the environment and investigation of aircraft accidents. Moreover, under the protocol, the IAC is responsible for performing, on behalf

131. IAC, 'Interstate Aviation Committee: presentation', (personal archives of the author, 2004).
132. Protocol No. 4/01-92 signed on 20 February 2006.

of the Russian Federation, certification of aircraft and their components, approval of production organisations, certification of international aerodromes and their equipment, and organisation and realisation of the investigation of aircraft accidents occurring within the territory of the Russian Federation or involving Russia as the 'State of Design', the 'State of the Operator' or the 'State of Registry' outside the Russian territory.

[i] The Role of IAC in Aviation Safety Rulemaking

In accordance with its statute, IAC 'shall issue inter-State regulatory instruments which shall be subject to mandatory compliance on the territory of all the founding States ...'.[133]

In practice the rule-making process within the IAC is based on the work of Commissions established in each relevant subject domain, that is the Commission for certification and aviation regulations – the Aviation Register, the Commission for aerodrome and equipment certification, and the Commission for accident investigation. Draft regulations are submitted by the Commissions to the Council for Aviation and Airspace Utilization for approval by consensus.

The regulations adopted by the Council for Aviation and Airspace Utilization, although legally binding under the Minsk Agreement, are not directly applicable in the domestic legal orders of the IAC Member States and need to be given such effect through enabling national legislation. For example, the Russian Federation has divided the responsibility for developing its aviation safety rules between the Ministry of Transport and the IAC,[134] with the latter authorised by the government[135] to develop and amend aviation rules on behalf of the Russian Federation, within the scope of the delegation protocol.

In addition to regulations, the IAC also issues detailed technical requirements for the design and certification of aircraft and their components, as well as aerodrome and navigation equipment and facilities used in the CIS.[136]

[ii] The Role of IAC in Aviation Safety Certification and Oversight

Under the Minsk Agreement the IAC has competence to issue certificates and other documents on behalf of its Member States. There is a two stage process to enable this. Firstly there needs to be an additional protocol concluded between the IAC and any of its Member State wishing to delegate certification competences. Secondly enabling State legislation must be adopted to implement the delegation into a national legal

133. 'IAC Statute', *supra* note 126, Article III.14.
134. Governmental Resolution No. 360 of 27 May 1998 provides that the rules of the Russian Federation that have been approved by the Council for Aviation and Airspace Utilization are enacted by the corresponding federal bodies.
135. Governmental Resolution No. 367 of 23 April 1994.
136. IAC, 'Авиационные Правила (Aviation Regulations)' http://www.mak.ru/russian/russian.html [accessed 10 August 2014].

system. For example, in the Russian Federation the IAC was given legal status as an authorised organ through the protocol concluded with IAC in 2006[137] and corresponding Presidential Decrees and Governmental Resolutions.[138] Accordingly, IAC acts on behalf of the Russian Federation for issues related to airworthiness, aerodromes, and environmental certification, including:

- certification of aircraft and their components (including aircraft noise type certification);
- approval of design and production organisations for aeronautical products;
- certification of international aerodromes and their equipment;
- accreditation of 'certification centres'.

For those States which have delegated to IAC aircraft certification competences, IAC will also be acting as a technical agent under BASAs or working arrangements concluded with third countries or foreign aviation authorities.[139]

[iii] The Role of IAC in Air Accident Investigation

Under the Minsk Agreement, and the IAC Statute, the IAC can accept delegation of State functions and duties related to aviation accident investigations.[140] A number of Contracting Parties to the Minsk Agreement, including the Russian Federation and Belarus have taken advantage of this possibility.[141] The legal modalities for the exercise of such delegations are presented in detail in section §3.05 dealing with RAIOs.

[c] Practical Aspects of Implementation

Originally twelve States signed the Minsk Agreement, but today the level of participation of the original signatories in IAC varies. For example since the establishment of IAC in 1991, countries such as Georgia,[142] Moldova[143] and Ukraine[144] have concluded,

137. Protocol No. 4/01-92, *supra* note 132.
138. Presidential Decrees No. 439 of 5 May 1992 and No. 904 of 13 June 1996, as well Governmental Resolutions No. 367 of 23 April 1994, No. 316 of 7 April 1995 and No. 1147 of 8 September 1997.
139. See section §5.05 of Chapter 5 for discussion about IAC's and other RASOs' international activities.
140. 'Minsk Agreement', *supra* note 124, Article 7(e); 'IAC Statute', *supra* note 126, Article II.5(e); IAC presentation (2004), *supra* note 131.
141. For Belarus see for example report issued by IAC, as the competent investigating authority, concerning the accident of BAe-125-800B, registration number RA-02807, which occurred on 26 October 2009 in the proximity of the Minsk airport.
142. 'Common Aviation Area Agreement between the European Union and its Member States and Georgia', 2 December 2010, (OJ L 321, 20.11.2012).
143. 'Common Aviation Area Agreement between the European Union and its Member States and the Republic of Moldova', 26 June 2012, (OJ L 292, 20.10.2012).
144. EC, 'EU and Ukraine skies to join forces', Press release IP/13/1181, (2013).

or are in the course of negotiations, of aviation agreements with the EU. These agreements provide or will provide for the participation of the civil aviation authorities of these countries, to various degrees, in the work of EASA. In practice today the Russian Federation, in whose territory IAC has its headquarters, is the most closely associated Member State of this RASO from a regulatory point of view.[145]

[4] The Banjul Accord Group Aviation Safety Oversight Organisation

[a] Legal Basis and Organisational Set-Up

BAGASOO was established by seven West African States[146] on the basis of an international agreement signed on 30 June 2009,[147] within the broader framework of the Banjul Accord Group (BAG) Agreement.[148] Its predecessor was the COSCAP-BAG – a technical cooperation project established by ICAO to enhance the safety oversight capabilities of the BAG States.[149] BAGASOO is one of the RSOOs which evolved from a COSCAP project (see Table 3.1).

Its founding agreement establishes BAGASOO as a self-accounting institution of the BAG. This in practice means that the BAG Council of Ministers and BAG Secretariat are involved in the review of the annual financial accounts of BAGASOO[150] through an audit, and facilitate dispute settlement procedures between the BAGASOO Member States.[151] At the same time, the Director Generals of the seven BAGASOO Member States, together with the Executive Director of BAGASOO constitute the governing Board of Directors which reviews and approves the budget of this RSOO.[152]

BAGASOO has legal personality under its founding agreement.[153] Its headquarters is located in Abuja, Nigeria.

145. Conclusion reached based on the review of the ICAO USOAP reports for the signatories of the Minsk Agreement, as well as experiences of the author who was responsible in EASA for international cooperation with a number of IAC Member States, including Ukraine, Moldova and Georgia.
146. Republic of Cape Verde, the Republic of Gambia, the Republic of Ghana, the Republic of Guinea, the Republic of Liberia, the Federal Republic of Nigeria, and the Republic of Sierra Leone.
147. 'Banjul Accord Group Aviation Safety Oversight Organisation Agreement', Montreal, 30 June 2009 ICAO Registration No. 5462. The BAGASOO agreement entered into force upon signature.
148. 'Agreement for the establishment of the Banjul Accord Group', Banjul, 29 January 2004, ICAO Registration No. 5455. The main objective of the BAG Agreement is to accelerate the implementation of the Yamoussoukro Declaration and the Yamoussoukro Decision which aim at the liberalisation of air transport in Africa. For further details on the BAG Agreement see: Schlumberger, *supra* note 37 in Ch. 1, at pp. 82-86.
149. Emmanuel Akatue, 'Institutionalization of the Banjul Accord Group Safety Oversight Organization', RASG-AFI/1 – IP/7, (First meeting of the Africa – Indian Ocean Regional Aviation Safety Group, RASG-AFI/1, 2012).
150. 'BAGASOO Agreement', *supra* note 147, Article 15(6).
151. *Ibid.*, Article 18.
152. BAGASOO official, 'Interview No 6', (2014).
153. 'BAGASOO Agreement', *supra* note 147, Article 2.2.

[b] *Main Safety Functions*

BAGASOO became operational in July 2010.[154] Under its founding agreement, the key objective of this RASO is the:

> Promotion of the safe and efficient use and development of civil aviation, and the provision of assistance to States for meeting their safety oversight obligations and responsibilities under the Chicago Convention and its related safety Annexes.[155]

BAGASOO's founding agreement does not specify the domains of aviation safety for which it is competent which means that in practice it can develop cooperation in any of the areas covered by ICAO Annexes. In 2013, its activities covered the areas of personnel licensing, airworthiness, flight operations and aerodromes, with the intention to extend its scope in the future to security and ATM.[156]

BAGASOO's functions are relatively broad and include development of harmonised safety requirements, procedures and manuals for adoption and use by the Member States, providing support to certification and surveillance, development and implementation of training programs and other. BAGASOO can also evaluate the safety oversight capabilities of its Member States and help with the implementation of USOAP corrective action plans, as well as accept delegation of certification and surveillance tasks.[157]

In the area of rulemaking, BAGASOO prepares regulations, guidance material, policies and procedures and submits them for adoption and use by the Member States. The regulations are not directly applicable and need to be transposed into the national legal systems.[158] The objective of BAGASOO is to ensure a harmonised regulatory environment in line with the ICAO SARPs.[159]

As far as implementation of legislation is concerned, BAGASOO does not enjoy delegated executive powers directly under its founding agreement. However, in accordance with its Article 5, BAGASOO can accept delegation of certification and surveillance functions when so requested by a Member State. At the time of writing this study in 2014, BAGASOO had not concluded any such delegation agreements.[160] In addition the BAGASOO is mandated to partake, with respect to all its Member States, and irrespective of the status of their safety oversight capability, in all initial certification exercises 'for the purpose of monitoring and ensuring the uniform application of common standards within the BAG Sub-Region.'[161]

So far BAGASOO focused primarily on human capacity building, including in particular the development of qualifications and training of aviation safety inspectors

154. Institutionalization of BAGASOO (RASG-AFI/1 - IP/7), *supra* note 149, at paragraph 5.
155. 'BAGASOO Agreement', *supra* note 147, Article 4(1).
156. BAGASOO, 'Revised Brochure' http://www.bagasoo.org/en/images/docs/downloads/bagasoo_brochure_revised.pdf [accessed 10 August 2014].
157. 'BAGASOO Agreement', *supra* note 147, Article 5. For a more detailed overview of BAGASOO's work see: Institutionalization of BAGASOO (RASG-AFI/1 - IP/7), *supra* note 149.
158. 'BAGASOO Agreement', *supra* note 147, Article 8(f)-(g).
159. *Ibid.*, Article 14(b).
160. 'Interview No 6', (2014), *supra* note 152.
161. 'BAGASOO Agreement', *supra* note 147, Article 5(f).

in the region. It has also been developing aviation safety oversight databases, participating in the AFI-CIS, and conducting visits to its Member States in order to carry out gap analysis and subsequently assist Member States in addressing identified deficiencies.[162]

[c] Practical Aspects of Implementation

BAGASOO has limited personnel and, at the moment of writing this study, did not expect to develop the capacity to act as a fully-fledged civil aviation authority.[163] Instead it intended to rely on inspectors from the region through a co-operative inspectorate scheme, similar to the one established by AFCAC and presented under section §3.04[A][3]. BAGASOO expects that the co-operative inspectorate scheme will enable it to maintain staffing levels that will ensure the effectiveness of its work programmes whilst, at the same time, significantly reduce operational cost.[164]

Since its establishment in 2010 BAGASOO has experienced financial challenges. This is because although the BAGASOO founding agreement envisages that BAGASOO is to be principally financed through a Passenger Service Charge to be collected from its Member States, as well as revenues deriving from BAGASOO's operational activities, in practice this scheme has not worked as planned, primarily because of Member States' different charging policies which proved difficult to harmonise.[165] BAGASOO had therefore to resort to sharing the budget amongst its Member States on a pro rata basis, but in practice only some States have actually been contributing fully to the budget.[166] At the beginning of 2014 BAGASOO was considering reverting back to the implementation of a Passenger Service Charge instead of relying on State contributions.[167]

Overall BAGASOO can be characterised as a RSOO with mainly expert advisory, consultancy and technical support functions, but which from a legal point of view also has the necessary mandate to exercise safety oversight functions on behalf of its Member States. It remains to be seen to what extent this mandate will actually be used in practice in the future.

---

162. Institutionalization of BAGASOO (RASG-AFI/1 – IP/7), *supra* note 149, at paragraph 7.2. See also: The Aviation & Allied Business Journal (12.10.2012), 'BAGASOO: Future Regional Safety Pivot', Interview with Mr Emmanuel Akatue, Executive Director of the BAGASOO' http://www.aviationbusinessjournal.aero/2012/10/12/bagasoo-future-regional-safety-pivot.aspx [accessed 23 July 2014].
163. BAGASOO Brochure, *supra* note 156. Also confirmed through: 'Interview No 6', (2014), *supra* note 152.
164. BAGASOO, 'Framework of the Banjul Accord Group Aviation Safety Oversight Organization (BAGASOO) and The Banjul Accord Group Accident Investigation Agency (BAGAIA)', C-WP/13396, (187th session of the ICAO Council, 2009), at paragraph 1.4.
165. BAGASOO: Future Regional Safety Pivot', Interview with Mr Emmanuel Akatue, Executive Director of the BAGASOO, *supra* note 162. Also confirmed through: 'Interview No 6', (2014), *supra* note 152.
166. Institutionalization of BAGASOO (RASG-AFI/1 – IP/7), *supra* note 149, at paragraph 6.1.
167. 'Interview No 6', (2014), *supra* note 152.

[5] Caribbean Aviation Safety and Security Oversight System

[a] Legal Basis and Organisational Set-Up

CASSOS was established in 2008 on the basis of the Agreement Establishing the Caribbean Aviation Safety and Security Oversight System (hereinafter the 'CASSOS Agreement'),[168] and is a successor of the Association of Civil Aviation Authorities of the Caribbean (ACCAC), a Type II pre-RASO. CASSOS is formally designated as an institution of the Caribbean Community (CARICOM) under Article 21 of the 'Revised Treaty of Chaguaramas Establishing the Caribbean Community including the CARICOM single Market and Economy (hereinafter the 'CARICOM Treaty').'[169] Part VI of the CARICOM Treaty addresses air transport and calls for harmonisation of licensing and certification, resource sharing and cooperation in accident investigation. In addition to safety, CASSOS mandate covers also aviation security and environmental issues.[170]

The transition from a pre-RASO, as well as its designation as a CARICOM institution 'gave CASSOS a much higher profile and allowed [it] to represent the region in aviation matters and to have official observer status at ICAO'.[171] At the same time, the analysis of the provisions of the CASSOS Agreement shows that this RASO, with the exception of the Caribbean Court of Justice, does not rely on the CARICOM institutions for its functioning, and for that reason has been classified as a RASO Type I rather than Type II under the typology proposed by this study.

Under its founding agreement CASSOS shall possess 'full juridical personality' and full capacity to 'acquire and dispose of immovable and movable property, contract and institute legal proceedings.[172] Its headquarters is located in Jamaica. In 2014, CASSOS had thirteen Member States.[173] The OECS, which is addressed under section §3.06 is a founding member of CASSOS and has one vote on the CASSOS Board of Directors.[174]

[b] Main Safety Functions

CASSOS is a RASO with advisory and coordination functions, and in 2014 did not have any executive competences formally delegated to it by Member States. In an interview

168. 'Agreement establishing the Caribbean Aviation Safety and Security Oversight System', Gros Islet, 9 May 2008. The CASSOS Agreement entered into force on 3 July 2008.
169. 'Revised Treaty of Chaguaramas Establishing the Caribbean Community including the CARICOM single Market and Economy', The Bahamas, 5 July 2001.
170. CASSOS, 'Caribbean Aviation Safety and Security Oversight System (CASSOS) – Report of activities and progress since the 37th General Assembly', A38-WP/328, (38th ICAO Assembly, 2013).
171. Official of the Caribbean Aviation Safety and Security Oversight System, 'Interview No 13', (2014).
172. 'CASSOS Agreement', *supra* note 168, at Article V(1).
173. Barbados, Guyana, Haiti, Jamaica, the Organization of Eastern Caribbean States (Antigua and Barbuda, Dominica, Grenada, St. Lucia, St. Kitts and Nevis, St. Vincent and the Grenadines), Suriname and Trinidad and Tobago.
174. 'Interview No 13', (2014), *supra* note 171.

conducted for the purpose of this study two reasons were mentioned by a CASSOS official to explain the fact that this RASO does not have executive competences, namely that: this would require the development of a much more complex treaty' and that 'States might view this [delegation of the exercise of safety functions] as a loss of sovereignty'.[175]

CASSOS has limited own resources (two staff members in 2013[176]), and primarily relies on inspectors drawn from member authorities and deployed in a cooperative resource-sharing manner.[177] CASSOS own staff performs certification and inspection tasks as authorised inspectors of the Member State for the benefit of which given tasks are performed, and not under CASSOS own authority.[178] In addition, in 2014 approximately twenty national inspectors were designated as CASSOS transnational aviation safety inspectors and made available to any of the CASSOS Member States.[179] Inspectors are included in the CASSOS 'pool of inspectors' after it has been determined by CASSOS that they meet pre-defined qualification criteria, including with respect to formal and on-the job training.[180]

When it comes to rulemaking, the primary objective of CASSOS is to coordinate harmonisation of Member State aviation safety legislation on the basis of ICAO Model Civil Aviation Regulations.[181] CASSOS also develops guidance and other supporting material for its Member States.[182]

[c] *Practical Aspects of Implementation*

Despite limited resources CASSOS believes that is had been able to help its Member States considerably. A number of CASSOS authorities managed to achieve FAA IASA Category I, and CASSOS is 'supporting the remaining authorities to achieve FAA IASA Category I and ICAO USOAP compliance'.[183]

CASSOS is also aiming at developing a common licensing system and mutual recognition of licenses and certifications, although in 2013 it was admitted by CASSOS that 'several years of work still remain before these goals will be achieved'.[184]

From the perspective of CASSOS Member States, the main challenge has been 'in attracting and retaining qualified flight operations inspectors, and CASSOS has been meeting some of this need by the transnational inspector mechanism',[185] which was described above. The following concrete examples of cooperation were mentioned by CASSOS in respect to inspector sharing:

---

175. *Ibid.*
176. A38-WP/328, *supra* note 170, at paragraph 4.2.
177. 'Interview No 13', (2014), *supra* note 171.
178. *Ibid.*
179. A38-WP/328, *supra* note 170, at paragraph 1.6.1.
180. *Ibid.*
181. *Ibid.*, at paragraph 1.3.
182. *Ibid.*
183. 'Interview No 13', (2014), *supra* note 171.
184. A38-WP/328, *supra* note 170, at paragraph 1.6.1.
185. *Ibid.*, at paragraph 4.1.

> Several States that needed a helicopter qualified flight operations inspector were able to share one from a State that had one; one State has had no flight operations inspector for several years and has used the CASSOS mechanism to meet its needs; and others had no Airbus inspector and had used CASSOS employee to meet those needs.[186]

Although, CASSOS had 'very stable budget since its earliest inception', it was also reported in the interview conducted for the purpose of this study that 'sustained funding is a challenge that needs to be addressed as expansion cannot happen unless there is a source of funds other than State contributions that do not always arrive on time.'[187]

CASSOS Member States are also considering establishing a RAIO in the future.[188]

[D] RASO (Type II): A Supranational Aviation Safety Agency

The second type of RASOs is a supranational aviation safety agency. In comparison with the previous category, the main feature of this type is that it evolves within the broader institutional and legal framework of a REIO.[189] From a policy point of view this means that a RASO is used by the REIO as its technical arm for the implementation of a single regional air transport market.

The extent to which a RASO can rely on the REIO's institutional framework and legislation is directly proportional to the level of integration of the latter. If a REIO has truly supranational character and can adopt through its institutions legally binding legislation, this legislation will also bind the RASO and will form the foundation of a single regional safety system. This is, for example, the case with the EU and EASA, which is currently the most prominent example of a supranational aviation safety agency and will be subject to a detailed presentation and analysis in the following chapter. A similar relationship is being developed between the Organisation of the Eastern Caribbean States (OECS) and the ECCAA, which is addressed in section §3.06 of this chapter.

If the level of the integration of a REIO is less deep, a RASO may be relying on the former to a lesser extent, as is the case with the CASSOA presented below. By mid-2014, there have still been very few truly supranational aviation safety agencies, but it can be expected that additional ones will be established, in particular in Africa, where some of the RECs have legislative competences and envisage establishing RASOs. This is the case for example with UEMOA which, as discussed under section §3.04[A][1], is planning to establish its own RASO type body.

Review of the existing practice also shows that RASOs established in a form of an organ of an international organisation and having a separate legal personality from the Member States of that organisation are created as a RASO Type II. In 2014, two RASOs were established in a form of an organ of an international legal person – that is EASA,

186. 'Interview No 13', (2014), *supra* note 171.
187. *Ibid.*
188. *Ibid.*
189. For examples of REIOs *supra* note 80.

and ASSA-AC. The latter is not presented in detail in the present study, as at the time of it writing ASSA-AC was not yet operational.[190]

[1] *East African Community Civil Aviation Safety and Security Oversight Agency*

[a] *Legal Basis and Organisational Set-Up*

CASSOA was established in 2007 as a self-accounting institution of the EAC. Its legal basis is a protocol signed by the three founding States, namely Kenya, Tanzania and Uganda on 18 April 2007, [191] and adopted under Article 92 of the EAC Treaty on 18 June 2007 (hereinafter the 'CASSOA protocol').[192] Subsequently two more States, Rwanda and Burundi, have joined the EAC and became parties to the CASSOA protocol.[193] CASSOA is therefore a specialised institution of the EAC responsible for aviation safety and security.

Although CASSOA is an institution of the EAC, in practice it relies to a small extent on the EAC institutional framework. With the exception of the privileges and immunities which CASSOA derives from the EAC Treaty, and the EAC Court of Justice, which is the designated forum for dispute resolution under the CASSOA protocol, CASSOA works largely independently. For example, the rules, procedures and manuals are developed by CASSOA Technical Committee(s) and following their endorsement by CASSOA's Board of Directors, are presented to the Member States for enactment in their national legal systems.[194]

At the same time the EAC has supranational institutions and a competence to adopt legislation which is binding upon the EAC Member States.[195] This institutional framework could be used by the EAC to develop supranational aviation safety legislation to be implemented by CASSOA. For this reason, the present study has qualified this organisation as a Type II RASO.

190. ASSA-AC was established by a Supplementary Act (Acte Additionnel) No 06/-CEMAC-204-CCE-11 of the EAC Heads of States Summit (La Conference des Chefs d'Etat) and CEMAC 'Regulation No 06/12-UEAC-204-CM-23, portant organisation et fonctionnement de l'Agence de Supervision de la Sècurité Aérienne en Afrique Centrale (ASSA-AC)', both adopted on 22 July 2012.
191. 'Protocol on the establishment of the East African Community Civil Aviation Safety and Security Oversight Agency', signed on 18 April 2007 and approved during the 5th Extraordinary Summit of EAC Heads of State held in Kampala, Uganda on 18th June 2007', http://www.cassoa.org/index.php/key-documents/cassoa-protocol [accessed 10 August 2014].
192. Article 92 of the EAC Treaty requires, among others, that the EAC partner States harmonise their policies, rules and regulations on civil aviation in order to promote the development of a safe, reliable, efficient and economically viable air transport system in the region in compliance with the international standards.
193. Treaties of Accession of the Republic of Rwanda and Burundi to the East African Community, both signed on 18 June 2007 are available at http://www.eac.int/legal/index.php?option=com_docman&Itemid=28 [accessed 10 August 2014].
194. 'CASSOA Protocol', *supra* note 191, Article 7(d)-(e).
195. Anne Pieter van der Mei, 'The East African Community: The Bumpy Road to Supranationalism', Maastricht Working Papers – Faculty of Law, 7 (2009).

CASSOA has legal personality.[196] Its headquarters is based in Entebbe, Uganda.[197]

[b] Main Safety Functions

Under its founding protocol, the mandate of CASSOA covers both aviation safety and security oversight, without however distinguishing further the specific domains of aviation safety for which it is competent.[198] In practice, it has been supporting its Member States in the areas of flight safety standards, including air operations, airworthiness and crew licensing, as well as aerodromes and ANS.[199]

The primary role of CASSOA is to assist the EAC Member States in meeting their safety and security oversight obligations under the Chicago Convention and its Annexes, as well as to provide a forum and structure to discuss, plan and implement common measures for the enhancement of safety and security of civil aviation.[200] From a legal point of view the structure and contents of the CASSOA protocol is similar to the BAGASOO founding agreement, with a major difference that CASSOA's mandate also covers security issues.

In contrast to BAGASOO, the CASSOA currently does not have a mandate to accept delegation of safety oversight functions from its Member States. For the time being, CASSOA performs mainly advisory and support functions. Since its establishment, it has been focusing primarily on harmonisation of regulations and procedures, providing assistance to States in reaching compliance with ICAO SARPs,[201] provision of training to national inspectors, exchange of safety information and implementation of operational projects, such as a common examination scheme for aviation personnel or EAC centre for aviation medicine.[202] It has also established – with mixed results – a system for the sharing of aviation safety inspectors.[203]

---

196. *Ibid.*, Article 3.
197. CASSOA, 'Regional cooperation for the enhancement of safety oversight: obstacles and lessons learnt', ACAC/ICAO Seminar/Workshop on Regional Safety Oversight Programmes, (Rabat, Morocco, 2012).
198. 'CASSOA Protocol', *supra* note 191, Article 2.
199. Regional cooperation for the enhancement of safety oversight: obstacles and lessons learnt, *supra* note 197.
200. 'CASSOA Protocol', *supra* note 191, Article 4(c). For a more detailed overview of CASSOA's activities see: Regional cooperation for the enhancement of safety oversight: obstacles and lessons learnt, *supra* note 197; and: CASSOA, 'Safety Initiatives and Regional Organizations in the AFI Region', RASG-AFI/1 – IP/8, (First meeting of the Africa Indian Ocean Regional Aviation Safety Group, 2012).
201. With some success, as for example Rwanda was removed in 2012 from the ICAO list of States with 'Significant Safety Concerns'. See: Regional cooperation for the enhancement of safety oversight: obstacles and lessons learnt, *supra* note 197.
202. Safety Initiatives and Regional Organizations in the AFI Region, *supra* note 200, at paragraph 3.
203. *Ibid.*

[c] *Practical Aspects of Implementation*

Similar to BAGASOO, CASSOA has been facing challenges in respect to its funding. The CASSOA protocol envisages various sources of funding, including a fees and charges scheme and sources provided by EAC.[204] In practice, the organisation is largely dependent on the funding from its Member States, which have their own priorities and whose contributions proved to be uneven.[205] This has resulted in difficulties in attracting and retaining sufficient number of qualified technical personnel, in particular pilots.[206]

Another challenge has been the difficulty in implementing an effective scheme for the sharing of inspector resources amongst the Member States due to 'relatively few qualified and skilled inspectors within the region.'[207] CASSOA has also highlighted resistance from civil aviation authorities based on perceptions of competition for safety oversight responsibilities, differences in legal frameworks, drafting principles and regulatory promulgation procedures of Member States, as some of the problems in discharging its mandate.[208]

It is the objective of CASSOA to evolve in the future into a RASO with some of the safety and security oversight competences formally delegated to it by the Member States. To this end, an organisational development plan has been prepared,[209] and expert assistance sought from ICAO as to how such a future mandate might best be structured.[210] However, as CASSOA is an institution of the EAC, such evolution would ultimately depend on the decision taken at the EAC level and would require a change to the CASSOA protocol. This in turn may depend on the future integration path of the EAC.[211]

§3.05 REGIONAL ACCIDENT INVESTIGATION ORGANISATIONS

[A] Introduction

Beyond regulation and oversight of civil aviation, which is the domain of RSOOs dealt with in the previous section, civil aviation accident investigation[212] is also an area

204. 'CASSOA Protocol', *supra* note 191, Article 15.
205. Regional cooperation for the enhancement of safety oversight: obstacles and lessons learnt, *supra* note 197.
206. *Ibid.*
207. Safety Initiatives and Regional Organizations in the AFI Region, *supra* note 200, at paragraph 3.2.
208. Regional cooperation for the enhancement of safety oversight: obstacles and lessons learnt, *supra* note 197.
209. CASSOA, 'Revised Strategic Plan 2010/11–2014/15' http://www.cassoa.org/index.php/key-documents/strategic-plan [accessed 10 August 2014].
210. ICAO, 'Cooperation with Regional Organizations and Regional Civil Aviation Bodies', C-WP/13885, (197th session of the ICAO Council, 2012), at paragraph 8.1.
211. Safety Initiatives and Regional Organizations in the AFI Region, *supra* note 200, at paragraphs 2.1.4 and 5.1.
212. According to Annex 13 to the Chicago Convention, States have an obligation to ensure the investigation of both accidents and serious accidents. This section, for the sake of brevity, will refer only to accident investigation and accident investigation bodies or authorities.

where regional cooperation can bring regulatory efficiencies and economies of scale. This study would therefore not be complete without also referring to RAIOs, which, although not yet as numerous as RSOOs, have also been gaining increasing attention in recent years.

Today, commercial aviation is overall a very safe sector of transport with fatal accidents occurring rarely as Chapter 1 demonstrated. This means that maintaining a permanent accident investigation authority with qualified staff and adequate facilities can be costly even for wealthy regions. When in 2009, the European Commission presented its proposal for a new EU regulation on air accident investigations, it highlighted, as one of the drivers for its initiative 'lack of a uniform investigating capacity in the EU',[213] and underlined that 'especially for smaller Member States it is difficult to mobilise the necessary expertise for more complex investigations and to be on par with large manufacturers or operators.'[214] and that 'in practice, only Member States with big manufacturing industry can justify budgets necessary to maintain a properly staffed and equipped [authorities].'[215]

The difficulties that States in general experience in meeting their legal obligations related to aviation accident investigations are best illustrated with the ICAO USOAP results. According to 2014 ICAO data concerning the level of effectiveness of safety oversight systems, accident investigation is an area where overall the States' capabilities *are the weakest,* with the level of effective implementation at only 50%.[216]

States can try to mitigate these difficulties through various means. This can include technical activities such as joint planning and conduct of training for investigators, or provision of assistance within the framework of a particular investigation. It may also entail formalisation of cooperation by means of memoranda of understanding, letters of intent or international agreements. The 2006 ECAC Code of Conduct on Co-operation can be given as an example of a non-legally binding arrangement providing a convenient framework for co-operation outside the context of a specific investigation.[217] The ECAC Code of Conduct addresses issues such as: collaboration during an investigation, management of resources, exchange of information and training activities.

States can also establish multimodal investigating agencies[218] or joint civil-military[219] aviation accident investigation bodies, in order to reduce the costs, and

213. EC, 'Impact Assessment accompanying the proposal of the European Commission for a Regulation of the European Parliament and of the Council on investigation and prevention of accidents and incidents in civil aviation', COM(2009) 611 final, (Brussels, 2009), p. 14.
214. *Ibid.*, at p. 15.
215. *Ibid.*
216. Regional Performance Dashboards, *supra* note 15 in Ch. 1.
217. ECAC, 'Code of Conduct on co-operation in the field of civil aviation accident/incident investigation' https://www.ecac-ceac.org//publications_events_news/ecac_documents/codes_of_conduct [accessed 7 August 2014].
218. Multimodal boards operate for example in the Netherlands, Bulgaria, Latvia and Sweden.
219. In Sweden for example, the Swedish Accident Investigation Board, which is a multimodal safety board reporting to the Ministry of Defence, is responsible for investigating accidents involving not only civil but also military aircraft, including Swedish military aircraft subject to an accident abroad unless stipulated otherwise in international agreements. See: Piotr

provide for efficiencies deriving from aggregation of knowledge and experience related to investigation of transport accidents.

In order to help States in meeting their accident investigation obligations ICAO started to promote the RAIO concept. This idea was formally introduced into the ICAO regulatory framework in 2010 with the adoption of an amendment to Annex 13 envisaging the possibility of delegation of investigations to RAIOs:

> The State of Occurrence shall institute an investigation into the circumstances of the accident and be responsible for the conduct of the investigation, but it may delegate the whole or any part of the conducting of such investigation to another State or a regional accident investigation organization by mutual arrangement and consent.[220]

The concept of a RAIO is not a new one. In Commonwealth of the Independent States, the IAC, in addition to being a RSOO as was presented in the previous section, also acts as a RAIO. Overall however, and in contrast to the RSOOs, the practical application of the RAIO concept has so far been rather limited. Until 2014, in addition to the IAC, only one other such organisation had been established – the Banjul Accord Group Accident Investigation Agency (BAGAIA).[221] In 2010, the EU established the European Network of Civil Aviation Safety Investigation Authorities (ENCASIA), but this organisation has only a supporting and coordinating role, and does not conduct investigations on behalf of EU Member States.[222] ENCASIA can be at best qualified as a pre-RAIO.

According to ICAO the key benefits of a RAIO are to:

- eliminate duplication of efforts by pooling human, technical and financial resources;
- achieve economies of scale leading to effectiveness and efficiency;
- demonstrate, as a responsible regional organisation, improved regional solidarity;
- enable investigators in the region to gain experience more quickly;
- facilitate the recruitment and retainment of investigators by States;
- help achieve the independence of investigations.[223]

The ICAO RSOO Symposium of 2011 similarly concluded that 'there are benefits to be derived from the establishment of Regional Accident and Incident Investigation

Kasprzyk, 'Legal Ramifications of the Investigations of the 2010 Polish President's Aircraft Accident', ASL, 36 (2011), p. 214.

220. Annex 13 to the Chicago Convention, at paragraphs 5.1 and 5.1.2.
221. 'Banjul Accord Group Accident Investigation Agency Agreement', Montreal, 30 June 2009, ICAO Registration No. 5463. The Member States of BAGAIA are: Republic of Cape Verde, the Republic of Gambia, the Republic of Ghana, the Republic of Guinea, the Republic of Liberia, the Federal Republic of Nigeria, and the Republic of Sierra Leone.
222. EU, 'Regulation (EU) No 996/2010 of the European Parliament and of the Council of 20 October 2010 on the investigation and prevention of accidents and incidents in civil aviation and repealing Directive 94/56/EC', (OJ L 295, 12.11.2010), Article 7.
223. ICAO Doc. 9946, *supra* note 3 in Ch. 1, at paragraph 2.2.

Organizations (RAIOs) and from close collaboration and coordination between RSOOs and RAIOs.'[224]

In the context of aviation accident investigations, the issue that must be particularly underlined, and which is fully applicable to a RAIO, is the requirement of independence and separation of the accident investigation process. Under Annex 13, the sole objective of the investigation of an accident or incident is the prevention of accidents and incidents. It is not the purpose of this activity to apportion blame or liability.[225] There are a number of consequences of this basic requirement at the legal, as well as operational and organisational levels, including that:

- the accident investigation authority shall have independence in the conduct of the investigation and have unrestricted authority over its conduct;
- air accident investigations shall be separate from any judicial or administrative proceedings to apportion blame or liability;
- air accident investigations should have unrestricted access to all evidential material without delay and not be impeded by administrative or judicial investigations or proceedings.[226]

Similar to accident investigation authorities at national level, a RAIO must be independent in its actions, impartial and be perceived as such. According to ICAO guidelines on RAIOs, 'it should be established in such a way that it can withstand political or other interference or pressure.'[227]

Today an aviation accident, especially in commercial air transport, is rarely a mono-national event, and almost routinely multiple States will be involved in the investigation either as a result of their technical interest, that is as a 'State of Registry', 'State of the Operator', 'State of Manufacture', 'State of Design', or by being a State whose citizens were injured or killed in the accident.[228] Press and politicians from the victims' countries, as well as the families and relatives, will also routinely follow the

224. Outcomes of the Symposium on Regional Safety Oversight Organisations (oral report to ICAO Council), *supra* note 4 in Ch. 1.
225. Annex 13 to the Chicago Convention, at paragraph 3.1.
226. For an overview of legal aspects of the independence of air accident investigations see: Paul S. Dempsey, 'Independence of Aviation Safety Investigation Authorities: Keeping the Foxes from the Henhouse', JALC, 75 (2010), pp. 223-284.
227. ICAO Doc. 9946, *supra* note 3 in Ch. 1, at Forward.
228. Under ICAO Annex 13, Standard 5.27, the rights of the State which has a special interest in an accident by virtue of fatalities or serious injuries to its citizens are formally more limited compared to the rights of States which have a technical interest in the investigation, and which are entitled to appoint an accredited representative. However there are cases where the interest of the State representing the fatally injured passengers will be so strong that this State may even take over the responsibility for the conduct of the investigation, upon delegation by the State of Occurrence. This has been the case with the shooting down of the Malaysian flight MH17 over Ukraine on 17 July 2014, and where Ukraine, as the 'State of Occurrence', delegated the conduct of the investigation to the Netherlands, as the State which represented the majority of the fatally injured passengers on that flight. For further details on this case see: Dutch Safety Board, 'Dutch Safety Board heads investigation: investigation effort in full swing, black boxes currently being read out', Press Release, (2014).

investigation and may try to exert pressure on the investigators or prematurely speculate about the probable cause(s).[229]

In this complex environment, establishing a RAIO can be beneficial from the perspective of strengthening independence of safety investigations, especially in States which do not have resources necessary to organise accident investigation individually at national level. In such cases, a technically competent RAIO would represent a strong counterpart to regulators and would be more likely to have resources adequate to be on a par with manufacturers and airlines.

In addition, in the case of States which already have independent accident investigation authorities, regional cooperation can offer benefits as well. In the EU, one of the reasons behind the 2010 establishment of ENCASIA (see section §3.05[B][3] below) was to 'improve the quality of investigations conducted by safety investigation authorities and to strengthen their independence.'[230]

According to IAC, it is also 'much easier to prevent conflicts of interests within the framework of regional organizations, as such an organization will, in a significant number of cases, present [sic] several States, which will make interaction as well as information exchange and publicity easier'.[231]

[B] Establishing a RAIO Legal Framework: Current Examples and Practice

According to ICAO, the most important consideration in setting up a RAIO is that it be established 'on a legal basis that clearly indicates its legal standing and the level of its responsibility within Member States'.[232] In 2014, there were two main types of RAIO in operation:

- with the competence to conduct the safety investigations on behalf of its Member States; and
- having a mainly coordinating and supporting role.

These are also the two types distinguished by ICAO in its RAIO manual as 'basic' and 'complex':[233]

- In a *basic set-up*, the national accident and incident investigation authority retains full responsibility for investigation activities within a Member State, while RAIO develops and provides common regulations, policies and procedures for accident and incident investigation, provides oversight of the

229. For a very good analysis of the general public, media and policy makers' reactions to aviation accidents (case studies from the US), see: Roger W. Cobb and David M. Primo, The plane truth: Airline crashes, the media and transportation policy, (2003).
230. Regulation (EU) No 996/2010, *supra* note 222, Article 7.
231. IAC, 'Regional Organizations in Accident and Incident Investigations', AIG/08-WP/22, (ICAO Accident Investigation and Prevention (AIG) Divisional Meeting, 2008), at paragraph 2.3.5.
232. ICAO Doc. 9946, *supra* note 3 in Ch. 1, at paragraph 3.4.2.
233. *Ibid.*, at paragraph 3.10.1.3.

implementation of such requirements, as well as advice, guidance and assistance to Member States.
- In a more *complex set-up*, the national accident investigation authorities may delegate the whole or part of their functions and responsibilities concerning accident and incident investigation to a RAIO, which conducts investigations on behalf of Member States.

The ICAO classification of RAIOs into basic and complex, broadly corresponds to the classification into pre-RASOs and RASOs which was proposed in section §3.04.

The first type of RAIO is currently represented by ENCASIA in the EU. The second type is represented by IAC and BAGAIA. Some other projects to establish RAIOs are under consideration in different parts of the world, including in the Gulf Region[234] and Central America,[235] but by mid-2014 had not yet materialised.

The key implication of the above distinction is that, if the delegation of the conduct of investigations is envisaged, it implies the granting of a legal personality to a RAIO. This is because, as will be demonstrated in Chapters 4 and 6, the carrying out by a RASO on behalf of its Member States of the functions and duties envisaged under the Chicago Convention presupposes the establishment of a relationship of an international agency between the RASO and its Member States. In such cases, the founding document of a RAIO will have to be an international agreement or a binding supranational legal framework.

Even if States do not delegate the conduct of investigations to a RAIO, they may decide to adopt common accident investigation regulations, with a view to ensuring uniform implementation of relevant Annex 13 SARPs. The EU regulation on air accident investigations can be given as an example here. Such regionally adopted legislation also offers an opportunity to organise some of the Annex 13 obligations in a collective manner. A good example in that respect is the European Database of Safety Recommendations.[236] Managed by the European Commission with the support of ENCASIA, the database constitutes a single repository of all the safety recommendations issued or received by the EU accident investigation authorities according to Annex 13. It allows information to be aggregated at the regional level with a view to identifying recommendations of EU-wide concern, or specific safety patterns emerging from the data which may not otherwise be visible.[237]

It is advisable that where States delegate the conduct of investigations to a RAIO, the investigations are based on common regional regulations, policies and procedures. Uniform regulatory framework is easier to apply from the perspective of a RAIO than a

234. In addition to RAIOs which are envisaged in Africa, as presented under section §3.03[A][1] of Chapter 3, a RAIO is also being considered by the Gulf Region. For more details see: UAE General Civil Aviation Authority, 'Regional Accident Investigation Organization', ACAC/ICAO Seminar/Workshop on Regional Safety Oversight Programmes (Rabat, Morocco, 2012).
235. El Salvador, 'Establishment of a central american accident and incident investigation organization', A38-WP/232, (38th ICAO Assembly, 2013).
236. Regulation (EU) No 996/2010, *supra* note 222, Article 18.
237. European Network of Civil Aviation Safety Investigation Authorities (ENCASIA), 'Annual Report', (2013), http://ec.europa.eu/transport/modes/air/safety/accident_investigation/authorities_en.htm [accessed 30 March 2014].

patchwork of national regulations. This may however not always be possible. For example in the case of interactions between the RAIO and local police and judiciary officers, the RAIO will have to abide by some, if not all, local regulations.

In addition, the 'State of Occurrence' may not always be able to delegate all of its responsibilities to a RAIO. For example the initial response responsibilities, such as ensuring the security of the accident site and protection of evidence, will have to be undertaken by the 'State of Occurrence', pending arrival of the RAIO investigation team and assumption of responsibility for the investigation by the RAIO.[238]

The founding document of a RAIO should ensure its independence from any other organisation whose interests or tasks may be in conflict with the objective of air accident investigations, and in particular the national civil aviation authorities or a RSOO if it has also been established. According to ICAO such separation should be achieved as a minimum at a functional level.[239] In the EU, the members of ENCASIA – even though this organisation does not conduct investigations – are legally prohibited to 'accept instructions from anybody which could affect the independent status of safety investigations.'[240]

The fact that a RAIO needs to meet the requirements of independence, does not mean that it should not be administratively supervised and accountable to governments of its Member States, or their supranational representatives, in relation to sound financial management, good administrative practices, and proper implementation of policies, working methods, and regulations. In fact, in the case of RAIOs which conduct safety investigations on behalf of their Member States, such supervision and accountability is necessary, given the fact that its Member States will continue to be ultimately responsible for ensuring compliance with their obligations under the Chicago Convention. The question of RASO oversight by its Member States will be further discussed in Chapter 6.

Where a RAIO may offer particular advantages is in the area of the protection of safety information coming from the accident investigation process or acquired under safety data collection and processing systems. If a RAIO is established in the form of an international organisation or supranational agency, its status – through the immunities and privileges granted by the Member States – may offer enhanced protection to the safety information it collects. For example in the EU, the protocol on privileges and immunities attached to the EU founding treaties and which ensures the inviolability of EU's archives, applies to EU agencies.[241] Such protection should be balanced by 'access to information' rules allowing the release of information to the public if it does not jeopardise the ability of the RAIO to gather such information in the future.[242]

238. ICAO Doc. 9946, *supra* note 3 in Ch. 1, at paragraph 3.10.1.5.
239. *Ibid.*at paragraph 2.4.9.
240. Regulation (EU) No 996/2010, *supra* note 222, Article 7(5).
241. For example Article 30 of Regulation (EU) No 216/2008, *supra* note 81 in Ch. 2, confirms that the 'Protocol on the Privileges and Immunities of the European Union' applies to EASA.
242. In the EU the information held by ENCASIA or EASA is without prejudice to: EU, 'Regulation (EC) No 1049/2001 of the European Parliament and of the Council of 30 May 2001 regarding public access to European Parliament, Council and Commission documents', (OJ L 145, 31.5.2001).

In assessing the feasibility of a RAIO, practical aspects of multinational cooperation such as language issues and knowledge of local circumstances should also be taken into account. RAIO inspectors will need to be *on the ground* to interview the witnesses, or to interact with the local police. They will also need rights, recognised and enforced by all the RAIO Member States, to take the necessary measures to ensure the effective conduct of the investigation. This may include the right to have access to the site of the accident, aircraft wreckage and flight recorders, to call and examine/interview witnesses, request the medical examination of the pilots, or to require the conduct of autopsy examination of the bodies of the fatally injured persons.

At the national level, experience shows that in some countries,[243] the rights of the air safety investigators can be in conflict with corresponding privileges of the justice authorities and police conducting a parallel investigation. This is a legally complex issue, and ICAO advises States to use a combination of legislation, protocols or agreements between the accident investigation and judicial authorities to ensure that the former are not 'impeded by administrative or judicial investigations or proceedings.'[244] A RAIO may similarly want to develop a template of advance arrangements to be used for the purpose of coordinating its investigations with judicial and police authorities of Member States. In the EU, for example, the use of such advance arrangements has been made mandatory for all the EU Member States.[245]

[1] The Interstate Aviation Committee

In 2014, the only example of a RAIO actually entitled to conduct accident investigations on behalf of its Member States was the IAC. This organisation, which is also a RSOO, has already been addressed under section §3.04[C][3], so here only its RAIO functions will be further presented.

IAC should be seen as part of a regional system for air accident investigations for the CIS States. This is because, in addition to the possibility to conduct the actual investigations on behalf of some of its Member States, it is also responsible for developing regional rules, procedures, manuals, training of investigators, checking compliance with such rules and procedures, as well as assisting the Member States in the conduct of investigations in case the delegation has not taken place.[246] Its objective is to ensure the greatest possible harmonisation of accident investigation procedures and requirements, and efficient application of Annex 13 at the regional level.[247]

243. France and Italy are often given as examples in this respect; See: EC Impact Assessment COM(2009) 611 final, *supra* note 213, at pp. 18-19. For an overview of the subject of criminalisation of aviation accidents see also: Sofia Michaelides-Mateou and Andreas Mateou, Flying in the Face of Criminalization: The Safety Implications of Prosecuting Aviation Professionals for Accidents, (2010).
244. Annex 13 to the Chicago Convention, at paragraph 5.4.3.
245. Regulation (EU) No 996/2010, *supra* note 222, Article 12(3). At the time of writing this study the implementation of this provision was still ongoing. For further details see: ENCASIA 2013 Annual Report, *supra* note 237, at p. 23.
246. 'Minsk Agreement', *supra* note 124, Article 7(b).
247. For a further overview of IAC accident investigation functions see: Sergey V. Zayko, 'Russia's Interstate Aviation Committee', ISASI Forum, 46 (2013), p. 16.

The delegation mechanism used by IAC is based on a combination of its founding agreement, which is the Minsk Treaty presented under section §3.04[C][3], and a bilateral delegation agreement concluded with a specific Member State.

For example the Russian Federation delegated to IAC investigation functions in the event of aircraft accident occurring in the territory of the Russian Federation, including in respect to accidents involving a foreign operated or registered aircraft, or involving an aircraft or aircraft engine of foreign design or manufacture.[248] The IAC also has responsibility for providing the Russian Accredited Representatives to investigations of accidents occurring on foreign territory and involving a Russian operated or registered aircraft or an accident/incident occurring in the foreign territory and involving an aircraft or aircraft engine of Russian design or manufacture.[249]

As far as the issue of independence of investigations is concerned, the situation of IAC is quite specific because, as mentioned above, it also acts as a RSOO with competences such as aircraft and aerodrome certification. Ideally both regulatory and investigative functions should be performed by separate organisations, and this is what this study recommends. However, according to ICAO, the separation should be ensured at least at the functional level.[250] In the case of IAC, the certification/regulatory functions, and accident investigations are performed by separate *commissions*, which are organisational units within the IAC with separate legal personalities, as was explained under section §3.04[C][3].

[2] The Banjul Accord Group Accident Investigation Agency

BAGAIA was formally established in 2009 on the basis of an international agreement. It has a status of an 'independent body under the Banjul Accord Group'. Contrary to IAC, BAGAIA's mandate is limited exclusively to air accident investigation matters.

At the time of writing this study in 2014, BAGAIA was not yet fully operational. It was therefore not possible to analyse practical aspects related to its functioning.

From a legal point of view, BAGAIA's founding agreement gives to this RAIO, at least formally speaking, the possibility to accept from its Member States the delegation of accident investigation functions and duties. Article 5(k) of the founding agreement states that BAGAIA can:

> Conduct, either in whole or any part of, an investigation into an aircraft accident or serious incident upon delegation be a State of Occurrence ... by mutual agreement and consent between the State of Occurrence and the BAGAIA.[251]

248. See for example: 'Memorandum of Understanding between the government of the United States of America and the government of the Russian Federation on cooperation in the field of civil aircraft accident/incident investigation and prevention', 2nd September 1998, 1998 TIAS 12983.
249. *Ibid.*
250. ICAO Doc. 9946, *supra* note 3 in Ch. 1, at paragraph 3.10.1.5.
251. 'BAGAIA Agreement', *supra* note 221, Article 5(k).

So far no such delegation agreements have been concluded, or are envisaged.[252] State sovereignty has been mentioned as one of the main principles to be taken into account when discussing possible future delegation agreements between BAGAIA and its Member States. It is also possible that such delegation agreements could be concluded between BAGAIA and its Member States on an ad hoc basis for the purpose of investigating specific accidents.[253] The fact that the conclusion of such delegation agreements, of either general or ad hoc nature, is foreseen in the BAGAIA founding agreement, presupposes that the BAGAIA's Member States envisaged, or at least did not exclude, this organisation having international legal personality, which is not explicitly envisaged under BAGAIA's founding agreement.

Similar to IAC, BAGAIA should be seen as part of a regional system for air accident investigations. This is because, beyond the possibility to conduct the actual investigations on behalf of its Member States, BAGAIA's founding agreement envisages this organisation also being responsible for a wide array of functions related to the strengthening of accident investigation capabilities of its Member States.[254]

Finally, concerning independence of investigations, the situation of BAGAIA is different from that of IAC, as it does not regulate civil aviation activities.

[3] The European Network of Civil Aviation Safety Investigation Authorities

ENCASIA has a different legal and organisational setup from that of the IAC or BAGAIA. It is essentially a *coordination* platform for national accident investigation authorities of the EU Member States. It does not have any supranational competences, and its main function is to 'encourage high standards in investigation methods and investigator training.'[255] To this end activities of ENCASIA include: coordinating and organising 'peer reviews'; training activities and skills development programmes for investigators; promoting best safety investigation practices; developing and managing a framework for sharing resources; and advising EU institutions on policy and regulation for safety investigations and the prevention of accidents and incidents.[256]

ENCASIA's Annual Report for 2013[257] and the ENCASIA work programme for 2014[258] provide examples of a wide range of activities which this organisation coordinates, such as:

- developing procedures for asking and providing assistance between the member authorities;

252. Official of the BAGAIA, 'Interview No 10', (2014).
253. *Ibid.*
254. 'BAGAIA Agreement', *supra* note 221, Article 5.
255. Regulation (EU) No 996/2010, *supra* note 222, Article 7.
256. *Ibid.*
257. ENCASIA 2013 Annual Report, *supra* note 237.
258. European Network of Civil Aviation Safety Investigation Authorities (ENCASIA), '2014 Work Programme', (2014), http://ec.europa.eu/transport/modes/air/safety/accident_investigation/authorities_en.htm [accessed 30 March 2014].

- establishing an inventory of best practices of investigation in Europe;
- developing a guidance manual on investigator training, and providing training courses on issues such as management of on-site hazards for investigators or responding to a major aviation accident;
- analysing information in a central EU database of safety recommendations;
- developing a programme of 'peer reviews' to help national authorities to increase their investigative capabilities and raise awareness of best practice.

From a legal point of view, the establishment of ENCASIA has been mandated by EU law, but the actual responsibility for the act of establishment has been given to the EU Member States.[259] This means that in legal terms the ENCASIA is not an EU agency or other body of the EU, and does not have legal personality under the EU legal system. This was a deliberate policy choice, because EU Member States were concerned that establishing ENACSIA through an act of EU law could make the organisation more subordinate to EU institutions and this in turn could weaken the independence of the national accident investigation bodies.[260]

The EU Member States quickly realised however that lack of legal personality can be a serious impediment to the effectiveness of ENCASIA, especially as they were intending to rely on the European Commission for its financial support. In order to overcome these difficulties, the concept of an association has been used, and in 2012, ENCASIA was registered in Belgium as an *association sans but lucratif.*[261] This was a solution similar to the one used in the past by the JAA and some other pre-RASOs which were presented under section §3.04[B], and allowed ENCASIA to set up a bank account and receive grants from the EU.[262]

It remains to be seen if in the future ENCASIA will evolve into an EU Air Accident Investigation Board, replacing the national investigation authorities. Such an evolution would in the first place depend on the political will of the EU Member States, and a clear demonstration by the European Commission that such an EU body would be a more efficient way of conducting air accident investigations than through the national authorities. In the Impact Assessment accompanying the proposal for the regulation mandating the establishment of ENCASIA, the European Commission considered, as one of the possible options, the establishment of such a Board, but finally decided that it would not be the best solution given the high implementation risks and associated costs for the EU budget.[263]

259. See: Regulation (EU) No 996/2010, *supra* note 222, Article 7(1), which provide that: 'Member States shall ensure that their safety investigation authorities establish between them a European Network of Civil Aviation Safety Investigation Authorities (the Network), composed of the heads of the safety investigation authorities in each of the Member States and/or, in the case of a multimodal authority, the head of its aviation branch, or their representatives ...'.
260. Source: Personal files of the author, who was responsible in the European Commission for coordinating the legislative process for the development of Regulation (EU) No 996/2010 of 20 October 2010.
261. Association Sans But Lucratif 'ENCASIA', 'Statuts et Acte de désignation des premiers administrateurs', Monitor Belge, 1 October 2012.
262. ENCASIA 2013 Annual Report, *supra* note 237, at p. 7.
263. EC Impact Assessment COM(2009) 611 final, *supra* note 213, at p. 59.

§3.06 TOWARDS A REGIONAL CIVIL AVIATION AUTHORITY

[A] Introduction

So far this chapter has been presenting examples of regional aviation safety bodies functioning in parallel with the national authorities of their Member States. To a certain extent, and especially in cases where regulatory competences are exercised in parallel by national authorities and a RASO, this is a model in which there is a risk of duplication of activities. This risk concerns not only the exercise of regulatory and oversight functions, but equally importantly the potential competition between a regional body and national authorities for resources and qualified personnel. Some of the experiences of CASSOA referred to in the preceding section illustrate well such difficulties.

Yet, there is another model of a RASO which eliminates the risk of such duplication. This is the concept of a RCAA, which acts as an aviation authority for multiple States. From a legal point of view a RCAA is a single entity, although organisationally it may operate on the basis of a headquarters office and local offices in the participating States. In the RCAA model, there is a *complete* delegation of safety oversight functions from a national to regional level.

The potential benefits of RCAA are economies of scale and associated savings for the governments on the one hand, and a single regulatory framework for the aviation industry on the other. This approach would best serve large groupings of small States with limited resources and/or States with low level of aviation activities which are unable to generate revenues big enough to support fully fledged national civil aviation authorities.

Putting in place a RCAA requires in the first place the political will of the States, which may be reluctant to transfer, to that extent, the exercise of their sovereign competences to an international organisation. It also requires a single legal framework and operating procedures to ensure that a RCAA operates as a truly unique aviation authority. How such a legal framework is to be achieved is a matter of choice. It is proposed here that a supranational REIO with binding legislative powers, such as the EU, would be the best solution for delivering a legal framework for a RCAA. Alternatively, instruments of traditional public international law could also be used.

In any case, the establishment of a RCAA requires an organisation established in a form which allows for large scale delegation of safety functions and duties by multiple States, and where such functions and duties can be exercised by a RCAA in a legally binding manner. In this respect, RCAA cannot be established in a pre-RASO form, but must have a legal status of either RASO Type I or RASO Type II in the typology proposed in section §3.04.

Finally, the feasibility of a RCAA would also depend on local circumstances such as the language(s) used, geographical considerations – which are important for the industry which needs to interact with the authority on a daily basis – and the presence, or lack, of a common administrative and legal culture/heritage.

In 2014, there was only one example of an operational RCAA – the ECCAA, established in October 2003 by Member States of the OECS as an international intergovernmental organisation with legal personality. The subsequent sections will present and analyse this organisation in more detail.[264]

[B] The Eastern Caribbean Civil Aviation Authority

[1] Origins and Evolution

The ECCAA is a unique organisation shaped by the history and geo-political status of the eastern Caribbean region in the second half of the twentieth century, when the Caribbean States gradually moved away from being British colonies towards full independence.

The origins of the ECCAA come from the 'Directorate of Civil Aviation – Eastern Caribbean States' which was established in 1957 by the United Kingdom:

> To advise the Governments of the Windward and Leeward Islands on all matters relating to Civil Aviation including airfields and airport developments, the implementation of ICAO conventions and the adequacy of air services.[265]

In 1982, the Directorate of Civil Aviation became an institution of the OECS through the Treaty of Basseterre.[266] Subsequently a decision was taken to transform it into 'a fully autonomous body ... with the responsibility to regulate civil aviation activities within OECS Member States.'[267] This decision gave the necessary political momentum for the conclusion of the ECCAA founding agreement which was signed at 21 October 2003.[268]

Although the OECS comprises nine States, including seven full members and two associated members,[269] these are very small entities with small economies and populations. According to the UN data, in 2013 the combined population of the nine

264. The concept of a RCAA has also been briefly presented at the: ICAO, 'Symposium on Regional Safety Oversight Organisations' 2011) http://www.icao.int/Meetings/RSOOSYMPO/Pages/default.aspx [accessed 6 August 2014]. See in particular: Michael Jennison, 'Is the RSOO a success story?', ICAO Symposium on Regional Safety Oversight Organisations (Montréal, Canada, 2011).
265. OECS, 'Eastern Caribbean Civil Aviation Authority' http://www.oecs.org/about-the-oecs/institutions/eastern-caribbean-civil-aviation-authority-eccaa [accessed 8 August 2014].
266. 'Treaty establishing the Organisation of Eastern Caribbean States', Basseterre, 18 June 1981, 1338 UNTS 97.
267. ECCAA website, *supra* note 265.
268. 'Agreement Establishing the Eastern Caribbean Civil Aviation Authority', Grenada, 21 October 2003, text can be found in: The Eastern Caribbean Civil Aviation Agreement Act, enacted by Parliament of Antigua and Barbuda, No. 24 of 2003. The ECCAA Member States are: Antigua and Barbuda, the Commonwealth of Dominica, Grenada, Saint Christopher (Kitts) and Nevis, Saint Lucia, Saint Vincent and the Grenadines. All ECCAA Member States with the exception of Dominica are signatories of the Chicago Convention. The OECS States which have the status of British Overseas Territories, namely Anguilla, British Virgin Islands and Montserrat are not parties to the ECCAA Agreement.
269. Antigua and Barbuda; Commonwealth of Dominica; Grenada; Montserrat (a British Overseas Territory); St Kitts and Nevis; St Lucia; St Vincent and the Grenadines. Anguilla and the British Virgin Islands are associate members of the OECS.

OECS States was 640,000 people,[270] which is comparable with the population of Washington D.C. in the US. It therefore made little economic or operational sense for these States to establish separate national civil aviation authorities, particularly in a context where civil aviation is indispensable for these island nations to maintain links with each other and the outside world.

In 2010, the legal status of ECCAA was further strengthened, as it has been formally listed as one of the institutions of the OECS, next to the Eastern Caribbean Supreme Court and the Eastern Caribbean Central Bank, under the Revised Treaty of Basseterre.[271] This in itself demonstrates the importance that the OECS, as an organisation of island nations, attaches to civil aviation.

Under the Revised Treaty of Basseterre, the OECS enhanced its supranational character and decided that in a number of areas, one of them being civil aviation, the Member States will exercise their legislative competences at the regional level. As far as civil aviation is concerned, this competence will be 'exercised on the recommendation of the Board of Directors of the Eastern Caribbean Civil Aviation Authority.'[272] In accordance with Article 5.3 of the Revised Treaty of Basseterre, such legislation should take precedence over the national laws of OECS Member States, and be directly applicable.[273] Yet in practice, at least for the time being, the regulations still have to be transposed into the national legal systems of the ECCAA Member States.[274]

In addition, being an institution of the OECS, means for the ECCAA that:

- the Heads of Governments of the OECS can override the Board of Directors of ECCAA;[275]
- the Director General of the ECCAA is appointed by the Heads of Governments of the OECS;[276]
- the amendments to the ECCAA Agreement have to be agreed by the Heads of Governments of the OECS;[277]
- the OECS institutions shall be exercising their legislative competence in matters of civil aviation on 'the recommendation of the Board of Directors of the Eastern Caribbean Civil Aviation Authority'.[278]

270. UN, United Nations Demographic Yearbook, Estimates of mid-year population: 2002-2011.
271. See Article 6 of 'Revised Treaty of Basseterre establishing the Organisation of Eastern Caribbean States Economic Union', Gros Islet, 18 June 2010.
272. *Ibid.*, Article 14(1).
273. Alfred Schipke, Aliona Cebotari, and Nita Thacker, The Eastern Caribbean Economic and Currency Union: Macroeconomics and Financial Systems, (2013), p. 60.
274. The first working session of the OECS Assembly took place in March 2013 and the Civil Aviation Regulations were the first laws enacted by that body. At the end of 2013 these regulations have not been promulgated by the individual Member States, and thus were not considered as being in force; Source: Official of the ECCAA, 'Interview No 7', (2014).
275. 'ECCAA Agreement', *supra* note 268, Article 10(1).
276. *Ibid.*, Article 10(2).
277. *Ibid.*, Article 23.
278. 'Revised Treaty of Basseterre', *supra* note 271, Article 14(1).

[2] ECCAA Legal and Organisational Status

The ECCAA, whose mandate covers both aviation safety and security,[279] is set up as 'an autonomous regional regulatory organization' and is responsible for 'regulating civil aviation and fostering competitiveness in the aviation industry in the Eastern Caribbean and for harmonising the application of the standards and recommended practices adopted by the International Civil Aviation Organisation'.[280] It is a 'body corporate, having a perpetual succession'.[281]

Under its founding agreement the ECCAA has legal personality,[282] and financial autonomy guaranteed by revenue from the fees and charges levied for the provision of its services, including issuance of certificates, as well as air navigation fees collected for the use of airspace of the OECS States.[283]

The ECCAA is located in St John's at Antigua and has 'outstations' in Member States. It is the only authority responsible for safety oversight of civil aviation activities in its Member States, meaning that there are no separate national civil aviation authorities. To this end the ECCAA has the competence, *inter alia,* to:

- regulate civil aviation in the participating States on behalf of and in collaboration with them;
- issue civil aviation documents under the national aviation legislation of the participating States;
- recommend to the participating States, rules, regulations and aviation standards;
- enforce existing rules, regulations and aviation standards and impose administrative fines and penalties for violations of the rules, regulations and aviation standards;
- require the payment of fees.[284]

From a legal point of view, the technique that was used to set up this RASO and empower it to act on behalf of its Member States was a combination of an international agreement and national laws. At the public international law level, the ECCAA founding agreement created the organisation, defined its mandate and functions, determined the organisational structure and funding principles, as well as granted to it the necessary privileges and immunities. The founding agreement was subsequently incorporated into the national laws of the ECCAA Member States through enabling legislation.[285]

In addition, there was a need to *internalise* the general competences of the ECCAA created under international law into the specific aviation laws and regulations

279. 'ECCAA Agreement', *supra* note 268, Article 4(a).
280. *Ibid.*, Preamble.
281. *Ibid.*, Article 3.
282. *Ibid.*, Article 5.
283. *Ibid.*, Article 17.
284. *Ibid.*, Article 5.
285. See for example: 'Chapter 85A, Eastern Caribbean Civil Aviation Authority Agreement Act', Laws of Grenada, Act No. 11 of 2004.

of its Member States. This was achieved through the adoption by each of the Member States of similar primary aviation legislation – *the Civil Aviation Act* – defining how the ECCAA would act on behalf of each of them. This includes the competence to issue certificates to personnel and organisations, as well to conduct the necessary oversight and enforcement activities.[286] For example, through such legislation the ECCAA Member States granted to ECCAA employees authorisations to act as their national aviation safety inspectors, including the rights to access buildings and facilities of the inspected entities, or to prevent an aircraft from flying if it were to be found in an unsafe condition.[287] The ECCAA has been so deeply integrated into the legal systems of its Member States that it has de facto and de lege become their organ.

Although ECCAA is an authorised agency for the conduct of safety oversight activities, issuance of certificates and enforcement of rules, including through imposition of administrative penalties, its competences in respect to rulemaking are more limited. This is because the mandate of the ECCAA is only to 'develop and seek approval for harmonized civil aviation regulations, policies and practices to be adopted by Participating States ...,'[288] while the responsibility for the adoption of such recommended regulations lies with the Member States, and since the entry into force of the Revised Treaty of Basseterre, with supranational institutions of the OECS.[289]

From the perspective of the Chicago Convention, the fact that ECCAA performs all safety oversight and certification functions on behalf of its Member States has a number of consequences. First of all, ICAO needs to audit ECCAA which is the only competent aviation authority of OECS States. By mid-2014, two such audits have been performed, in 2007,[290] and in 2013.[291]

Secondly, where safety related non-compliances have been identified by ICAO with respect to the ECCAA, it is also this RSOO which will need to follow-up these findings. This in turn requires close coordination between the ECCAA and all its Member States. Indeed, it is the ECCAA that prepares and submits responses to ICAO on behalf of the OECS Member States in a single corrective action plan.[292]

The ECCAA, as a single aviation authority, is the beneficiary of all the revenues generated from the provision of safety oversight services, and does not have to *share* them with national authorities. It can also finance its activities from navigation service fees which are usually an adequate and stable source of revenue. This would imply that overall it should have sufficient financial resources to perform the required regulatory activities. The interview performed for the purpose of this study suggests however that ECCAA has experienced 'challenges in recruiting staff due to the small size of the

286. See for example: 'Chapter 54A, Civil Aviation Act', Laws of Grenada, Act No. 12 of 2004, amended by Act No. 18 of 2006; 'Civil Aviation Regulations', Laws of Grenada, SRO 12 of 2005.
287. 'Civil Aviation Regulations of Grenada', *supra* note 286, at Part XIII.
288. 'ECCAA Agreement', *supra* note 268, Article 4(b).
289. Schipke, Cebotari, and Thacker, *supra* note 273, at p. 60.
290. ICAO, 'Final report on the safety oversight audit of the civil aviation system of the Organization of Eastern Caribbean States (Antigua and Barbuda; Grenada; St. Kitts and Nevis; Saint Lucia; and Saint Vincent and the Grenadines)', (2007).
291. ICAO, 'Final Report on the ICAO Coordinated Validation Mission in the Organization of Eastern Caribbean States', (2013).
292. 'Interview No 7', (2014), *supra* note 274.

aviation industry in the region.'[293] These challenges have also been confirmed by ICAO.[294]

ECCAA provides an example in which, even if sufficient financial resources are available to a RASO, it may be difficult for it to recruit, even on a regional basis, suitably qualified personnel, if they are simply not available in the region in sufficient numbers. Still, the ECCAA confirms that it has 'permitted OECS States to achieve effective civil aviation safety oversight at a fraction of the cost of establishing their own civil aviation authorities.'[295]

To conclude, the ECCAA is both de lege and de facto, part of a regional civil aviation safety system based on the sharing of tasks and responsibilities between the national and supranational levels. It is currently the only example of an organisation functioning as a single aviation authority for more than one State.

In the future, it will be interesting to see how the OECS institutions will exercise their newly acquired competences to regulate civil aviation at the supranational level, and how ECCAA will be involved in this process. Potentially the OECS has an opportunity to become the first region in the world to both regulate aviation safety and to implement the regulations exclusively through supranational institutions.

Another question that needs to be asked is whether any of the other RASOs, and in particular EASA which is currently the only RASO which has been operating for over ten years in a supranational legal environment, could potentially evolve into a RCAA type organisations in the future. This question will be addressed in Chapter 4 which deals with the EU and EASA.

§3.07 GENERAL CONCLUSIONS

So far ICAO has not developed a definition of a RASO and the current approach of ICAO and of the international aviation community is to treat this type of organisation as a broad concept covering a wide range of very different forms of cooperation. In practice RASOs fall into two general categories – RSOO and RAIO – depending on whether their function is safety regulation and oversight, or investigation of aviation accidents and incidents.

In 2014, there were over twenty initiatives in almost all parts of the world, which could be considered as RASOs, if looked at from the perspective of the broad approach currently followed by ICAO. In addition, a number of projects aimed at establishing additional RASOs were also ongoing at the time of the finalisation of this study, in particular in Africa, South America and Middle East.

This study has found that the recent boom in the establishment of RASOs has resulted, in particular in Africa, in establishment of significant number of such organisations, sometimes with overlapping membership, and functioning in parallel with national authorities. Similar duplications exist, to a certain extent, in Europe

293. *Ibid.*

294. ICAO ICVM report on the OECS (2013), *supra* note 291, at Appendix 2.1 (used with the permission of the ECCAA).

295. 'Interview No 7', (2014), *supra* note 274.

where a number of regional aviation organisations, for historical reasons, continue to function in parallel, as the next chapter will show in more detail.

In line with the recommendations for greater clarity of the RASO concept expressed by the international civil aviation community at the 2011 ICAO Symposium on regional aviation safety oversight organisations, this chapter proposes the following definition of a RASO:

> An organisation established by States from the same geographical region, which has legal personality under international law or is established in a form of an organ of an international legal person, and whose principal purpose is the provision of support for the carrying out of safety-related functions and duties set out by the Chicago Convention and its Annexes, and preferably the actual carrying out of some or all of such functions and duties on behalf of its participating States.

The development of such a definition is considered necessary for two main reasons.

Firstly, it is necessary because the notions of RSOO and RAIO are being used increasingly often in ICAO documentation, including Assembly resolutions and Annexes to the Chicago Convention. Such definition would help in ensuring clarity as to who exactly is an addressee of these documents, especially where they give to a RSOO or a RAIO a right to carry out functions or duties so far normally exercised only by States.

Secondly, the proposed definition was constructed in a way to promote the most efficient forms of RASOs, and notably those which have the competence to carry out, on behalf of States, safety related functions and duties set out by the Chicago Convention, in a legally binding manner. As will be demonstrated in Chapters 4 and 6, the granting of such powers results in a relationship of an international agency between the organisation and the States concerned, and presupposes that the RASO either possesses a separate international legal personality, or is established in a form of an organ of an international legal person.

The objective of the proposed definition is therefore, in addition to clarifying the roles of States and RASOs, to promote those forms of RASOs which are able to accept the most advanced forms of delegations. This capability will make RASOs more suitable to constitute strong building blocks of the GASON, which was proposed in the preceding chapter.

In addition to proposing a RASO definition, this chapter has also introduced a RASO typology. For the sake of completeness, and because regional aviation safety bodies have tendency to evolve over time (see section §5.04[B] of Chapter 5), this typology distinguishes between pre-RASOs, which do not fall, strictly speaking, within the scope of the definition as proposed above, and RASOs proper.

Although every type of a pre-RASO and RASO has its *pros* and *cons*, the purpose of the proposed classification is not to present better or worse types, but rather to systematise knowledge about these organisations and to study their achievements and problems that they have encountered, so that lessons may be learned for the future.

Pre-RASO typology:

The *first type* of pre-RASO forms are *regional cooperation projects of a technical nature.* They are considered as a pre-RASO form, due to the fact that some of such projects have a tendency to evolve into RASOs with separate international legal personality or a body established in a form of an organ of an international legal person. Two main categories of this type have been distinguished, that is COSCAPs and cooperative inspector schemes:

- *COSCAPs* can play a role in establishing RASOs by upgrading the safety oversight capabilities of its member authorities and building confidence between them in working together. So far the process of transitioning COSCAPs into RASOs is still ongoing, and in the first half of 2014, out of the nine ICAO COSCAP projects only two had fully transitioned into RASOs. In addition one COSCAP has transitioned into a form which can be placed in-between a technical cooperation project and a RASO, and continues to rely on ICAO for management – that is the SRVSOP in South America. ICAO and States need to accelerate the transition of COSCAPs into RASOs, where it is possible.
- *Cooperative inspector schemes*, with the most prominent example of them being currently the AFI-CIS, are a simple and practical tool to organise pooling and sharing of aviation safety inspectors. Experience of AFI-CIS showed however that cooperative inspector schemes do not seem to be a total remedy for the problem of shortage of qualified resources for the AFCAC States. This is mainly due to the inability of the participating authorities to finance the costs of the assistance missions, and the overall shortage of qualified inspectors in the region.

The *second type* of pre-RASO forms are *regional associations of aviation safety authorities*. Whilst not having the status of an international organisation, such associations can have legal personality under the domestic law of some of their member authorities, and experience shows that this form can be a practical way to launch cooperation, which over time can evolve into a legally more solid structure with international legal personality or an organ of an international organisation. The main shortcoming of this RASO type is the fact that lack of a binding legal status under international law does not permit an association to mandate common requirements or to deliver certificates on behalf States. This, over time, can result in a heterogeneous regulatory environment.

RASO proper typology:

The *first type* of RASOs proper can be referred to as *international regional aviation safety organisations*. In 2014 this was the most common RASO category. This type is established on the basis of an international agreement and may exercise, in a legally binding manner, certain safety functions on behalf of its Member States. This type of RASO, as opposed to the next category, will also normally be established outside the institutional framework of a REIO.

The *second type* of RASOs proper is the *supranational aviation safety agency*. The main difference between this and previous category is that a supranational aviation safety agency evolves within the broader legal and institutional framework of a REIO. The extent to which a RASO can rely on the REIO institutional framework and legislation is directly proportional to the level of integration of the latter. If a REIO has supranational character and can adopt, through its institutions, legally binding legislation, this legislation will also bind the RASO and will form the foundation of a single regional safety system. So far there are very few RASOs in operation which could be truly considered as falling within this category.

The RAIO typology:

This chapter also presented the concept of a RAIO, which in theory can be established in a pre-RASO form as an association of accident investigation authorities (Pre-RASO Type II), or a RASO proper. In practice, in 2014, only two RAIOs were actually in operation (IAC: RASO Type I; and ENCASIA: Pre-RASO Type II), with only one of them, that is IAC, being able to conduct accident investigations on behalf of its Member States. In addition one more RAIO has been formally established, but in 2014 was not yet fully operational (BAGAIA: RASO Type I), and a number of other RAIO projects were under consideration in Africa, South America and Middle East.

The RCAA model:

Finally, this chapter distinguished a very specific sub-group of RASOs, namely the RCAA. In 2014, there was only one example of such an authority - the ECCAA. The main feature of the RCAA is that, whilst the RASOs normally do not replace the national authorities and function in parallel with them, under a RCAA model there is almost a *complete* delegation of safety oversight functions and duties from a national to regional level. RCAA eliminates therefore the risk of duplication of functions and resources. This approach would best serve large groupings of small States with limited resources and/or States with low levels of aviation activities, and which are unable to generate revenues large enough to support fully fledged national civil aviation authorities. RCAA can be established either as a RASO Type I or a RASO Type II.

Having proposed a RASO definition and typology of RASO and pre-RASO forms, the following chapter will present a detailed case study of the EU civil aviation safety system, and of EASA - a Type II RASO, which is currently a point of reference for many such organisations around the world, and has a number of features which make it very well placed to form one of the building blocks of a future GASON.

CHAPTER 4

The European Aviation Safety Agency: Case Study of a Supranational Aviation Safety Organisation

> This Europe must be born. And she will, when Spaniards say 'our Chartres', Englishmen say 'our Cracow', Italians 'our Copenhagen' and Germans 'our Bruges'. Then will Europe live.
>
> Salvador de Madariaga (1886-1978)[1]

§4.01 INTRODUCTION

This chapter presents a case study of the European Union's Aviation Safety Agency, which is considered as a supranational aviation safety agency (RASO Type II) from the perspective of the RASO typology proposed in Chapter 3. This means that EASA is part of and relies for its functioning on a REIO – the EU.

Although EASA is not a single aviation authority for EU Member States, similar to the ECCAA described in the preceding chapter, the volume of aviation activity for which it is responsible together with the EU national aviation authorities (NAAs),[2] the legal powers it enjoys as part of the supranational EU system, and the resources it has at its disposal[3] definitely makes it the most relevant RASO functioning today.

The EU aviation safety system, including EASA, has over the last twelve years undergone a dynamic evolution, including two extensions of its scope.[4] This evolution

1. Salvador de Madariaga y Rojo was a Spanish diplomat, writer, historian and pacifist. He was also a co-founder of the College of Europe and a promoter of the vision of a united Europe.
2. EASA, 'Annual Safety Review', (2013), http://easa.europa.eu/system/files/dfu/199751_EASA_ASR_2013_ok.pdf [accessed 6 August 2014], at Chapter 3.
3. EASA, 'Annual General Report', (2013), http://easa.europa.eu/system/files/dfu/TOAC14001ENN.pdf [accessed 6 August 2014], at Annexes 6 and 8.
4. EASA, '10th Anniversary Chronicle', (2013), p. 36.

is expected to continue in the years to come and thus provides a lot of interesting material for analysis.[5]

Europe has also been, for many years, an arena for a number of regional aviation organisations, which in addition to the EU included or still includes ECAC, JAA and EUROCONTROL. As a result of the interactions between these organisations, some of them ceased to exist (JAA) or had to reform (ECAC, EUROCONTROL), while others benefitted and increased their influence on the European aviation scene (EASA). From this perspective, Europe as a whole is an interesting *laboratory* for studying regional cooperation in civil aviation matters and its impact on aviation safety.

The purpose of this chapter is to demonstrate to what extent and how exactly EASA contributes to the improvement of global aviation safety and to the objective of uniformity in civil aviation, as set out by the Chicago Convention (section §4.04). Particular emphasis will be placed on the on fact that EASA functions within the legal and institutional framework of the EU as a supranational REIO (section §4.02). The role of EASA in international relations and its status under the Chicago Convention will be also addressed (section §4.03). Finally the question of whether EASA could one day become a single aviation authority for Europe and the impact this could have on aviation safety will be addressed (section §4.06).

For the purpose of this chapter, when referring to Europe this means – unless otherwise indicated – the geographical boundaries of Member States of ECAC.[6] In 2014, ECAC consisted of 44 Member States, which is much broader than the membership of the EU.[7] This ECAC area is an arena for a number of aviation organisations, which in addition to ECAC, EU and EASA include also EUROCONTROL,[8] as shown on Figure 4.1. Up to June 2009, there was also the JAA, which was a predecessor of EASA and which will be briefly addressed in the following section.

While non-EU States also participate in the work of EASA on the basis of international agreements or working arrangements, this chapter will refer primarily to the EU Member States. The question of associating non-EU States with the work of EASA will be dealt with specifically in section §4.05 of this chapter.

5. EC, 'Roadmap for a policy initiative on aviation safety and a possible revision of Regulation (EC) No 216/2008 on common rules in the field of civil aviation and establishing a European Aviation Safety Agency', (2014), http://ec.europa.eu/smart-regulation/impact/planned_ia/docs/2015_move_001_revision_easa_regulation_en.pdf [accessed 19 April 2014].
6. ECAC was established in 1955 following a recommendation of the Council of Europe. See: ECAC, 'About ECAC' https://www.ecac-ceac.org//about_ecac [accessed 3 January 2014].
7. In addition to the 28 Member States of the EU, ECAC membership consists also of: Albania, Armenia, Azerbaijan, Bosnia and Herzegovina, Georgia, Iceland, Republic of Moldova, Monaco, Montenegro, Norway, San Marino, Serbia, Switzerland, former Yugoslav Republic of Macedonia (fYROM), Turkey and Ukraine.
8. EUROCONTROL, 'About EUROCONTROL' http://www.eurocontrol.int/articles/who-we-are [accessed 3 January 2014].

Figure 4.1 The European Aviation Safety Landscape (2014)

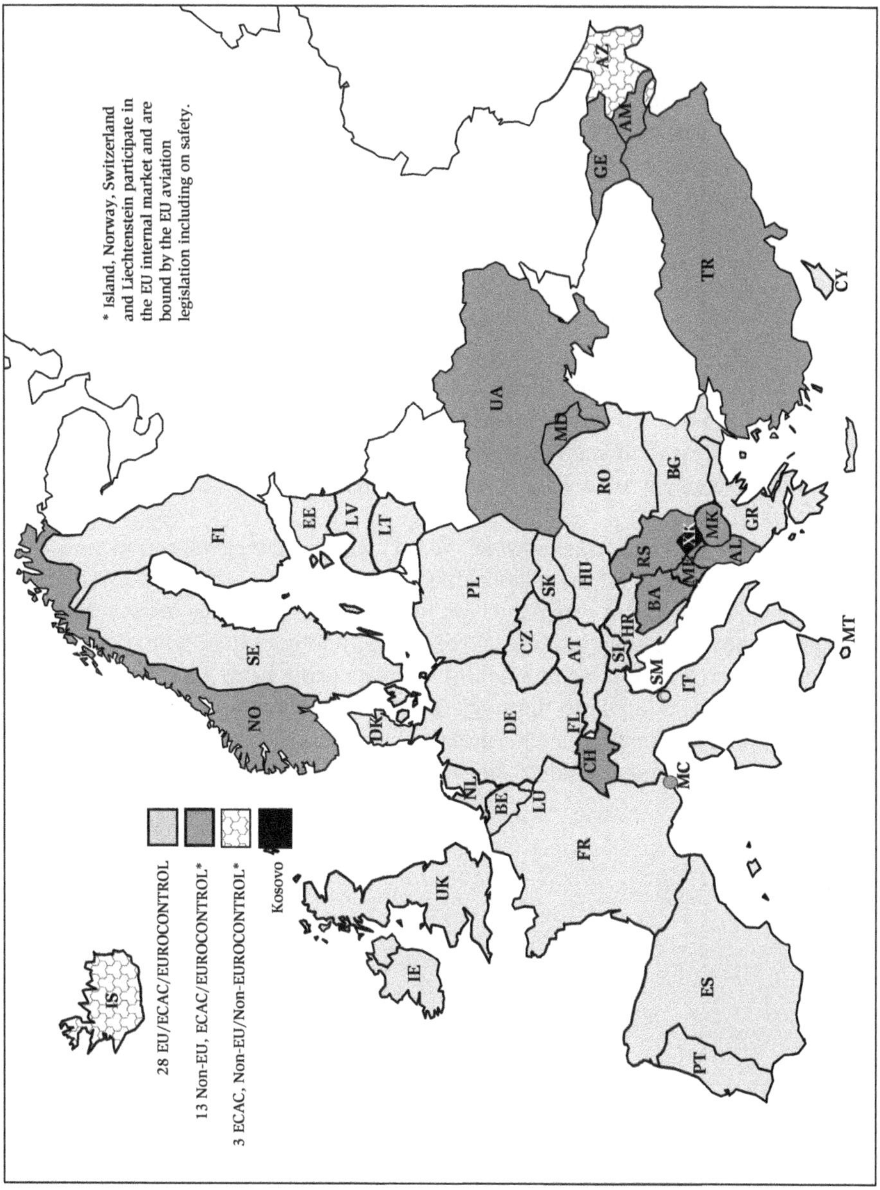

§4.02 EASA AS PART OF THE EU CIVIL AVIATION SAFETY SYSTEM

[A] Introduction

It is not possible to understand the functioning of EASA and the benefits that it brings for aviation safety without apprehending the fact that it is an integral part of the EU legal and institutional framework and could not exist without the EU. In this respect, it is appropriate to refer to this system as the 'EU civil aviation safety system' rather than the 'EASA system'.

The EU civil aviation safety system encompasses not only EASA and EU institutions,[9] but also EU Member States which have the primary responsibility for the implementation of the EU aviation safety legislation.[10] In this respect, it is a multi-layered and multifaceted system, with the tasks and responsibilities shared between all its actors.

The establishment of the EU civil aviation safety system should also not be seen in isolation from other EU policies, but as a logical consequence of the development of the single EU aviation market which started in the 1990s, and which in itself constituted an element of a greater effort to create a single internal market for the EU.[11]

The necessity of a linkage between the EU civil aviation safety system and other EU policies was essential for the establishment of EASA. EASA's predecessor, the JAA, lacked this linkage whilst it was regulating issues at the crossroads of aviation safety and socio-economic matters, such as aircrew flight and duty time limitations, certification of cabin crew or leasing of aircraft.[12] Whilst clearly having a safety dimension such issues were also linked to the single aviation market and thus required greater involvement of the EU institutions.[13] The existence of this disharmony was used by the EU as one of the arguments against the JAA and in favour of EASA which ultimately replaced the former.[14]

---

9. Primarily the European Commission, which has the monopoly of the legislative initiative, the European Parliament and the Council which act as co-legislators, and the European Court of Justice, which exercises the judiciary control.
10. Regulation (EU) No 216/2008, *supra* note 81 in Ch. 2, at Preamble clause 3.
11. Isabella H. Ph. Diederiks-Verschoor, An Introduction to Air Law, (2006), pp. 72-77.
12. Sulocki and Cartier, 'Continuing Airworthiness in the framework of the transition from JAA to EASA', *supra* note 53 in Ch. 1, at p. 313; Jon Pierre and Guy B. Peters, 'From a club to a bureaucracy: JAA, EASA, and European aviation regulation', JEPP, 16 (2009), p. 350.
13. Pierre and Peters, 'From a club to a bureaucracy: JAA, EASA, and European aviation regulation', *supra* note 12, at p. 350.
14. *Ibid.*

[B] The Initial Attempts to Establish EASA in the Form of an International Organisation

Initially, there were attempts to establish EASA as an international organisation by means of a treaty.[15] However, these attempts failed, largely as a result of the inability of EU Member States to find a politically acceptable and legally sound solution which would allow EASA to adopt binding and directly applicable decisions and regulations.[16]

Finding such a solution was necessary to address the shortcomings of the previous system, where the JAA – because of its legally non-binding status – could only recommend the adoption of harmonised regulations and was not able to deliver certificates on behalf of its member authorities. This was not considered as sufficient by the industry,[17] and was criticised by the European Commission which believed that the JAA 'has not produced the single system sought by the industry.'[18]

At that time, some EU Member States argued that direct applicability of rules adopted outside the EU legal framework would require a change to their constitutions and possibly also a referendum.[19] From the EU law point of view, and based on the principles established by the Court of Justice of the European Union (CJEU), it was also questionable if it is possible to delegate such broad regulatory competences to an external organisation,[20] as this could amount to:

> A surrender of the independence of action of the Community in its external relations and a change in the internal constitution of the Community by the alteration of essential elements of the Community structure as regards both the prerogatives of the institutions and the position of the Member States *vis-à-vis* one another.[21]

The EU could agree to such delegation only if the provisions of a future EASA treaty defined and limited the powers in question so clearly that they would be

15. EU, 'Recommandation de décision du Conseil autorisant la Commission à engage des négociations en vue de la création d'une organisation européenne pour la sécurité de l'aviation civile', SEC(96) 2152 final, (EU Council archives, Brussels, 1996).
16. EASA 10th Anniversary Chronicle, *supra* note 4, at p. 9.
17. In December 1992, the JAA Board held a meeting with the European aviation associations to discuss the concept of a single European airworthiness organisation, which the industry saw as urgently needed; see: ECAC, 'Report on 'JAA activities'', DGCA/86, (ECAC archives, Paris, 1992). See also: Pierre and Peters, 'From a club to a bureaucracy: JAA, EASA, and European aviation regulation', *supra* note 12, at p. 351.
18. Neil Kinnock, Member of the European Commission responsible for Transport, 'Meeting the global challenge: the outlook for civil aviation in the EU', SPEECH/98/1, (Forum Europe, Brussels, 1998).
19. See: Interventions of the Irish and Italian delegations during the 2108th Council (Transport) meeting, 17-18 June 1998, (EU Council archives, Brussels, 1998).
20. EU, 'European Organisation Responsible for Civil Aviation Safety: Report on the Work of the Expert Group on Legal Issues', Working Party on Aviation of 19 February 1998, Working Document AER/98/17, (EU Council archives, Brussels, 1998).
21. 'Opinion 1/76 concerning the draft agreement establishing a European laying-up fund for inland waterway vessels', in: [1977] ECR I-741, (CJEU,1977), (p. 758).

exclusively executive powers.[22] In the context of the EASA treaty, this meant that the EU could probably only agree to the transfer of competences to take individually binding decisions, but not to adopt directly applicable regulations of a general nature. This, in practice, meant that the main legal *flaw* of the JAA, namely its inability to 'produce the single system sought by the industry' would persist.

As a result, alternative proposals started to emerge, with some EU Member States arguing that an EU-type organisation 'would solve the legal and political problems arising from the setting up of an international organisation ...'.[23] All in all, the idea of establishing EASA by means of a treaty was finally abandoned and it became clear that an alternative solution had to be found within the institutional framework of the EU. To this end the European Commission presented an outline for the setting up of EASA as an EU agency.[24] This was soon after followed by a proposal for the 'Regulation of the European Parliament and of the Council setting up the European Aviation Safety Agency'.[25]

[C] The Benefits of Establishing EASA in the Form of an EU Agency

EASA is one of the EU's regulatory agencies and, like most of the other such agencies, was created by an act of EU secondary legislation – regulation of the European Parliament and the Council (hereinafter the 'EASA Basic Regulation'),[26] which is of general applicability and binding in its entirety and directly applicable in all EU Member States by virtue of Article 288 of the Treaty on the Functioning of the European Union (TFEU).[27]

Under its Basic Regulation, EASA was given the status of an 'EU body' with legal personality.[28] This means that it has independent legal standing under public EU law, can conclude contracts with EU institutions,[29] and can be a party to the proceedings in

22. *Ibid.*, at p. 759. See also: EC, 'Proposal for a Regulation of the European Parliament and of the Council on establishing common rules in the field of civil aviation and creating a European Aviation Safety Agency', (COM(2000) 595 final), p. 4.
23. See: Intervention of the German delegation during the 2074th Council (Transport) meeting of 17 March 1998, (EU Council archives, Brussels, 1998). On the other hand the UK, fearing further transfers of power from London to Brussels, continued to back the original concept of an international organisation, see: Airline Business, 'EASA delayed by debate over powers' www.flightglobal.com/news/articles/easa-delayed-by-debate-over-powers-63801/ [accessed 7 August 2014].
24. EC, 'Commission Working Document: In view of the discussions within the Council on the creation of the European Aviation Safety Authority in the Community framework', COM (2000) 144 final, (Brussels, 2000).
25. EC proposal for the 'EASA Basic Regulation' (COM(2000) 595 final), *supra* note 22.
26. EU, 'Regulation (EC) No 1592/2002 of 15 July 2002 on common rules in the field of civil aviation and establishing a European Aviation Safety Agency', (OJ L 240, 7.9.2002).
27. EU, 'Treaty on the Functioning of the European Union (TFEU)', in: Consolidated Treaties and Charter of Fundamental Rights, (2010).
28. Regulation (EU) No 216/2008, *supra* note 81 in Ch. 2, Article 28.
29. For example EASA concludes agreements with the European Commission under which it provides technical assistance to third countries in the area of aviation safety. See: EASA, 'Management Board Decision 02-2014 adopting the first 2014 amending budget (Annex)' 2014) http://easa.europa.eu/the-agency/governance/management-board/decisions/easa-mb-decision-05-2014-adopting-2014-first [accessed 7 August 2014].

the CJEU.[30] Its legal personality extends to domestic legal orders of all EU Member States, where EASA enjoys 'the most extensive legal capacity accorded to legal persons under their laws.'[31]

Thus two main benefits stem from EASA's legal basis:

- the legally binding and directly applicable nature of the regulatory framework on the basis of which EASA was established and in which it operates together with the EU Member States, and
- the possession of a legal personality which is valid in the domestic legal orders of all EU Member States.

These two benefits address the shortcomings of the previous JAA system which was based on a non-binding arrangement between NAAs of the ECAC Member States and where the JAA executed legal personality through a foundation which was established under the Dutch law.[32] However, as section §4.02[D] below demonstrates, the fact that EASA is based on a legally binding and directly applicable legal framework does not mean that it can itself adopt rules with similar status. This is not unusual for RASOs. In fact this study did not identify a single RASO with competence to adopt legally binding and directly applicable measures of general applicability which would be of legislative nature (see Chapter 5 for further details).

[D] The Limits of EASA Powers as an EU Agency

The main consequence of EASA being an EU agency is that its competences have to fit 'within the EU's existing institutional structure and balance of powers.'[33] This means that EASA itself cannot adopt legally binding acts of general applicability other than of executive nature, as the competence to adopt legislative measures is, under Article 288 of the TFEU, reserved exclusively for the EU institutions.[34]

The question of whether EU institutions can delegate to agencies the powers to adopt legally binding acts of general applicability is subject to jurisprudence of the CJEU. Of key importance to this debate is the *Meroni* doctrine, which stems from the 1956 case law.[35] It is to date consistently applied by EU institutions,[36] and re-confirmed in subsequent rulings of the CJEU.[37]

30. Regulation (EU) No 216/2008, *supra* note 81 in Ch. 2, Article 50.
31. *Ibid.*, Article 28(2).
32. Roadmap for JAA (2005), *supra* note 76 in Ch. 3.
33. Regulation (EU) No 216/2008, *supra* note 81 in Ch. 2, Preamble clause 12.
34. TFEU, Article 288: 'To exercise the Union's competences, the institutions shall adopt regulations, directives, decisions, recommendations and opinions.'
35. 'Case C-9/56 Meroni and Co., Industrie Metallurgiche S.p.A. v. Highly Authority', in: [1957-1958] ECR I-133, (CJEU,1958).
36. EC, 'European Governance: A White Paper', (COM (2001) 428 final), p. 35; EC, 'Communication from the Commission to the European Parliament and the Council: European Agencies: The Way Forward', COM (2008) 135 final, pp. 9-10; EC, 'Draft Interinstitutional Agreement on the operating framework for the European regulatory agencies', COM (2005) 59 final, p. 5.
37. 'Joined Cases C-154/04 and C-155/04, The Queen v. Secretary of State for Health and National Assembly for Wales', in: [2005] ECR I-06451, (CJEU,2005), (p. 6514). See also: 'Case C-270/12,

The *Meroni* doctrine is based on the concept of institutional balance, which requires that 'the powers of any rule-making body ultimately should be traced back to the authority of a democratically elected parliament.'[38] On this basis, the CJEU developed a number of principles which the EU institutions must respect when delegating powers to bodies not established by the Treaties:

- The delegating institution cannot delegate broader powers than it itself possesses or allow their exercise under the conditions other than it would have to observe itself.
- Only clearly defined, executive powers can be delegated, the exercise of which can be subject to strict review in the light of objective criteria determined by the delegating authority.
- Delegation of discretionary powers implying a wide margin of discretion is not allowed, since by replacing the choices of the delegator by the choices of the delegate it would bring about an actual transfer of responsibility.[39]

The *Meroni* doctrine does not in itself prohibit EU agencies from adopting acts of general application, as this possibility is explicitly envisaged by the TFEU.[40] What it does however prohibit is adoption by an EU agency of an act of general application which would be of *legislative nature*, as this would amount to the transfer of responsibility, which is prohibited by *Meroni*.[41] It is therefore perfectly consistent with the EU institutional framework to delegate to an EU agency, such as EASA, the powers to adopt legally binding measures of general applicability which would be of *executive nature*.

Although the *Meroni* doctrine excludes giving EASA powers to adopt legislative acts, the practical necessities of regulating aviation safety challenged this principle. This is because the EASA Basic Regulation is built on a hierarchy of norms, which distinguishes between, the binding measures of general applicability which are contained in EU regulations, and more detailed texts: certification specifications (CS), acceptable means of compliance (AMC) and guidance material (GM).

United Kingdom v. Parliament and Council ', in: not yet published (available on-line), (CJEU,2014), (paragraphs 41-53).

38. Koen Lenaerts and Amaryllis Verhoeven, 'Institutional Balance as a Guarantee for Democracy in EU Governance', in: Good Governance in Europe's Integrated Market, ed. by Christian Joerges and Renaud Dehousse (2002), p. 37; Ellen I. L. Vos, 'Reforming the European Commission: What Role to Play for EU Agencies?', CMLR, 37 (2000), p. 1123.
39. 'Case C-9/56, Meroni', *supra* note 35, (pp. 150-152).
40. See in particular Article 277 of the TFEU. The CJEU has also recalled in its rulings that 'institutional framework established by the TFEU, in particular the first paragraph of Article 263 TFEU and Article 277 TFEU, expressly permits Union bodies, offices and agencies to adopt acts of general application' (See: 'Case C-270/12, United Kingdom v. Parliament and Council ', *supra* note 37, ([aragraph 65)).
41. See also the 'Romano Case' where the CJEU Stated that an EU body such as an administrative commission may not be empowered by the Council to adopt acts having the force of law ('Case C-98/80, Giuseppe Romano v. Institut national d'assurance maladie-invalidité', in: [1981] ECR I-1241, (CJEU,1981), (p. 1256)).

While the measures of the first type are adopted through the EU legislative machinery,[42] the other type can be adopted directly by EASA.[43] This distinction was necessary to enable technical standards to be adapted quickly in view of operational experience and rapid scientific progress which characterises the aviation sector.

Although formally non-binding, it can be asserted that some of the measures adopted by EASA, and especially CS, have in practice, a value of law. This reasoning is based on the following:

- In some jurisdictions, the CSs used to approve aircraft design are legally binding requirements. For example, in the US they are contained in Federal Aviation Regulations.[44] This was also the case in Europe before the establishment of EASA, when the JARs had to be transposed into the national legal orders of JAA member authorities.[45]
- In addition, although general in nature, the CS are *tailor-made* by EASA for each individual product and notified to the applicant as a final *certification basis*, which makes the CS binding in individual cases.[46] The objective of this notification is to create certainty for the applicant, and a clear reference against which demonstration of compliance can take place.
- Similarly, the AMCs although not legally binding, create a presumption of compliance with essential requirements of the EASA Basic Regulation, implementing rules and CS.[47] By following them, the applicant's task of demonstrating compliance is thus greatly facilitated.

The CS and AMC issued by EASA can be considered as measures, which in legal studies are sometimes referred to as *quasi-law*[48] or *soft law*.[49] This somewhat controversial concept is based on the premise that certain normative material such as codes

42. EASA prepares proposals for binding measures of general applicability. These proposals, which are formally referred to as 'opinions', are submitted to the European Commission, who on this basis formulates proposals to the European Parliament and Council, or, in case of implementing measures, directly to the Member States. See: Regulation (EU) No 216/2008, *supra* note 81 in Ch. 2, Article 19(1).
43. *Ibid.*, Article 19(2).
44. See for example 14 CFR, Part 25 in the US, which establishes airworthiness standards for transport category airplanes.
45. For example in Poland the JARs were transposed into the national legal system by means of implementing regulations issued by the minister of infrastructure. See: Regulation of the Minister of Infrastructure of 5 October 2004 concerning the introduction of European requirements of aviation safety 'JAR' and European requirements concerning facilitation of civil aviation (Official Journal Nr 2004.224.2282 of 15 October 2004).
46. Regulation (EU) No 216/2008, *supra* note 81 in Ch. 2, Article 20. See also: EASA, 'General Principles Related to the Certification procedures to be applied by the Agency for the issuing of certificates for products, parts, and appliances (Product Certification Procedures) ', (Decision of the EASA Management Board No 07-2004, and amended by Decision No 12-2007).
47. See for example: Commission Regulation (EU) No 748/2012, *supra* note 86 in Ch. 2, Article 10.
48. Huang, *supra* note 29 in Ch. 1, at p. 187.
49. Gregory Shaffer and Mark A. Pollack, 'Hard and Soft Law', in: Interdisciplinary Perspectives on International Law and International Relations: The State of the Art, ed. by Jeffrey L. Dunoff and Mark A. Pollack (2013), pp. 197-218.

of practice, guidelines or resolutions can produce legal effects,[50] or in practice 'influences State and corporate behaviour but lacks judicial enforceability'.[51]

In addition there are sui generis measures that EASA can adopt, such as the Airworthiness Directives (ADs), which EASA issues on behalf of EU Member States,[52] as part of its responsibility for continuing airworthiness of aircraft design.[53] ADs apply to all aircraft of a given type or model, and therefore have a status which puts them between an individual decision and a regulation of general applicability. An EASA AD is a powerful tool and can even be used to ground all aircraft of a given type on the registries of the States on behalf of which it was issued.[54]

It could be argued that the competence of EASA to issue ADs, which have a general scope of application, is not compatible with *Meroni*. In the case of EASA however, this competence stems from the relationship of *agency* which exists between EASA and EU Member States, as will be demonstrated in the following section. Under this relationship, it is the EU Member States not the EU institutions which delegate to EASA the exercise of certain competences.

EASA competence to issue ADs is therefore a *Europeanization* of certain domains of national competence, rather than a delegation from an EU institution to an EU body, which would be governed by the *Meroni* doctrine. In addition, as was pointed out in preceding paragraphs, the EU institutional framework explicitly permits EU agencies to adopt legally binding acts of general applicability if they are of executive nature only and do not replace the choices which have been made by the EU legislator.[55]

§4.03 THE ROLE OF EASA IN INTERNATIONAL RELATIONS AND ITS STATUS UNDER THE CHICAGO CONVENTION

[A] The Question of International Legal Personality of EASA

As was described under section §4.02[B], initially there was an attempt to establish EASA by means of an international treaty and in the form of an international organisation, which was however ultimately abandoned.[56]

50. Ingo Venzke, How Interpretation Makes International Law: On Semantic Change and Normative Twists, (2012), p. 228.
51. Laurence Boulle, The Law of Globalization: An Introduction, (2009), p. 363.
52. For examples of EASA Airworthiness Directives see: EASA, 'Airworthiness Directives Publishing Tool' http://ad.easa.europa.eu/ [accessed 02 March 2014].
53. Regulation (EU) No 216/2008, *supra* note 81 in Ch. 2, Article 20(1); Commission Regulation (EU) No 748/2012, *supra* note 86 in Ch. 2, at Annex I (Part 21), paragraph 21A.3B.
54. See for example: Aviation Safety Network, 'EASA grounds all Dassault Falcon 7X aircraft pending incident investigation' http://news.aviation-safety.net/2011/05/26/easa-grounds-all-dassault-falcon-7x-aircraft-pending-incident-investigation/ [accessed 14 June 2014].
55. *Supra* note 40.
56. The EU institutional practice also provides examples of bodies which were established in a form of an international organisation but functioning under close control of EU institutions. This was the case with Europol, which was originally created by an international convention concluded by EU Member States and subsequently transformed into an EU agency. For further discussion see: Andrea Ott, Ellen I. L. Vos, and Florin Coman-Kund, 'European Agencies on the Global

The fact that EASA was established in the form of an EU agency did not diminish the importance of international cooperation for the functioning of this agency. Indeed one of the main objectives set by the EASA Basic Regulation, is to 'promote [EU] views regarding civil aviation safety standards and rules throughout the world by establishing appropriate cooperation with third countries and international organisations'.[57] In this respect the primary role of EASA is to:

> Assist the [EU] and its Member States in the field of international relations, including the harmonisation of rules, recognition of approvals and technical cooperation, and be entitled to establish the appropriate relations with the aeronautical authorities of third countries and international organisations ... .[58]

The use of the word *assist* above is symptomatic of the fact that EU institutions and Member States do not consider EU agencies, including EASA, as being entitled to represent the EU position to an outside audience or commit the EU to international obligations.[59] This is yet another consequence of EASA being part of the EU legal system. In practice, however, the situation is more complex, especially if one tries to analyse the question of EU agencies' legal status not from the perspective of EU law, but from the perspective of public international law.

While EASA's legal personality in the territories of EU Member States is explicitly envisaged under its Basic Regulation,[60] the question of EASA's international legal personality is not so clear. This is not a surprise as the question of international legal personality of EU agencies in general is subject to divergent views in academic writings.[61] The controversies around legal status of EU agencies as international actors[62] can be viewed as an emanation of a more general discussion on the relationship between international law and the EU law, which 'to some extent still remains quite an esoteric issue'.[63]

The question of international legal personality of EU agencies is primarily approached in the academic writings from the perspective of potential treaty making powers of these bodies. While there are differences of opinion in the literature

Scene: EU and International Law Perspectives', in: European Agencies in between Institutions and Member States, ed. by Michelle Everson, Cosimo Monda, and Ellen I. L. Vos (2014).

57. Regulation (EU) No 216/2008, *supra* note 81 in Ch. 2, Article 2(d).
58. *Ibid.*, Preamble clause 23.
59. EU, 'Joint Statement of the European Parliament, the Council of the EU and the European Commission on decentralised agencies', (2012), http://ec.europa.eu/commission_2010-2014/sefcovic/documents/120719_agencies_joint_statement_en.pdf [accessed 9 January 2014].
60. Regulation (EU) No 216/2008, *supra* note 81 in Ch. 2, Article 28.
61. See in particular: Gregor Schusterschitz, 'European Agencies as Subjects of International Law', IOLR, 1 (2004), pp. 163-188; Andrea Ott, 'EU regulatory agencies in EU external relations: Trapped in a legal minefield between European and International Law', European Foreign Affairs Review, 13 (2008), pp. 515-540; Melanie Fink, 'Frontex Working Arrangements: Legitimacy and Human Rights Concerns Regarding 'Technical Relationships'', Utrecht Journal of International and European Law, 28 (2012), pp. 25-26.
62. The question of international activities of EU agencies has so far been studied only scarcely. At the time of writing this study a research project was being finalised on this topic at the Maastricht University, and the author has consulted one of the researchers involved in that project when preparing this section of Chapter 4.
63. Enzo Cannizzaro, Peolo Palchetti, and A. Ramses Wessel, 'International law as law of the European Union', (2012).

concerning the international status of some working arrangements concluded by EU agencies, including EASA[64] this study stands on a position that such working arrangements cannot be considered as international agreements. The CJEU in its ruling *French Republic v. Commission* of 1994 clearly stated that the EU legal order does not know the concept of administrative agreements and that only the Council and not the European Commission can conclude international agreements with third countries following the procedures set out in the EU founding treaties.[65] Reasoning *a fortiori*, if the European Commission cannot conclude international agreements with third countries on behalf of the EU, it would be even more difficult to argue that an EU agency, which is overseen by the Commission, could conclude them. The legal status of EASA working arrangements is further addressed under section §4.03[D].

In addition, some commentators argue that international legal personality of EU agencies can be established in case they conclude headquarters agreements with host States.[66] By the end of 2013, over eighteen EU agencies had concluded headquarters agreements.[67] However, even though the provisions of headquarters agreements and associated State practice closely resembles treaty making under international law, as was demonstrated by Schusterschitz,[68] headquarters agreements are not a very reliable indicator of international legal personality. This is because they are concluded not with third countries but with one of the Member States, or in a case of an EU agency with an EU Member State, and concern the status of the organisation within the internal legal order of the host state.[69] In addition, so far EASA has not been granted the capacity to conclude a headquarters agreement, although in 2013 a proposal to this end was made by the European Commission.[70] EASA also does not have its own privileges and immunities on the international field, but relies on the privileges and immunities of the EU, which have been granted to the EU on the basis of its founding Treaties.[71]

In view of the above it could be concluded that EASA does not have any features indicating possession of international legal personality. Before such a definitive statement can be made, there is however a need to analyse one more feature of EASA's

---

64. See in particular: Fink, 'Frontex Working Arrangements: Legitimacy and Human Rights Concerns Regarding 'Technical Relationships'', *supra* note 61, at pp. 25-26; Ott, Vos, and Coman-Kund, *supra* note 56, at pp. 104-105.
65. 'Case C-327/91, French Republic v. Commission', in: [1994] ECR I-03641, (CJEU,1994), (pp. 3676-3678).
66. Schusterschitz, 'European Agencies as Subjects of International Law', *supra* note 61, at p. 188.
67. EC, 'Decentralised agencies: 2012 Overhaul (analitical fiches)' http://europa.eu/agencies/documents/fiche_3_sent_to_ep_cons_2010-12-15_en.pdf [accessed 9 January 2014].
68. Schusterschitz, 'European Agencies as Subjects of International Law', *supra* note 61, at pp. 176-177.
69. Vincent Correia, 'La contribution des agences de régulation à l'action extérieure de l'Union européenne', in: L'Europe face au monde, ed. by Loic Grard (2013), pp. 36-37.
70. EC, 'Proposal for a Regulation of the European Parliament and of the Council amending Regulation (EC) No 216/2008 in the field of aerodromes, air traffic management and air navigation services', (COM(2013) 409 final).
71. The application of the 'Protocol on the Privileges and Immunities of the EU' to EASA is confirmed by Article 30 of Regulation (EU) No 216/2008. This means, in particular, that the premises, buildings and archives of EASA are inviolable and exempt from search, requisition, confiscation or expropriation. Also the property and assets of EASA cannot be the subject of administrative or legal measures without the authorisation of the CJEU.

legal set-up, namely its competence to implement the Chicago Convention on behalf of EU Member States. This topic is dealt with in the following section.

[B] The Relationship of 'International Agency' between EU and Its Member States

The fact that EASA has been established in the form of an EU agency and not international organisation is not necessarily, on its own, a showstopper to this body having competences the execution of which could pre-suppose international legal personality. International law literature identifies cases which suggest that organs of an international organisation could act on the international plane independently from the *mother* organisation.[72]

As explained by Brownlie in his principles of public international law, 'entities acting with delegated powers from States, may appear to enjoy a separate personality and viability on the international plane',[73] and that 'joint agencies of States ... may have restricted capacities and limited independence but be regarded as a separate legal person'.[74]

The question of international legal personality is today primarily approached from a functional perspective, meaning that it is important to look at the totality of the factors, including the powers and competences that were given to a given organisation, as well as its relevant practice, and on this basis to assess whether these powers, competences and practice pre-suppose that the organisation is a separate legal person under international law.[75] This approach is in-line with the famous *Reparation for Injuries* ruling of the International Court of Justice (ICJ).[76]

When looking at EASA from the functional perspective, of primary importance are Articles 17(e) and 20(1) of the EASA 'Basic Regulation', which provide that the Agency shall:

> In its fields of competence, carry out, on behalf of Member States, functions and tasks ascribed to them by applicable international conventions, in particular the Chicago Convention.[77]

and:

> With regard to the products, parts and appliances ..., the Agency shall, where applicable and as specified in the Chicago Convention or its Annexes, carry out on

72. For discussion on (in)divisibility of international legal personality see: Henry G. Schermers and Niels M. Blokker, International Institutional Law, (2011), p. 994.
73. James Crawford, Brownlie's principles of public international law, (2012), p. 120.
74. *Ibid.*, at p. 169-170.
75. See: Schermers and Blokker, *supra* note 72, at pp. 989-990; Crawford, *supra* note 73, at p. 170; Jan Klabbers, An Introduction to International Institutional Law, (2009), pp. 49-50.
76. In this case the ICJ concluded that UN is an international legal person because its member States 'by entrusting certain functions to it, with the attendant duties and responsibilities have clothed it with the competence required to enable those functions to be effectively discharged' ('Reparation for Injuries Suffered in the Service of the United Nations, Advisory Opinion', in: [1949] ICJ Reports 174, (ICJ,1949), (p. 179).
77. Regulation (EU) No 216/2008, *supra* note 81 in Ch. 2, Article 17(e).

> behalf of Member States the functions and tasks of the State of design, manufacture or registry when related to design approval.[78]

The legal and practical consequence of the above provisions is that, whenever the EASA Basic Regulation grants to the Agency competences which are also covered by international conventions and in particular the Chicago Convention, then EASA in this respect will be acting as an authorised representative, or agent, of EU Member States. This includes EASA having the powers to make decisions that are binding for EU Member States under the Chicago Convention. An example of such a decision would be the issuance by EASA of a Type Certificate confirming that an aircraft design complies with an appropriate certification basis.[79] Such a decision creates effects under Annex 8 to the Chicago Convention, including the triggering of obligations which this Annex attributes to the 'State of Design'.[80]

The existence of a relationship of agency between EASA and EU Member States is also supported by diplomatic practice, and where following the establishment of EASA each EU Member State has notified ICAO that EASA is 'now its authorised representative for the fulfilment of its obligations, as State of design or manufacture, as specified in Part II of Annex 8 to the Chicago Convention'.[81]

At the same time, the concept of direct delegation of the exercise of competences from EU Member States to an EU agency has so far been addressed in the literature only scarcely and primarily from the perspective of EU law. Hofman and Moroni in their analysis of 'pluralisation of EU executive' observe that the model of direct delegation:

> Might seem at first sight attractive in that it could be capable of explaining the most far-reaching delegations of powers to EU agencies such as the power to take externally binding implementing acts and engage in international relations in absence of any clear Treaty authorisation to do so.[82]

They conclude however that the consequence of direct delegation from EU Member States to EU agencies:

> Would result in EU agencies, which are established under EU law, and apply EU procedural law, exercising Member State competences. This concept and mix of approaches would lead, in effect, to nothing less than the creation of agencies as bodies, legally speaking, occupying a place in between EU and Member States law. Conceptualising delegation to agencies in the European Union as direct or horizontal delegation – although it might be an apt description of delegation of powers from a political scientist's point of view – *is thus difficult to establish in terms of EU law* (emphasis added).[83]

78. *Ibid.*, Article 20(1).
79. Regulation (EU) No 216/2008, *supra* note 81 in Ch. 2, Article 20.
80. See for example: Annex 8 to the Chicago Convention, at paragraph 4.2.1.1.
81. EC, 'Template for EU Member States démarche to ICAO on the transfer of regulatory tasks to EASA', (EU Council archives, Brussels, 14 November 2003).
82. Herwig C.H. Hofmann and Alessandro Morini, 'The Pluralisation of EU Executive – Constitutional Aspects of "Agencification"', ELR, 37 (2012), p. 431.
83. *Ibid.*, p. 432.

The question of direct delegation from EU member States to EU agencies, in the specific context of EASA, has also been looked at by Vos, Ott and Koman-Kund, who came to a conclusion that this construction '... is quite peculiar, as we see that Member States "borrow" EASA for tasks relating to powers for which they are responsible. Consequently *this necessitates more empirical research on this matter* (emphasis added)'.[84]

The difficulty that researchers experience in fully explaining the legal basis and consequences of the direct delegation of implementing powers from EU Member States to an EU agency, or more specifically to EASA, suggests that a different approach may be necessary. In particular, given the fact that in the case of EASA the delegation concerns powers to implement international law, namely the Chicago Convention, the public international law perspective has to be employed, in addition to the EU law perspective.

The concept which allows to explain, from an international law perspective, the ability of EASA to implement the Chicago Convention on behalf of the EU Member States is the notion of *international agency*.[85] As was demonstrated by Sarooshi, the concept of international agency is recognised in the rulings of international courts, by practitioners as well as in academic writings.[86]

Sereni describes this relationship as follows:

> In the field of international law every subject generally acts in person, through its own organs, without resorting to cooperation with other subjects. However, international practice shows that members of the community of nations sometimes act on behalf of other members, with the legal effect that the transactions performed by the acting subject in the name and for the account of the other person have for the latter the same legal consequences as if it had acted in person. ... This legal phenomenon implies a split between the immediately acting international person and the person to whom the legal effects of these acts are imputed.[87]

Sereni argues that, given the fact that the international agency[88] concerns the performance of international activities, it is governed by international law, and can therefore exist 'only between parties recognised as subjects of international law'.[89]

---

84. Ott, Vos, and Coman-Kund, *supra* note 56, at p. 105.
85. For an overview of the concept of agency in international law see in particular: Sarooshi, *supra* note 19 in Ch. 2, at pp. 33-51; Angelo P. Sereni, 'Agency in International Law', American Journal of International Law, 34 (1940), pp. 638-660; Curtis A. Bradley and Judith G. Kelley, 'The concept of international delegation', Law and Contemporary Problems, 71 (2008), pp. 1-36.
86. Sarooshi, *supra* note 19 in Ch. 2, at p. 33.
87. Sereni, 'Agency in International Law', *supra* note 85, at p.638.
88. The relationship of an international agency between a State and organisation, as described in this section, has to be distinguished from the notion of a 'joint organ', which is a different category of State cooperation under international law. A 'joint organ' is a body *composed* of the States, and does not have a separate legal personality. Two most prominent examples of such joint organs, often referred to in the literature, are the Nauru Administering Authority established under the 'Trusteeship Agreement for the Territory of Nauru', New York, 1 November 1947, UN General Assembly Resolution 140(II); and the Intergovernmental Commission under the 'Treaty between the United Kingdom of Great Britain and Northern Ireland and the French Republic concerning the Construction and Operation by Private Concessionaires of a Channel Fixed Link', Canterbury, 12 February 1986, UKTS No. 15 (1992).
89. *Ibid.*, p. 639.

Similar view is expressed by Sarooshi:

> An important precondition for the existence of an agency relationship in both international and domestic law is that the principal and agent are separate legal entities. This flows from the principle of representation inherent in an agency relationship: that an agent acts on behalf of its principal to change certain of its rights and obligations.[90]

It has also to be underlined that in this case we are dealing with a constitutional agency, and not a factual agency which 'does not hinge specifically on the nature of personality of the organisation nor does it flow from the constitutional relationship between the organization and its members'.[91]

The requirement that the principal and agent are separate international legal persons when it comes to the implementation of the Chicago Convention and its Annexes may also be derived from the practice of ICAO, which in its Resolution on nationality and registration of aircraft operated by international operating agencies, had defined international aircraft registration as:

> The cases where the aircraft to be operated by an international operating agency would be registered not on a national basis but with an international organization having legal personality, whether or not such international organization is composed of the same States as have constituted the international operating agency.[92]

As EASA acts today on behalf of EU member States as a 'State of Registry' for all issues related to aircraft design, and this has been found acceptable by ICAO as the subsequent section demonstrates, it should not be excluded that it could similarly act on behalf of EU Member States for the purpose of international aircraft registration

If applied directly to EASA, the above reasoning would lead to a conclusion that the relationship of agency which was established under Articles 17(e) and 20(1) of the EASA Basic Regulation presupposes the possession by EASA of a separate legal personality not only under public EU law, but also public international law. Such a conclusion would be however at odds with the founding treaties of the EU, which treat agencies, such as EASA, as organs of the EU.[93] As pointed out by Hoffmeister, the EU Treaties establish the principle of EU responsibility, from an international law point of view, for all acts of its instrumentalities, including institutions, bodies, offices, agencies

90. Sarooshi, *supra* note 19 in Ch. 2, at p. 34.
91. Chittharanjan F. Amerasinghe in: Institute of International Law (IIL), 'Yearbook', Volume 66, Part I, Session of Lisbon, (1995), p. 353.
92. ICAO, 'Resolution on Nationality and Registration of Aircraft Operated by International Operating Agencies', (Reproduced in ICAO Doc. 9587 'Policy and Guidance Material on the Economic Regulation of International Air Transport').
93. When referring to its internal organs, the EU founding treaties use a standard formula: 'Union institutions, bodies, offices or agencies.' For further discussion see: Jan Pieter Kuijper and Esa Paasivirta, 'EU International Responsibility and its Attribution: From the Inside Looking Out', in: The International Responsibility of the European Union: European and International Perspectives, ed. by Malcolm Evans and Panos Koutrakos (2013), p. 50. See also: Correia, *supra* note 69, at p. 40, who observes that: 'Les agences, créées par des actes de droit dérivé qui rappellent le plus souvent qu'elles sont des organismes de l'Union, ne sont pas individualisables, au plan externe, de l'organisation international qui les a créées.'

and their servants.[94] Also analysis of international aviation safety agreements concluded by the EU suggests that EASA is considered only as a technical agent of the EU and its Member States and not as a separate international legal person.[95] Under international law, the conduct of organs and agents of an international organisation is normally attributed to the latter.[96]

In order to reconcile the theory of the international agency, as developed under public international law, and the legal status of EASA under public EU law, this study argues that, although Articles 17(e) and 20(1) of the EASA 'Basic Regulation' speak about EASA acting 'on behalf of EU Member States', from the international law perspective the agency relationship must be considered as having been established between the EU and its Member States. This means that the EU, which is an international organisation, exercises the aforementioned competences through EASA, as its organ. Indeed, during the discussions on the establishment of EASA in the form of an EU agency, it has been considered that the certification functions which are today performed by EASA could be also exercised, on behalf of the EU Member States, by the European Commission.[97]

From the international law perspective, the above means that the EU Member States are using the EU law to implement the obligations which are incumbent on them under the Chicago Convention. It will be also the EU and not EASA which is responsible under international law for breaches of EU's international obligations towards third countries or international organisations – an issue which will be further addressed in Chapter 6.

To conclude, while EASA has separate legal personality under public EU law, from the international law perspective EASA must be treated as an organ of the EU, which in turn exercises, through EASA, the competences which have been transferred to the European level by EU Member States. This includes the taking of decisions, on behalf of EU Member States, which create legal consequences under the Chicago Convention.

The existence of the relationship of international agency between the EU and its Member States does not mean however, as will be demonstrated in Chapter 6, that EU Member States ceased to be responsible for compliance with their obligations as contracting parties to the Chicago Convention.

In 2014, apart from EASA, there has been only one other RASO which was established in a form of an organ of an international organisation with separate legal personality – this is the case of ASSA-AC, a central African RASO which was referred

94. Frank Hoffmeister, 'Litigating against the European Union and its Member States – Who responds under the ILC's Draft Articles on International Responsibility of International Organizations?', EJIL, 21 (2010), p. 740.

95. See in particular the definition of 'Technical Agent' under the EU-US BASA, *supra* note 97 in Ch.2.

96. UN, 'Commentary to draft articles on the responsibility of international organizations', Yearbook of the International Law Commission, Volume II, Part 2 (2011), pp. 17-18.

97. COM (2000) 144 final, *supra* note 24, at pp. 6-7. The EU has also established agencies which only deliver technical opinions, but where the actual legal decision is taken by the Commission. This is the case for example for the European Medicines Agency, which recommends to the European Commission the issuance of market authorisations for human and veterinary medicines.

to in Chapter 3.[98] In order to take account of that specific category of regional aviation safety bodies, the RASO definition which was proposed in Chapter 3, covers, in addition to international organisations, also RASOs which are established in the form of an organ of an international organisation.

[C] Practical Consequences of the Relationship of 'International Agency' between EU and Its Member States

The relationship of international agency between the EU, acting through EASA, and EU Member States is in the first place a consequence of a decision which was driven by arguments of safety and efficiency – namely to perform certain certification tasks centrally, on behalf of all EU Member States, and with binding legal effects. Given that these tasks are also governed by the Chicago Convention, meant that the creation of EASA necessarily had to have effects under international law.

From the Chicago Convention point of view there are a number of practical consequences of the establishment of the international agency relationship.

First of all, under Article 83 of the Chicago Convention ICAO Member States:

> May make arrangements not inconsistent with the provisions of this Convention. Any such arrangement shall be forthwith registered with the Council, which shall make it public as soon as possible.[99]

Because the relationship of international agency between the EU and its Member States alters the way in which the latter discharge their responsibilities under the Chicago Convention, such relationship falls within the scope of Article 83. The analysis of State practice indicates that this is also the understanding of the EU Member States which have notified ICAO about the fact that EASA exercises on their behalf the 'functions and tasks of the State of design, manufacture or registry when related to design approval.'[100] This is in line with the theory of international agency:

> Since international agency is intended to function with relation to third parties, it is necessary that they be informed of the extent of the authority conferred upon the agent. ... Every international transaction is so closely connected with the special characteristics and qualities of each subject involved that each of them must necessarily know the other parties to whom rights and duties are to be assumed. There is no place in international law for the doctrine of the undisclosed principal.[101]

The second consequence of EASA, as an EU agency, acting on behalf of EU Member States is the fact that this reflects on the scope of the ICAO USOAP activities. As a result, ICAO had to conduct audits of EASA to verify the compliance of EU Member

---

98. *Supra* note 190 in Ch. 3.
99. 'Chicago Convention', Article 83.
100. ICAO, 'Final Report on the safety oversight audit of the civil aviation system of the European Aviation Safety Agency', (2008), http://cfapp.icao.int/fsix/AuditReps/CSAfinal/EASA_USOAP_Final%20Report_en.pdf [accessed 9 August 2014], at paragraph 1.1.10.
101. Sereni, 'Agency in International Law', *supra* note 85, at p. 649.

States with the relevant ICAO SARPs, in particular Annex 8 to the Chicago Convention.[102] This was a major benefit for ICAO and EU Member States, as instead of conducting an audit of each individual State, ICAO could conduct just one audit of EASA and subsequently link its results with the USAOP reports of each EU Member State.[103]

The Chicago Convention is not the only international legal instrument which is impacted by this agency relationship. The other two instruments are BASAs concluded by the EU, and working arrangements concluded by EASA. The following section will look at the benefits of these two instruments and associated legal problems.

[D] Legal Status of EASA under BASA and Working Arrangements

When it comes to the conclusion of BASAs, which were addressed in Chapter 2, the role of EASA is only to assist the European Commission in their negotiations - this is clear from the provisions of EU Treaties,[104] EASA Basic Regulation,[105] and practice.[106]

Compared with the situation under the JAA, EU BASAs offer considerable benefits from a safety and efficiency perspective. Whilst in the past not all EU Member States had such agreements, today when the EU concludes a BASA, it applies, in principle, to all EU Member States.[107] This is because EU BASAs, although being *bilateral in form* - that is they are concluded between the EU and the third country only - have a *multilateral effect*, meaning that they bind also EU Member States.

The EU BASAs also create a level playing field by replacing the national BASAs, which EU Member States were allowed to continue using even after the adoption of the EASA Basic Regulation.[108] In addition, because they are above secondary legislation in the hierarchy of EU laws, EU BASAs allow derogating from the provisions of EASA Basic Regulation and its implementing rules.[109] This brings benefits such as automatic acceptance of foreign approvals,[110] or the possibility to issue certificates in a simplified manner, that is by checking only the differences between the EU and foreign requirements.[111] Not all countries have this possibility. For example in the US, BASAs are

102. ICAO USOAP report on EASA (2008), *supra* note 100.
103. *Ibid.*, at paragraph 1.1.9.
104. TFEU, Article 218.
105. In accordance with Regulation (EU) No 216/2008, *supra* note 81 in Ch. 2, Article 27: 'the Agency shall assist the Community and the Member States in their relations with third countries in accordance with the relevant Community law.' The Agency shall, in particular, '[A]ssist in the harmonising of rules and mutual recognition regarding approvals attesting the satisfactory application of rules.'
106. EASA Information Note on the EU-US BASA, *supra* note 118 in Ch. 2.
107. For examples of BASA concluded by the EU with third countries see: List of EU Bilateral Aviation Safety Agreements, *supra* note 108 in Ch. 2.
108. Regulation (EU) No 216/2008, *supra* note 81 in Ch. 2, Article 12(2).
109. *Ibid.*, Article 12(1).
110. This is the case for example under the EU-US BASA with approvals of production and design organisations, and certain minor repair and design change approvals. See: Annex I to 'EU-US BASA', *supra* note 97 in Ch. 2.
111. This is the case for example in respect of the approval of repair stations under the EU-US BASA. See Annex 2, paragraph 4.4 of the EU-US BASA, *supra* note 97 in Ch. 2.

treated as executive agreements only which means that they cannot derogate from the national requirements.[112]

In addition to assisting in BASA negotiations, EASA also plays an important role in their implementation. Each of the agreements concluded so far by the EU designates EASA as a technical agent of the EU and its Member States for matters falling within the scope of EASA's competence.[113] This role of EASA as a technical agent implies that it may act in the international arena as a body designated by the EU under a BASA.

The legal situation is different in the case of working arrangements (WA), which EASA can conclude with third country aviation authorities or international organisations under Article 27(2) of its Basic Regulation. Such WAs require however prior approval of the European Commission, to ensure their consistency with EASA's mandate and EU's international aviation policy.

The legal status of EASA WAs creates some difficulties for academic writers. For example, Ott observes that certain formulations they use, such as the *entry into force* clauses, suggest that EASA WAs could be considered as internationally legally binding and that this results:

> In a grey area which is legally not acceptable and creates problems of legal uncertainty with regard to their implications and consequences for the internal and external division of [EU] competences in external relations.[114]

Also other sources suggest that, looking from the international law perspective, some of the EASA WAs could be considered as having the status of an international agreement.[115]

The above uncertainties regarding the legal status of EASA WAs can be explained by referring to the relationship of international agency which exists between EASA and EU Member States. The fact that a WA stipulates that EASA acts on behalf, or represents EU Member States, is a recognition of the delegation provisions already contained in the EASA Basic Regulation, and should not be understood as implying that a WA in any way binds the EU institutions or EU Member States under international law. In this situation, the WA is a tool used by EASA to exercise the implementing powers which have been given to it as a technical agent. Under the EU institutional framework, the principle is that only the 'Union may conclude an agreement with one or more third countries or international organisations'.[116]

It is however true that EASA is not always consistent in clarifying the legal status of its WAs, and some of them do not explicitly State that they are without prejudice to international agreements.[117] Divergences of interpretations also do happen, as was the

112. Jennison, 'The Future of Aviation Safety Regulation: New US-EU Agreement Harmonizes and Consolidates the Transatlantic Regime, but What is the Potential for Genuine Regulatory Reform', *supra* note 117 in Ch. 2, at p. 344.
113. See for example Article 1F of the EU-US BASA, *supra* note 97 in Ch. 2.
114. Ott, 'EU regulatory agencies in EU external relations: Trapped in a legal minefield between European and International Law', *supra* note 61, at p. 539.
115. Ott, Vos, and Coman-Kund, *supra* note 56, at p. 103-104.
116. TFEU, Article 216.
117. The list of EASA working arrangements can be found at: EASA, 'Working Arrangements' http://easa.europa.eu/document-library/working-arrangements [accessed 6 August 2014].

case in 2013 when the Turkish aviation authority argued in a case involving aircraft certification that it delegated to EASA the exercise of its 'State of Design' responsibilities on the basis of a WA, and where EASA had to clarify that this is possible only on the basis of an international agreement.[118]

Finally, because WAs do not have a binding status under international law, they cannot derogate from EU law, which is in fact their main limitation. As a consequence, when implementing a WA, EASA must follow the provisions of EU law. This also means that any provision in a WA suggesting obligations for third parties, such as aircraft manufacturers or designers would have to be considered as *ultra vires*, and therefore void.[119]

§4.04 CONTRIBUTION OF EASA TO THE IMPROVEMENT OF GLOBAL AVIATION SAFETY AND OBJECTIVES OF THE CHICAGO CONVENTION

This section will provide an analysis of the safety functions of EASA and demonstrate how and to what extent these functions contribute to global aviation safety and the Chicago Convention objectives of ensuring 'the highest practicable degree of uniformity in regulations, standards, and procedures.'[120]

In this context, it has to be recalled that EASA is not a single EU authority for aviation safety, and has to work in partnership and share tasks with the NAAs of EU Member States. In addition, similarly to EASA's legal status, the performance of its safety functions is also impacted by the fact that it is part of the EU institutional system.

The scope of EASA's Basic Regulation and EASA's mandate has gradually evolved, starting with airworthiness matters in 2002,[121] and then extended to flight operations and aircrew in 2008,[122] and in 2009 further extended to safety aspects of ATM/ANS and aerodromes.[123]

The following sub-section will address three aspects of EASA's functioning as a RASO: rulemaking, certification and finally oversight and enforcement. This should not be understood as an exhaustive study of EASA's safety functions but rather as a critical analysis of those of their aspects which are most relevant from the perspective of this study.

118. Author was involved personally in the clarification of this case.
119. This does not mean however that the working arrangements do not affect third parties from a practical point of view. For example if EASA concludes an arrangement on participation of a foreign authority in the EU SAFA programme, this means that this authority may have access to information on ramp inspections performed by EU Member States.
120. 'Chicago Convention', Article 37.
121. Regulation (EC) No 1592/2002, *supra* note 26.
122. Regulation (EU) No 216/2008, *supra* note 81 in Ch. 2.
123. EU, 'Regulation (EC) No 1108/2009 of the European Parliament and of the Council of 21 October 2009 amending Regulation (EC) No 216/2008 in the field of aerodromes, air traffic management and air navigation services and repealing Directive 2006/23/EC', (OJ L 309, 24.11.2009).

[A] The EU Aviation Safety Regulatory Process

The primary objective of the EASA Basic Regulation is to ensure 'a high and uniform level of protection of the European citizen'.[124] One of the means to ensure this objective is 'the preparation, adoption and uniform application of all necessary acts.'[125]

A single regulatory framework is also essential for a level playing field for the industry, facilitating free movement of goods, persons and services, and promoting cost-efficiency in the regulatory and certification processes. This harmonisation is also in line with the Chicago Convention objective of ensuring 'the highest practicable degree of uniformity in regulations, standards, and procedures.'[126]

It is important to recall that aviation safety rulemaking in the EU is based on the division of work between EASA, and the European Commission, European Parliament, Council and specialised regulatory committees.[127] As demonstrated under section §4.02[D], EASA can only adopt non-legally binding documents, but when it comes to adoption of legally binding EU regulations, its role is limited to assisting the European Commission.[128]

The EU aviation safety regulations, unlike ICAO SARPs are not minimum requirements. They are directly binding in their entirety,[129] and with the exception of conditions envisaged under Article 14 of the EASA Basic Regulation (see section §4.04[A][1] below) EU Member States are not allowed to derogate from them or to impose additional requirements. This principle of EU law, which is reflected in the founding treaties,[130] and confirmed by rulings of the CJEU,[131] is essential for the functioning of the single aviation market which requires uniform conditions of operation for undertakings.

---

124. Regulation (EU) No 216/2008, *supra* note 81 in Ch. 2, at Preamble clause 1.
125. *Ibid.*, Article 2.3(a).
126. 'Chicago Convention', Article 37.
127. Paul Craig and Gráinne de Búrca, EU Law: Text, Cases, and Materials, (2011), pp. 121-141.
128. Regulation (EU) No 216/2008, *supra* note 81 in Ch. 2, Article 19, which states that: 'In order to assist the Commission in the preparation of proposals for basic principles, applicability and essential requirements to be presented to the European Parliament and to the Council and the adoption of the implementing rules, the Agency shall prepare drafts thereof. These drafts shall be submitted by the Agency as opinions to the Commission.'
129. TFEU, Article 288.
130. *Ibid.*
131. 'Case C-6/64, Flaminio Costa v. ENEL', in: [1964] ECR I-585, (CJEU,1964), (p. 594), where the CJEU stated that: '[T]he law stemming from the Treaty, an independent source of law, could not, because of its special and original nature, be overridden by domestic legal provisions, however framed, without being deprived of its character as Community law and without the legal basis of the Community itself being called into question. The transfer by the States from their domestic legal system to the Community legal system of the rights and obligations arising under the Treaty carries with it a permanent limitation of their sovereign rights, against which a subsequent unilateral act incompatible with the concept of the Community cannot prevail.' See also: 'Case C-26/62, Van Gend en Loos v. Administratie der Belastingen', in: [1963] ECR I-1, (CJEU,1963), (p. 12), where the CJEY stated that: '[T]he Community constitutes a new legal order of international law for the benefit of which the States have limited their sovereign rights, albeit within limited fields, and the subjects of which comprise not only Member States but also their nationals. Independently of the legislation of Member States, Community law therefore not only imposes obligations on individuals but is also intended to confer upon them rights which become part of their legal heritage. These rights arise not only where they are

[1] *Benefits and Shortcomings of the EU Aviation Safety Regulatory Process*

The benefits brought about by the establishment of the EU aviation safety regulatory process are so far mixed. On the one hand, the EU regulations are directly applicable and legally binding for all EU Member States, as was demonstrated in the preceding section. There is thus no need to transpose them into the national legal systems to make them binding for individuals.[132] This is the most significant benefit, as compared with the previous JAA system, which could only recommend adoption of harmonised requirements to its member authorities.[133]

On the other hand, the establishment of this process did not seem to result in substantial efficiencies in terms of resource savings for the EU national authorities. A study conducted in 2010 for the European Parliament concluded that:

> More than half of the European national agencies stated that their costs had increased since the establishment of the EU rulemaking procedure. Only very few countries had a reduced workload following the change to the rulemaking process compared with the JAA process. Their workload is still heavy in general, as it encompasses the wider number of consultations. The largest NAAs who were particularly active in the JAA negotiations (e.g. Germany) are the ones who experienced a reduction in their workload.[134]

The above can be attributed to two facts. Firstly, following its establishment and subsequent two extensions of its mandate, EASA had to undertake a large number of rulemaking tasks in order to help build the system. The review of rulemaking deliverables of EASA for the years 2004-2013 shows that on average EASA published nineteen 'Notices of Proposed Amendment' (NPA) a year, with an upwards trend towards the end of the analysed period.[135] Secondly, the EASA rulemaking process was already preceded by a regional system set up under the JAA, and – as far as ATM/ANS is concerned – by EUROCONTROL.[136] It is likely that if the EASA rulemaking system had not built upon the largely harmonised JAA/EUROCONTROL system, but on the

expressly granted by the Treaty, but also by reason of obligations which the Treaty imposes in a clearly defined way upon individuals as well as upon the Member States and upon the institutions of the Community.'

132. This is also because a general trend can be observed in the air transport sector towards replacing EU Directives, which need transposition, with EU regulations, which do not need transposition.
133. As it the case with the 'differences' to ICAO SARPs, the JAA authorities committed only to 'declare all their national regulatory differences to existing JARs ... and to work towards the deletion of these national regulatory differences or their embodiment in the appropriate JAR.' See Cyprus Arrangements, *supra* note 71 in Ch. 3, at paragraph 3.
134. Pricewaterhouse Coopers on behalf of the European Parliament's Committee on Budgets, 'The impact on the EU and national budgets of EU agencies: case studies, PricewaterhouseCoopers study prepared for the European Parliament's Committee on Budgets', (2012), http://www.europarl.europa.eu/studies [accessed 2 March 2014], p. 82.
135. EASA, 'Notices of Proposed Amendment (NPAs)' http://easa.europa.eu/document-library/notices-of-proposed-amendment [accessed 3 June 2014].
136. For an overview of the EUROCONTROL safety related rulemaking activities before the extension of the EASA competence to ATM/ANS safety see: Van Antwerpen, *supra* note 52 in Ch. 1, at p. 54.

twenty-eight different national frameworks of EU Member States the cost savings would be more visible.

The fact that the EU system is based on directly applicable and binding regulations does not mean that all regulatory differences have been eliminated. The possibility of such differences, although considered as exceptional, is envisaged under Article 14 of the EASA Basic Regulation, which gives to EU Member States the possibility to: (1) adopt additional safety measures in case they need to immediately react to a safety problem; (2) grant exemptions in the event of unforeseen urgent operational circumstances or operational needs of a limited duration, provided the level of safety is not adversely affected; and (3) issue individual approvals derogating from the common requirements where an equivalent level of protection can be achieved by other means.

The application of Article 14 is subject to the control of the European Commission and EASA.[137] An evaluation of the application of this Article 14 conducted by the European Commission in 2013 showed that an increasing number of EU Member States are submitting a growing number of notifications under this article, and especially under its provisions referred to in points 2 and 3 above.[138]

Another observation is that the EU civil aviation safety system does not encompass all aviation activities. Two examples can be given in this respect. Firstly, so called Annex II aircraft[139] are excluded, unless they are used in commercial air transport.[140] The second exclusion concerns aerodrome safety, as the EASA Basic Regulation applies only to:

> Aerodromes, including equipment, located in the territory subject to the provisions of the Treaty, open to public use and which serve commercial air transport and where operations using instrument approach or departure procedures are provided, and:
>
> (a) have a paved runway of 800 meters or above; or
> (b) exclusively serve helicopters.[141]

Such exclusions principally stem from the subsidiarity principle enshrined in Article 5 of the Treaty on the European Union (TEU), which limits EU regulations to only those issues which by reason of the scale or effects of the proposed action, can be better achieved at Union level than at the national level.[142] In practice they mean

137. Regulation (EU) No 216/2008, *supra* note 81 in Ch. 2, Article 14.
138. EC, 'Information Note: Handling of notifications in the context of the flexibility provisions under Articles 14(1), 14(4) and 14(6) of EU Regulation No 216/2008', (meeting of the EASA committee No 3/2013).
139. 'Annex II aircraft' include a wide category ranging from amateur built or historic aircraft, to modern ultralight aircraft built in serial production. See: Regulation (EU) No 216/2008, *supra* note 81 in Ch. 2, Annex II.
140. Regulation (EU) No 216/2008, *supra* note 81 in Ch. 2, Article 4(4) and (5).
141. *Ibid.*, Article 4(3a).
142. EU, 'Treaty on the European Union (TEU)', in Consolidated Treaties and Charter of Fundamental Rights, (2010).

however that Member States still need to maintain and correctly implement national rules to the extent necessary to regulate activities falling outside the EU competence.[143]

The other feature of the EU regulatory framework is that not all aviation safety regulations fall within the scope of the EASA Basic Regulation. This is the case *inter alia* for regulations on accident investigation,[144] occurrence reporting,[145] or SES.[146] The practical consequence of that is that they are adopted in a separate rulemaking process not involving EASA and their implementation is not necessarily monitored through the EASA standardisation inspections. At the same time the Agency can be given certain tasks and responsibilities under such legislation.[147]

While in certain cases such separation can be justified - for example accident investigation which has to be independent from EASA as a certifying authority - this dichotomy is proving to be an increasing source of problems. This is most visible in ATM/ANS where, following the extension of EASA competences to this domain, safety is regulated in parallel under the SES and the EASA Basic Regulation. As pointed out by the European Commission, this creates duplication and is not efficient because it necessitates involvement of two specialised bodies, meaning EUROCONTROL and EASA to deal with technical aspects of civil aviation regulation.[148] Although the European Commission believes that it is possible to 'eradicate the overlap between SES and EASA regulations' through better coordination between EASA and EUROCONTROL,[149] this study advocates a partial or even complete merger of these two organisations for reasons explained under section §4.06.

[2] Compliance of EU Aviation Safety Requirements with Annexes to the Chicago Convention

Under the EASA Basic Regulation one of the obligations of the Agency is to:

> Assist Member States in fulfilling their obligations under the Chicago Convention, by providing a basis for a common interpretation and uniform implementation of its provisions, and by ensuring that its provisions are duly taken into account in this Regulation and in the rules drawn up for its implementation.[150]

143. EASA, 'The EASA system as an integral part of the EU (Aviation) legal system', in EASA International Cooperation Forum Legal Workshop, (Brussels, 12-14 October 2009).
144. Regulation (EU) No 996/2010, *supra* note 222 in Ch. 3.
145. EU, 'Regulation No 376/2014 of the European Parliament and of the Council of 3 April 2014 on the reporting, analysis and follow-up of occurrences in civil aviation, amending Regulation (EU) No 996/2010 of the European Parliament and of the Council and repealing Directive 2003/42/EC of the European Parliament and of the Council and Commission Regulations (EC) No 1321/2007 and (EC) No 1330/2007', (OJ L 122, 24.4.2014).
146. EC, 'Framework for creation of the Single European Sky (SES)' http://europa.eu/legislation_summaries/transport/air_transport/l24020_en.htm [accessed 29 March 2014].
147. See for example: Regulation (EU) No 996/2010, *supra* note 222 in Ch. 3, Article 8, which sets outs the rights and responsibilities of EASA in the course of an air accident investigation.
148. EC, 'Communication from the Commission to the European Parliament, the Council, the European Economic and Social Committee and the Committee of the Regions: Accelerating the implementation of the Single European Sky', (COM(2013) 408 final, 2013), p. 9.
149. *Ibid.*
150. Regulation (EU) No 216/2008, *supra* note 81 in Ch. 2, Article 2(d).

Under the above provision EASA should be assisting EU Member States in identifying differences between ICAO SARPs and EU regulations. So far however the practical implementation of this function is not ideal, as EASA does not seem to systematically identify the differences between the rules that it proposes and the ICAO SARPs.

A review of thirty opinions published by EASA between 2010 and 2013, shows that although EASA compares the proposed rules with ICAO SARPs, there is no uniform process followed by EASA in this respect, and the comparisons are either very general,[151] or not documented in a way which would allow EU Member States to correctly discharge their obligations under Article 38 of the Chicago Convention.[152] In addition, none of the opinions analysed presented the identified differences using the ICAO recommended classification methodology.[153]

The closest to ideal in identifying differences with SARPs is the EU regulation 'laying down the common rules of the air and operational provisions regarding services and procedures in air navigation'[154] which contains a list of 'commonly agreed differences' to ICAO Annexes 2 and 11. This regulation also obliges the EU Member States to notify to ICAO the 'commonly agreed differences' and mandates the European Commission to update them if justified by subsequent amendments to ICAO SARPs.[155] The fact that the differences are commonly agreed is important for maintaining uniformity. As experience shows – knowing that a difference exists is not sufficient for the proper assessment and classification of such a difference.[156] This method of keeping track of the differences could be usefully extended to other ICAO Annexes, for example by mandating EASA under its Basic Regulation to develop and make available to EU Member States an inventory of differences.

---

151. Many of the EASA Opinions simply state that: 'with the proposed changes ICAO compliance is ensured' (Opinion 5/2013), that the proposed rule 'has taken into account the development of international law (ICAO)' (Opinion 2/2013) or 'the proposed rules are compliant with ICAO Standards and Recommended Practices' (Opinion 4/2012). Some Opinions do not provide a correlation table indicating differences with SARPs, although the Opinion itself admits that some of the provisions it proposes are below ICAO requirements (Opinion 07/2010, Opinion 03/2013).
152. See for example EASA Opinion 11/2013 on 'Licensing and medical certification of air traffic controllers' at: EASA, 'Agency Opinions' http://easa.europa.eu/document-library/opinions [accessed 28 July 2014]. Although Opinion 11/2013 is a rare example of an EASA proposal containing a single consolidated correlation table between the ICAO SARPs and the proposed EU requirements, it does not identify in which ICAO category each of the differences falls.
153. ICAO classifies the differences into three categories, that is: (1) more exacting or exceeds the ICAO Standard or Recommended Practice (Category A); (2) different in character or other means of compliance (Category B); (3) less protective or partially implemented/not implemented (Category C). See: C-WP/12412, *supra* note 42 in Ch. 2, at Appendix A (as approved by ICAO Council by C-DEC 177/14).
154. EU, 'Commission Implementing Regulation (EU) No 923/2012 of 26 September 2012 laying down the common rules of the air and operational provisions regarding services and procedures in air navigation and amending Implementing Regulation (EU) No 1035/2011 and Regulations (EC) No 1265/2007, (EC) No 1794/2006, (EC) No 730/2006, (EC) No 1033/2006 and (EU) No 255/2010', (OJ L 281, 13.10.2012). The proposal for this regulation was prepared jointly by EASA and EUROCONTROL.
155. *Ibid.*, Article 5.
156. 'Interview No 1', (2013), *supra* note 37 in Ch. 2.

By the end of 2013, EASA had also identified differences between EU regulations and SARPs contained in ICAO Annex 8 and, partially, in Annexes 1 and 6, which had been undertaken for the purpose of ICAO USOAP audits of EASA conducted in 2005 and 2009.[157] Comparison had also been done between EU regulations and the latest ICAO Annex 19 on safety management.[158]

The shortcomings concerning the identification of differences with ICAO SARPs need to be addressed as a matter of priority. From a legal point of view, it is not easy for EU Member States today to discharge their obligations under Article 38 of the Chicago Convention without full knowledge of the differences. Secondly, this hampers the ability of ICAO to rely on the EU system for the purpose of monitoring EU Member States under the USOAP, as envisaged under the recently signed EU–ICAO Memorandum of Cooperation.[159] This last point will be further addressed under section §4.04[C][3].

At the same time, the fact that in addition to 28 EU Member States there is also a number of non-EU European States associated with the work of EASA (see section §4.05) offers an opportunity for helping ICAO to standardise the application of Article 38 of the Chicago Convention and make it more focused, as was advocated in Chapter 2. If over 30 European States came to a common interpretation of what constitutes a difference under Article 38 of the Chicago Convention and filed with ICAO such differences in a uniform and consistent manner, this would not only be a resource efficiency and safety benefit for ICAO and Europe but could also pave the way for an internationally agreed manner of interpreting Article 38 of the Chicago Convention.

[B] The Role of the EU System in Certification of Civil Aviation Activities

The main benefit of the EU system from the perspective of certification[160] of civil aviation activities is the principle of *automatic recognition* of certificates which is enshrined under Article 11 of the EASA Basic Regulation. This provision requires EU Member States to:

> Recognise, without further technical requirements or evaluation, certificates issued in accordance with that regulation and related implementing rules.[161]

The precondition for automatic recognition of certificates is the existence of the common regulatory framework presented under section §4.04[A] above. In the case of

157. ICAO USOAP report on EASA (2008), *supra* note 100.
158. 'Interview No 4', (2014), *supra* note 41 in Ch. 2.
159. 'Memorandum of Cooperation between the European Union and the International Civil Aviation Organization providing a framework for enhanced cooperation', 4 May 2011, (OJ L 232, 9 September 2011).
160. In the EU civil aviation safety system certification is understood as: 'any form of recognition that a product, part or appliance, organisation or person complies with the applicable requirements ..., as well as the issuance of the relevant certificate attesting such compliance.' See: Regulation (EU) No 216/2008, *supra* note 81 in Ch. 2, Article 3(e).
161. Regulation (EU) No 216/2008, *supra* note 81 in Ch. 2, Article 11(1).

the EU, it is not appropriate to speak about *reciprocal recognition* of certificates, as the defining criteria triggering EU-wide acceptance of a certificate is its issuance in compliance with the applicable regulations. Making recognition conditional on reciprocal benefits offered by other EU Member States would not be allowed under the EASA Basic Regulation.

Automatic recognition is an advantage when compared with the previous system of mutual recognition 'recommendations' under the JAA, which referred to different levels of JAR amendments, and in practice lead, as the example of aircrew licensing shows, to a patchwork of recognition arrangements.[162]

The second feature of the EU system is that certain certification tasks are performed centrally by EASA on behalf of EU Member States. This is however an exception, as under the '[EU] institutional system, implementation of ... law is primarily the responsibility of the Member States', in line with the subsidiarity principle.[163] Conceptually, this principle of implementation of EU law at the national level can be summarised as *locally approved, globally accepted.*

Therefore, certification tasks were given to EASA only when this was deemed to be more cost efficient and practical, or if justified by need for uniformity of action *vis-à-vis* third countries. In 2014, EASA was competent to issue certificates in the areas of: approval of design of aeronautical products, parts and appliances,[164] third country organisations and operators,[165] and organisations providing pan-European air navigation services.[166] EU Member States may also delegate to EASA certain certification responsibilities on a voluntary basis – this is for example the case for production, and where France, United Kingdom, Spain and Germany delegated to EASA certification and oversight of the Airbus consortium.[167]

The EASA certification process represents a *one-stop-shop* for the aeronautical industry. From a technical point of view, similar to the previous JAA process, EASA conducts one technical investigation on behalf of all the EU Member States. However, and this is an important difference with the previous system, the EASA certificate is valid in all EU Member States.[168] There is no need for issuance of the certificate in each of the States as was the case under the JAA regime.[169] In addition, EU Member States

162. See for example the last version of JAA mutual recognition recommendations for aircrew licensing at: *supra* note 73 in Ch. 3.
163. Regulation (EU) No 216/2008, *supra* note 81 in Ch. 2, Preamble clause 13.
164. *Ibid.*, Article 20.
165. *Ibid.*, Articles 20.2(b)(iii), 21.1(b), 21.2(iii), 22a(b), 22b(b) and 23.
166. *Ibid.*, Article 22(a).
167. The legal basis for such approval is: Regulation (EU) No 216/2008, *supra* note 81 in Ch. 2, Article 20.2(b)(ii). See also: EASA, 'Agency issues first European Single Production Organisation Approval to Airbus', Press release of 21.07.2008.
168. Regulation (EU) No 216/2008, *supra* note 81 in Ch. 2, Article 11.
169. Sulocki and Cartier, 'Continuing Airworthiness in the framework of the transition from JAA to EASA', *supra* note 53 in Ch. 1, at p. 321. See also: Günter Verhaugen, Vice-President of the European Commission responsible for Enterprise and Industry, 'The role of the Aviation Safety Agency from an industry point of view', SPEECH/04/536, (Speech at the occasion of the inauguration of EASA in Cologne, 2004).

cannot modify the certificate or add additional conditions - something which had been possible under the JAA.[170]

Review of the available reports assessing the functioning of EASA does not offer a clear picture as to the cost efficiency impacts that the transfer of certification tasks had on the national authorities. The initial evaluation of the functioning of EASA conducted in 2007 was inconclusive on this point and stated that:

> With detailed information on cost structures under the former system being unavailable, no significant cost reductions in certification procedures compared to the former system could be identified.[171]

On the other hand, the evaluation performed in 2010 for the European Parliament, somewhat surprisingly came to a conclusion that:

> The expected effect of shifting both the responsibility and the execution of some tasks is usually a budget reduction. However, the perception-based results of our survey show that, all in all, the impact of the task transfer at national level has been toward an increase in budget pressure with very few exceptions. [172]

The available reports are more consistent about the impact of centralisation on the industry. The EU-wide legal value of a single EASA certificate is identified as a major benefit.[173] There seems to also be a consensus that the EASA certification processes are better suited for the larger industries,[174] and that the smaller industry faced challenges stemming from the complexity of the regulations and operational distance of the Agency,[175] which outsources only around 20% of the technical work to local NAAs when it comes to approval of aircraft design.[176]

[1] Implications from the Perspective of the Chicago Convention

The principle of automatic recognition and centralisation of certain tasks at EASA level has a number of implications from the perspective of the Chicago Convention. The first one is the establishment of the international agency relationship between EU, acting through EASA, and EU Member States along with the associated consequences under the USOAP, as was presented in section §4.03[C].

The second consequence is the separation of the functions and tasks of the 'State of Design' which are related to aircraft airworthiness and investigation of aviation

170. Ramboll-Euréval-Matrix on behalf of the European Commission, 'Evaluation of the EU decentralised agencies: Final Report - Volume III, Agency level findings', (2009), p. 56.
171. Horváth & Partners Management Consultants on behalf of the EASA management board, 'Evaluation on the Implementation of EU Regulation 1592/2002: Final Report ', EASA evaluation prepared on the basis of Article 51 of Regulation (EC) 1592/2002, (2007), p. 12.
172. The impact on the EU and national budgets of EU agencies, *supra* note 134, at p. 75.
173. Evaluation of the EU decentralised agencies (2009), *supra* note 170, at p. 56; EASA evaluation (2007), *supra* note 171, at p. 100.
174. *Ibid.*
175. EASA evaluation (2007), *supra* note 171, at p. 100.
176. Certification tasks internalisation rate on the basis of: EASA, 'Business Plan 2014-2018', EASA Management Board Decision Nr 12-2013, (2013).

accidents, which will be presented in more detail in Chapter 5 as an example of unintended consequences that establishment of a RASO may have on the responsibilities of States under the Chicago Convention.

In addition, the following consequences were identified with respect to Article 32 of the Chicago Convention which deals with recognition of certificates for the purpose of international air navigation:

(1) With regard to Article 32(a) of the Chicago Convention, which states that:

> The pilot of every aircraft and the other members of the operating crew of every aircraft engaged in international navigation shall be provided with certificates of competency and licenses issued or rendered valid by the State in which the aircraft is registered.

- The EASA Basic Regulation should be considered as a mechanism for automatic validation or 'rendering valid' of aircrew licences between EU Member States. This is because under Article 11 of the EASA Basic Regulation, an EU 'State of Registry' must automatically accept an aircrew licence which was issued by any other EU Member State 'in accordance with that regulation and related implementing rules'. Given that it is not possible to file differences with the provisions of the Chicago Convention, this is the only possible explanation of consistency between Article 11 of EASA Basic Regulation and Article 32 (a) of the Chicago Convention.

(2) With regard to Article 32 (2) of the Chicago Convention, which provides that:

> Each contracting State reserves the right to refuse to recognize, for the purpose of flight above its own territory, certificates of competency and licenses granted to any of its nationals by another contracting State.

- The EU Member States have waived the possibility of such refusal of recognition in relationships between themselves. Exercise of the right provided in Article 32 (b) by one EU Member State in respect of another EU Member State would not only be in contradiction of Article 11 of the EASA Basic Regulation but also of the principle of non-discrimination established by EU Treaties.[177]

Finally, the EASA Basic Regulation also has consequences from the perspective of Article 83bis of the Chicago Convention, which provides for the possibility of a transfer of certain 'State of Registry' responsibilities to the 'State of the Operator'.[178] For such

177. TFEU, Article 18.
178. 'Chicago Convention', Article 83 bis (a), which states that: 'Notwithstanding the provisions of Articles 12, 30, 31 and 32(a), when an aircraft registered in a contracting State is operated pursuant to an agreement for the lease, charter or interchange of the aircraft or any similar arrangement by an operator who has his principal place of business or, if he has no such place

transfer to take place an agreement is needed between the States concerned and to make the transfer binding for third countries, they have to be notified about the existence of such agreement either directly or through ICAO.[179]

As observed by Manuhutu, in the EU 'any aircraft - regardless in which EU Member State that aircraft is registered - must comply with the same aviation safety rules and standards if that aircraft is operated within the territory of an EU Member State.'[180] This study agrees that 'as between EU Member States there is no need for EU Member States to conclude among them arrangements as envisaged under Article 83bis.'[181] Such a position is supported by the arguments of efficiency and uniformity of safety levels which are the objectives of the EU system. For legal certainty purposes such interpretation could be enshrined in the EASA Basic Regulation, and subsequently notified by EU Member States to ICAO to ensure the international recognition of such a multilateral Article 83bis agreement.[182]

[C] The Benefits of the EU System for Oversight and Enforcement

The EU aviation safety system has its own oversight and enforcement mechanisms which complement those available in EU Member States.[183] As with rulemaking and certification, these mechanisms must be seen in the context of the EU as a whole, and involve multiple actors, which in addition to EASA include the NAAs and EU institutions, notably the European Commission - each with its own role, competences and responsibilities.

The multifaceted nature of the EU system requires close cooperation between all the actors involved. This cooperation is a necessity due to legal considerations, which are analysed in subsequent paragraphs, but primarily from a safety point of view, as none of the actors has a complete picture, or can address problems on its own. For example, while a safety issue can be identified at a national level, it may require resolution through EU legislation. Similarly, a problem identified by EASA may have to be addressed by an NAA.

---

of business, his permanent residence in another contracting State, the State of registry may, by agreement with such other State, transfer to it all or part of its functions and duties as State of registry in respect of that aircraft under Articles 12, 30, 31, and 32(a). The State of registry shall be relieved of responsibility in respect of the functions and duties transferred.'

179. Chicago Convention, Article 83bis (b), which states that: 'The transfer shall not have effect in respect of other contracting States before either the agreement between States in which it is embodied has been registered with the Council and made public pursuant to Article 83 or the existence and scope of the agreement have been directly communicated to the authorities of the other contracting State or States concerned by a State party to the agreement.'
180. Frank Manuhutu, 'Article 83bis (Revisited): Transfer of Safety Oversight Responsibilities Seen from a European's Regulator Perspective', in: From Lowlands to High Skies: A multilevel Jurisdictional Approach towards Air Law, ed. by Pablo Mendes de Leon (2013), pp. 89-95.
181. *Ibid.*
182. *Ibid.*
183. Regulation (EU) No 216/2008, *supra* note 81 in Ch. 2, Article 68, which mandates the EU Member States to lay down penalties for infringement of this regulation and its implementing rules.

[1] EASA Standardisation and Monitoring Activities

Key oversight and enforcement features of the EU system are the EASA standardisation inspections and other monitoring activities, which constitute a regional mechanism mandated by EU law to control the application by EU Member States of the EASA Basic Regulation and its implementing rules, as well as to verify the uniform implementation of these rules across the EU.[184]

In a regional system, an additional level of monitoring independent from national continuing oversight functions is useful to ensure the consistent implementation of the common regulatory framework. This is especially important if a regional system is based on the principle of recognition of certificates which requires trust between the Member States. A reliable, independent verification mechanism is a guarantor of this confidence.

EASA standardisation inspections and monitoring activities are mandatory.[185] This is an advantage over the previous JAA system of standardisation visits which a national authority could reject.[186] The mandatory nature of the EASA activities is justified because, while JAA was issuing only mutual recognition 'recommendations', in the EU the recognition is automatically granted by law as section §4.04[B] demonstrated.

In addition, while the JAA standardisation visits were organised by the aviation authorities themselves and could thus be considered more as 'peer reviews', the EASA process is independent from the NAAs.[187]

[2] Enforcement Competences of the European Commission

The EASA standardisation inspections and other monitoring activities are ancillary to the enforcement competences of the European Commission. Their purpose is to assist the Commission, as the *Guardian of the Treaties* in monitoring the application of the EASA Basic Regulation and its implementing rules.[188] They are also 'without prejudice to the enforcement powers conferred by the Treaty on the Commission.'[189]

Therefore when EASA identifies a serious non-compliance, it must report back to the European Commission, possibly with a recommendation to suspend recognition of

184. EU, 'Regulation (EU) No 628/2013 of 28 June 2013 on working methods of the European Aviation Safety Agency for conducting standardisation inspections and for monitoring the application of the rules of Regulation (EC) No 216/2008 of the European Parliament and of the Council and repealing Commission Regulation (EC) No 736/2006', (OJ L 179, 29.06.2013), Articles 1.1(a) and 3.1.
185. Regulation (EU) No 216/2008, *supra* note 81 in Ch. 2, Articles 24 and 54.
186. Francesco Banal, former EASA Quality and Standardisation Director, 'EASA Standardisation', in Aircraft Engineers International Conference, (Belgrade 2006).
187. *Ibid.*
188. Regulation (EU) No 216/2008, *supra* note 81 in Ch. 2, Article 54(1).
189. *Ibid.* The enforcement powers are vested into the European Commission through Article 258 of the TFEU.

certificates under Article 11 of EASA Basic Regulation.[190] In this respect the position of EASA is similar to the previous JAA which could only withdraw the mutual recognition recommendations, as was explained in section §3.04[B] of Chapter 3.

The European Commission is not obliged to act upon a recommendation of EASA.[191] The Commission may also initiate an infringement action directly against a Member State without a prior EASA recommendation using its enforcement competences under the EU Treaty.[192] This discretion of the European Commission stems from Article 11 of the EASA Basic Regulation, standardisation regulation,[193] and is confirmed by the jurisprudence of the CJEU.[194]

The fact that enforcement is dependent on the discretion of the European Commission could be subject to criticism. The very purpose of establishing an independent safety agency was to insulate technical decisions from political considerations and associated discretion. This is, however, an inevitable consequence of the initial decision to establish EASA as an EU agency, as launching infringement actions is a discretionary competence the delegation of which to EASA would be incompatible with the *Meroni* doctrine presented in section §4.02[D].[195]

By mid-2014, with the exception of safeguard measures adopted by the European Commission at the time of Bulgaria's accession to the EU in 2007,[196] there had been no cases of non-compliance with the EU safety requirements which necessitated an enforcement action by the European Commission under Article 11 of the EASA Basic Regulation.[197] Whether this is an indication of a system which functions well, or rather a symptom of the system's genuine inability to deal decisively with serious deficiencies could of course be a point for discussion.

On the one hand, the review of EASA annual reports indicates that between 20% - 34% of the overall number of standardisation findings can be classified as 'significant

190. In case of non-compliance or ineffective compliance, the European Commission shall require the issuer of a certificate to take appropriate corrective action and safeguard measures, such as limitation or suspension of the certificate. Moreover, the EU-wide recognition of the certificate ceases to apply from the date of the notification of the Commission's decision to the Member States. See: Regulation (EU) No 216/2008, *supra* note 81 in Ch. 2, Article 11(2).
191. See: Regulation (EU) No 216/2008, *supra* note 81 in Ch. 2, Article 11, which States that the Commission *may* initiate such procedure.
192. Infringement procedures are actions taken by the European Commission under Article 258 of the TFEU against a Member State which is in breach of EU law, and involve judicial control by the CJEU. Originally, they were intended to be the primary mechanism for enforcement of EU law. However since the development by the CJEU of the doctrines of direct effect and State liability which allow for enforcement of EU law by national courts, infringement procedures are only one element of the EU enforcement system. See in particular: 'Joint Cases C-6 and C-9/90, Francovich and Bonifaci v. Republic of Italy', in: [1991] ECR I-05375, (CJEU,1991).
193. Regulation (EU) No 628/2013, *supra* note 184.
194. This discretion of the Commission has been confirmed in the CJEU ruling: 'Case C-247/87, Star Fruit Company v. Commission', in: [1989] ECR I-291, (CJEU,1989), (p. 301). See also: 'Case T-571/93, Lefebvre and Others v. Commission ', in: [1995] ECR II-02379, (CJEU,1995), (p. 2403).
195. Regulation (EU) No 216/2008, *supra* note 81 in Ch. 2, Preamble clause 18 and Article 25.
196. EU, 'Commission Regulation (EC) No 1962/2006 of 21 December 2006 in application of Article 37 of the Act of Accession of Bulgaria to the European Union', (OJ L 408, 30.12.2006).
197. Official of the European Commission, 'Interview No 9', (2014).

deficiencies that may raise safety concerns if not duly corrected.'[198] It also seems that the main cause of such findings is 'insufficient availability of adequate inspecting staff, in terms of qualification and/or number',[199] which is an important observation given that one of the main advantages of regional systems is supposed to be enhancement of safety oversight capabilities of States.

On the other hand, looking at the actual safety record, it is clear that the EU system delivers a consistently low accident rate, although now stabilised following the significant reductions achieved in the first half of the previous decade.[200] Between 2003 and 2013, the average rate of scheduled passenger and cargo fatal accidents per 10 million flights, oscillated around two for the aircraft operators under responsibility of the States participating in the work of EASA.[201] This is one of the best safety records in the world.[202]

[3] *Interaction between EASA Standardisation and Monitoring Activities and ICAO USOAP-CMA*

While EASA monitoring activities are justified by the regional nature of the EU system, they are also an additional layer of oversight which requires resources. In 2012 the EASA standardisation department had in total 48 members of personnel,[203] and an operational budget of 635,000 EURO.[204] EASA also involves inspectors from EU Member States. In 2012, EU Member States provided 134 inspectors which constituted 50% of all EASA standardisation inspection team members.[205] The inspections also require preparation on the part of EU Member States and continuous monitoring and follow up of results by EASA and the European Commission.

In addition, EASA conducts inspections in non-EU European States on the basis of international agreements or working arrangements concluded by EU or EASA respectively. In 2012, EASA was involved in standardisation activities in 46 countries.[206]

Such an effort to a certain extent duplicates the ICAO USOAP-CMA monitoring activities, which apply equally to States which are subject to EASA standardisation activities. The EU could eliminate this overlap and realise efficiencies for ICAO and EU Member States by relying on the 2011 EU-ICAO Memorandum of Cooperation (hereinafter the 'EU-ICAO MoC') which provides for the possibility of coordinating the EASA

198. EASA, 'Annual General Reports for the years 2010-2013' http://easa.europa.eu/newsroom-and-events/general-publications [accessed 28 July 2014].
199. EASA, 'Annual General Report', (2012), http://easa.europa.eu/system/files/dfu/EASA-Annual_General_Report_2012.pdf [accessed 20 December 2013], at p. 31.
200. EASA Annual Safety Review (2013), *supra* note 2, at p. 27.
201. *Ibid.*, at p. 15.
202. *Ibid.*
203. EASA, 'Staff Policy Plan for the years 2014-2016: Annex I', EASA Management Board Decision 2/2013, (2013).
204. EASA, 'Amended Budget', EASA Management Board Decision 02/2012, (2012).
205. EASA Annual General Report (2012), *supra* note 199, at p. 31.
206. *Ibid.*, at p. 30.

standardisation inspections and the ICAO USOAP-CMA.[207] Paragraph 7 of the safety Annex to the EU-ICAO MoC States that:

> In order to verify compliance by EU Member States with ICAO safety-related Standards and adherence to ICAO Recommended Practices ... , the Parties shall establish a framework for conducting, as appropriate ... : ICAO oversight of the EU Standardisation Inspections conducted by EASA of the national competent authorities of EU Member States regarding safety-related SARPs that are addressed by EU legislation.[208]

Establishing such a link would allow ICAO to recognise the results produced by the EU system, at least in those areas where the EASA standardisation inspections and monitoring activities and those of USOAP-CMA are deemed to be equivalent. This could ultimately reduce the duplication of inspection and monitoring activities of EU Member States by ICAO, as is already the case in the area of aviation security.[209]

In 2014, ICAO and EASA signed a 'Working Arrangement on Continuous Monitoring Activities', to implement the provisions of the EU-ICAO MoC and its safety annex related to the coordination of the ICAO USOAP and EU standardisation inspections. It is expected that such coordination will be put into effective operation in the near future.[210]

One of the primary obstacles to realising efficiencies between ICAO USOAP and EASA standardisation remains the inadequate knowledge by EASA of the differences between EU regulations and ICAO Annexes as was demonstrated in section §4.04[A][2]. In addition, due to the split of responsibilities between EASA and the European Commission, ICAO would also probably need to monitor the latter, notably in view of the European Commission's legislative and enforcement competences which are related to CEs seven and eight under the ICAO safety oversight model which was presented in Chapter 2.

[4] Independent EASA Enforcement Actions

The only independent enforcement actions that EASA can take, *de lege lata*, is the possibility to suspend, revoke or amend a certificate that EASA granted to an organisation, operator or designer of an aeronautical product.[211] Such decisions can be subject to an appeal process, and include a judicial control by the CJEU.[212] Revoking or suspending a certificate is however an ultimate measure. Therefore if a more 'nuanced,

207. 'EU-ICAO MoC (2011)', *supra* note 159.
208. 'Decision of the EU-ICAO Joint Committee of 21 September 2011 on the adoption of an Annex on aviation safety to the Memorandum of Cooperation between the European Union and the International Civil Aviation Organization providing a framework for enhanced cooperation', (OJ L 172, 25.6.2013).
209. 'Memorandum of Cooperation between the International Civil Aviation Organisation and the European Community regarding security audits/inspections and related matters', 17 September 2008, (OJ L 36, 5.2.2009).
210. 'Interview No 4', (2014), *supra* note 41 in Ch. 2.
211. See for example: Regulation (EU) No 216/2008, *supra* note 81 in Ch. 2, Article 20.1(i).
212. *Ibid.*, Articles 40-51.

flexible and graduated response to a breach of the rules, is warranted',[213] the EU legislation provides the possibility of imposing financial penalties or periodic penalty payments on holders of certificates issued by EASA which have intentionally or negligently breached the provisions of EU law.[214]

Such penalties or payments are imposed not by EASA but by the European Commission upon the Agency's recommendation.[215] This is another consequence of EASA being an EU agency, because launching infringement actions is a discretionary competence, the delegation of which to EASA would contradict the *Meroni* doctrine. The fact that EASA cannot impose financial penalties is a key difference with a traditional set-up, where national authorities may have competences to fine operators or individuals for breaches of aviation legislation.[216]

By mid-2014, the European Commission had not used its competences to impose financial penalties or periodic penalty payments on EASA certificate holders.[217] It was therefore not possible to assess the effectiveness of this instrument.

§4.05 ASSOCIATION OF NON-EU EUROPEAN COUNTRIES WITH EASA

In addition to EU Member States, non-EU European countries can also participate in the work of EASA and be associated with the EU aviation safety system. The legal basis for this association is Article 66 of the EASA Basic Regulation, which provides that:

> The Agency shall be open to the participation of European third countries which are contracting parties to the Chicago Convention and which have entered into agreements with the European Community whereby they adopted and apply Community law in the field covered by this Regulation and its implementing rules.[218]

This Pan-European dimension of the EU aviation safety system is driven by two developments. The first one was the closure of the JAA in 2009, which necessitated offering ex-JAA non-EU countries 'an alternative forum to express interests regarding aviation safety matters.'[219] The second one is the European Neighbourhood Policy

---

213. *Ibid.*, Preamble clause 18.
214. EU, 'Commission Regulation (EU) No 646/2012 of 16 July 2012 laying down detailed rules on fines and periodic penalty payments pursuant to Regulation (EC) No 216/2008 of the European Parliament and of the Council', (OJ L 187, 17.7.2012).
215. *Ibid.*, Article 10.
216. For example in the US, the FAA has a competence to impose civil penalty payments for violations of aviation regulations under: Title 14 CFR, Part 13 'Investigative and Enforcement Procedures' ('Code of Federal Regulations', http://www.gpo.gov/fdsys/pkg/CFR-2014-title 14-vol1/pdf/CFR-2014-title14-vol1.pdf [accessed 29 March 2014].
217. 'Interview No 9', (2014), *supra* note 197.
218. Regulation (EU) No 216/2008, *supra* note 81 in Ch. 2, Article 66.
219. At the time of the dissolution of the JAA, there were fifteen non-EU European States whose aviation authorities were members or candidate members of the JAA. For more information about the transition from the JAA to EASA, see: JAA, 'FUJA II Working Group: Final Report (2008)' www.jaa.nl/fuja/fuja_report.html [accessed 28 March 2014].

(ENP)[220] and its aviation component – the Common Aviation Area – which is based on uniform conditions of doing business, including as regards aviation safety.[221]

The main precondition for associating a non-EU European country with the EU aviation safety system and EASA is the conclusion of an international agreement meeting conditions of Article 66 of EASA Basic Regulation. By mid-2014 the EU had signed five such agreements,[222] although none of them is limited solely to aviation safety: [223]

- Agreement on the European Economic Area;[224]
- Agreement between the European Community and the Swiss Confederation on Air Transport;[225]
- Multilateral Agreement between the European Community and its Member States, the Republic of Albania, Bosnia and Herzegovina, the Republic of Bulgaria, the Republic of Croatia, the former Yugoslav Republic of Macedonia, the Republic of Iceland, the Republic of Montenegro, the Kingdom of Norway, Romania, the Republic of Serbia and the United Nations Interim Administration Mission in Kosovo on the Establishment of a European Common Aviation Area (ECAA);[226]

220. The ENP was established in 2004 and is the EU's policy for promoting political association and economic integration with the sixteen neighbouring countries of the EU. For more information on the ENP see: EC, 'A new response to a changing Neighbourhood: Joint Communication by the High Representative of The Union For Foreign Affairs And Security Policy and the European Commission', COM (2011) 303, (Brussels, 2011).
221. Common Aviation Area aims at establishing a single aviation market comprising, in addition to the EU Member States, also the ENP countries. It is based on aviation agreements encompassing gradual market opening and regulatory convergence towards EU aviation legislation and regulations. For more information about the Common Aviation Area see: EC, 'The EU's External Aviation Policy: Addressing Future Challenges, Communication from the Commission to the European Parliament, the Council, the European Economic and Social Committee and the Committee of the Regions', COM(2012) 556, (Brussels, 2012).
222. In addition to 'Article 66' agreements the EU has signed, in the framework of the ENP, agreements with non-European countries which also extend, to various degrees, the EU aviation safety legislation but which do not create regulatory consequences under the EASA 'Basic Regulation' such as recognition of certificates or delegation of State safety functions to EASA. These are for example the agreements signed with Morocco, Jordan and Israel.
223. 'Article 66' agreements can be: (i) aviation specific agreements, (ii) more general and free-standing association agreements providing for the adoption and implementation by third countries of EU legislation, including in the area of aviation safety, or (iii) agreements specifically aimed at adopting and implementing existing EU legislation on aviation safety, concluded specifically to enable third countries to participate in the work of EASA. See: EC, 'Participation of European third countries in the work of the European Aviation Safety Agency, Commission Staff Working Paper', SEC(2002) 1090, (Brussels, 2002).
224. 'Agreement on the European Economic Area', 2 May 1992 (OJ L 1, 3.1.1994). Provides for integration of the EEA countries (Norway, Iceland and Liechtenstein), into the EU internal market, including the air transport market.
225. 'Agreement between the European Community and the Swiss Confederation on Air Transport', 21 June 1999, (OJ L 114, 30.4.2002). It is an aviation specific agreement providing for integration of the Swiss Confederation into the EU internal air transport market.
226. 'Multilateral Agreement between the European Community and its Member States, the Republic of Albania, Bosnia and Herzegovina, the Republic of Bulgaria, the Republic of Croatia, the former Yugoslav Republic of Macedonia, the Republic of Iceland, the Republic of Montenegro, the Kingdom of Norway, Romania, the Republic of Serbia and the United Nations Interim

- Common Aviation Area Agreement between the European Union and its Member States and Georgia;[227]
- Common Aviation Area Agreement between the European Union and its Member States and the Republic of Moldova.[228]

Under the above agreements the partner countries commit to implement the EU aviation safety legislation, and in exchange have the possibility of acquiring status equivalent to an EU Member State, including as regards recognition of certificates, participation in EASA rulemaking process and other technical initiatives, as well as delegation of safety certification functions to EASA. The main limitation of 'Article 66 agreements' is lack of the possibility of granting to non-EU countries voting rights in the EASA Management Board and regulatory committees which take legally binding decisions.[229]

[A] Implementation and Safety Benefits of 'Article 66 Agreements'

The evaluation of the implementation of the five 'Article 66 agreements' signed until mid-2014 reveals mixed results. The main problem is that most of these agreements take a long time to actually enter into force. Here a clear distinction must be made between 'Article 66 agreements' negotiated as *mixed*, which necessitate ratification by both the EU and its Members States, and *EU only* meaning that EU Member States are not parties to the agreement and do not need to ratify it.[230]

Only two out of five 'Article 66 agreements' actually entered into force by mid-2014, and both of them were negotiated as *EU only* agreements: the Agreement on the European Economic Area[231] which is not aviation specific, and the EU–Switzerland

Administration Mission in Kosovo on the establishment of a European Common Aviation Area', 9 June 2006, (OJ L 285, 16.10.2006). Signed with States candidates for EU membership and providing for their gradual integration into the single EU aviation market. The agreement also covers Norway and Iceland. Since the signature of the agreement a number of its contracting parties (Bulgaria, Romania, and Croatia) have become EU Member States.

227. 'EU-Georgia Common Aviation Area Agreement', *supra* note 142 in Ch. 3. This agreement provides for implementation by Georgia of EU aviation legislation and exchange of traffic rights between EU Member States and Georgia. The agreement does not provide for full integration of Georgia into the EU's common aviation market.
228. 'EU-Moldova Common Aviation Area Agreement', *supra* note 143 in Ch. 3. This agreement provides for implementation by the Republic of Moldova of EU aviation legislation and exchange of traffic rights between EU Member States and the Republic of Moldova. The agreement does not provide for full integration of the Republic of Moldova into the EU's common aviation market.
229. Any participation by a third party's representative in the decision-making process of an EU body must always respect the principle of EU decision-making autonomy. See: 'Opinion 1/76', *supra* note 21. Similarly: *Participation of European third countries in the work of EASA (SEC(2002) 1090), supra note 223, at p. 4.*
230. The legal justification for 'an EU only' agreement is that EU's competences cover the entire agreement. See: Piet Eeckhout, External Relations of the European Union: Legal and Constitutional Foundations, (2004), p. 191.
231. In force since 1 January 1994.

Air Transport Agreement.[232] It took on average two and a half years for these agreements to enter into force.[233]

The other agreements – with the Western Balkan States (ECAA), Republic of Georgia and Republic of Moldova – were signed as *mixed*, and in mid-2014 none of them was in force, or provisionally applied, due to either lack of sufficient number of ratifications by EU Member States, or lack of completion by the EU and its Member States of procedures necessary for enabling provisional application.[234] In mid-2014, the ECAA agreement was closest to entering into force, but only after over seven years following signature.[235]

The fact that an 'Article 66 agreement' is not in force, has a number of consequences. Firstly, it prevents a Joint Committee established under such agreement to update the list of EU legislation which the EU's partner country must apply.[236] A review of the five 'Article 66 agreements', including relevant Joint Committee decisions, shows that in the case of agreements which are not in force, the lists of EU aviation safety legislation are largely outdated.[237] Although this does not prevent the partner countries from implementing the latest EU aviation legislation on a voluntary basis, the present situation creates a lack of legal certainty and contributes to a patchwork of regulatory requirements.

The second consequence of an 'Article 66 agreement' not being in force or provisionally applied is that even if a partner country implements EU aviation safety legislation, its certificates continue to be treated as coming from a third country. This is because activation of the recognition of certificates requires a formal decision by the Joint Committee to be taken under the agreement. In 2014 only Norway, Switzerland, Iceland and Liechtenstein had a status equivalent to an EU Member State, and benefited from recognition of certificates.[238]

232. In force since 1 June 2002.
233. Based on the analysis of information available in: Council of the EU, 'International Agreements Database' http://www.consilium.europa.eu/policies/agreements?lang=en [accessed 28 March 2014].
234. *Ibid.*
235. *Ibid.*
236. In the case of the five 'Article 66' agreements such decisions were taken on regular basis only by the Joint Committees established under the EEA Agreement and the EU-Switzerland Air Transport Agreement. The Joint Committee established under the ECAA Agreement took only one such decision since the signature of the agreement. This analysis was conducted on the basis of information from: European External Action Service, 'Treaty Office Database' http://ec.europa.eu/world/agreements/default.home.do [accessed 30 March 2014].
237. International Agreements Database, *supra* note 233. In addition the author reviewed a registry of decisions of joint committees set up pursuant to an international agreement and comprising representatives of the signatories for the purpose of administering the agreement, at: EU, 'EUR-Lex, International Agreements' http://eur-lex.europa.eu/collection/eu-law/inter-agree.html [accessed 30 March 2014].
238. 'Decision No 1/2013 of the Joint European Union/Switzerland Air Transport Committee set up under the Agreement between the European Community and the Swiss Confederation on Air Transport of 2 December 2013 replacing the Annex to the Agreement between the European Community and the Swiss Confederation on Air Transport', 2 December 2013, (OJ L 12, 17.1.2014); 'Decision of the EEA Joint Committee No 179/2004 of 9 December 2004 amending Annex XIII (Transport) to the EEA Agreement', 9 December 2004, (OJ L 133, 26.5.2005).

It is also legally not possible to establish a relationship of international agency between the EU and the partner countries on the basis of an 'Article 66 agreement' which is not in force or at least provisionally applied. As was demonstrated in section §4.03[D], a country cannot delegate to EU the exercise of its safety functions on the basis of a working arrangement which is not binding under international law. In 2014, only the countries party to the EEA agreement and EU-Switzerland Air Transport agreement have effectively delegated to EU the exercise of safety tasks as envisaged under the EASA Basic Regulation.[239]

Last but not least, not all States parties to 'Article 66 agreements' are able to apply directly EU aviation safety legislation in their internal legal orders. In 2014, this has been the case only for Liechtenstein and Switzerland, which do not need implementing regulations to apply the EU aviation safety standards.[240] All other States which are parties to 'Article 66 agreements' do not consider such agreements as self-executing and need to enact national legislation to give effect to EU aviation safety regulations.[241]

§4.06 EASA AS A SINGLE AVIATION AUTHORITY FOR EUROPE: POLITICAL FICTION OR LONG-TERM VISION?

Although sometimes compared with the FAA, EASA is today still far from becoming a similar authority. Of course, the main difference between the US and EU is that while the former is a federal State, the latter is composed of 28 independent countries, each with its own airspace, interests, language and culture. EASA, which recently celebrated its tenth anniversary,[242] is also a young organisation if compared with the FAA, which in 2014 had its 56th birthday.[243]

Although some discussions have taken place in 2014 about the possibility of establishing a single European aviation (safety) agency, it does not seem that such a scenario would materialise soon.[244] A further discussion on this subject is however worthwhile especially in view of the mounting pressure on national and EU budgets, coupled with continuing demand for aviation transportation from the public, and increasing market competition from other regions of the world that Europe has to face.[245]

239. *Ibid.* Such delegation is possible when a partner country completes transitional periods under the relevant agreement. Successful transition is confirmed by a decision of the Joint Committee established under the agreement, and which also establishes the precise conditions for participation of the country in question in the work of EASA.
240. Official of the Swiss Civil Aviation Authority (FOCA), 'Interview No 3', (2014). For information about the transposition of EU law by the EEA States see: EFTA Surveillance Authority, 'Internal Market Scoreboard No 33', (2014), http://www.eftasurv.int/media/scoreboard/Scoreboard_No_33_pdf.PDF [accessed 30 March 2014], p. 22.
241. In the case of the former Yugoslav Republic of Macedonia (fYROM) and Kosovo such transposition can also take place by reference to a specific piece of EU law.
242. EASA 10th Anniversary Chronicle, *supra* note 4.
243. Theresa L. Kraus, The Federal Aviation Administration: A historical perspective, 1903-2008, (2008), p. 9.
244. This discussion has been undertaken in the framework of the EASA Management Board based on the report presented by the Finish Director General of Civil Aviation, Mr Pekka Hentu.
245. EASA 2013 Article 62 evaluation, *supra* note 29 in Ch. 3, at pp. 10-12.

In this respect, a comparison with the US is not entirely inappropriate. While in the US all aspects of aviation safety, interoperability, deployment of large infrastructure programmes like NextGen,[246] and even provision of ANS are under the responsibility of one body, the FAA, on the European side these issues are dealt with by multiple organisations which include the European Commission, EASA, NAAs, EUROCONTROL, ECAC, and various joint technology initiatives such as SESAR[247] or Clean Sky.[248]

A good illustration of the inefficiencies which this fragmentation creates is ATM, where the US system is capable of handling 70% more aircraft movements than in Europe at a total cost that is 23% lower.[249] Similarly, any significant aviation initiative in Europe requires elaborate coordination to ensure that the different organisations contribute to it in a coherent way, and have a common understanding of the objectives. This can be illustrated with the example of SESAR deployment, which requires involvement of multiple authorities and bodies at both the EU and national levels,[250] while in the US the responsibility for NextGen development and deployment rests largely with the FAA.[251]

This structural problem is well defined and recognised in Europe. The 2007 High Level Group for the Future European Aviation Regulatory Framework has already underlined that the current 'patchwork of responsibilities and regulatory structures' is a 'major bottleneck in improving the performance of the European aviation system.'[252]

Focusing on aviation safety, a recent evaluation of the EASA system concluded that 'there are too many actors in the System with different or overlapping responsibilities and roles', which makes it 'unsustainable in the medium to long term' and that therefore:

> The required processes to create a genuine European Aviation Safety System through the convergence of the various existing actors in the System towards a single entity responsible for all aviation safety regulation and oversight should be embarked upon.[253]

The following paragraphs will try to identify the legal and institutional enablers of such a change, and obstacles to implementation.

---

246. NextGen is a US project for the deployment of a Next Generation Air Transportation System in the national airspace. See: SESAR, 'Discover SESAR' http://www.sesarju.eu/discover-sesar [accessed 30 March 2014].
247. SESAR or Single European Sky ATM Research is the EU's equivalent of the US NextGen project.
248. Clean Sky is an EU aeronautical research programme which mission is to significantly increase the environmental performances of airplanes and air transport. See: Clean Sky, 'About Us' http://www.cleansky.eu/content/homepage/about-us [accessed 30 March 2014].
249. EC, 'Single European Sky 2 + , Cost and Flight efficiency' http://ec.europa.eu/transport/modes/air/single_european_sky/doc/ses2plus/cost-flight-efficiency.pdf [accessed 30 March 2014].
250. EC, 'Communication from the Commission: Governance and incentive mechanisms for the deployment of SESAR, the Single European Sky's technological pillar', COM(2011) 923 final, (Brussels, 2011).
251. United States Government Accountability Office, 'Report to Congressional Requesters on NextGen Air Transportation System', GAO-13-264, (2013).
252. 'Report of the High Level Group for the Future European Aviation Regulatory Framework: A framework for driving performance improvement', (2007), http://ec.europa.eu/transport/modes/air/doc/hlg_2007_07_03_report.pdf [accessed 2 February 2014], p. 7.
253. .EASA 2013 Article 62 evaluation, *supra* note 29 in Ch. 3, at p. 29.

[A] Milestones towards a European Aviation (Safety) Authority

Although slow, the process of establishing a single aviation safety entity for Europe has already started. The major milestone in this respect was the transition from the JAA to EASA, and the closure of the former in 2009. EASA also effectively took over from EUROCONTROL the development of ATM safety standards[254] and inspects national authorities' ATM oversight capabilities, as part of its standardisation programme.[255] In 2013, the European Commission proposed renaming EASA as the 'European Aviation Agency', which is a symbolic reflection of these changes.[256]

The next milestones that would need to be accomplished to realise the vision of 'a single entity responsible for all aviation safety regulation and oversight', would be a merger of EASA and EUROCONTROL, and a much closer integration between such a future European Aviation Authority (EAA) and the NAAs.

The main challenge for a potential EASA-EUROCONTROL merger is that these two organisations belong to different political and legal worlds. While EASA is a body governed by EU public law, EUROCONTROL is an intergovernmental organisation governed by public international law.[257] The membership of EUROCONTROL is also broader than EU,[258] and while 'Article 66 agreements' enable participation of non-EU States in the work of EASA, they cannot grant voting rights, which the partner countries enjoy in EUROCONTROL.[259] This absence of voting rights is difficult to accept for important aviation countries such as Turkey,[260] and underlines even more the need for efficient and prompt implementation of 'Article 66' agreements by the EU.

Concerning the relationship between EASA and the NAAs, the fact that EASA operates in an environment comprising multiple national States is not in itself an obstacle to transforming it into a single EU aviation safety authority. As the example of the ECCAA (see Chapter 3) showed, it is legally possible to create a single aviation authority spanning across multiple States, although of course the EU is not a small

254. EASA, 'Revised 4-year Rulemaking Programme 2014-2017', Annex I to EASA Executive Director's Decision No 2013/029/R, (2013), http://easa.europa.eu/document-library/rulemaking-programmes/revised-2014-2017-rulemaking-programme [accessed 6 August 2014], p. 5.
255. By mid-2014, all EUROCONTROL Member States with the exception of Ukraine and Turkey have accepted this competence of EASA, based on working arrangements signed with the Agency. See: EASA, 'Working Arrangements' http://easa.europa.eu/document-library/working-arrangements [accessed 6 August 2014].
256. COM(2013) 409 final, *supra* note 70.
257. For an overview of EUROCONTROL's legal status see: Pablo Mendes de Leon, 'The Relationship between Eurocontrol and the EC: Living Apart Together', IOLR, 4 (2008), pp. 305–320.
258. EUROCONTROL's membership consists of 40 States. Except for Estonia, which is planning to join EUROCONTROL in January 2015, all EU Member States are also EUROCONTROL's Member States. See: EUROCONTROL, 'Who we are' https://www.eurocontrol.int/articles/who-we-are [accessed 3 March 2014].
259. Non-EU States can at best enjoy observer status in EU committees and bodies such as the Single Sky Committee or the EASA Management Board. For details of the status given to non-EU States please consult the international agreements signed between the EU and such countries, as presented in section §4.05.
260. Aytaç Aras, 'European aviation safety regulatory framework and Turkey: A critical analysis', University of Turkish Aeronautical Association, Faculty of Business Working Papers (2011), pp. 13, 17.

community of Caribbean islands sharing common language and legal heritage - issues which from a practical point of view cannot be ignored.

The setting up of such a single authority would probably require transformation of the EASA Basic Regulation into a much more elaborate European Aviation (Safety) Act, which would need to go into much more detail concerning the relationship between the EAA and EU Member States and possibly also harmonising the national administrative procedures.[261] Under such a scheme the NAAs would become local offices, or outstations of EAA.

The main rationale for establishing EAA would be the pooling of the technical resources available at the EU and national levels, and deploying them in a way which would best correspond to the actual needs of the system. This would necessitate giving to the EAA the authority to close and open local offices-NAAs and to redistribute the workforce among them as necessary. The geographical scope of responsibility of such local offices-NAAs could span across multiple EU Member States, if justified by the volume of aviation activity. This structure would be similar to the FAA, which has a highly decentralised structure and operates with a nation-wide network of specialised local offices.[262]

Irrespective of the political will to actually put such a structure in place, and practical difficulties, such as language differences, transformation of EASA and EUROCONTROL into an EAA would also pose legal challenges. It is not clear whether the legal form of an EU agency and the limitations that it brings could actually hinder the effectiveness of the EAA. For example, given that EU agencies cannot impose penalties on individuals (see section §4.04[C][4]), the enforcement function in such a system could become difficult to manage.

From the perspective of the Chicago Convention, the setting up of such a system would require delegation by EU Member States of all safety functions and tasks to the EU, which would implement them through the EAA. This could have consequences such as, for example, the setting up of a multinational aircraft registry managed by EAA on behalf of EU Member States. As Chapter 6 will demonstrate, there are limitations in respect of such far reaching delegations stemming from the provisions of the Chicago Convention.

While the above scenario is an ambitious, long-term vision, there are intermediate steps which could make the current EU aviation safety system more resource-efficient in the short to mid-term. These include, for example, the extension of the possibility for EU Member States to delegate to EASA, on a voluntary basis, certification and oversight tasks, or to link, by means of the EASA Basic Regulation, the NAAs and EASA into a single EU aviation safety oversight network within which all the authorities could pool their resources and share the oversight work more flexibly.

261. In the past the JAA has been harmonising also the procedures of member authorities through the issuance of the Joint Implementation Procedures (JIPs).

262. This includes: nineteen Manufacturing Inspection District Offices (MIDOs), over eighty Flight Standards District Offices (FSDOs), ten aircraft certification offices (ACOs), twenty-two Certificate Management Offices (CMOs), five Aircraft Evaluation Groups (AEGs), and one aeronautical centre and one technical centre. See: FAA, 'Offices' http://www.faa.gov/about/office_org/ [accessed 12 March 2014].

§4.07 GENERAL CONCLUSIONS

In 2014, EASA was still the only example of an operational RASO which fully relies for its functioning on a supranational REIO. In this respect, the purpose of this chapter was to demonstrate how EASA contributes to the improvement of global aviation safety and to the objective of uniformity in civil aviation regulation and oversight, as set out by the Chicago Convention. In addition, this chapter verified what the limitations of EASA are in respect to the achievement of the above mentioned objectives.

While initially there has been an attempt to establish EASA in the form of an international organisation, EASA has been ultimately set up in the form of an EU agency, which means a body governed by EU public law.

The main benefit of EASA being an EU agency is the fact that it can take advantage of the EU's legally binding and directly applicable legal framework. This is an advantage compared with the previous legally non-binding JAA framework, which could not mandate any legislation and relied on voluntary compliance of participating authorities. The second benefit is that the EU law grants to EASA legal personality which is valid in domestic legal orders of all EU Member States – this is also an advantage over the previous JAA, which exercised a legal personality only as a foundation under the Dutch law.

Being an EU agency also brings certain limitations for EASA, the main one being that it cannot adopt acts of general application which would be of legislative nature. This, in practice, does not constitute a problem for the EU aviation safety system as a whole, because the EU Treaties allow delegation of more detailed, implementing rulemakings to the European Commission, which in turn relies on the technical advice of EASA. On the other hand EASA can adopt certain executive measures such as ADs, which are legally binding and of general applicability. In addition, although formally non-binding, certain other measures adopted by EASA such as CS or AMC, produce legal effects because they determine how people will act in practice.

This chapter also examined the position of EASA from the perspective of public international law in view of the fact that EASA has been authorised by EU legislation to implement, on behalf of the EU Member States, the provisions of the Chicago Convention and its Annexes. This authorisation concerns in particular the exercise of the 'functions and tasks of the State of design, manufacture or registry when related to design approval'. In order to reconcile the EU law with the theory of international agency, which presupposes that the principal and agent are separate legal persons under international law, this chapter explained that while EASA has separate legal personality under public EU law, from the international law perspective EASA must be treated as an organ of the EU. This means that, at the international level, it is the EU which exercises, through EASA, the competences which have been transferred to the European level by EU Member States. The practical benefit of this international agency relationship is that EASA has the powers to make decisions that are binding for EU Member States under the Chicago Convention.

The relationship of international agency which exists between EU, acting through EASA, and EU Member States has been recognised by ICAO under the USOAP, as well as by a number of non-EU States which have concluded international aviation safety agreements with the EU or working arrangements with EASA.

From the point of view of the Chicago Convention, the establishment of the relationship of an international agency has brought benefits for EU Member States, which now do not need to be audited under the USOAP in those areas where EASA acts on their behalf. Instead ICAO is now able to conduct just one audit of EASA and to subsequently link its results with the USAOP reports of each EU Member State. This provides an example of an interaction between a RASO and ICAO which constitutes an important building block of the GASON concept which was proposed in Chapter 2.

As far as rulemaking is concerned, the main benefit of the EU system is the fact that EU regulations are directly applicable and legally binding for all EU Member States. On the other hand, the fact that the EU system is based on directly applicable and binding regulations does not mean that all regulatory differences have been completely eliminated, as there are still some possibilities of exemptions.

In addition, the EU civil aviation safety system does not encompass all aviation activities, which means that EU Member States still need to maintain national rules - and the resources to maintain them - to the extent necessary to regulate activities falling outside the EU competence.

Finally a review of the EASA rulemaking proposals from the period 2010-2013 demonstrates that EASA does not systematically identify the differences between the rules that it proposes and the ICAO SARPs. This is potentially an obstacle to ICAO relying more closely on the EU oversight system for the purpose of monitoring EU Member State compliance with their obligations under the Chicago Convention. This discrepancy should be fully eliminated, as it is not in line with the GASON concept.

From the certification point of view, the EU created a multilateral regime for automatic recognition of certificates amongst all the EU Member States - which is a big benefit the EU system has to offer to the aviation industry. In addition, certain certification tasks are exercised centrally and in a legally binding manner by EASA where this has been found to be more efficient, or where the requirements of unity vis-à-vis third countries so justify. This is an advantage compared to the previous system of mutual recognition recommendations under the JAA.

Although this study was not able to identify clear evidence of cost efficiencies that the transfer of certification tasks had on authorities of EU Member States, the current system, and especially the single EASA certificate which is valid across the EU, is an obvious benefit for the industry, especially large aircraft manufacturers. This large scale, automatic recognition of certificates, the issuance of which is based on a uniform and legally binding legal framework is in line with the GASON concept.

When it comes to oversight, the key feature of the EU system are the standardisation inspections and other monitoring activities, which are of mandatory nature and are used to control, in an independent manner, the application by EU Member States of the EASA Basic Regulation and its implementing rules, as well as to verify the uniform implementation of these rules across the EU. This verification mechanism is important in view of the fact that the EU system is based on the principle of wide scale recognition of certificates which requires trust between all the EU Member States.

From the point of view of ICAO, but also the GASON concept proposed in Chapter 2, the EU system of standardisation inspections and monitoring activities offers an opportunity to optimise the monitoring of EU Member States' obligations under the USOAP and the Chicago Convention. This could ultimately reduce the duplication of inspection and monitoring activities of EU Member States by ICAO, as is already the case in the EU in the area of aviation security.

As far as enforcement is concerned, EASA, with the exception of withdrawing, suspending or limiting a certificate that it has issued, has so far not been granted by the EU legislator own enforcement competences, and can only recommend to the European Commission suspension of recognition of certificates in a given EU Member State, or recommend imposition of a fine or periodic penalty payment on a certificate holder. The fact that enforcement is dependent on the discretion of the European Commission could be subject to criticism, but the fact that the EU system consistently produces a good safety record, is an indication that overall the system works effectively.

The EU civil aviation safety system is Pan-European in scope. Up to mid-2014 the EU had signed five international agreements with non-EU European countries on the basis of which such countries can participate in the work of EASA and be part of the EU aviation safety system as per Article 66 of the EASA Basic Regulation. The analysis of these agreements shows that, as far as legal aspects are concerned, the safety benefits which they offer are the greatest when they are negotiated as *EU only*, which significantly speeds up their entry into force.

Although the EU partner countries can implement the EU legislation on a voluntary basis, the main benefits offered by the EU aviation safety system, such as uniform regulatory framework, automatic acceptance of certificates, and centralisation of certification tasks at the level of EASA, are possible only on the basis of an 'Article 66 agreement' which is in force or at least provisionally applied. The 'Article 66 agreements' are generally not able to provide for direct applicability of the EU aviation safety legislation, and the majority of the EU partner countries require implementing legislation to make the EU requirements part of their internal legal orders.

The EU should therefore consider making more use of 'Article 66 agreements' negotiated as *EU only*, similar to the one concluded with Switzerland or the EEA countries. In order to overcome the political reluctance of EU Member States towards *EU only* agreements, their scope could be limited to aviation safety matters, leaving commercial aspects and exchange of traffic rights to more comprehensive Common Aviation Area type agreements to be negotiated in parallel.[263]

Finally, this chapter considered the feasibility of merging EASA and EUROCONTROL into a single European Aviation Authority, or EAA. The main reason for establishing such an entity is the fact that the current architecture of the EU aviation safety system is not efficient enough and maybe even not sustainable in the long-term perspective, as some reports on the functioning of EASA argue. This is due to the fact that the system is institutionally fragmented and that there are too many actors

263. For an overview of the reasons why EU Member States prefer 'mixed' agreements see: Eeckhout, *supra* note 230, at p. 198.

involved. The inefficiencies in this respect have been well documented in the ATM sector but also affect other domains.

Whilst establishing a single entity in Europe responsible for aviation safety, or even all technical aspects of aviation regulation and oversight, would be a very challenging undertaking, this possibility should not be excluded in the long-term perspective. The main rationale for establishing such an authority would be the pooling of EU technical resources, and deploying them in a way which would best correspond to the actual needs of the system.

The major steps that would need to be considered in this respect are the merger of EASA and EUROCONTROL and transformation of EU NAAs into local offices of the new EAA. In addition, while legally feasible, the setting up of the new EAA would need to consider the impacts from the perspective of the Chicago Convention, and practical difficulties such as related to language differences. The legal form of an EU agency could also bring limitations for such a single authority, in particular as far as enforcement of aviation safety regulations is concerned.

Irrespective of the above challenges, intermediate steps could be taken to make the EU system more resource-efficient. This could be achieved for example by extending the possibility for EU Member States to delegate to EASA, on a voluntary basis, certification and oversight tasks, or to link the NAAs and EASA into a single EU aviation safety oversight network within which the authorities could pool their resources and share the oversight work more flexibly.

[illegible] ... [illegible] ... [illegible] ... [illegible] ... [illegible] ... [illegible] ... [illegible] ... [illegible] ... [illegible]

CHAPTER 5

The Functioning and Evolution of Regional Aviation Safety Organisations

To exist is to change, to change is to mature,
to mature is to go on creating oneself endlessly.

Henri L. Bergson (1859-1941)[1]

§5.01 INTRODUCTION[2]

Based on the analysis of different types of RASOs and the detailed case study of EASA presented in Chapters 3 and 4, this chapter will offer more general observations and conclusions on the extent to which the various functions of RASOs and the continuing evolution of these organisations contribute to the improvement of global aviation safety and achievement of the objectives of uniformity in regulations, procedures and operations in civil aviation.

More specifically, this chapter will first offer a classification of the different levels of delegation arrangements that States use when creating RASOs (section §5.02). It will then present, in a systematic way, the different types of safety functions that RASO bodies may exercise and propose a methodology for the setting up of RASOs using a 'tool-box' approach (section §5.03). It will also analyse key trends that can be observed around the world regarding the setting up and functioning of RASOs (section §5.04), and finally review the functioning of RASOs as international actors (section §5.05). Where relevant this chapter will also refer to pre-RASOs as defined in Chapter 3.

1. Henri L. Bergson was a French philosopher and 1927 Nobel Prize laureate in literature.
2. This Chapter is an expanded version of a paper that the author submitted to the 2011 ICAO Symposium on Regional Safety Oversight Organisations. See: Mikołaj Ratajczyk, 'Features and Evolution of Regional Safety Oversight Organisations: Comparative Analysis', ICAO Symposium on Regional Safety Oversight Organizations (Montréal, 2011), *supra* note 2 in Ch. 3.

§5.02 TYPOLOGY OF DELEGATION ARRANGEMENTS

Some of the RASOs, such as EASA or IAC have been empowered by their Member States to exercise, in a legally binding manner, certain safety functions, normally attributed to States by the Chicago Convention. Such delegation can be a powerful tool, allowing States to simplify exercise a safety function in a uniform manner across the whole region.

Delegating the exercise of State safety functions can be far reaching, and indeed, as was demonstrated in section §3.06 of Chapter 3, there is one example today, the ECCAA, where almost all safety functions have been delegated by Member States to a regional body, which has de facto and de lege become a single civil aviation authority for all of them. However, such far reaching delegations still remain exceptional.

In the same way, that there is no single template for establishing a RASO (see section §5.04[A]), the delegation of State safety functions does not follow a single model and can take place at many levels. The analysis of the different regional bodies shows that this applies both to: (1) the depth of delegation, and (2) legal methods of delegation.

As far as the depth of delegation is concerned, or the extent to which a given function is delegated to a RASO or pre-RASO, three levels of delegations can be identified:

(1) *Level 1 (Coordination level):* At the basic level, States may decide to delegate specific competences to individuals not employed by their national civil aviation authorities. Such authorisations then give the underlying authority to inspectors of a regional body to perform audits, inspections and other oversight or investigative work on behalf of the national authority which gave the authorisation. The authorisations given may entail the right to enter the premises of the regulated organisation and to review and inspect its documentation and facilities.

In such cases, although an inspector is employed by a RASO/pre-RASO, he or she will be working under the regulatory authority of the host State. This is for example the case with the AFCAC AFI-CIS, as was demonstrated under section §3.04[A][3] of Chapter 3, or some services provided by PASO[3] and COSCAP projects.[4]

Under this type of delegation, the beneficiary or host State continues to remain responsible for the issuance of certificates or other approvals on the basis of the technical work conducted by the inspectors of the regional body.

3. PASO inspectors, when carrying out their duties on behalf of a PASO Member State, are deemed to be officers of the civil aviation administration of that State, and have rights, privileges and responsibilities no less favourable than those granted to civil aviation officers of that State. See: 'PICASST', *supra* note 100 in Ch. 3, Article 8(2).

4. See for example: 'Model bilateral agreement between COSCAP South Asia and States for obtaining Services of Technical Experts from COSCAP South Asia to perform Safety Oversight functions', *supra* note 15 in Ch. 3.

Current State practice indicates that, in addition to envisaging the possibility of such delegation/authorisation in the RASO/pre-RASO founding document, enabling State legislation may be also necessary to give authorisations the necessary legal value in domestic legal orders of host States. For example under the AFI-CIS programme, the State receiving services of the regional inspectors will be obliged to issue them credentials in accordance with a national civil aviation act.[5]

(2) *Level 2 (Harmonisation level):* The next level, which goes beyond authorisation of individuals only, is a delegation to a RASO/pre-RASO, as an organisation, of the competence to perform specific technical work on behalf of its Member States or member authorities. In other words, this type of delegation means that a regional body will perform the *technical findings*, such as inspections, tests, examinations, on behalf of all or selected Member States/aviation authorities, and then submit the results, together with recommendations, for further legal action at the national level(s).

One of the most prominent examples of a regional body using this type of delegation has been the European JAA (see section §3.04[B] of Chapter 3), and its multinational aircraft type certification procedures.[6] Another example of this type of delegation is the process envisaged by the AAMAC States in Africa (see section §3.04[C][1] of Chapter 3) for the oversight of ANSPs, and in particular ASECNA.[7]

Under this option, States remain legally responsible under their national legislation for the issuance of a certificate or other type of approval. So whilst from a technical point of view, Level 2 delegations provide for efficiencies by virtue of centralisation of technical work, aviation organisations are still holders of multiple approvals and have to meet legal obligations towards multiple civil aviation authorities.

(3) *Level 3 (Unification level):* Finally States may want to delegate to a regional body both the conduct of the technical work, and responsibility for the issuance of the certificate/approval confirming that the applicable requirements have been met. Under this option efficiencies are potentially most significant, because it effectively results in centralisation of a given safety function at regional level. There is only one technical process and one

5. See Appendix 5 'Sample AFCAC AFI-CIS Inspector Credentials' to the AFI-CIS MoU, *supra* note 58 in Ch. 3, which provides that: 'The Director General of the *[host State]* Civil Aviation Authority hereby delegates, in accordance with *Article XX* of the Civil Aviation Act and paragraph 4 of the Memorandum of Understanding (MoU) signed between the *[host State]* and the African Civil Aviation Commission (AFCAC) on *[Date]*, to the holder of this credential ....'

6. JAA would conduct only one technical investigation to establish compliance of an aircraft design with the applicable certification basis. Upon completion of the work, JAA would submit technical recommendations to its member authorities which remained responsible for the issuance of a type certificate, and were also free to add additional technical requirements. For more details see section §3.04[B] of Chapter 3.

7. AAMAC is responsible for the 'conduct for the benefit of the Parties, of the technical tasks of certification and surveillance of ASECNA and other providers of air navigation services ... and to provide recommendations for the issuance and follow-up by the Parties of corresponding certificates.' See: 'AAMAC Treaty', *supra* note 81 in Ch. 3, Article 6(d).

approval issued at its end. From the perspective of the aviation industry this is a *one-stop-shop* for obtaining the approvals that they need to provide services on the market.

The most prominent example of a RASO using this type of delegation is EASA in Europe which was addressed in Chapter 4. In 2014 EASA was carrying out the functions and tasks of the State of design, manufacture or registry when related to design approval on behalf of 32 European States, including the competence to perform the technical investigations, as well as to issue type certificates and other aircraft design related approvals. As was demonstrated in the preceding chapter, EASA also has the competence to issue legally binding ADs, as well as to approve certain organisations both in the EU and non-EU countries. It conducts surveillance of approved organisations and can suspend or revoke certificates if their holders are no longer complying with the applicable legislation. Another organisation with similar competences is the IAC (see section §3.04[C][3] of Chapter 3).

ECCAA is a specific case of a regional body which combines Level 1 and 3 delegations. This is because, although it is a RASO, it is fully empowered to perform the functions of national civil aviation authorities of all its Member States. This is reflected in the civil aviation legislations of ECCAA Member States, which essentially treat it as a national authority and grant to its inspectors the authorisations and powers as if they were national inspectors of each of the States concerned. The main difference between ECCAA and organisations like EASA or IAC is therefore not the *depth* of the delegation but its *breadth* which will be addressed in subsequent paragraphs – while EASA and IAC carry out only *certain* safety functions on behalf of their Member States, ECCAA carries out almost all of these functions, thus effectively becoming a civil aviation authority for all its Member States.

Level 3 delegations currently remain the most important criteria distinguishing the different types of RASOs, as in the internal legal orders of the Member States they shift responsibility for the issuance of certificate / approval or conduct of accident investigation from national to regional level. At the same time, it is important to underline, as will be demonstrated in Chapter 6, that from the perspective of the Chicago Convention, States remain ultimately responsible for the carrying out of these safety functions even when Level 3 delegations are used.

The majority of the RASOs from the core sample selected for the purpose of this study enjoy Level 1 or 2 delegations and provide mainly advisory and support services to their Member States not resulting in binding legal effects. In 2014, there were only four organisations with delegation actually granted at Level 3 (EASA, IAC and ECCAA, ASSA-AC). In addition, two organisations had the necessary mandate to agree Level 3 delegations with their Member States on a bilateral basis (BAGASO and BAGAIA).

Both the type of a safety function to be delegated and local circumstances have to be taken into account when taking a decision about the level of delegation to be used. For example, while centralisation of aircraft certification may make perfect sense for regions with aeronautical production activities, it may make little sense for small States with limited aeronautical activity. Some functions, such as pilot licensing, may be, because of their local nature, better suited to remain at the national level, unless a single regional aviation authority, such as the ECCAA, is envisaged. In such cases, the establishment of RASO local offices may be a good solution to ensure the proximity of the service to the applicants. Alternatively, a regional body may be empowered to outsource some of the technical work back to the national authorities, especially for smaller projects, where local proximity and language issues may play a role.[8] Table 5.1 gives an overview of the levels of delegation used by some of the RASOs studied.

As far as the method of the delegation is concerned, States use various legal tools and combinations thereof. For Level 3 delegations a legally binding international agreement or an equivalent supranational regulation is needed, as it entails the shift of legal responsibility from national to regional level, and in the case of a safety function provided for by the Chicago Convention also results in a relationship of international agency as was explained in section §4.03[B] of Chapter 4. All Level 3 RASOs that were in operation in 2014 were based on such legally binding agreements or regulations. This means that in order to use Level 3 delegation a RASO will have to be set up as either an International Regional Aviation Safety Organisation (RASO Type I) or Supranational Aviation Safety Agency (RASO Type II), from the perspective of the typology proposed in Chapter 3.

With the exception of EASA in the EU, whose founding regulation is part of the domestic legal orders of the EU Member States, there may also be a need for implementing national legislation to make the Level 3 delegation effective (ECCAA, IAC).[9]

Table 5.1 Level of Delegation of State Safety Functions to Selected RASOs

RASO	Level of Delegation
Eastern Caribbean Civil Aviation Authority	Level 3 and Level 1 (acting as unique authority for all the Member States
European Aviation Safety Agency	Level 3
Interstate Aviation Committee	Level 3 (on the basis of a bilateral arrangement)
Banjul Accord Group Aviation Safety Oversight Organisation	Level 2 (Level 3 on the basis of a bilateral arrangement)
Banjul Accord Group Accident Investigation Agency	Level 2 (Level 3 on the basis of a bilateral arrangement)

8. In the EU, the EASA is entitled, through a tendering process, to outsource the technical work it is doing to national aviation authorities or 'qualified entities' (essentially commercial entities), if they meet specific safety and quality criteria which is confirmed through an accreditation process. In such cases the EASA continues however to be responsible for the issuance of the certificate / approval. See: EASA, 'Guidelines for the allocation of certification tasks to National Aviation Authorities and Qualified Entities', (Decision of the EASA Management Board No 01-2011).
9. Non-EU European countries which participate in the work of EASA on the basis of Article 66 agreements may also need to enact implementing legislation (see section §4.05 of Chapter 4).

RASO	Level of Delegation
East African Community Civil Aviation Safety and Security Oversight Agency	Level 2
Civil Aviation Authorities of Africa and Madagascar	Level 2
Pacific Aviation Safety Office	Level 1 or Level 2

Some RASOs, such as IAC, BAGAIA and BAGASO, have their Level 3 delegations made conditional upon conclusion of additional bilateral agreements. This may result in a patchwork of delegations, making it much more difficult to achieve a homogenous regional system. States may also establish specific conditions under which Level 3 delegation would take place,[10] or give States the possibility of *opting into* a Level 3 delegation if they consider it useful for them.[11]

For Level 2 delegations, a legally binding legal framework can be used as well, but is not absolutely necessary. This means that a Pre-RASO Type II will be sufficient to enable this type of delegation. The JAA for example was based on a non-binding multilateral arrangement concluded at the authority level, but nevertheless managed to successfully conduct its technical work for many years. The weak point of this solution is lack of a legal obligation on the part of Member States to recognise the validity of the recommendations and findings made by the regional body. The States also need to continue to issue multiple certificates, even if the technical work is centralised. In the EU these drawbacks were important reasons behind the establishment of EASA and dissolution of the JAA, as was explained in Chapter 4. International agreement, on the other hand, although providing for delegation of technical work only, may oblige States to give uniform legal value to the work of a RASO and from this perspective is a better solution to ensure uniformity, as is the case for instance under the AAMAC Treaty, which was addressed under section §3.04[C][1] of Chapter 3.

Finally, in the case of Level 1 delegations, that is authorisations of individual inspectors, a combination of a RASO/pre-RASO founding document and national legislation will be necessary. The founding document does not necessarily have to be a binding international agreement, as is the case with the AFCAC AFI-CIS MoU, but there is nothing which prevents States from using this type of instrument, especially if functions other than sharing of inspectors are envisaged as well, as is the case for instance with PASO. The use of national law will also be necessary, because otherwise

10. In the EU, the ANSPs are, par default, under the regulatory responsibility of the national authorities. However, under EU law, in case of organisations providing such services on a pan-European basis, the competent authority is EASA. See: Regulation (EU) No 216/2008, *supra* note 81 in Ch. 2, Article 22a(c).
11. In the EU production organisations are, par default, under the responsibility of national authorities. However this responsibility may be transferred to EASA on a voluntary basis. This has been the case with the Airbus company which is a multinational consortium involving France, Germany, United Kingdom and Spain. In this case, the States concerned requested EASA to take over the regulatory competence. As a result, a single production organisation approval has been issued by EASA and covers all facilities of Airbus located in the EU and also abroad, such as in China.

the authorisations of the regional inspectors performing tasks for the national authority will not be valid in the national legal systems.

In addition to the *depth* and the *method* of delegation, the *breadth* of the delegation can also be distinguished. This can be looked at from two perspectives: (1) the *subject matter* of the delegation, and the (2) *type of the function*:

(1) Concerning the *subject matter*, States need to decide in which domains of civil aviation they intend to empower the regional body. This means domains such as airworthiness, flight operations, personnel licensing, aerodromes, ATM, accident investigation, or even aviation security. The level of delegations, that is 1, 2 or 3, does not necessarily have to be the same for each of the domains. Also, the competence of the regional body may be extended over time, as was the case for example with EASA.

(2) As far as the *type of the function* is concerned, the crucial observation that emerges from the analysis of the available material is that none of the fourteen organisations from the core sample enjoy legislative functions. This shows that States essentially treat RASOs as technical agencies implementing and enforcing the law but not creating it. This is an approach different from that under traditional national set-ups, where aviation authorities may have a competence to enact legally binding rules of general application.[12] Even EASA in the EU, or ECCAA in the Pacific, does not enjoy legislative competences. The lack of legislative competences of RASOs also stems from the fact that States, as a matter of principle, rarely vest international organisations with competence to adopt decisions or regulations which are legally binding for individuals.[13] In those limited cases where they do delegate legislative competences, such as in the EU, this is done within the framework of a REIO with appropriate checks and balances put in place, such as a regional parliament and judicial control of the RASO decisions, if Level 3 delegations have been used. In the case of EASA in the EU and ECCAA in the OECS – that is RASOs which operate within a framework of supranational organisations with legislative powers – the technical proposals developed by these RASOs have first to be submitted to supranational legislators, that is the European Commission, Council and European Parliament in the EU, and the OECS Authority and Assembly in the OECS, for adoption.[14]

12. This is the case for example in the US where the FAA Administrator has an authority to issue regulations. See: 49 USC, Subtitle I, paragraph 106 at: US House of Representatives, 'US Code' http://uscode.house.gov/browse.xhtml [accessed 3 April 2014].
13. Schermers and Blokker, *supra* note 72 in Ch. 4, at pp. 831-832.
14. When in the mid-1990s the EU debated the possibility of establishing EASA on the basis of a self-standing international treaty, some of the EU Member States argued that direct applicability of rules adopted outside the EU framework would require a change of their constitutions and possibly also a referendum. As a result the idea of setting up EASA in the form of an international organisation with legislative powers was abandoned (see section §4.02[B] of Chapter 4).

In the case of RSOOs, when executive competences are transferred, such as the power to deliver certificates, States should ensure the possibility of independent judicial review of RSOO decisions. The applicants, in case they have been denied rights, should have the possibility of challenging the decision, similarly to the rights that they would enjoy under a traditional national system.[15]

Finally, regardless of the level, method or breadth of the delegation, the fundamental issue that must be ensured by States when setting up a RASO/pre-RASO, is to clearly delineate the boundaries of responsibility between the regional body and the national authorities. There should be no overlap of competences or regulatory loopholes, as this can result in unintended consequences or even non-compliances with the international safety requirements of ICAO, as will be demonstrated under section §5.04[E] below.

§5.03 THE FUNCTIONS OF RASOs: SETTING UP A RASO USING A 'TOOL BOX' APPROACH

The purpose of this section is to present, using practical experience of various RASOs/pre-RASOs,[16] concrete examples of the safety functions or tasks that these organisations can perform to the benefit of States and the aviation industry.

The information in this section has been structured along the ICAO eight CEs of State safety oversight, which is an internationally recognised method for discussing safety oversight in civil aviation. It should however not be considered as an exhaustive list of all regional safety functions but as an illustration based on selected examples.

Where relevant, the different types of potential RASO/pre-RASO functions are presented taking into account the three levels of delegation as proposed in the preceding section. Attention is also drawn to the specific points which should be given particular consideration from a legal and organisational point of view, and which are based on experience from real life implementation.

The intention of this section is to serve as a 'tool-box', which together with the typology of RASOs/pre-RASOs proposed in Chapter 3, the three levels of delegations developed under the preceding section, and the already existing ICAO RSOO and RAIO manuals could be used by States for setting up RASO/pre-RASO type bodies. In this respect, as pointed out by ICAO:

15. In the EU the decisions of EASA, if challenged, are reviewed first by an internal appeal body within the Agency, and then if needed also by the CJEU (See: Regulation (EU) No 216/2008, *supra* note 81 in Ch. 2, Articles 44-51). In the OECS, the decisions of ECCAA can be subject to an appeal in front of the Eastern Caribbean Supreme Court (see: 'Civil Aviation Act of Grenada', *supra* note 286 in Ch. 3, at section 39; 'Civil Aviation Regulations of Grenada', *supra* note 286 in Ch. 3, at section 92).
16. This section is primarily based on the analysis of material from three RASO conferences, two of which the author attended as a speaker: ICAO RSOO Symposium (2011), *supra* note 2 in Ch. 3; ICAO/AFCAC/EASA, 'Symposium on regional civil aviation agencies', (Livingstone, Zambia, 2009); ACAC/ICAO, 'Seminar/Workshop on Regional Safety Oversight Programmes', (Rabat, Morocco, 2012).

> It is important that States wishing to establish an RSOO commit themselves, at the very beginning of the process, to a strategy that is well defined in terms of the intended purpose and objectives of the organization they wish to establish. The strategy should therefore include a comprehensive analysis of the needs of the States involved.[17]

The table below should help States when making such a determination, by providing them with a *menu* of potential options from which they could choose, taking into account that they should normally focus on 'those activities that demonstrate a higher impact on regional safety oversight and contribute towards developing an effective aviation safety oversight framework.'[18] Such determination will necessarily involve taking into account the local circumstances and specific needs of both States and the industry.

<table>
<tr><td colspan="2">CE-1. Primary aviation legislation</td></tr>
<tr><td colspan="2">The provision of a comprehensive and effective aviation law consistent with the environment and complexity of the State's aviation activity and compliant with the requirements contained in the Convention on International Civil Aviation.</td></tr>
<tr><td>Possible types of regional safety functions:</td><td>Points of attention:</td></tr>
<tr><td>Level 1/Level 2:
Harmonised aviation legislation: RASO/pre-RASO develops generic legislation for submission to States for adoption / transposition (e.g., BAGASOO, COSCAPs, SRVSOP, CASSOA and JAA);</td><td rowspan="2">- Possibility of filing differences erodes the uniformity of the regulatory framework and should be avoided.
- Uniform regulatory framework is a prerequisite for enabling region-wide recognition of certificates.
- RASO/pre-RASO should centrally track amendments to SARPs, in order to keep the regional regulations ICAO compliant.
- RASO/pre-RASO should centrally identify eventual differences with SARPs and help States to notify ICAO in a uniform manner.</td></tr>
<tr><td>Level 3:
Common aviation legislation: Regulations can be adopted through a supranational regional mechanism (e.g. REIO) and be directly binding in a uniform manner in all the participating States (e.g. EU/EASA);</td></tr>
</table>

17. ICAO Doc. 9734 Part B, *supra* note 3 in Ch. 1, at paragraph 2.2.1.
18. *Ibid.*, at paragraph 2.2.3.

<table>
<tr><td colspan="2">CE-2. Specific operating regulations</td></tr>
<tr><td colspan="2">The provision of adequate regulations to address, at a minimum, national requirements emanating from the primary aviation legislation and providing for standardized operational procedures, equipment and infrastructures (including safety management and training systems), in conformance with the SARPs contained in the Annexes to the Convention on International Civil Aviation.</td></tr>
<tr><td>Possible types of regional safety functions:</td><td>Points of attention:</td></tr>
<tr><td><u>Level 1/Level 2:</u>
Harmonised operating regulations: RASO/pre-RASO develops generic regulations for submission to States for adoption / transposition (e.g., BAGASOO, COSCAPs, SRVSOP, CASSOA and JAA);</td><td rowspan="2">- Possibility of filing differences erodes the uniformity of the regulatory the framework and should be avoided.
- Uniform regulatory framework is a prerequisite for enabling region-wide recognition of certificates.
- RASO/pre-RASO should centrally track amendments to SARPs, in order to keep the regional regulations ICAO compliant.
- RASO/pre-RASO should centrally identify eventual differences with SARPs and help States to notify ICAO in a uniform manner.
- A system of 'hierarchy of texts' should be considered to enable operating regulations to be amended more easily than primary legislation.</td></tr>
<tr><td><u>Level 3:</u>
Common operating regulations: Operating regulations can be adopted through a supra-national regional mechanism and be directly binding in a uniform manner in all the participating States (e.g., EU/EASA);</td></tr>
</table>

<table>
<tr><td colspan="2">CE-3. State civil aviation system and safety oversight functions</td></tr>
<tr><td colspan="2">The establishment of a Civil Aviation Authority and/or other relevant authorities or government agencies, headed by a Chief Executive Officer, supported by the appropriate and adequate technical and non-technical staff and provided with adequate financial resources. The State authority must have stated safety regulatory functions, objectives and safety policies.</td></tr>
<tr><td>Possible types of regional safety functions:</td><td>Points of attention:</td></tr>
<tr><td>- Development of a regional safety programme/plan (e.g., EASA);
- Setting up regional aviation safety teams in partnership with industry (e.g., EASA, COSCAPs);</td><td>- Separation, at least at the functional level, of safety oversight and accident investigation functions, and service provision from regulatory functions;</td></tr>
</table>

- Assisting States in preparation for USOAP audits and addressing follow up actions (e.g., BAGASOO, COSCAPs, SRVSOP, PASO); - Setting up common examination systems (e.g., CASSOA); - Setting up a regional centre for aviation medicine (e.g., CASSOA); - Setting up a regional system for collection and analysis of safety information (e.g., EASA); - Coordinating replies to ICAO State Letters (e.g., EASA, BAGASOO);	- Need to take into account the interdependencies between ICAO State safety functions when transferring the exercise of some of them to the regional level (see section §5.04[E] below for illustration); - States remain ultimately responsible under the Chicago Convention for safety oversight (see Chapter 6);

CE-4. Technical personnel qualifications and training	
The establishment of minimum knowledge and experience requirements for the technical personnel performing safety oversight functions and the provision of appropriate training to maintain and enhance their competence at the desired level. The training should include initial and recurrent (periodic) training.	
Possible types of regional safety functions:	Points of attention:
- Joint use and sharing of training facilities (e.g., BAGASOO); - Establishment of a regional inspector training programme and training criteria for inspectors (e.g. BAGASOO, SRVSOP, ACSA, COSCAP); - Common training database and training planning and recording system (e.g. BAGASOO, SRVSOP);	- Common inspector training and qualifications should be a prerequisite for setting up a regional inspector sharing scheme, or joint surveillance initiatives such as ramp inspection programmes (e.g. SAFA in the EU);

CE-5. Technical guidance, tools and provision of safety-critical information
The provision of technical guidance (including processes and procedures), tools (including facilities and equipment) and safety-critical information, as applicable, to the technical personnel to enable them to perform their safety oversight functions in accordance with established requirements and in a standardized manner. In addition, this includes the provision of technical guidance by the oversight authority to the aviation industry on the implementation of applicable regulations and instructions.

Possible types of regional safety functions:	Points of attention:
- Production of harmonised guidance material, handbooks and checklists for safety inspectors (e.g. EASA, SRVSOP, COSCAP, CASSOA); - Setting up regional aviation databases of aircraft, AOC holders, approved maintenance or training organisations (e.g., BAGASOO);	- Harmonised guidance material is important to standardise implementation, which in turn may be a pre-requisite for enabling region-wide recognition of certificates

<table>
<tr><td colspan="2">CE-6. Licensing, certification, authorization and/or approval obligations</td></tr>
<tr><td colspan="2">The implementation of processes and procedures to ensure that personnel and organizations performing an aviation activity meet the established requirements before they are allowed to exercise the privileges of a licence, certificate, authorization and/or approval to conduct the relevant aviation activity.</td></tr>
<tr><td>Possible types of regional safety functions:</td><td>Points of attention:</td></tr>
<tr><td><u>Level 1:</u>
- Regional inspector sharing schemes (e.g., AFI-CIS, COSCAPs);</td><td rowspan="3">States need to pay attention to the legal status of the RASO/pre-RASO inspectors, which may also be coming from a national aviation authority, during the conduct of safety oversight activity in a Member State . Typical issues to be addressed are: legal authority, credentials and the liability protection of the inspectors.</td></tr>
<tr><td><u>Level 2:</u>
- Perform technical tasks of certification on behalf of pre-RASO/RASO States (e.g., JAA, AAMAC, SRV-SOP);
- Provide certification/surveillance assistance and advice to RASO/pre-RASO States (e.g., PASO, COS-CAPs);</td></tr>
<tr><td><u>Level 3:</u>
- In addition to performing the technical tasks of certification/licensing, RASO can also be authorised to issue the approvals/certificates on behalf of RASO States (e.g., EASA, IAC);
- States can delegate to a RASO all their safety oversight functions, effectively creating a regional civil aviation authority (e.g., ECCAA);</td></tr>
</table>

<table>
<tr><td colspan="2">CE-7. Surveillance obligations</td></tr>
<tr><td colspan="2">The implementation of processes, such as inspections and audits, to proactively ensure that aviation licence, certificate, authorization and/or approval holders continue to meet the established requirements and function at the level of competency and safety required by the State to undertake an aviation-related activity for which they have been licensed, certified, authorized and/or approved to perform. This includes the surveillance of designated personnel who perform safety oversight functions on behalf of the CAA.</td></tr>
<tr><td>Possible types of regional safety functions:</td><td>Points of attention:</td></tr>
<tr><td><u>Level 1:</u>
Regional inspector sharing schemes (e.g., AFI-CIS, COSCAPs);</td><td rowspan="3">States need to pay attention to the legal status of the RASO/pre-RASO inspectors, which may also be coming from a national aviation authority, during the conduct of safety oversight activity in a Member State. Typical issues to be addressed are: legal authority, credentials and the liability protection of the inspectors.</td></tr>
<tr><td><u>Level 2:</u>
- Perform technical surveillance tasks on behalf of RASO/pre-RASO States (e.g., JAA, AAMAC, SRV-SOP);
- Provide safety oversight advice to RASO/pre-RASO States (e.g., PASO, COSCAPs);
- Setting up regional ramp inspection programmes (e.g., EASA, SRVSOP);
- Development of regional safety oversight support tools/software (e.g., EASA, SRVSOP, ACSA);</td></tr>
<tr><td><u>Level 3:</u>
- In addition to performing the technical surveillance tasks, RASO can also be authorised to issue the approvals/certificates on behalf of RASO States (e.g., EASA, IAC);
- States can delegate to a RASO all their safety oversight functions, effectively creating a regional civil aviation authority (e.g., ECCAA)</td></tr>
</table>

<table>
<tr><td colspan="2">CE-8. Resolution of safety concerns</td></tr>
<tr><td colspan="2">The implementation of processes and procedures to resolve identified deficiencies impacting aviation safety, which may have been residing in the aviation system and have been detected by the regulatory authority or other appropriate bodies.</td></tr>
<tr><td>Possible types of regional safety functions:</td><td>Points of attention:</td></tr>
</table>

Level 1/Level 2: - Advise and make recommendations to States on actions to be taken in the event that a license or certificate holder fails to correct deficiencies within specified deadlines (e.g., COSCAP, PASO);	In the absence of a harmonised or common regulatory framework RASO/pre-RASO inspectors may need to be familiar with the enforcement procedures and means of each of the Member States.
Level 3: - States may want to delegate to a RASO the authority to take enforcement action. This will be necessary in particular where a RASO is empowered to take legally binding certification decisions (e.g., EASA, IAC); - The RASO may also rely on the enforcement competences already vested in a supranational regional organisation (e.g., EASA/EU); - Where States set up a regional civil aviation authority, the RASO will take over enforcement competences normally exercised by the national authorities (e.g., ECCAA);	

§5.04 MAIN TRENDS IN RASOs FUNCTIONING AND EVOLUTION

[A] There Is No 'One Size Fits All' Approach to RASOs Establishment

The first conclusion that can be reached as regards the overall trends in the establishment of regional aviation safety bodies is that there is no single template that States use in this respect. Although RASOs/pre-RASOs can be classified into certain general types as proposed in Chapter 3, overall the legal and organisational frameworks of these organisations are far from being uniform.

This diversity results in the first place from the fact that the needs of States differ in terms of strengthening their safety oversight and accident investigation capabilities, as well as providing efficiencies for the industry. As a result, the RASO/pre-RASO has to be tailored to the circumstances of a particular situation. For example, if there is little aeronautical manufacturing industry in a region, it may make little sense for the States to use their limited resources on establishing an expensive type-certifying agency, and instead to focus on a RSOO which would help them in the oversight of airlines and AMOs.

The solutions chosen by States when setting up a RASO/pre-RASO do not depend on safety considerations alone. Regulating aviation can be a highly political issue, as it is often associated with national sovereignty and strategic interests.[19] So although from a purely technical point of view a solution calling for a safety agency with legal personality and strong executive powers could have a lot of advantages, this may not

19. Erwin von den Steinen, National interest and international aviation, (2006), pp. 1-25.

always be possible because of lack of political will. This reluctance of States to delegate the exercise of competences to an external body is an issue which is brought up quite often by RASOs as an example of practical problems they experience – the 2011 ICAO symposium on RSOOs identified the 'presence of strong sovereignty issues that could impede regional cooperation' as one of the obstacles to RSOO establishment.[20] As a result, where a RASO has a mandate to act on behalf of its Member States, in the majority of cases today this is dependent on an additional bilateral arrangement (BAGASOO, BAGAIA, or IAC). Only EASA and the ECCAA have general mandates to act on behalf of their Member States.

RASOs or regional civil aviation safety cooperation schemes more generally also have a clear tendency to evolve over time, as section §5.04[B] below will demonstrate. Thus an organisation which today has legal personality and exercises safety related competences on behalf of Member States, yesterday could have been only an informal network of civil aviation safety regulators. This evolution has to be taken into account when comparing different organisations at a given moment in time.

Most of the RASOs which were reviewed for the purpose of this study deal only with aviation safety issues. However some of them, in addition to aviation safety, also deal with aviation security, as is the case for instance with PASO, ECCAA and CASSOA.

Finally, so far RASOs have not replaced the national authorities but supplement them. In 2014, there was only one example of a RCAA common for all its Member States, namely the ECCAA.

[B] RASOs Tend to Evolve into 'Institutionalised' Structures

The concept of a regional aviation safety body is not new, with JAA dating back to the 1970s or IAC to 1991. However, the last twelve years can be seen as real boom years for these organisations, especially on the African continent where five of them have been established between 2008 and 2014 (BAGASOO and BAGAIA in 2009, CASSOA in 2007/2008, AAMAC in 2009, and ASSA-AC in 2012).

Overall, nine organisations have been established in the last twelve years (2003-2014), as Table 5.2 demonstrates. Even taking into account that some of them evolved from other organisations, this still means that six were established after 2004 (ENCASIA, BAGASOO, BAGAIA, CASSOA, PASO, and ASSA-AC). Overall RASOs/pre-RASOs in existence today are therefore still relatively young organisations.

In addition, in 2014 a number of additional RASO type bodies were planned by States and ICAO. In particular, six additional RASOs – two RSOOs and four RAIOs – were planned for the African region,[21] and at least one RSOO and one RAIO were being considered for the States of the ACAC.[22] There were also discussions about a RAIO for Latin America.[23]

20. Outcomes of 2011 RSOO Symposium (C-WP/13810), *supra* note 4 in Ch. 1, at paragraph 2.3.1.
21. AFI Plan Steering Committee Report, AFI SC/2013/12, *supra* note 3 in Ch. 2, at Appendix B.
22. ACAC/ICAO seminar on regional safety oversight programmes (2012), *supra* note 16, at 'Summary of Conclusions'.
23. A38-WP/232, *supra* note 235 in Ch. 3.

Although the institutional frameworks and legal basis of RASOs/pre-RASOs are very varied, it is clear that there is a strong tendency for these organisations to evolve over time into more formal entities. This is especially true for the young organisations. Of the nine RASOs/pre-RASOs established since 2003, six have already undergone an evolution from a less formal into a more formal structure (Table 5.2).

Some of these organisations, such as CASSOA, are considering further evolution in the future. ICAO also supports and encourages the transition of COSCAPs into RASO type bodies, although this process is still ongoing, as was demonstrated in section §3.04[A][1] of Chapter 3.

Identified examples of the types of evolutions involve: moving from a technical cooperation project (Pre-RASO Type I) into an international regional safety organisation with legal personality (RASO Type I), which was the case for BAGASOO or ASSA-AC; or a network of aviation safety authorities (pre-RASO Type II) evolving into an international regional safety organisation with legal personality (RASO Type I), which was the case for AAMAC. Older organisations demonstrate similar patterns of evolution – for example the JAA (pre-RASO Type II) evolving into EASA (RASO Type II) in Europe.

States establishing RASOs/pre-RASOs generally seem to consider it necessary, or at least useful, for these organisations to have some form of legal personality. In the case of pre-RASOs, a useful way of granting legal personality is to establish an association or foundation under the law of one of the Member States. Out of the fourteen organisations from the core sample, four were established, at a certain point in time, as an association or foundation under private law or evolved from such an association or foundation (JAA/EASA, AAMAC, EUROCONTROL, and CASSOS/ACAAC). In 2014, at least eleven organisations studied had some sort of legal personality.[24]

Table 5.2 RASOs/Pre-RASOs Established since 2003 and Their Predecessors

Name of the Organisation	*Predecessor Organisation (If Any)*
European Network of Civil Aviation Safety Investigation Authorities (2010/2011)	Council of European Air Safety Investigation Authorities (2008)
Banjul Accord Group Aviation Safety Oversight Organisation (2009)	COSCAP – BAG (2004)
Banjul Accord Group Accident Investigation Agency (2009)	none
East African Community Civil Aviation Safety and Security Oversight Agency (2007/2008)	none
Civil Aviation Authorities of Africa and Madagascar – *international organisation* (2009)	Civil Aviation Authorities of Africa and Madagascar – *association of regulators* (2001)

24. For a more detailed overview of the question of RASO legal personality see Chapter 6.

Name of the Organisation	*Predecessor Organisation (If Any)*
- Pacific Aviation Safety Office (2004/2005)	none
Eastern Caribbean Civil Aviation Authority (2003/2004)	Directorate of Civil Aviation - Eastern Caribbean States (1957)
Caribbean Aviation Safety and Security Oversight System (2008)	Regional Aviation Safety Oversight System of the Caribbean (2001)
Central African Aviation Safety Oversight Agency (2012)	COSCAP-CEMAC (2008)

ICAO supports the transition of less formalised RASOs or pre-RASOs, to more institutionalised regional safety bodies established on the basis of formal legal agreements. According to ICAO, the more formalised types gain better commitment from their Member States, enable better delegation of tasks and functions and provide better for sustainability.[25]

[C] Efficiencies Stemming from a RASO Should Not Be Taken for Granted

The primary purpose of this study is not to quantify the efficiencies gained by States as a result of the establishment of a RASO, but to identify the legal and institutional features of RASOs which make these organisations more efficient and allow them to best contribute to the improvement of aviation safety and uniformity of regulations and procedures in civil aviation. Nevertheless, based on a review of experiences involved in establishment and functioning of these organisations, some general observations can also be formulated in respect of their overall effectiveness.

As explained in Chapter 2, the main reason behind the current RASO *boom* is the strong conviction of the international aviation community that these organisations provide a good way of addressing the difficulties experienced by States, in particular those with weak safety oversight systems. RASOs are in particular supposed to enable more efficient use of limited resources and be in a better position than national aviation authorities to attract and retain qualified aviation personnel.

Yet, the real life experiences of some of the RASOs and their Member States indicate that such efficiencies and benefits should not be taken for granted. As was demonstrated above, in the vast majority of cases a regional organisation does not replace the national authorities. This means that States may have to finance a regional body in addition to their national aviation authorities. There may even be a need to create new functions, which did not exist before the RASO establishment, such as a regional inspection-standardisation scheme. Where a regional body has not completely taken over at least some of the safety functions from States, both the RASO and the national authorities may be competing to attract similar safety experts from the market.

25. ICAO Doc. 9946, *supra* note 3 in Ch. 1, at Forward.

A technical and legal review of PASO conducted by external auditors in 2007 concluded that:

> It should not be assumed that the engagement of PASO's services will result in a reduction in the resources required by the States. On review of some States' responses to USOAP audit findings it was noted that this assumption formed the basis of many of the individual finding responses. There could actually be significant additional resource implications for each of the States in order to achieve the improved safety and security outcomes intended to be achieved.[26]

Similarly, a study conducted by the European Parliament (EP) in 2012 on the impact of the establishment of EASA on the EU's and national budgets, offers, somewhat surprisingly, the following observation:

> The centralisation of tasks impacted the national budget in different ways according to the nature of the transferred task. The expected effect of shifting both the responsibility and the execution of some tasks is usually a budget reduction. However, ..., all in all, the impact of the task transfer at national level has been toward an increase in budget pressure with very few exceptions.[27]

The EP study further clarifies that this has been in particular due to the fact that '[t]o comply with the new standard defined by EU regulations ..., some Member States had to invest more in the area of aviation safety.'[28] This is a similar observation to that which was formulated in respect to PASO.

The above indicates that if the additional costs resulting from establishment of a RASO are not offset by efficiencies stemming from its operations, or additional revenues, States may actually be worse off in terms of their overall budgets. If States cannot reduce their costs, whilst at the same time they will need to contribute to the financing of a RASO, this may actually lead to lack of sustainable funding of the latter and putting in danger its operations. This has been the case for example with PASO, which experienced serious financial difficulties due to the lack of contributions from its Member States, as was presented in section §3.04[C][2] of Chapter 3. Similarly CASSOA reported in 2012 that the lack of a sustainable funding mechanism was affecting its ability to 'execute the planned activities and recruitment and retention of technical personnel'.[29]

The above can be especially true for RASOs which depend on donor support for functioning. As pointed out in 2011 by a representative of the U.S. Department for Transport responsible for the 'Safe Skies for Africa' programme: 'RSOOs can be a solution, but much remains to be done to prove that the regional oversight model provides value for donor expenditures and sustainable results for the regions and States that wish to implement them.'[30]

---

26. PASO Legal and Technical Review Report, *supra* note 105 in Ch. 3, at p. 70.
27. The impact on the EU and national budgets of EU agencies, *supra* note 134 in Ch. 4, at p. 75.
28. *Ibid.*, at p. 76.
29. Regional cooperation for the enhancement of safety oversight: obstacles and lessons learnt, *supra* note 197 in Ch. 3.
30. Cornelia Wilson-Hunter, 'Remarks', ICAO Symposium on Regional Aviation Safety Organisations 2011).

An interview conducted with an official of BAGASOO characterises the problems of African RASOs in the following way:

> The main challenge facing RSOOs is financing. In most cases it is contributions from States, yet this contribution is left to CAAs to pay. For RSOO to attract and retain qualified, skilled personnel, the remuneration must be significantly higher than that of CAAs, otherwise it would be better to work in the CAA as there, the job is more guaranteed. To the extent that the CAAs are the ones paying the contributions directly to sustain the RSOOs ... that puts RSOOs and its Member States in competition for limited resources.[31]

A similar opinion was expressed by ECCAA, which is, from an organisational point of view, a very efficient form of RASO:

> The main challenges facing the ECCAA are managing the increasing costs of providing effective oversight and the recruitment of qualified personnel.[32]

Due to the above, this study recommends that RASOs should be vested, to the largest extent possible, with the competence to exercise safety functions on behalf of States. Only this solution guarantees lack of duplication between the national and regional levels and the desired economies of scale. As pointed out by ICAO:

> The major benefits of establishing an RSOO can be achieved only if the RSOO is enabled to act on behalf of Member States, to the highest possible extent, and if States maintain supervisory control so that the RSOO can succeed in enabling them to effectively meet their international obligations.[33]

Strong delegation arrangements are also preferable from a legal point of view, because they are more likely than informal arrangements to ensure uniformity of standards and operating procedures required by the Chicago Convention. Where States just *endeavour* to harmonise their regulations and procedures this will most likely result in national differences and will subsequently make standardisation and cross border recognition of certificates and approvals more difficult. This problem was demonstrated in the case of EASA and its predecessor, the JAA, in Chapter 4.

Another reason why regional safety bodies may not provide the desired benefits can be due to duplication between different aviation safety improvement initiatives. For example, in Africa some States have multiple memberships in COSCAPs and RASOs, and additional RASO projects are planned which involve overlapping membership, as was demonstrated in section §3.04[A][1] of Chapter 3. This situation, instead of focusing limited resources spreads them further amongst a number of similar initiatives. In mid-2013 several African States which had been members of RASOs for some years, were also subject to review by ICAO's Monitoring and Assistance Review Board (MARB) which is a body set up to consider the situation in States experiencing

31. 'Interview No 6', (2014), *supra* note 152 in Ch. 3.
32. 'Interview No 7', (2014), *supra* note 274 in Ch. 3.
33. ICAO Doc. 9734 Part B, *supra* note 3 in Ch. 1, at paragraph 4.1.35.

serious safety oversight problems.[34] As admitted by AFCAC, this very fact means that 'these regional bodies are not yet as effective as they could be.'[35]

Duplication of structures and inefficiencies resulting from this fact are also evident in Europe, where multiple regional aviation organisations exist in parallel, most of them with overlapping membership, and to a certain extent mandates, as was demonstrated in Chapter 4.

The above does not mean however that delegation should be considered as the *ultimate panacea*, and used by States without prior assessment as to where this would yield maximum benefits. Such assessment is always necessary and its result should primarily depend on a particular situation of States in a given region. As pointed out by an official of BAGASOO: 'RSOO should identify and concentrate its efforts on those activities that are better handled at a regional level.'[36] This has been the case in Europe, where due to the presence of a large aeronautical manufacturing industry, the main impetus behind the establishment of EASA has been the regionalisation of certification and oversight functions incumbent upon a 'State of Design', as was demonstrated in Chapter 4.

[D] Implications of Institutional Choices for the Functioning of RASOs

Legal issues, while important in their own right, generally prove not to be an obstacle in the process of establishing a RASO/pre-RASO. At the same time it is crucial that, when States consider establishing such an organisation, or undertake its evolution, they fully understand the consequences of their legal and institutional choices.

Reaching such an understanding can be greatly assisted by organising the whole process of establishing a regional body in a structured way. The *tool-box* approach proposed under section §5.03 above could help to achieve the most appropriate combination, given the specific needs of States. A similar approach was used in the EU during the initial EASA establishment process, in which States first created a list of potential functions and tasks, such as rulemaking, certification, standardisation, and then considered the implications of the different institutional solutions on each of them.[37]

In terms of legal tools used to establish a RASO, the tendency that can be observed is that States are inclined, more and more often, to use legally binding instruments – mainly international agreements. This can be associated with the overall

34. In march 2013 these were: Benin, Cameroon, Central African Republic, Chad, Comoros, Congo, Equatorial Guinea, Gabon, Guinea Bissau, Madagascar, Mali, Mauretania (Member States of AAMAC); Guinea, Liberia, Sierra Leone (Member States of BAGASOO); and Rwanda (Member State of CASSOA). See: ICAO, 'ICAO plans of action for States under the review of the MARB', AFI Plan-SC/2013/11-DP/02, (11th AFI Plan Steering Committee, 2013).
35. A37-WP/166, *supra* note 220 in Ch. 2, at paragraph 2.2.
36. 'Interview No 6', (2014), *supra* note 152 in Ch. 3.
37. Working papers tabled at the aviation working group of the Council in the context of the discussions on the establishment of EASA in the years 1996-1998 (Archives of the EU Council, Brussels).

tendency of the regional safety bodies to evolve into more formal structures, as was demonstrated under section §5.04[B] above.

As a consequence of the trend to use legally binding instruments, organisations based on MoUs, working arrangements or private law associations have almost completely disappeared. In 2014, only one of the fourteen organisations from the core sample was based on a non-binding legal instrument, namely the SRVSOP, as opposed to six in the previous decade.[38] Non-binding instruments continue to be used for specific cooperation projects such as regional inspector schemes. Table 5.3 gives an overview of the legal instruments which were used to establish the presently functioning RASOs/pre-RASOs.

Table 5.3 Legal Instruments Used to Establish RASOs/Pre-RASOs

Supranational Regulation	*International Agreement*	*Working Arrangement – MoU*
- European Aviation Safety Agency (EU regulation of 2002); - European Network of Civil Aviation Safety Investigation Authorities (EU regulation of 2010 combined with a private law association); - Central African Aviation Safety Oversight Agency (protocol adopted by chiefs of CEMAC States in 2012, and a CEMAC Regulation of 2012);	- The European Organisation for the safety of air navigation: EUROCONTROL (agreement of 1963, as variously amended); - Interstate Aviation Committee (agreement of 1991); - Banjul Accord Group Aviation Safety Oversight Organisation (agreement of 2009); - Banjul Accord Group Accident Investigation Agency (agreement of 2009); - East African Community Civil Aviation Safety and Security Oversight Agency (Agreement of 2007); - Civil Aviation Authorities of Africa and Madagascar (agreement of 2009);	- Regional Cooperation System on Safety Oversight in Latin America (ICAO – LACAC MoU of 1 October 1998)

38. In addition, ENCASIA is based on a combination of a legally binding EU regulation and an association established under Belgian law (*supra* note 261 in Ch. 3).

Supranational Regulation	*International Agreement*	*Working Arrangement – MoU*
	- Pacific Aviation Safety Office (agreement of 2004); - Eastern Caribbean Civil Aviation Authority (agreement of 2003) - Caribbean Aviation Safety and Security Oversight System (agreement of 2008); - Central American Aviation Safety Agency (agreement of 1960, and a ministerial decision of 2000).	

This study also recommends the use of legally binding instruments, such as appropriately internalised international agreements, or supranational acts creating direct legal effects, due to the fact that they are essential to enable Level 3 delegations, and by providing for legal personality of RASOs eliminate the need for establishing additional associations or foundations under private law.

As was demonstrated in the preceding chapter, in Europe, the EU developed a special legal method for associating non-EU countries into its aviation safety framework, including EASA. Under this method, international agreements are used to extend the EU aviation safety legislation to neighbouring countries, as well as to enable the delegation of safety functions by those countries to EASA. Upon transposition of the EU aviation safety legislation into their national legal systems, the partner countries acquire status similar to EU Member States. This means that their certificates benefit from recognition in the EU system, they can participate in the work of EASA, albeit without the right to vote, and are subject to EASA standardisation inspections. In 2014, four non-EU States had already been fully associated in such a manner, while a number of others were on the way to acquiring a full association status, as was explained in section §4.05 of Chapter 4.

[E] RASOs as Part of the Civil Aviation Safety System of Their Member States

A RASO should be considered, similar to a national civil aviation authority or aviation accident investigation body, as part of the civil aviation safety system of its Member States, and RASO functions should be fully integrated into that system. This is not always obvious, as at the national level all State safety functions envisaged under the system of the Chicago Convention are maintained within a single regulatory framework and under the responsibility of one government. When one or more of those functions is *taken out* of the national framework and transferred to the regional level some essential links may be lost.

For example, even after establishing a RASO, States will continue to be subject to ICAO USOAP, which is of a universal character. In this respect, States have to be mindful that even though the ICAO findings will be formally raised against them, it may be up to a RASO to address these findings from a practical point of view, which will require close coordination between States and their RASO. This coordination can sometimes be a complex undertaking, as a single State may not necessarily have full control over the way remedial actions are developed and put into effect. For example, if ICAO findings require a change in legislation, a collective action of all the States may be needed, or, as is the case in the EU, the additional involvement of the supranational legislator acting on the basis of EASA's technical recommendation.

In the case of certain Level 3 delegations, ICAO may have to audit a RASO, in addition to its Member States. In this case, if there are any findings raised against the RASO, ICAO will link them with the States' USOAP reports, based on the understanding that they ultimately remain responsible for compliance with ICAO requirements.[39]

Another aspect that States have to bear in mind is the notification of differences to ICAO in case of non-compliance with SARPs. Such notification is an obligation of every State party to the Chicago Convention, as Chapter 2 explained. If a regional system is based on a harmonised or single set of regulations, such notifications will only make sense if they are done in a uniform manner for all the States concerned. In such case, States should ensure that their RASO plays a coordinating role, reviewing ICAO SARPs on a regular basis and providing Member States with recommendations for notification.

[1] Unintended Consequences Related to the Establishment of a RASO

The necessity to look at RASOs holistically and as an integral part of States' civil aviation safety system can be very well illustrated with a practical example taken from the EU, and which is related to the functions assigned by ICAO Annexes to the 'State of Design'.

With the establishment of EASA in 2003, EU Member States delegated to this agency the functions and tasks of the 'State of Design' as envisaged under the system of the Chicago Convention.[40] This was however not a complete transfer of all the functions of the 'State of Design', but only of those related to aircraft airworthiness, including aircraft design approval and follow up of its continuing airworthiness, as addressed in Annex 8 to the Chicago Convention. Given the fact that EASA is not an air accident investigation agency, the functions of the 'State of Design' associated with air accident investigations, which are covered by Annex 13 to the Chicago Convention, remained at the national level. This relationship is illustrated by Figure 5.1.

39. See for example: ICAO USOAP report on EASA (2008), *supra* note 100 in Ch. 4, at paragraph 1.1.9.
40. Regulation (EU) No 216/2008, *supra* note 81 in Ch. 2, Article 20(1).

Figure 5.1 Transfer of State Safety Functions from a National to a Regional Level

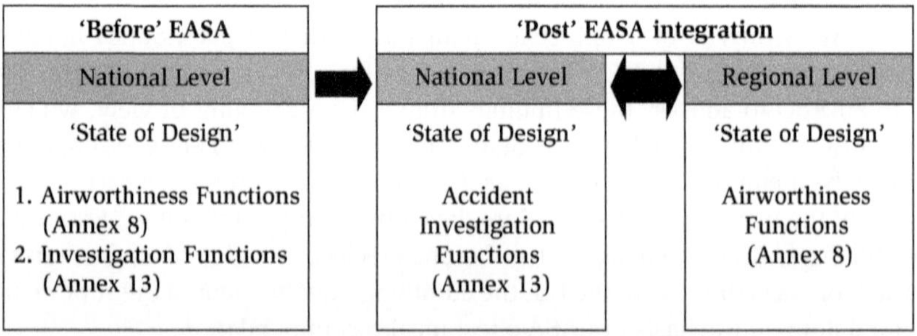

When in 2008 ICAO assessed EASA under USOAP it raised a finding against the agency in respect to lack of formal agreements with EU Member States regarding:

> The modalities and status of participation of representatives of EASA and representatives of Member States' bodies in accident and serious incident investigations involving aircraft whose type certificate is delivered by EASA.[41]

This finding was resolved only after the adoption by the EU of a regulation defining the rights and obligations of EASA as a participant in air accident investigations.[42] The regulation was adopted following unsuccessful attempts by EASA and EU Member States to address this issue through non-legislative measures, and in the wake of a number of cases where EASA had been denied the right to participate in an investigation by some of the EU air accident investigation authorities.[43]

Follow-up of safety recommendations resulting from air accident investigations is yet another example where a vital link may be lost when State safety functions are moved from a national to regional level. This is because when a RSOO, such as EASA, has been vested with actual regulatory competences, accident investigation bodies should consider it as a potential addressee of safety recommendations, and the RSOO should be bound by Annex 13 responsibilities applicable to such addressees, including as regards the obligation to analyse and reply to a safety recommendation within a prescribed deadline.[44]

At the same time, the implementation of safety recommendations coming from air accident investigation bodies may become more complex at the regional level. This is because where States have agreed that their rulemaking competences will be exercised collectively, they may need to activate the regional machinery in order to address a particular recommendation.[45]

41. ICAO USOAP report on EASA (2008), *supra* note 100 in Ch. 4, Audit Finding ORG/01.
42. Regulation (EU) No 996/2010, *supra* note 222 in Ch. 3, Article 8.
43. EC Impact Assessment COM(2009) 611 final, *supra* note 213 in Ch. 3, at paragraph 3.4.1.1.
44. Annex 13 to the Chicago Convention, at paragraph 6.10.
45. For example, on 1 April 2011 EASA initiated a rulemaking task concerning airworthiness and operational aspects for maintenance check flights (Task No MDM.097 (a)&(b)), which results from recommendations issued by Bureau d'Enquêtes et d'Analyses in the aftermath of an accident of Airbus A320-232 aircraft operated by XL Airways Germany and which occurred on

§5.05 RASOs AS INTERNATIONAL ACTORS

RASOs actively participate in international aviation relations, including ICAO sponsored activities, international conferences and symposia.[46] Especially after the adoption by ICAO of its new policy on cooperation with regional organisations and bodies, the international aviation community has become well aware of RASOs' existence. At the same time RASOs cannot, at present, be parties to the Chicago Convention which is open for membership of States only.[47]

From an international law point of view, as was demonstrated under section §5.04[D], the majority of RASOs are set up by international agreements or supranational law. Even though not all the treaties explicitly provide for it, those RASOs that are created by international agreements can be considered as international organisations, or in some cases as treaty organs,[48] as they are governed by international law. EASA is a specific case of an EU agency, and is not considered as an international organisation but as a body governed by public EU law, as was explained in Chapter 4.[49] A similar status of an organ of an international organisation can be attributed to ASSA-AC.

The international agreements establishing RASOs are not always clear whether the organisation in question is vested with international legal personality. This is not a unique situation, as 'constitutions of most international organizations lack explicit provisions on the legal status of the organization under international law.'[50] In the core sample of RASOs, only two out of ten international agreements, that is the AAMAC Treaty and PICCAST, explicitly provide that the RASO has international legal personality. In practice, this may not be a significant problem as 'many organisations can be seen to perform international legal activities despite the absence of an explicit grant of personality.'[51] What is important therefore is to analyse internationally relevant RASO activities, which means activities which derive their origin or have consequences under international law.

The first observation that has to be made in this respect is that some RASOs enjoy a limited degree of treaty making powers, which are functionally oriented. Most often RASOs are authorised to conclude headquarters agreements.[52] In addition, as was

27 November 2008 off the coast of Canet-Plage (France). See: EASA, 'Terms of Reference (ToRs) and Group Compositions (GCs)' http://www.easa.europa.eu/document-library/terms-of-reference-and-group-compositions/rmt0589 [accessed 10 August 2014].

46. *Supra* note 16.
47. 'Chicago Convention', Articles 92-93.
48. This is the case for example with IAC, which is a 'standing executive body' of the 'Minsk Agreement', *supra* note 124 in Ch. 3, Article 8. IAC considers itself as an international organisation, see: AIG/08-WP/22, *supra* note 231 in Ch. 3, at paragraph 2.1. In practice the distinction between an international organization and a treaty organ is not so important, as demonstrated by: Klabbers, *supra* note 75 in Ch. 4, at p. 9.
49. Regulation (EU) No 216/2008, *supra* note 81 in Ch. 2, Article 28.
50. Schermers and Blokker, *supra* note 72 in Ch. 4, at p. 988.
51. Klabbers, *supra* note 75 in Ch. 4, at p. 51.
52. The conclusion of headquarters agreements are explicitly envisaged in the constituent documents of BAGASOO, BAGAIA, AAMAC and CASSOS. However headquarters agreements can be

already explained above, some RASOs, such as IAC, BAGASOO or BAGAIA can conclude delegation agreements with their Member States.

Only organisations enjoying 'Level 3' delegations are designated by their Member States for the purpose of executing international agreements. Two examples can be given in this respect: (1) Agreement between the Government of the Russian Federation and the Government of the United States of America for the Promotion of Aviation Safety of 1998,[53] and (2) the Agreement between the United States of America and the European Community on cooperation in the regulation of civil aviation safety.[54] Under these agreements the IAC and EASA were designated as technical agents of the Russian Federation and of the EU respectively, for the purpose of the implementation of these agreements. In the first case, the agreement explicitly States that 'the IAC shall act under the authority and on behalf of the Government of the Russian Federation.'[55]

Under both of the above mentioned agreements, EASA and IAC are authorised to conclude with the FAA more detailed implementation procedures. Under these implementation procedures 'the IAC designates the Aviation Register of the IAC as its executive agent to carry out these Implementation Procedures.'[56] This was possible because of the independent legal standing of the different IAC committees under the Minsk Agreement.[57]

As was demonstrated in Chapter 4, where States grant to a RASO Level 3 delegations in respect of aviation safety functions which are governed by the Chicago Convention, this will result in the establishment of an international agency relationship between a RASO and its Member States. Such a relationship requires that the agent and principal are separate international legal persons. Where a RASO does not have own international legal personality, as is for example the case for EASA, the international agency relationship will be established between States and the international organisation of which the RASO is an organ.

In addition to executing international agreements, RASOs can also be authorised to conclude, within the scope of their competence, technical working arrangements. Such working arrangements are of a technical nature only and do not create legally binding effects for third parties. As a result, their scope of application is limited to issues which concern the working procedures of the RASO. The 2004 working

sometimes concluded also by RASOs which do not have this competence explicitly envisaged in their founding documents, which is the case for example with IAC.

53. 'Agreement between the government of the Russian Federation and the Government of the United States of America for the promotion of aviation safety', (Moscow, 1998), www.faa.gov/aircraft/air_cert/international/bilateral_agreements/baa_basa_listing/media/RussiaEA.pdf [accessed 10 August 2014].
54. 'EU-US BASA', *supra* note 97 in Ch. 2.
55. US-Russian Federation BASA, *supra* note 53, Article 1.D.
56. 'Implementation procedures for design approval, production activities, export airworthiness approval, post design approval activities, and technical assistance between authorities, done under the Agreement between the Government of the United States of America and the Government of the Russian Federation for Promotion of aviation safety', (1998), https://www.faa.gov/aircraft/air_cert/international/bilateral_agreements/baa_basa_listing/media/RussiaIPA.pdf [accessed 10 August 2014], section I (1.0).
57. See section §3.04[C][3] of Chapter 3.

arrangement between IAC and EASA can be given as an example of an arrangement concluded by two RSOOs carrying out executive tasks on behalf of States.[58]

§5.06 GENERAL CONCLUSIONS

It is clear that States do not follow a *one-size-fits-all* approach to establishing RASOs. This results from the fact that the needs of States in terms of strengthening their safety oversight or accident investigation capabilities differ, and therefore regional cooperation initiatives have to be tailored to the circumstances of a particular situation.

Political considerations also play a role when decisions are taken by States regarding the form of the RASO to be set-up.

Although the RASO concept is not entirely new, based on the analysis of the latest information, it is evident that the last twelve years have been real boom years for these organisations. Of the core sample of fourteen RASOs reviewed for the purpose of this study, nine have been established in the last twelve years. Even taking into account that some of them evolved from other organisations, this still means that six of the fourteen were only established after 2004. In addition, based on the available information about the projects which were being considered in 2014 by States and ICAO, more of such organisations can be expected to be set up in the coming years. According to ICAO, in Africa alone it is envisaged to have six additional RASO type organisations established in the coming years.

This clear trend towards increasing regionalisation of civil aviation safety oversight and accident investigation functions is a demonstration of the strong conviction of the international civil aviation community about RASOs' contribution to the improvement of civil aviation safety, worldwide harmonisation of standards, and cost-effectiveness of regulatory functions.

This study argues that, because of the above mentioned trend, it is important to collect and analyse the experience coming from RASO functioning so that it can be used to optimise their performance and help future organisations in avoiding some of the mistakes made by their predecessors. In this respect, whilst the findings of this chapter in principle confirmed that RASOs can bring benefits expected from them by the international aviation community, it is also clear from the existing experience that such benefits should not be taken for granted. Some of the RASOs experienced problems related to their sustainability and this aspect of RASOs functioning clearly requires further research in the future.

One of the principal reasons why RASOs which are in operation today are probably not as efficient as they could be is the fact that, in a vast majority of cases, they do not replace national authorities but supplement them. In 2014, there was only one example of a true RCAA, which acts as an aviation authority for multiple States.

The fact that RASOs generally do not replace national authorities, means that there may be additional costs for States deriving from their establishment which need

58. EASA, 'Working Arrangement on Airworthiness between the European Aviation Safety Agency and the Interstate Aviation Committee', (St. Petersburg, 2004), http://www.easa.europa.eu/system/files/dfu/intl_appro_IAC_EASA.pdf [accessed 10 August 2014].

to be offset by economies of scale and more efficient regulatory processes. Existing experience also shows that RASOs may be competing with States for aviation experts, especially if State safety functions continue to be exercised by the national authorities with parallel support of a RASO. This chapter identified at least two sources stating that 'these regional bodies are not yet as effective as they could be'.

Whilst it would not be realistic to expect that many RASOs be set up in the form of a RCAA due to the strong sovereignty issues which States associate with civil aviation oversight and regulatory functions, existing State experience and ICAO guidance shows that RASO efficiencies are strongest when safety functions are pooled at a regional level. This is because such pooling allows duplication with the national level to be avoided and makes functions such as certification or rulemaking more cost efficient through economies of scale. At the same time, regulatory centralisation at regional level is not an obstacle to local implementation, as the example of ECCAA, which operates with a network of local outstations, shows.

In order to assist States in choosing the best method and type of delegation, this chapter proposed to classify delegation arrangements into three levels:

(1) *Level 1* (Coordination level), under which States authorise individual inspectors of a regional body to perform audits, inspections and other oversight or investigative work on their behalf.
(2) *Level 2* (Harmonisation level) which goes beyond authorisation of individuals only, and entails a delegation to a regional body, as an organisation, of the competence to perform specific technical work on behalf of its Member States or member authorities.
(3) *Level 3* (Unification level) under which States delegate to a regional body both the conduct of the technical work, and responsibility for the issuance of the certificate/approval confirming that the applicable requirements have been met.

This chapter found that, despite the benefits of centralisation of safety functions at RASO level, the delegation of not only technical work but also legal responsibility (Level 3) is still quite rare. In 2014, there were only four RASOs which enjoyed such a level of delegation, while the majority of the RASOs studied provided mainly advisory and support services to their Member States which do not result in legally binding legal effects.

At the same time a tendency can be observed of RASOs gradually evolving into more institutionalised structures, which means towards organisations set up on the basis of international agreements and having legal personality. In 2014, twelve of the fourteen RASOs studied had some sort of legal personality, and only one of the fourteen organisations was based on a non-binding legal instrument as opposed to six in the previous decade.

The fact that RASOs evolve over time into organisations based on international law and having legal personality strengthens their mandate and allows them to accept more advanced levels of delegations of safety functions from their Member States. This is an important trend from the point of view of civil aviation safety and regulatory efficiency, given the identified correlation between the level of delegation of safety oversight tasks to RASOs and the resulting dividends for States in terms of efficiency of the regulatory processes and the effective use of resources. From the perspective of the main proposition of this study, that is the proposal for a GASON, this evolution also means that RASOs are overall moving towards forms which make them better suited to take the role of effective GASON building blocks.

In order to assist States in setting up RASO type bodies, this chapter reviewed practical examples of the different safety functions that these bodies perform and structured them along the eight ICAO CEs of State safety oversight. This *tool-box* approach provides States with a menu of potential options from which they could choose, taking into account that, as advocated by ICAO, when setting up RASOs, States should focus on 'those activities that demonstrate a higher impact on regional safety oversight and contribute towards developing an effective aviation safety oversight framework'.[59]

When analysing the different safety functions exercised by RASOs, this chapter also found that none of the organisations enjoy legislative functions. This demonstrates that States essentially treat RASOs as technical agencies implementing and enforcing the law but not creating it.

Another finding of this chapter was that a RASO should be considered as part of the overall civil aviation safety system of its Member States, and that RASO functions should be fully integrated into that system. This is because when one or more State safety functions is *taken out* of the national framework and transferred to the regional level, some essential safety links may be lost, as was demonstrated by the example of the transfer of 'State of Design' functions in the context of EASA in the EU.

Finally, this chapter addressed the role of RASOs as international actors. In this respect, it was found that RASOs are now well-established and recognised on the international level, and that some of them may enjoy competences to act under international law. In particular, RASOs can have treaty-making powers, including the competence to conclude headquarters and delegation agreements with their Member States. In addition, organisations enjoying Level 3 delegations can be authorised to act as authorised representatives of States for the purpose of executing international aviation safety agreements.

The legal standing of RASOs under international law and the delegation of the exercise of State safety functions to RASOs may also have consequences in terms of international responsibility and civil liability for wrongful acts in relation to the Member States of the RASO, third countries, as well as the regional body itself. This issue will be the subject matter of the following chapter of this study.

59. ICAO Doc. 9734 Part B, *supra* note 3 in Ch. 1, at paragraph 2.2.1.

CHAPTER 6

Responsibility and Liability of Regional Aviation Safety Organisations and of Their Member States

It would be difficult to find a topic beset with greater confusion and uncertainty.

Francisco V. García Amador
First International Law Commission's Special Rapporteur on State Responsibility (1956-1961)[1]

§6.01 INTRODUCTION

The success of the GASON proposed in Chapter 2, measured by more effective and uniform implementation of ICAO SARPs and efficiencies in terms of the use of resources by ICAO and its Member States, will to a large degree depend on whether the RASOs which form GASON's building blocks are appropriately empowered by their Member States to exercise civil aviation safety functions – either on behalf of these Member States or in RASOs own name.

Chapter 5 analysed and classified the various RASO delegation arrangements from an operational point of view. However, such delegations also raise questions related to the legal consequences, in terms of international responsibility and civil liability, for the RASO Member States and the regional body itself.[2] The precise legal source and nature of these consequences, which are the subject matter of this chapter, will depend on the legal form of the RASO, its relationship with Member States and

1. Francisco V. García Amador was the UN International Law Commission first special rapporteur on State responsibility.
2. In this Chapter the term 'responsibility' is used when referring to obligations stemming from international law, while the term 'liability' is used when referring to situations where a breach of a legal obligation results in damages the recovery of which is being pursued in national courts.

third countries, the applicable international legal framework and finally the domestic legislation of the States concerned.

In order to resolve the above issues, this chapter will first clarify and systematise the general principles and concepts concerning the attribution and delegation of State safety functions to aviation authorities from the perspective of domestic and international law (section §6.02). It will then verify if there are any provisions in the Chicago Convention or its Annexes which could limit the possibility of delegating State safety functions to RASOs, or more generally to exercising these functions on a non-national basis (section §6.03). Following on from that, this chapter will address the issue of RASO and State responsibility for internationally wrongful acts (sections §6.04 and §6.05), and domestic civil liability (section §6.06). Finally, this chapter will examine the need to amend the Chicago Convention in view of the emergence of RASOs (section §6.07).

§6.02 THE PRINCIPLE OF LEGALITY AND DELEGATION OF STATE SAFETY FUNCTIONS IN CIVIL AVIATION

[A] Attribution of Competences to Civil Aviation Authorities under Domestic Law

State organs can only act within the scope of the competences which have been *attributed* to them, which is a reflection of the *principle of legality*, as applied in administrative law.[3] This principle of attribution is also valid for civil aviation authorities dealing with aviation safety matters, and where the constituting acts of such bodies specify in detailed manner their competences, functions and duties.[4]

In some countries, such as the United Kingdom, the civil aviation authorities are established as an independent agency.[5] In other countries, such as the Netherlands, they are part of the organisational framework of one of the ministries.[6] Sometimes, such as in Poland, the competences are shared, with the ministry having competences for the legislation, and the civil aviation administration for its execution. Finally, in some jurisdictions, such as Germany, more than one administrative body was given the

3. Hofmann, Rowe, and Türk, *supra* note 116 in Ch. 2, 148-151; Michael Nierhaus, 'Administrative Law', in: Introduction to German Law, ed. by Mathias Reimann and Joachim Zekoll (2005), pp. 88-89; Philippos K. Spyropoulos and Théodore Fortsakis, Constitutional Law in Greece, (2009), p. 180; Lionel N. Brown and John Bell, French Administrative Law, (2003), pp. 213-215.
4. For example, for the competences, functions and duties of the UK civil aviation authority see: the Civil Aviation Act of 1982, Chapter 16; For the competences, functions and duties of the Polish Civil Aviation Authority see: Civil Aviation Act (Ustawa 'Prawo Lotnicze') of 3 July 2002 (Consolidated text in: Official Journal of the Republic of Poland of 28 November 2013, Item 1393).
5. The UK CAA is a body corporate which is not considered to be a servant or the agent of a Crown in accordance with the Civil Aviation Act of 1982.
6. In the Netherlands, the Minister of Transport is considered as the national aviation authority and is supported by Human Environment and Transport Inspectorate (ILT) which is an integral part of the Ministry of Transport.

competence to exercise the certification and oversight tasks placed upon a State by the Chicago Convention and its Annexes.[7]

Whether a national civil aviation authority or an administrative body in general can delegate its statutory responsibilities to other entities or individuals is in the first place a matter of domestic law, in line with the above mentioned principle of legality.[8]

In practice, it is not rare for States to delegate the conduct of some of their civil aviation safety tasks outside governmental structures. A study conducted in 2010 by the NLR Air Transport Safety Institute on 32 of the 44 ECAC States showed that in 2008 sixteen ECAC States were making use of inspecting staff contracted from external organisations.[9] The study also showed that fifteen States sub-contracted or delegated specific tasks to a separate organisation.[10] In the EU, legislation was even adopted setting out requirements that should be met by such *qualified entities* when contracted by EU Member States' aviation authorities or by EASA.[11]

In some cases, entities which are not part of the governmental structures are not only authorised to provide technical oversight services, but may also be authorised to issue certificates on behalf of States. This is the case, for example, in the Czech Republic, where the Light Aircraft Association is a competent authority for certification of microlight aircraft and licensing of persons involved in their operation.[12] In Austria, Austrocontrol GmbH was set up in 1994 as a limited liability company with 100% shares owned by the State[13] and is responsible for providing, on behalf of the Austrian government, air navigation services as well as, through a separate division, regulatory

7. In Germany, which is a federation of sixteen States (*Länder*), the competence has been split between the federal aviation authority and the *Länder* authorities, with the latter being responsible in particular for general aviation policing activities and for administration and licensing of aerodromes; Source: ICAO, 'Final Report on the safety oversight audit of the civil aviation system of the Federal Republic of Germany', (2005), http://cfapp.icao.int/fsix/AuditReps/CSAfinal/Germany_CSA_%20Final_Report.pdf [accessed 21 July 2014]. The UK also has more than one civil aviation authority, this however stems from the fact that in addition to the mainland, the UK is also composed of the Overseas Territories. Although from the perspective of the Chicago Convention the UK Overseas Territories are an integral part of the UK, the aviation activities in the Overseas Territories are under the responsibility of their Governors, which in practice either establish their own aviation safety administrations or can rely on the Air Safety Support International, which is a subsidiary company of the UK Civil Aviation Authority charged with supporting the development of civil aviation safety regulation in the Overseas Territories; for further details see: 'About ASSI', http://www.airsafety.aero/about/ [accessed 15 March 2014].
8. In addition to manuals concerning RSOOs and RAIOs, ICAO has also published guidelines concerning the establishment of State safety oversight system, which follows the logic of the eight CEs which were presented in Chapter 2. See: ICAO Doc. 9734, Part A, *supra* note 86 in Ch. 3.
9. NLR Air Transport Safety Institute, 'Safety Oversight Comparative Analysis Study', NLR-CR-2009-260, (2010), pp. 20-21.
10. *Ibid.*
11. Regulation (EU) No 216/2008, *supra* note 81 in Ch. 2, at Annex V.
12. Light Aircraft Association of the Czech Republic, http://en.laacr.cz/about-laa.htm [accessed 20 July 2014]. See also the case of Austrian Aeroclub (Österreichischer Aeroclub), a non-profit organization, which acts as an official body in areas such as: licensing of companies which maintain or design and manufacture parachutes, hang-gliders and paragliders; licensing of glider, hang glider and paraglider pilots; maintaining the register for gliders, balloons, micro-lights, hang gliders and paragliders.
13. Austrocontrol, 'Company Profile', (on file with author, 2012).

tasks including certification and inspection of aircraft, supervision of maintenance and flight operations, the performance of ramp checks on foreign aircraft, the issuance of civil aviation pilots' licenses and certification and oversight of pilot schools.[14]

Some jurisdictions envisage the concept of approved organisations which, in addition to being commercial enterprises, are also given privileges to make statements which under the Chicago Convention are the responsibility of States. This is the case, for example, with the approved design organisations in the EU, which have privileges to approve certain changes to aircraft design.[15] Under Annex 8 to the Chicago Convention, approval of aircraft design is one of the responsibilities of the 'State of Design'.[16]

Finally, in the US and some other countries which have their civil aviation safety regulatory system based on the American one, the national legal system envisages the concept of authorised *designees*. These individuals, which are not employees of the national aviation authority, may be authorised, on the basis of provisions of law, to conduct regulatory tasks. For example, in the US regulatory system, such individuals, when authorised by the FAA administrator,[17] can perform tasks such as 'determining whether aircraft designs, manufacturing, and maintenance meet specific safety standards and certifying the competency of persons that operate aircraft.'[18]

The main benefit of delegation arrangements, such as the ones described above, is to leverage resources and to allow the aviation authority to focus on most important tasks, while leaving routine or low-risk activities to approved organisations, designees, or external contractors. For example, in the US, the designees and designated organisations at a certain point performed 'more than 90 percent of FAA's certification activities, thus greatly leveraging the agency's resources.'[19] On the other hand, such delegation arrangements, especially when they involve delegating State tasks to commercial organisations or their employees, can sometimes face political criticism for supposedly allowing industry to *self-regulate*.[20]

While it is therefore clear that a civil aviation authority does not have to discharge all of its statutory responsibilities through in-house resources, a question arises as to what are the legal pre-requisites to enable such delegations, as well as what are their legal consequences.

In the case of two main jurisdictions which were reviewed for the purpose of this study, that is the EU and US, the delegations are allowed only on the basis of a clear

14. Austrocontrol, 'Annual Report', (2011), http://www.austrocontrol.at/jart/prj3/austro_control/data/uploads/pdfs/report_11.pdf [accessed 12 August 2014].
15. Commission Regulation (EU) No 748/2012, *supra* note 86 in Ch. 2, at Annex I, paragraph 21.A.263.
16. Annex 8 to the Chicago Convention, paragraph 1.3.4.
17. Title 14 CFR Part 183 'Representatives of the Administrator' (see: Code of Federal Regulations', http://www.gpo.gov/fdsys/pkg/CFR-2014-title14-vol1/pdf/CFR-2014-title14-vol1.pdf [accessed 29 July 2014].
18. US GAO, 'FAA Needs to Strengthen the Management of Its Designee Programs', GAO-05-40, (2004), at p. 7.
19. *Ibid.*, at p. 3.
20. Reuters, 'Will Dreamliner drama affect industry self-inspection?' http://www.reuters.com/article/2013/03/02/us-boeing-787-oversight-idUSBRE92104W20130302 [accessed 20 July 2014].

statutory provision.[21] In the EU, the principle is that national aviation authorities can delegate only the exercise of certification and oversight tasks, but cannot delegate the responsibility for the final regulatory decision, that is the issuance or revocation / suspension of an approval.[22] Only in limited cases which are clearly envisaged under the EASA Basic Regulation, an EU Member State can delegate to EASA the whole regulatory responsibility, including the audits and inspections, as well as the competence to issue a certificate.[23]

This *numerus clausus* of delegation scenarios in the US and EU aviation law is a reflection of the general principle applicable to delegation arrangements in administrative law according to which delegation cannot be presumed and must be clearly authorised by law. This means that '[a]n administrative agency with statutory responsibility for an exercise of powers cannot delegate them without statutory authorization.'[24] This principle, which is also expressed by a Latin maxim *delegatus non potest delegare*,[25] had been confirmed in the EU in the *Meroni* rulings, which were addressed in Chapter 4,[26] and in the US, through extensive case law.[27]

[B] Attribution and Delegation of Civil Aviation State Safety Functions under Public International Law

Having looked at the general principles concerning attribution and delegation of civil aviation safety functions under domestic law, this section will address the question of delegation of such functions to RASOs from the perspective of public international law. This analysis is an essential pre-requisite for the subsequent discussion about States' and RASOs' potential responsibility for wrongful acts under public international law.

As is the case in the domestic legal systems, where competences have to be clearly attributed to State organs by law, also in the case of international organisations the competence to act is governed by a *principle of attribution*. This principle means, as explained by Blokker, that 'international organizations are competent to act only as far as powers have been attributed to them by the Member States.'[28] This principle can

21. For the US this authorisation is contained Title 14 CFR Part 183 'Representatives of the Administrator', *supra* note 17. For the EU the authorisations for EASA and EU Member States are contained in: Regulation (EU) No 216/2008, *supra* note 81 in Ch. 2.
22. *Ibid.*, Article 13, which States that 'qualified entities shall not issue certificates'.
23. This is the case for organisations responsible for production of aeronautical products, and flight simulation training devices. See: Article 20.2 (b)(ii) and Article 21.2 (b)(ii) of Regulation (EU) No 216/2008, *supra* note 81 in Ch. 2.
24. Neil Hawke and Neil Parpworth, Introduction to Administrative Law, (1996), p. 138.
25. Stephen H. Bailey, Cases materials and Commentaty on administrative law, (2005), pp. 463-464.
26. 'Case C-9/56, Meroni', *supra* note 35 in Ch. 4, (p. 151), which states that: 'A delegation of powers cannot be presumed and even when empowered to delegate its powers the delegating authority must take an express decision transferring them.' See also: 'Case T-311/06, FMC Chemical SPRL v. European Food Safety Authority (EFSA)', in: [2008] ECR II-88, (CJEU,2008), (paragraph 66).
27. For an overview of the delegation doctrine in US administrative law see: William F. Funk and Richard H. Seamon, Administrative Law: Examples and explanations, (2009), pp. 30-43.
28. Schermers and Blokker, *supra* note 72 in Ch. 4, at p. 157.

also be referred to as the *principle of speciality*,[29] or the principle of *conferral of powers*.[30] Such attribution can be either explicit, or, although not explicitly envisaged in the constituent instrument of the organisation, implied 'as being essential to the performance of its duties.'[31]

The most comprehensive analysis of the methods by which States attribute or confer powers on international organisations was conducted by Sarooshi, who distinguishes, at the basic level, between the attribution by means of the constituent treaty and ad hoc conferrals.[32] This basic distinction is valid also for RASOs, where, as was demonstrated in Chapter 5, in case of RASOs which are established by international agreements or, in the case of EASA or ASSA-AC, by supranational law, competences are granted either in the RASO founding document or specific delegation agreements which can be concluded between a RASO and its Member States.

When it comes to a further typology of attribution of competences to international organisations, the situation is more complicated. This is because, as pointed out by Sarooshi:

> There is a considerable lack of clarity and consistent usage in the conceptual labels used to describe different types of conferrals by States of powers on international organizations. Such terms as 'ceding', alienation', 'transfer', 'delegation' and 'authorization' are used interchangeably by international and domestic courts as well as by commentators, often to refer to the same type of conferral of powers or the same conceptual label is used in a general way to refer to different types of conferrals. However not all conferrals of powers are the same, and there are important differences that flow from the types of conferrals for the legal relationship that is thereby established between States conferring powers and organizations.[33]

Based on the analysis of RASOs' founding documents this study found that where competences are allocated to regional aviation safety bodies, States, rather than using terms such as *transfer*, *delegation* or *authorisation*, prefer to simply list the different competences and refer to them as RASO *functions* or *objectives*.[34] The term *delegation* appears only in the case of one of the organisations studied, that is BAGAIA.[35] Therefore, rather than relying on a specific term, in order to determine the legal consequences of a conferral by a State of competences on a RASO it is necessary to

29. See: 'Legality of the Threat or Use of Nuclear Weapons, Advisory Opinion', in: [1996] ICJ Reports 66, (ICJ,1996), (p. 78). In this ruling the ICJ stated that: 'International organizations are subjects of international law which do not, unlike States, possess a general competence. International organizations are governed by the 'principle of speciality', that is to say they are invested by the States which create them with powers, the limits of which are a function of the common interests whose promotion those States entrust to them.'
30. Sarooshi, *supra* note 19 in Ch. 2.
31. 'Reparation for Injuries', *supra* note 76 in Ch. 4, (p. 182).
32. Sarooshi, *supra* note 19 in Ch. 2, at p. 18.
33. *Ibid.*, at p. 28.
34. This is the case for example for PASO (see: 'PICASST', *supra* note 100 in Ch. 3, Article 7), AAMAC (see: 'AAMAC Treaty', *supra* note 81 in Ch. 3, Article 3), ECCAA (see: 'ECCAA Agreement', *supra* note 268 in Ch. 3, Articles 5-6), or BAGASOO (see: 'BAGASOO Agreement', *supra* note 147 in Ch. 3, Article 5).
35. 'BAGAIA Agreement', *supra* note 221 in Ch. 3, Article 5(k).

assess all the circumstances of a particular case, including the provisions of the RASO founding agreement, as well as State, ICAO and RASO practice.

Referring back to the theory of international delegations, academic writers generally tend to classify the different arrangements using as the main criterion the degree to which the State powers have been given away to an international organisation. Sarooshi, for example, distinguishes three types of conferrals, that is, agency relationships, delegations, and transfers, depending on the criteria such as the revocability of the conferral, the level of control exercised by a State over the organisation, the possibility to exercise a given power in parallel by a State and the organisation, and other criteria.[36] He also specifies the consequences that each of these three types of conferrals may have for a State and international organisation from the perspective of international responsibility for wrongful acts.[37]

Similarly, Bradley and Kelly propose a typology of what they call *international delegation*, according to criteria related to the legal effect that the delegation has and the degree of independence of the international body to which a delegation is given.[38] They rightly point out that 'delegations that allow international bodies to create binding legal obligations are more extensive than similar delegations of only advisory or agenda-setting authority.'[39] This is in line with the findings of this study, which, as Chapter 5 demonstrated, found that delegations to RASOs which create legally binding effects (Level 3 delegations), are in practice much more difficult to achieve and implement than more simple delegations which concern advisory and technical assistance functions, and which do not create legally binding effects for States or aviation undertakings.

While the typologies of international delegation arrangements proposed in the existing literature are useful for this study in the sense that they allow the different types of RASOs to be put in the more general context of discussions on conferrals of powers to international organisations or bodies, this study came to the conclusions that these typologies need adaptation before they can be applied in the specific context of RASOs. For this reason, it has been decided that the 3-Level typology of delegation arrangements that was proposed in Chapter 5, although of an operational nature, is also a good starting point for discussing RASO delegation arrangements from the perspective of public international law.

The first conclusion that was reached in this respect, is that a distinction has to be made, as is the case under the domestic law, between the *delegation of tasks* and the *delegation of the competence to take a decision*. The theory of international law and the practice of international organisations recognise the possibility of delegating the exercise of tasks only, or using outside experts. In such cases, although the exercise of tasks is allocated to outside experts, the competence to take a decision remains with the delegating organisation,[40] or in our case with a RASO Member State. Level 1 and 2

36. Sarooshi, *supra* note 19 in Ch. 2, at pp. 28-31.
37. *Ibid.*, at pp. 33-104.
38. Bradley and Kelley, 'The concept of international delegation', *supra* note 85 in Ch. 4, at pp. 17-25.
39. *Ibid.*, at p. 17.
40. Schermers and Blokker, *supra* note 72 in Ch. 4, at pp. 339-340.

delegations, as proposed in Chapter 5, are considered as delegation of tasks, while Level 3 delegations also entail the competence to take a decision. For example, RASOs may be given the task of preparing proposals of legislative measures, but the actual adoption of these measures is the responsibility of States, as is clear from the cases reviewed for the purpose of this study.

The second conclusion is that a distinction has to be made between (1) the delegation of State safety functions and duties which are created by the Chicago Convention, and (2) functions and duties which are not dealt with under this international law instrument.

In the first case, regardless of the term used, we will be talking about a relationship of an international *agency*, as was demonstrated on the example of EASA in Chapter 4. This is because, when the delegation concerns a function which is already envisaged under the Chicago Convention, a State is only mandating an organisation to exercise, on its behalf, the functions for which this State is already responsible under international law. This conclusion is also supported by ICAO practice concerning registration of aircraft by RASOs as will be shown in section §6.03[A][1] below.

In the second case, we will be talking about an *attribution* of a new competence to an international organisation or body. This distinction is important from the perspective of international State responsibility, as will be demonstrated in sections §6.04 and §6.05.

§6.03 THE OBLIGATION TO ESTABLISH AVIATION AUTHORITIES, AS ENVISAGED IN THE CHICAGO CONVENTION AND ITS ANNEXES

Before addressing the question of international responsibility of States and RASOs for wrongful acts, the final point which needs to be resolved is whether either the Chicago Convention or its Annexes establish any restrictions or conditions with regard to the delegation to RASOs of State safety functions. In order to resolve this issue, the provisions of the Chicago Convention, as well as all safety-related ICAO Annexes and ICAO interpretative manuals concerning RSOOs and RAIO were reviewed.

When it comes to the provisions of the Chicago Convention, most of them are formulated in a way which establishes obligations at State level only and do not provide further details as to the nature or structure of the authority which should be actually tasked by a State with discharging these obligations. However, some of the articles of the Chicago Convention make a more specific reference to the *appropriate authorities of each of the contracting States* (Article 16 – Search of Aircraft), State *own authorities* (Article 25 – Aircraft in Distress), *appropriate authorities of the State* (Article 30 – Aircraft radio equipment), *appropriate national authorities for certification* (Article 41 – Recognition of existing standards of airworthiness), or *authorities of the other contracting State or States* (Article 83bis – Transfer of certain functions and duties).

Similarly the review of the safety related Annexes to the Chicago Convention reveals a mosaic of different formulations and solutions with regard to the authorities and entities through which ICAO allows or requires States to discharge their obligations. Depending on the technical domain, the Annexes use formulations such as *licensing authority,*[41] *appropriate authority,*[42] *competent authority,*[43] *appropriate national authority,*[44] *issuing authority,*[45] *appropriate certifying authority,*[46] *appropriate airworthiness authority,*[47] *State authority,*[48] *common mark registering authority,*[49] and *responsible authority.*[50]

The most recently adopted Annex 19, which deals with safety management, contains a Standard, which obliges every State to:

> Establish relevant authorities or agencies, as appropriate, supported by sufficient and qualified personnel and provided with adequate financial resources. Each State authority or agency shall have stated safety functions and objectives to fulfil its safety management responsibilities.[51]

An explanatory note to the above cited Annex 19 Standard clarifies that:

> The term 'relevant authorities or agencies' is used in a *generic sense* to include all authorities with aviation safety oversight responsibility which may be established by the State as separate entities, such as: Civil Aviation Authorities, Airport Authorities, ATS Authorities, Accident Investigation Authority, and Meteorological Authority (emphasis added).[52]

Based on the analysis of the context in which the above and other formulations are used, as well as the analysis of ICAO and State practice, the following conclusions were reached:

(1) Although there is no consistency in the way the different formulations regarding aviation authorities are used in the ICAO Annexes, the vast majority of the ICAO SARPs use broad formulations which refer to a *State*[53] and/or to an *authority* in a generic sense without specifying that it has to be a *national*

41. See: Annex 1 to the Chicago Convention, at 'Definitions'.
42. See: ICAO, 'Annex 2 to the Chicago Convention: Rules of the Air', (2005), 'Definitions'; ICAO, 'Annex 10 to the Chicago Convention: Aeronautical Telecommunications, Volume I – Radio Navigation Aids', (2006), paragraph 12.13.11; Annex 14 to the Chicago Convention, at paragraph 1.2.1.
43. See: ICAO, 'Annex 4 to the Chicago Convention: Aeronautical Charts', (2009), paragraph 11.10.15; Annex 10, Volume I to the Chicago Convention, at paragraph 3.1.7.1.
44. See: Annex 6, Part I to the Chicago Convention, at 'Note' to paragraph 6.12; Annex 8 to the Chicago Convention, at paragraph 10.3.1; ICAO, 'Annex 18 to the Chicago Convention: The Safe Transport of Dangerous Goods by Air', (2011), at paragraph 2.7.
45. See: Annex 6, Part I to the Chicago Convention, at paragraph 4.2.1.5 (a).
46. *Ibid.*, at Appendix 8, paragraph 1.5.
47. *Ibid.*, at Attachment F, paragraph 7.
48. See: ICAO, 'Annex 6 to the Chicago Convention: Operation of Aircraft, Part II – International General Aviation with Aeroplanes', (2008), at paragraph 2.3.1.1.
49. See: ICAO, 'Annex 7 to the Chicago Convention: Aircraft Nationality and Registration Marks', (2012), at 'Definitions'.
50. See: ICAO, 'Annex 12 to the Chicago Convention: Search and Rescue', (2004), paragraph 2.1.1.2.
51. Annex 19 to the Chicago Convention, at Appendix 1, paragraph 3.1.
52. *Ibid.*, Appendix 1, Note 2.
53. ICAO uses broad concepts such as: 'State of the Operator' (The State in which the operator's principal place of business is located or, if there is no such place of business, the operator's permanent residence), 'State of Registry' (The State on whose register the aircraft is entered), 'State of Design' (The State having jurisdiction over the organization responsible for the type

authority. Annex 6 for example, distinguishes between the 'State of the Operator' which is the 'State in which the operator's principal place of business is located or, if there is no such place of business, the operator's permanent residence', and the *issuing authority* which is specifically responsible, on behalf of the 'State of the Operator' for the determination that the operator complies with the provisions of Annex 6 and the issuance of an AOC.[54]

(2) In the rare cases where an ICAO Annex uses the term *national*, the relevant State and ICAO practice demonstrates that this term is actually also interpreted as covering RASO type authorities. This is, for example, the case with aircraft design certification, where Annexes 6 and 8 refer in this context to *appropriate national authority*,[55] but where in practice RASOs have been established, such as EASA, which approve aircraft design on behalf of States and this has been found acceptable to ICAO.[56] Similarly, with respect to the transport of dangerous goods by air, where paragraph 2.7 of Annex 18 explicitly requires each ICAO Member State to designate 'an appropriate authority *within its administration* to be responsible for ensuring compliance with this Annex (emphasis added)', the ECCAA discharges these responsibilities on behalf of the OECS States, and this had been accepted by ICAO.[57]

(3) Many of the ICAO Annexes explicitly envisage that a State has an obligation to designate an authority, which is to discharge on its behalf relevant safety related responsibilities or provide services which are necessary for international air navigation. This is, for example, the case, in addition to the above mentioned issuing authority under Annex 6, for: aircrew licensing,[58] publication of aeronautical information publication,[59] provision of meteorological information,[60] international aeronautical telecommunications services,[61] air

---

design) or 'State of Manufacture' (The State having jurisdiction over the organization responsible for the final assembly of the aircraft).

54. Annex 6, Part I to the Chicago Convention, at Appendix 6.
55. *Ibid.*, at paragraph 6.3.1.2.8; Annex 8 to the Chicago Convention, at Part 11, paragraph 1.1.1.
56. ICAO USOAP report on EASA (2008), *supra* note 100 in Ch. 4.
57. ICAO USOAP report on OECS (2007), *supra* note 290 in Ch. 3, at paragraph 3.3.8 (used with the permission of the ECCAA).
58. Annex 1 to the Chicago Convention uses the term 'Licensing Authority' which means: 'The Authority designated by a Contracting State as responsible for the licensing of personnel'.
59. A State may provide the aeronautical information itself, agree with one or more other Contracting State(s) for the provision of a joint service, or delegate the authority for the provision of the service to a non-governmental agency, provided the Standards and Recommended Practices of this Annex are adequately met (see: Annex 2 to the Chicago Convention, at paragraph 2.1.1).
60. Under paragraph 2.1.4 of Annex 3 to the Chicago Convention, each ICAO Member States 'shall designate the authority ..., to provide or to arrange for the provision of meteorological service for international air navigation on its behalf.'
61. Under paragraph 2.4.1 of Annex 10 – Volume II to the Chicago Convention, each ICAO Member State has an obligation to 'designate the authority responsible for ensuring that the international aeronautical telecommunications service is conducted in accordance with the procedures of this Annex.'

traffic services,[62] and search and rescue.[63] These provisions are general in nature and do not explicitly limit the authority to be designated as having a *national* status.

In addition, as was mentioned under section §2.04[C] of Chapter 2, Annexes 13 and 19 explicitly refer to RASOs. A more detailed review of these references reveals however that ICAO still struggles somewhat with the use of this concept. In the case of Annex 19, ICAO explains in the 'Foreword' that:

> Certain State safety management functions required in Annex 19 may be delegated to a regional safety oversight organization or a regional accident and incident investigation organization on behalf of the State.

The above formulation and especially the use of the word *certain* suggests that there may be limitations as to the scope or depth of the subject matter delegation. Unfortunately however Annex 19 does not offer further guidance in this respect.

Even more confusing are the provisions of Annex 13, which is the only Annex which actually contains SARPs referring to RASOs. Although Standard 5.1 of this Annex gives to the 'State of Occurrence' the possibility to: 'delegate *the whole* or any part of the conducting of such investigation to another State or a regional accident investigation organization (emphasis added)', the explanatory note which accompanies this provision does not mention a RAIO when clarifying the consequences of *the whole* delegation:

> When the whole investigation is delegated to another State or a regional accident investigation organization, *such a State* is expected to be responsible for the conduct of the investigation, including the issuance of the Final Report and the ADREP reporting. When a part of the investigation is delegated, the State of Occurrence usually retains the responsibility for the conduct of the investigation (emphasis added).[64]

Similarly, the ICAO manual on RAIOs seems to suggest that the possibility of delegating investigative functions to a regional body does not relieve a State from establishing a national investigation authority:

62. Under paragraph 2.1.1 of Annex 11 to the Chicago Convention each ICAO Member State has an obligation to arrange for air traffic services 'to be established and provided in accordance with the provisions of this Annex, except that, by mutual agreement, a State may delegate to another State the responsibility for establishing and providing air traffic services in flight information regions, control areas or control zones extending over the territories of the former.' An explanatory note to this provision further clarifies that: 'If one State delegates to another State the responsibility for the provision of air traffic services over its territory, it does so without derogation of its national sovereignty. Similarly, the providing State's responsibility is limited to technical and operational considerations and does not extend beyond those pertaining to the safety and expedition of aircraft using the concerned airspace ...'.
63. Under paragraph 2.5.1 of Annex 12 to the Chicago Convention each ICAO Member State has an obligation to 'designate as search and rescue units elements of public or private services suitably located and equipped for search and rescue operations.'
64. Annex 13 to the Chicago Convention, at explanatory note to paragraph 5.1.

> In a more complex regional organization, the *national accident investigation authorities* may delegate the whole or part of their functions and responsibilities concerning accident and incident investigation to the RAIO, which would conduct the actual investigation on behalf of Member States. Such investigations would be based on common regional regulations, policies and procedures, while Member States would retain responsibility for the oversight of the system, in accordance with the Chicago Convention (emphasis added).[65]

The above interpretation in the RAIO manual seems to be shared by the ICAO ANC, which at the end of 2013 discussed a proposal for an amendment to Annex 13 introducing an obligation for States to establish an independent accident investigation authority,[66] and where the team which developed the proposed amendment 'felt that a regional accident and incident investigation organization (RAIO) was not an alternative to the national accident and incident investigation authority.'[67]

This study does not agree with such a restrictive approach. As was demonstrated above, the vast majority of the ICAO Annexes do not oblige States to establish *national* authorities as a means of discharging their safety related obligations, and in those rare cases where such limiting language was included in the SARPs the subsequent State practice has demonstrated that such limitations are not sensible.

In addition, as was pointed out by an official of one of the RAIOs, there are at present between 50 and 60 States which do not have resources and expertise to establish permanent accident investigation authorities.[68] For such countries a requirement to establish a permanent investigation authority would probably result in filing of differences – which is not an answer – or establishing a one person authority to satisfy the ICAO requirement from a formal point of view, but which in practice would not have, on its own, the resources necessary to effectively investigate aviation accidents.[69]

To conclude, ICAO Annexes should be drafted in a way which recognises that it is perfectly acceptable for a State to discharge its safety related obligations under Annex 13 or any other safety related Annex to the Chicago Convention by relying either on a national authority(ies) or, in part or even entirely, on a RASO type body as long as the State concerned can demonstrate that the relevant SARPs are effectively implemented.

[A] 'State of Registry' and 'State of the Operator' in the Context of Establishing RASOs: Limitations of the Chicago Convention

The analysis of the legal consequences of establishing RASOs from the perspective of State responsibility under the Chicago Convention would not be complete without also addressing the concepts of the 'State of Registry' and 'State of the Operator', which are

65. ICAO Doc. 9946, *supra* note 3 in Ch. 1, at paragraph 3.10.1.5.
66. ICAO, 'Final review of proposed amendment to Annex 13 relating to independence of accident and incident investigations', AN-WP/8803, (Air Navigation Commission, 2013).
67. ICAO, 'Minutes of the Sixth Meeting', AN Min. 195-6, (195th Session of the Air Navigation Commission, 2014).
68. 'Interview No 10', (2014), *supra* note 252 in Ch. 3.
69. *Ibid.*

linked to basic State responsibilities in the context of international air navigation and stem directly from the provisions of the Chicago Convention.

[1] RASO as a 'State of Registry'

The 'State of Registry' is one of the fundamental concepts in the Chicago Convention, and the one with which the Convention associates a number of legal consequences, such as the obligation to issue certificates of airworthiness,[70] to validate pilot licenses,[71] or the right to appoint observers to an accident investigation.[72] There are also numerous other rights and obligations which are attached to the 'State of Registry' through the technical Annexes of the Chicago Convention.[73]

A contracting State to the Chicago Convention acquires the status of the 'State of Registry' when an aircraft is entered on its national aircraft registry.[74] This act of registration also creates a unique link between the aircraft and its 'State of Registry' which the Chicago Convention refers to as *nationality of aircraft*.[75] Under the Chicago Convention, the general principle is that an aircraft can have a nationality of only one State – the 'State of Registry'.[76]

In the context of this study the question emerges whether there are any legal limitations as to the ability of a RASO to carry out on behalf of a State the functions of a 'State of Registry'. The general answer to this question is that such a delegation is legally acceptable. Relevant State and ICAO practice demonstrates that it is possible to establish, in compliance with the Chicago Convention, a RASO which would discharge the functions of a 'State of Registry' with respect to, for example, aircraft design (IAC, EASA) or accident investigation matters (IAC).

It is also possible to have a RASO discharging on behalf of States the functions associated with aircraft registration, including the issuance of certificates of registration and airworthiness. In 2014, there was one RASO (ECCAA), having such competences. In such cases however aircraft still have the nationality of the State on behalf of which they are registered in accordance with Article 17 of the Chicago Convention. For example, in the case of aircraft registered by ECCAA, each OECS Member State retains its national registration marks as assigned by ICAO.[77] It is not possible to overcome this limitation without an amendment to the Chicago Convention.

A limited exception to the general principle of registering aircraft on a national basis is contained in Article 77 of the Chicago Convention. This exception is available only to aircraft operated by an *international operating agency*, which is an airline

70. 'Chicago Convention', Article 31.
71. *Ibid.*, Article 32.
72. *Ibid.*, Article 26.
73. See for example Annexes 6, 8 and 13 to the Chicago Convention.
74. The Annexes to the Chicago Convention define the 'State of Registry' as 'The State on whose register the aircraft is entered'. For further commentary on legal aspects of aircraft registration and nationality from aviation safety perspective see: Huang, *supra* note 29 in Ch. 1, at pp. 24-32.
75. 'Chicago Convention', Article 17.
76. *Ibid.*, Article 18.
77. 'Interview No 7', (2014), *supra* note 274 in Ch. 3.

established by two or more of the ICAO Member States on the basis of an international treaty.[78] According to an ICAO Council determination made in 1967 on the basis of Article 77 of the Chicago Convention, aircraft of international operating agencies can be registered either *jointly* by the States constituting the agency or on an *international basis*.[79] In both cases, all aircraft of an international operating agency which are registered on other than a national basis will bear the same common registration mark.[80]

The only practical example of application of the possibility of non-national aircraft registration has so far been the case of Arab Air Cargo, which is an international operating agency set up in 1983 by Iraq and Kingdom of Jordan and still functioning today.[81] Although all aircraft of Arab Air Cargo have a common non-national registration mark assigned by ICAO (4YB), the actual registration tasks are performed by the Kingdom of Jordan, which also carries out the functions of the 'State of Registry' on behalf of Iraq,[82] and is considered as a 'Common mark registering authority' from the perspective of Annex 7 to the Chicago Convention which deals with aircraft registration.[83] Furthermore, according to the ICAO determination concerning Arab Air Cargo, the governments of Iraq and Jordan are:

> Jointly and severally bound to assume the obligations and responsibilities which under the Convention on International Civil Aviation attach to the State of registry; any complaints by other contracting States will be accepted by both the Governments of Jordan and Iraq.[84]

The example of Arab Air Cargo represents a case of a *joint* aircraft registration by a number of ICAO Member States. However, from the perspective of this study of greater relevance is the second possibility envisaged by the ICAO Council, namely that of *international aircraft registration*. So far however there have been no cases of using this possibility in practice.

The above mentioned ICAO resolution of 1967, defines international aircraft registration as:

---

78. Pablo Mendes de Leon, Cabotage in Air Transport Regulation, (1992), pp. 128-134.
79. Resolution on International Operating Agencies, *supra* note 92 in Ch. 4.
80. *Ibid.*, at paragraph 1.
81. For an overview of this case see: Michael Milde, 'Nationality and registration of aircraft operated by Joint Air Transport Operating Organizations or International Operating Agencies', AASL, X (1985). For a critical analysis of the ICAO Council resolution see: Khairy El - Hussainy, 'Registration and Nationality of Aircraft operated by International Agencies in Law and Practice', Air Law, X (1985), pp. 15-27.
82. A similar solution is envisaged under Article 18 of the Convention on offences and certain other acts committed on board aircraft, signed at Tokyo, on 14 September 1963 (Tokyo Convention) which provides that: 'If Contracting States establish joint air transport operating organizations or international operating agencies, which operate aircraft not registered in any one State those States shall, according to the circumstances of the case, designate the State among them which, for the purposes of this Convention, shall be considered as the State of registration and shall give notice thereof to the International Civil Aviation Organization which shall communicate the notice to all States Parties to this Convention.'
83. Annex 7 to the Chicago Convention, at 'Definitions' and at paragraph 3.5.
84. Milde, 'Nationality and registration of aircraft operated by Joint Air Transport Operating Organizations or International Operating Agencies', *supra* note 81, at p. 149.

> The cases where the aircraft to be operated by an international operating agency would be registered not on a national basis but with an international organization having legal personality, whether or not such international organization is composed of the same States as have constituted the international operating agency.[85]

The ICAO has further clarified in its Resolution that:

> In arriving at its determination [the Council], shall be satisfied that any system of international registration devised by the States constituting the international operating agency gives the other Member States of ICAO sufficient guarantees that the provisions of the Chicago Convention are complied with.[86]

Finally, according to the subject matter Resolution, the following criteria have to be met, as a minimum, by States envisaging international aircraft registration:

(1) The States constituting the international operating agency shall be jointly and severally bound to assume the obligations which, under the Chicago Convention, attach to a State of registry.
(2) The operation of the aircraft concerned shall not give rise to any discrimination against aircraft registered in other Contracting States with respect to the provisions of the Chicago Convention.
(3) The States constituting the international operating agency shall ensure that their laws, regulations and procedures as they relate to the aircraft and personnel of the international operating agency when engaged in international air navigation shall meet in a uniform manner the obligations under the Chicago Convention and the Annexes thereto.[87]

According to Milde 'in the discussions leading to the Council Resolution, it has been suggested that even ICAO itself or the United Nations or other international organizations could become such a registering authority.'[88] This leads to the conclusion that a RASO or an international organisation of which the RASO is an organ, could be considered as an international aircraft registering authority subject to the following conditions and limitations:

(1) The RASO should be established as an entity with a separate legal personality. This requirement set by the ICAO Council is also in line with the findings of this study, according to which the establishment of a relationship of an international agency requires the organisation which acts on behalf of States to possess a separate international legal personality (see section §4.03[B] of Chapter 4). In case of RASOs, such as EASA, which are established in the form of an organ of an international organisation, the registering authority will be the international organisation acting through the RASO.

85. Resolution on International Operating Agencies, *supra* note 92 in Ch. 4, at 'Appendix 1'.
86. *Ibid.*, at Appendix 2, Part II.
87. *Ibid.*
88. Milde, 'Nationality and registration of aircraft operated by Joint Air Transport Operating Organizations or International Operating Agencies', *supra* note 81, at p. 150.

(2) The international registration functions performed by a RASO or by an international organisation of which the RASO is an organ, would be applicable only to aircraft of joint operating agencies as envisaged under Article 77 of the Chicago Convention. This is the main practical limitation of the Chicago Convention with regard to non-national aircraft registration. In respect to aircraft operated by operators not having status of joint operating agencies a RASO can only carry out, on behalf of States, the national responsibilities of the 'State of Registry, as is the case today with ECCAA.

(3) From the perspective of Annex 7 to the Chicago Convention a RASO or an international organisation of which the RASO is an organ, carrying out international registration functions should be considered as a common mark registering authority, and in this respect would be obliged to establish and maintain a dedicated 'non-national register or, where appropriate, a part thereof, in which aircraft of an international operating agency are registered.'[89]

Finally it has to be reiterated that the ICAO Council Resolution concerning non-national aircraft registration is clear that the setting up of an international aircraft registration scheme does not relieve the States participating in such a scheme from the responsibilities that the Chicago Convention attaches to the 'State of Registry', and that the States concerned shall be jointly and severally responsible for assuming these obligations.[90]

Given the fact that so far there has been no practical case of application of international aircraft registration, it is not clear what the position of the ICAO Council would be as to the possibility of joint and several responsibility of the States and the international aircraft registering authority. This study argues that such possibility should not be excluded, given the fact that the international aircraft registering authority would be exercising on behalf of States safety critical tasks such as the issuance of certificates of airworthiness.

Should such parallel responsibility of the international registering authority be allowed, this would be the only case of an international organisation directly bound by the provisions of the Chicago Convention.[91] The legal basis for such responsibility would then be the determination of the ICAO Council made in accordance with Article 77 of the Chicago Convention.

[2] RASO as a 'State of the Operator'

The second basic State safety function under the Chicago Convention is the 'State of the Operator', which was introduced through Article 83bis of the Convention, and is defined as 'the State where the operator has his principal place of business or, if he has

89. Annex 7 to the Chicago Convention, at 'Definitions'.
90. Resolution on International Operating Agencies, *supra* note 92 in Ch. 4, at Appendix 2, Part 1.
91. For cases where an international organisation could be bound indirectly by the provisions of the Chicago Convention see section §6.05[D] below.

no such place of business, his permanent residence'.[92] As is the case with the 'State of Registry', the details of the tasks and responsibilities of the 'State of the Operator' are defined in the technical Annexes to the Chicago Convention, and notably Annex 6.

There is no doubt that under the current international legal framework a RASO can discharge on behalf of a State the functions of a 'State of the Operator'. As was already mentioned above, Annex 6 clearly distinguishes between the 'State of the Operator' and the authority responsible for the issuing of the AOC. This gives States the possibility of designating a RASO as the latter. ECCAA is the only example of a RASO which in 2014 was discharging 'State of the Operator' functions on behalf of its Member States.

However, there are certain legal pitfalls that States should be aware of when deciding to discharge their 'State of the Operator' responsibilities on other than a national basis.

The first point of attention is the fact that ICAO does not readily accept all schemes where several States act jointly as the 'State of the Operator', even though such situations are in practice very rare. The most notable, and so far the only case where two or more States act jointly as the 'State of the Operator' is the Scandinavian Airline System (SAS), which is a multinational operating consortium established in 1951 by Sweden, Norway and Denmark under an international agreement.[93] For the purpose of safety oversight of SAS, the three participating States concluded an agreement under which they share oversight responsibilities and issue approvals and certificates for this company, which means in practice that the approvals are granted on one document issued jointly by the civil aviation authorities of these three States.[94] In relation to this arrangement the ICAO USOAP audit of Norway conducted in 2006 has raised a finding according to which:

> No evidence was provided to show that there was appropriate legal basis for such an oversight mechanism and that Norway had established a means to ensure that its national and international obligations for safety oversight in the delegated areas were fulfilled.[95]

As a result ICAO has recommended to Norway to:

> Ensure that there is an appropriate legal basis for it to assume responsibility on the oversight of SAS International and for the delegation of oversight tasks to STK.[96] When and if applicable, Norway should also establish a means to ensure that its

92. 'Chicago Convention', Article 83 bis (a).
93. Mendes de Leon, *supra* note 78, at pp. 125-127.
94. The SAS is under oversight of OPS-Utvalget (Scandinavian Surveillance System), which was established by an Agreement signed on 20 December 1951 by the Foreign Ministers of Sweden, Denmark and Norway for the purpose of promoting cooperation among Scandinavian flight safety authorities. The AOC of SAS is signed by the Directors General of the three authorities on behalf of OPS-Utvalget (Source: ICAO, 'Final report on the safety oversight audit of the civil aviation system of the Kingdom of Norway', (2006), http://cfapp.icao.int/fsix/AuditReps/CSAfinal/Norway_USOAP_Final_Audit_Report.pdf [accessed 12 August 2014].
95. *Ibid.*, at Appendix 1-1-05.
96. *Ibid.*

national and international obligations for safety oversight in the delegated areas are fulfilled.[97]

The Scandinavian aviation authorities have subsequently submitted a corrective action plan to ICAO to ensure that their national and international obligations for safety oversight of SAS in the relevant areas are fulfilled. This corrective action plan was accepted by ICAO.[98]

The above demonstrates that ICAO seems to accept that a number of its Member States could act jointly as a 'State of the Operator', provided that there is a clear legal basis for the delegation of safety oversight tasks, and the States concerned can demonstrate that national and international obligations for safety oversight are met. Furthermore, the above suggests that it should be likewise possible for a number of States to delegate the exercise of the functions of 'State of the Operator' to a RASO.

The second point to which States should pay attention is the split between the 'State of Registry' and the 'State of the Operator'. Such a scenario is possible under Article 83bis of the Chicago Convention, which in such cases provides for the possibility of *transferring* all or part of the functions and duties of the 'State of Registry' to the 'State of the Operator'. Such transfers allows the exercise of all safety functions related to international air navigation to be kept under the responsibility of a single State, which then has a holistic view of the safety performance of both the operator and its aircraft. However, given the fact that international organisations cannot be party to the Chicago Convention, the conclusion of Article 83bis agreements is only possible between States. From a RASO perspective this has two consequences:

(1) Where a RASO exercises on behalf of its Member States the functions and duties of the 'State of the Operator' or 'State of Registry' it will not be able to conclude Article 83bis with third countries, at least in its own name.[99]

(2) Where a RASO exercises on behalf of its Member States only the functions and duties of the 'State of Registry', while the RASO Member States continue to exercise the functions and duties of the 'State of Operator', any agreement concerning the transfer of responsibilities which may be concluded between the RASO and its Member States, may not be recognised by third countries.[100]

97. *Ibid.*

98. *Ibid.*

99. It could be envisaged however, that a RASO is authorised to conclude Article 83bis agreements on behalf of its Member States.

100. It cannot be excluded however that a RASO which is designated by its Member States as a joint registering authority under Article 77 of the Chicago Convention could be a party to a transfer agreement which could be recognised as valid under the Chicago Convention. Indeed, Article 83bis (c) of the Chicago Convention provides that its provisions of paragraphs a) and b) shall also be applicable to cases covered by Article 77 of the Chicago Convention. The deliberations of the legal committee which led to the formulation of the Article 83bis considered this issue, but finally decided not to go into more details as it was believed that it would be difficult to 'consider all different cases of transfer of functions and duties from joint and international operating organizations to the contracting States which were not members of such organizations'. For further details see: Burkhart von Erlach, 'Public law aspects of lease, charter and interchange of aircraft in international operations', in: Master Thesis, (McGill University: Institute of Air and Space Law, 1990), (pp. 84-87).

§6.04 GENERAL PRINCIPLES OF INTERNATIONAL STATE RESPONSIBILITY

[A] Act or Omission Attributable to a State under International Law

The starting point for analysing the implications of establishing regional aviation safety bodies for international State responsibility is the basic principle of international law according to which every internationally wrongful act of a State entails the international responsibility of that State. This principle was applied in a number of cases by the Permanent Court of International Justice (PCIJ) and the ICJ,[101] and is reflected in Article 1 of the International Law Commission's (ILC) 'Draft Articles on State Responsibility' (DASR).[102] It essentially means that if a State breaches an obligation created by international law, this entails that State's responsibility and as a consequence an obligation of reparations.[103] The reparations can take the form of restitution, compensation or satisfaction.[104]

An internationally wrongful act occurs when there is an act or omission which is *attributable* to a State under international law, and which constitutes a breach of an international obligation of that State.[105] The notion of attribution in this sense is a different concept from empowering a body or organisation to act under administrative or international law, as was addressed under section §6.02 above, and denotes 'an operation of attaching a given action or omission to a State.'[106]

Firstly, the notion of an act or omission has to be considered. In the context of this study, these would be primarily acts or omissions related to the conduct of safety oversight activities, such as certifications, inspections, or the taking of enforcement actions to address identified non-compliances. Legislative activities could also be considered as a potential act or omission triggering international State responsibility. This could be the case for example where a State has an obligation stemming from the

101. 'Phosphates in Morocco (Italy v. France), Judgement', in: [1938] PCIJ Series A/B-No 74, (PCIJ,1938), (p. 28); 'Corfu Channel, Judgement', in: [1949] ICJ Reports 4, (ICJ,1949), (p. 23); 'Military and Paramilitary Activities in and against Nicaragua (Nicaragua v. United States of America)', in: [1986] ICJ Reports 14, (ICJ,1986), pp. 142-143).

102. UN, 'Draft articles on responsibility of States for internationally wrongful acts (DASR)', Yearbook of the International Law Commission, Volume II, Part 2 (2001). For further commentary see: James Crawford, The International Law Commission's Articles on State Responsibility: Introduction, Text and Commentaries, (2002), p. 77. The DASR do not have a status of an international treaty, and have been only noted by the UN General Assembly, and commended to the attention of States (UN General Assembly Resolution 65/19 of 6 December 2010). It is however considered that the DASR is largely a codification of customary international law; see: James Crawford, State Responsibility: The General Part, (2013), pp. 42-44.

103. UN, 'DASR (2001)', *supra* note 102, Article 31. See also: 'Case concerning the Factory at Chorzów (Germany v. Poland), Judgement', in: [1928] PCIJ Series A-No 17, (PCIJ,1928), (p. 29). In this case the PCIJ stated that: 'it is a principle of international law, and even a general conception of law, that any breach of an engagement involves an obligation to make reparation.'

104. UN, 'DASR (2001)', *supra* note 102, Articles 34-37.

105. *Ibid.*, Article 2. See also: 'Phosphates in Morocco (1938)', *supra* note 101, (p. 28); 'United States Diplomatic and Consular Staff in Tehran (United States of America v. Iran), Judgement', in: [1980] ICJ Reports 3, (ICJ,1980), pp. 29-31).

106. Crawford, *supra* note 102, at p. 84.

Chicago Convention to adopt a rule, and does not fulfil this obligation in due time or fulfils it incorrectly.[107]

Concerning the attribution aspects, as was demonstrated under section §6.02, States discharge their civil aviation safety responsibilities either through governmental departments, but also through private entities such as subcontractors or authorised organisations and persons. When it comes to the civil aviation authorities, the situation is straightforward, as regardless of a particular setup, all these agencies and ministries constitute parts of a State's government and therefore the acts of their civil servants, acting within their official capacity, will be the acts of the State itself, and thus attributable to the State. As stated by the ICJ:

> According to a well-established rule of international law, the conduct of any organ of a State must be regarded as an act of that State. This rule ... is of customary character.[108]

When it comes to international State responsibility for actions undertaken by entities which are not part of the governmental structures, the case of ATM and provision of ANS offers a useful analogy, given that many States provide such services today through corporatized or privatised ANSPs.[109]

As pointed out by Van Antwerpen:

> Notwithstanding the organizational format, the underlying State in whose airspace ... air navigation services are being provided is ultimately responsible for the conduct of the air navigation service provider that is involved with the service provision, whether or not through its agents or through an entity outside its governmental structures.[110]

The above stems from the fact that under Article 28 of the Chicago Convention, a State has a general responsibility towards other contracting parties to provide in its territory ANS and facilitates, and to ensure that these meet the minimum standards as established under the Chicago Convention.[111] According to ICAO, the territorial State

---

107. For example when a State fails to transpose a particular ICAO SARP into its national legal order and does not notify a difference under Article 38 of the Chicago Convention.
108. 'Difference Relating to Immunity from Legal Process of a Special Rapporteur of the Commission on Human Rights, Advisory Opinion', in: [1999] ICJ Reports 62, (ICJ,1999), (p. 87). Also as pointed out by Crawford (*supra* note 102, at p. 83): 'Under many legal systems, the State organs consist of different legal persons (ministries or other legal entities), which are regarded as having distinct rights and obligations ... . For the purposes of international law of State responsibility the position is different. The State is treated as a unity, consistent with its recognition as a single legal person under international law.'
109. CANSO, 'Guide to Separation of Service Provision and Regulation', (2011), at p. 36.
110. Van Antwerpen, *supra* note 52 in Ch. 1, at p. 115.
111. Some treaties explicitly provide for attribution to States of actions undertaken by operational entities. For example the 'Outer Space Treaty' in its Article VII attributes to a State responsibility for any damage caused to other States-parties, including their nationals, by objects launched from its territory or facilities, and it is irrelevant if the launch is performed by a governmental or non-governmental entity. See: 'Treaty on Principles Governing the Activities of States in the Exploration and Use of Outer Space, including the Moon and other Celestial Bodies', London, Moscow and Washington, 27 January 1967, 610 UNTS 205.

remains responsible to fulfil these obligations, even when it has decided to delegate their practical implementation to another State.[112]

Does a similar principle apply in the case of delegation by State of civil aviation safety oversight, regulatory and enforcement activities outside of governmental structures?

From the perspective of the Chicago Convention the reply to the above question is affirmative, which means that the acts and omissions of corporate law entities which exercise elements of governmental authority can be attributed to States from an international law point of view. This is clear both from the general principles of international law of State responsibility, and the provisions of Chicago Convention and its Annexes.

In this respect, the main guidance is offered by Article 5 of the DASR which clarifies that:

> The conduct of a person or entity which is not an organ of the State under Article 4 but which is empowered by the law of that State to exercise elements of the governmental authority shall be considered an act of the State under international law, provided the person or entity is acting in that capacity in the particular instance.

As explained by Crawford, the entities referred to in Article 5 of the DASR may include:

> Public corporations, semi-public entities, public agencies of various kinds and even private entities, provided that in each case the entity is explicitly empowered by the law of the State to exercise functions of a public character normally exercised by State organs.[113]

However, it has to be underlined that, in accordance with Article 5 of the DASR, actions of corporate entities will be attributable to States only in those cases where they 'exercise elements of the governmental authority.' This point is important in view of the fact that such entities may provide similar services to governments as well as to other companies on the market. For example, some airlines may wish to contract certification services with a view to helping them to prepare for audits conducted by aviation authorities.[114] Such commercial services will not be considered as falling with the scope of Article 5 of DASR.

---

112. See: ICAO, 'Assembly Resolution A38-12: Consolidated Statement of continuing ICAO policies and associated practices related specifically to air navigation', (38th ICAO Assembly, 2013), which States, at Appendix G that: 'Any delegation of responsibility by one State to another or any assignment of responsibility over the high seas shall be limited to technical and operational functions pertaining to the safety and regularity of the air traffic operating in the airspace concerned.' Similarly: ICAO, 'Annex 11 to the Chicago Convention: Air Traffic Services', (2001), at Note to paragraph 2.1.
113. Crawford, *supra* note 102, at p. 100.
114. For example Austrocontrol, which is a corporatized entity authorized by law to conduct civil aviation certification and oversight tasks in Austria, has also established a subsidiary company – Austro Control GmbH International – which provides training, consultancy and project support services to civil aviation industry.

In addition, as was demonstrated under section §6.03, most of the ICAO Annexes actually explicitly envisage the possibility for a State to designate authorities or organisations which are tasked to exercise, on its behalf, the various responsibilities and tasks codified in these Annexes. From the perspective of the Chicago Convention it does not matter if such organisations or bodies are set up under public or private law of the State concerned. It is up to the State to decide how best to organise the discharge of its safety related responsibilities. However, States have to be aware that if such organisations are empowered by law to exercise elements of the governmental authority, their acts may be attributable to States under international law.

[B] Breach of an International Legal Obligation

Up to 2014, there had been very limited number of cases considered, even preliminarily, from a perspective of international State responsibility under the Chicago Convention.[115] Most of the cases which emerged did not reach the stage of the ICJ, and were usually settled through negotiations between the States concerned.[116] However, it is also true that the ICAO Council had, on a number of occasions, determined that certain State actions constituted infractions of the Chicago Convention within the meaning of its Article 54(j)-(k). These cases concerned aviation security, and more precisely the shoot-down or interception of civil aircraft.[117]

As far as the concept of the breach of an international obligation is concerned, the first point that has to be made is that such a breach does not have to result in *damage* in order to trigger the responsibility.[118] This is a different formulation from that in domestic law, where the responsibility and resulting civil liability typically occurs when there is damage resulting from an act, based on fault/negligence or conduct of abnormally dangerous activity, attributable to a person and with a clear causal link between the damage and the act.[119]

The breach of an international obligation which is attributable to a State is sufficient to trigger the responsibility under international law. In practice however, when it comes to aviation safety, cases involving questions of State responsibility are not likely to arise unless they involve material damages.

It is also irrelevant what the origin or source of the legal obligation is, because international law does not distinguish between responsibility *ex contractu* or *ex delicto*.[120]

---

115. Weber, *supra* note 48 in Ch. 1, at pp. 40-44.
116. *Ibid.*
117. ICAO, 'Infractions of the Convention on International Civil Aviation', C-WP/11186, (185th session of the ICAO Council, 1999).
118. Crawford, *supra* note 102, at p. 84.
119. European Group on Tort Law, Principles of European Tort Law: text and commentary, (2005).
120. 'Any violation by a State of any obligation, of whatever origin, gives rise to State responsibility and consequently, to the duty of reparation'; See: 'Rainbow Warrior (New Zealand v. France)', in: [1990] RIAA, Volume XX, (New Zealand-France Arbitral Tribunal,1990), (p. 251).

There is also a clear distinction between State *responsibility* under international law and domestic *liability*, which is addressed under section §6.06. In general, liability has a broader meaning and may also involve acts that are not unlawful under international law, but which cause damage or injury, and which on this basis create an obligation of compensation.[121]

As was demonstrated in Chapter 2, the system of the Chicago Convention establishes a number of safety related obligations for States, including, the obligation to implement SARPs or to notify the differences (Article 37 and 38), to issue or validate the certificates of airworthiness and pilot licences (Article 31 and 32), to licence the usage of on-board radio equipment (Article 30), to enforce rules related to the flight and manoeuvre of aircraft (Article 12), or to investigate accidents occurring it its territory (Article 26). States can potentially be found in breach of any of them.

In addition, as was demonstrated by Huang in his study of international obligations related to safety and security of civil aviation, it could be argued that failure by a State to establish an effective safety oversight system is a breach of an obligation which every State owes towards all other States, hence a breach of an obligation effective *erga omnes*.[122] This could occur especially if the deficiencies in a State's safety oversight system were confirmed by ICAO in an objective manner.[123] Such a breach could arguably lead to State responsibility, as international law does not limit State responsibility to breaches of obligations established by treaties only.[124]

The above leads to the conclusion that a breach of an obligation of effective civil aviation safety oversight, including resulting from acts or omissions conducted by non-governmental entities acting on behalf of a State, can result in an international responsibility of that State, and subsequently an obligation of reparations if the breach has resulted in an injury.[125] However, as underlined by Crawford in his commentary to DASR, 'there is no such thing as breach of an international obligation in the abstract',[126] which means that each case has to be analysed separately taking into account, in the first place, the obligation of the State concerned, the substance of the conduct required, the standard to be observed, the result to be achieved and relevant circumstances and facts of a particular case.[127]

The question that now needs to be addressed is whether the above principles also apply when States delegate their State safety functions to a RASO.

121. For further discussion see: Schermers and Blokker, *supra* note 72 in Ch. 4, at p. 1006; Crawford, *supra* note 102, at p. 75.
122. Huang, *supra* note 29 in Ch. 1, at p. 231.
123. This would be for example the case when ICAO, following the USOAP monitoring activities, issues a Significant Safety Concern (SSC) in respect to one of its Member States.
124. 'Rainbow Warrior', *supra* note 120, (p. 251).
125. Injury includes any damage, whether material or not, caused by the internationally wrongful act of a State. See: UN, 'DASR (2001)', *supra* note 102, Article 31(2).
126. Crawford, *supra* note 102, at p. 124.
127. *Ibid.*

§6.05 INTERNATIONAL RESPONSIBILITY OF RASOS AND THEIR MEMBER STATES

[A] Determining International Legal Personality of RASOs

The international law regarding responsibility of international organisations is still not settled and many issues are open to interpretation or even disputes.[128] Leckow and Plith characterise the current situation in this respect in the following way:

> While it is recognised that States should be held responsible for their actions, the rules governing responsibility of international organizations are less clear. As a general principle, there is little doubt that international organizations should bear responsibility for wrongful acts. But the international legal jurisprudence and practice governing the circumstances in which responsibility will be imposed on international organizations is not extensive or well-defined.[129]

In 2011, the UN ILC presented to the UN General Assembly 'Draft Articles on the Responsibility of International Organizations' (DARIO)[130] with associated commentary, [131] which is a result of ten years of work by the ILC on this subject. The ILC in its general commentary to DARIO recognised the difficulties in codifying this area of law by referring to limited availability of pertinent practice and limited use of procedures for third-party settlement of disputes to which international organisations are parties.[132] As a result, DARIO constitutes more of a progressive development of international law than its codification.[133]

Regardless of the above controversies, there are a number of principles, which are considered as of customary character in relation to responsibility of international organisations under international law.

First of all, the very principle that an international organisation can be held responsible for breaches of international law is of customary character,[134] and was confirmed in the rulings of the ICJ.[135]

128. Chittharanjan F. Amerasinghe, Principles of the International Law of International Organisations, (2005), p. 384.
129. Ross Leckow and Erik Plith, 'Codification, Progressive Development or Innovation? – Some Reflections on the ILC Articles on the Responsibility of International Organizations', in: Responsibility of international organizations: essays in memory of Sir Ian Brownlie, ed. by Maurizio Ragazzi (2013), p. 225.
130. UN, 'Draft articles on the responsibility of international organizations (DARIO)', Yearbook of the International Law Commission, Volume II, Part 2 (2011).
131. UN, 'DARIO commentary (2011)', *supra* note 96 in Ch. 4.
132. *Ibid.*, at 'General Commentary', paragraph 5.
133. In 2011 the UN General Assembly took note of the articles on the responsibility of international organizations, presented by the International Law Commission and commended them to the attention of the governments and international organizations without prejudice to the question of their future adoption or other appropriate action (see: United Nations General Assembly Resolution 66/100 of 9 December 2011). For a more general discussion about the relevance of DARIO see: Maurizio Ragazzi, 'Responsibility of international organizations: essays in memory of Sir Ian Brownlie', (2013).
134. UN, 'DARIO commentary (2011)', *supra* note 96 in Ch. 4, at p. 13.
135. 'Difference Relating to Immunity from Legal Process', *supra* note 108, (pp. 88-89).

It is also clear that in accordance with international law, only organisations vested with international legal personality have a legal existence separate from their Member States, and thus can have their international responsibility potentially engaged, or can demand responsibility of other international persons. This has been confirmed both by the ICJ,[136] and the ILC, which in Article 2(a) of DARIO provided the following definition of an international organisation:

> International organization means an organization established by a treaty or other instrument governed by international law and *possessing its own international legal personality*. International organizations may include as members, in addition to States, other entities (emphasis added).[137]

A contrario therefore, if an organisation does not possess international legal personality separate from its Member States, then it constitutes merely an extension of States and thus when an organisation acts, it is as if the States were acting themselves.[138] For the purpose of this study the latter would be the case with the pre-RASOs established in the form of national foundations / associations and / or on the basis of MoUs or working arrangements.

As pointed out by Schermers and Blokker, 'today it is generally recognised that international organizations have international legal personality, unless there is clear evidence to the contrary.'[139] They further point out, that the prevailing school of thought at present is that:

> [International] organizations are international legal persons not *ipso facto*, but because the status is given to them either explicitly, or if there is no constitutional attribution of this quality, *implicitly*. If organizations are empowered to conclude treaties, to exchange representatives, and to mobilize international forces ... how can such powers be exercised without the organization having the status of an international legal person?[140]

In view of the above, for the purpose of the present analysis, only RASOs proper will be taken into account, with a caveat that – as was demonstrated under section §5.05 of Chapter 5 – only some of the agreements constituting RASOs explicitly provide for their international legal personality.

Furthermore, a distinction has to be made between, on the one hand, RASOs established in a form of an international organisation and, on the other hand, established in a form of an organ of an international organisation, which in 2014 was

136. 'Reparation for Injuries', *supra* note 76 in Ch. 4, (pp. 178-179, 184-185).
137. UN, 'DARIO (2011)', *supra* note 130, Article 2(a).
138. This has been confirmed by the ICJ in the case: 'Certain Phosphate Lands in Nauru', *supra* note 10 in Ch. 3, (p. 258). See also: Sarooshi, *supra* note 19 in Ch. 2, at p. 34.
139. Schermers and Blokker, *supra* note 72 in Ch. 4, at p. 991.
140. *Ibid.*, p. 989.

the case with EASA and ASSA-AC. In the latter case, it is not the RASO which is a separate international legal person but its mother organisation, such as the EU or CEMAC.

As sections §6.05[B] and §6.05[D] will explain, distinction also has to be made between the attribution of the international legal personality to an organisation in relations with the Member States of that organisation, and vis-à-vis third countries. In the latter case, the question of recognition of the organisation as an international legal person becomes relevant. Finally, a distinction has to be made between international legal personality and domestic legal personality (the latter will be dealt with in section §6.06[D][1]).

Overall, at least eight RASOs from the core sample can be considered as having international legal personality, given the fact that they have been established by international agreements in the form of an international organisation. In two cases, the RASO international legal personality has been explicitly envisaged in its founding treaty (AAMAC, PASO). In addition, in two cases (EASA, ASSA-AC) a RASO has been established as an organ of an international organisation. In six cases the organisation has been granted or has the legal competence to accept Level 3 delegations (EASA/EU, IAC, ECCAA, BAGASOO, BAGAIA and ASSA-AC/CEMAC).

Table 6.1 presents a summary of possible indicators for determining international and domestic legal personality for selected RASOs.

Table 6.1 Indicators for Determining International and Domestic Legal Personality of Selected RASOs

	Established by an International Agreement	*International Personality Explicit in the Founding Document*	*Domestic Personality Explicit in the Founding Document*	*Audited Independently by ICAO under USOAP*	*Concluded or May Conclude Delegation Agreements or Other International Agreements*	*Authorised Agent of Its Member States under the Chicago Convention*	*Designated as a Technical Agent under BASAs*	*Third Countries Recognise Certificates Issued by the RASO*
EU /EASA	X (EU)	X (EU)	X (EASA)	X (EASA)	X (EU)	X (EASA)	X (EASA)	X
IAC	X		X		X	X	X	X
BAGASOO	X		X		X			
BAGAIA	X				X			
CASSOA	X		X					
AAMAC	X	X	X					
PASO	X	X	X					
ECCAA	X		X	X		X		X
CASSOS	X		X					

[B] The Substance of RASOs Responsibility under International Law

[1] Preliminary Remarks

When discussing international responsibility of RASOs', or in the case of organisations like EASA and ASSA-AC of their mother organisations,[141] a distinction has to be made, on the one hand, between such international responsibility of a RASO towards its Member States and, on the other hand, towards third-countries. This distinction is important in view of the principle *pacta tertiis nec nocent nec prosunt*, which does not permit an imposition of an obligation on a State, or international organisation, without its consent.[142]

The relationship between a RASO and its Member States will in the first place be regulated by the constituent act and other relevant documents, such as the headquarters / host State agreement,[143] or bilateral delegation agreements. These documents, as well as general rules of international law can be a source of rights and obligations in the bilateral relations between a RASO and its Member States. If such obligations are breached, international responsibility could, in principle, be invoked by the organisation[144] or its Member States.[145] The main difficulty in such cases would of course be the fact that 'there is no compulsory system for review of the acts of international organizations by external bodies'.[146] In the case of RASOs only some of their constituent documents explicitly provide for such mandatory dispute resolution mechanisms,[147] which

141. In the case of RASOs established in the form of an organ of an international organisation, the notion of RASO as used in this section should be read as referring to the international organisation of which the RASO is an organ.
142. 'Vienna Convention on the Law of the Treaties', *supra* note 63 in Ch. 2, Articles 35-36.
143. The conclusion of headquarters agreements is explicitly envisaged in: 'BAGASOO Agreement', *supra* note 147 in Ch. 3, Article 17; 'BAGAIA Agreement', *supra* note 221 in Ch. 3, Article 15; 'AAMAC Treaty', *supra* note 81 in Ch. 3, Article 7; 'CASSOS Agreement', *supra* note 168 in Ch. 3, Article XVI.
144. In the 'Reparations for Injuries' case, the ICJ stated that 'it cannot be doubted that the Organization has the capacity to bring an international claim against one of its Members which has caused injury to it by a breach of its international obligations towards it'; see: 'Reparation for Injuries', *supra* note 76 in Ch. 4, (p. 180).
145. The RASO Member States have various ways of exerting influence on the functioning of the organisation, notably through the control of its budget and work programme, so an international action would be used as a means of a last resort.
146. Crawford, *supra* note 73 in Ch. 4, at p. 196.
147. For example CASSOA, if it fails to resolve any dispute with a Member State through a dispute resolution mechanism can bring the case to the East African Court of Justice, whose decisions are final; see: CASSOA Protocol, *supra* note 191 in Ch. 3, Article 18. Similarly the ECCAA can be party to the proceedings in front of arbitration tribunals in cases involving its disputes with Member States; see: 'ECCAA Agreement', *supra* note 268 in Ch. 3, Article 24. Also EUROCONTROL can be a party in dispute resolution proceedings with its Member States, and which involve a possibility of arbitration at the Permanent Court of Arbitration in The Hague, as provided in: 'Consolidated version of the EUROCONTROL international Convention relating to co-operation for the safety of air navigation of 13 December 1960, as variously amended', Brussels, 27 June 1997, Final Act of the Diplomatic Conference. The position of EASA is specific, as eventual disputes related to the implementation of the EU legislation are resolved between EU institutions and EU Member States in front of the CJEU.

from the perspective of DARIO could be referred to as special rules of international law, or *lex specialis*.[148]

The question of international responsibility of a RASO vis-à-vis the non-Member States is even more complicated in view of the above invoked principle *pacta tertiis nec nocent nec prosunt*, and the consequent lack of a third party effect of the RASO founding documents. This issue is probably most relevant from the perspective of the Chicago Convention and the safety related obligations that it establishes for the vast majority of the States around the world.

At present, the safety related obligations established by the Chicago Convention and its Annexes, including in particular the obligation to transpose and apply the SARPs are applicable to the 191 Contracting Parties to the Convention. Currently no RASO can accede to the Chicago Convention, because this instrument is not open for the participation of international organisations.[149] Some practice of ICAO and its Member State is emerging which gives RSOOs a status similar to States, but today this practice is still not consistent and thus far away from constituting a rule of customary international law.[150]

[2] Ultimate State Responsibility under the Chicago Convention

Based on the fact that only States can be parties to the Chicago Convention, ICAO has formulated the principle of *ultimate State responsibility*, which is expressed in the following formulation:

> Responsibility/accountability: The state of being responsible for an undertaking, person, thing or action and for which an organization or individual or both are liable to be called to account. An ICAO Contracting State and its respective civil aviation authority are ultimately responsible for the implementation of ICAO SARPs within their State. A State may either perform these obligations or, through mutual agreement, have another organization perform and be accountable for these functions; however, the State retains the responsibility under its duties of sovereignty.[151]

The principle of ultimate State responsibility under the Chicago Convention was further elaborated by ICAO in the specific context of RASOs. The ICAO Safety Oversight Manual explains that 'only the State has responsibility for safety oversight, and this

148. See Article 64 of DARIO, *supra* note 130, which states that: 'These articles do not apply where and to the extent that the conditions for the existence of an internationally wrongful act or the content or implementation of the international responsibility of an international organization, or a State in connection with the conduct of an international organization, are governed by special rules of international law. *Such special rules of international law may be contained in the rules of the organization applicable to the relations between an international organization and its members* (emphasis added).
149. 'Chicago Convention', Articles 92-93.
150. So far only one Assembly resolution has been adopted which States that, where applicable: 'word "States" ... should be read to include RSOOs'; see: Assembly Resolution A37-5, *supra* note 71 in Ch. 2.
151. ICAO Doc. 9734 Part B, *supra* note 3 in Ch. 1, at p. xi.

responsibility may not be transferred to a regional body ...,'[152] and that this principle applies 'regardless of the level of authority delegated to the RSOO.'[153]

The above approach is also followed by ICAO under the USOAP, where even when a State discharges certain of its safety oversight functions through a RASO, ICAO links the findings made during audits of such a RASO with the USOAP audit results of the State concerned.[154]

In the domain of ATM the principle of non-transferability of responsibility has even been confirmed by an ICAO Assembly Resolution A38-12 which states, that:

> Any delegation of responsibility by one State to another or any assignment of responsibility over the high seas shall be limited to technical and operational functions pertaining to the safety and regularity of the air traffic operating in the airspace concerned.[155]

The principle of ultimate State responsibility has also been raised in the initial process of establishing EASA in the form of an international organisation, and where the report of the Expert Group on Legal Issues stated that:

> The group took the view that the Chicago Convention does not prevent Member States from delegating such certification and/or licensing tasks to EASA, provided that it is clearly established that, for the purpose of the Chicago Convention, the ultimate responsibility remains with the Member States.[156]

The principle of non-transferability of responsibilities under the Chicago Convention applies not only in relations between States and RASOs but also in between the States themselves. This means that the Chicago Convention does not allow, through an act of delegation, a State to be relieved from ultimate legal responsibility associated with the obligation towards other States-parties to the Chicago Convention – so in other words, to transfer such responsibility.

De lege lata the only exception in the Chicago Convention from the principle of non-transferability of responsibilities is its Article 83bis, which allows a 'State of Registry' to be 'relieved of responsibility in respect of the functions and duties transferred' to a 'State of the Operator'.[157] The crucial issue is the third party effect of Article 83bis, which means that any transfer agreement signed between States party to

152. *Ibid.*, at paragraph 2.1.8.
153. *Ibid.*, at paragraph 4.1.35.
154. For example, following the USOAP audit of EASA, ICAO linked the findings of this audit with the results of the USOAP audits of EU Member States and clarified that: 'ICAO Contracting States that are members of EASA will always maintain their individual responsibility for such competencies and, hence, for all audit results that are derived from the audit carried out on EASA. Once an EASA Member State's audit is completed, the latest EASA safety oversight audit report will be linked to the final safety oversight audit report of the State concerned.' See: ICAO USOAP report on EASA (2008), *supra* note 100 in Ch. 4, at paragraph 1.1.9.
155. Assembly Resolution A38-12, *supra* note 112. Similar principle is expressed in: Annex 11 to the Chicago Convention, at Note to paragraph 2.1.
156. Report on the Work of the Expert Group on Legal Issues (AER/98/17), *supra* note 20 in Ch. 4, at p. 11.
157. For more information on practical implementation of Article 83bis see: ICAO, 'Guidance on the Implementation of Article 83 bis of the Convention on International Civil Aviation', Circular 295, (2003).

Article 83bis will have to be recognised by other States bound by Article 83bis,[158] on condition that the transfer agreement had been duly notified to them.[159] The implications of Article 83bis from the perspective of RASOs were addressed under section §6.03[A][2].

In view of the above, even in the case of RASOs which enjoy Level 3 delegations, the transfer of Chicago Convention related safety tasks and associated responsibilities takes place only *inter se,* which may have relevance for civil liability of Member States of a RASO in their internal relations (an issue which is addressed under section §6.04), but does not create effects vis-à-vis third countries from the perspective of the Chicago Convention. In such cases we should be speaking essentially about an *agency relationship*, whereby the regional body is acting on behalf of and in the name of its Member States.

The above understanding is confirmed by the intention of States expressed in RASO founding documents. In those cases where safety functions have been delegated, even potentially, at Level 3, the founding documents speak about a RASO acting 'on behalf of its Member States' or 'upon delegation'. This is the case even in the EU, where the tasks and responsibilities of the 'State of Design', 'State of Registry' and 'State of Manufacture' when related to design aspects, have been transferred to EU, which from the international law point of view acts through EASA, on an exclusive basis, but where nevertheless the EASA Basic Regulation speaks about EASA as acting 'on behalf of Member States'.[160] Similar language can be found in constituent documents of BAGASOO,[161] BAGAIA,[162] and ECCAA.[163]

---

158. Article 83bis was introduced into the Chicago Convention through an amending protocol adopted by the ICAO Assembly on 6 October 1980, and in force since 20 July 1997; see: ICAO, 'Protocol Relating to an Amendment to the Convention on International Civil Aviation (Article 83bis)', ICAO Doc 9318, (1980).
159. See: Chicago Convention, Article 83bis (b), which states that: 'The transfer shall not have effect in respect of other contracting States before either the agreement between the States in which it is embodied has been registered with the Council and made public pursuant to Article 83 or the existence and scope of the agreement have been directly communicated to the authorities of the other contracting State or States concerned by a State party to the agreement.'
160. See: Regulation (EU) No 216/2008, *supra* note 81 in Ch. 2, Article 17(2)(e), which states that: 'For the purposes of ensuring the proper functioning and development of civil aviation safety, the Agency shall: ... in its fields of competence, carry out, on behalf of Member States, functions and tasks ascribed to them by applicable international conventions, in particular the Chicago Convention.' See also: *Ibid.*, Article 20(1), which states that: 'With regard to the products, parts and appliances referred to in Article 4(1)(a) and (b), the Agency shall, where applicable and as specified in the Chicago Convention or its Annexes, carry out on behalf of Member States the functions and tasks of the State of design, manufacture or registry when related to design approval.'
161. See: 'BAGASOO Agreement', *supra* note 147 in Ch. 3, Article 5(e) which states that: 'The functions of the BAGASOO shall be to: Perform certification and surveillance tasks on behalf of Member States CAAs, as required.'
162. See: 'BAGAIA Agreement', *supra* note 221 in Ch. 3, Article 5(k), which states that: 'The functions of the BAGAIA shall be to: Conduct, either in whole or any part of, an investigation into an aircraft accident or serious incident upon delegation by a State of Occurrence in the BAG Sub-Region, by mutual arrangement and consent between the State of Occurrence and the BAGAIA.'
163. See: 'ECCAA Agreement', *supra* note 268 in Ch. 3, Article 5(k), which states that: 'For the attainment of its purposes the Authority may regulate civil aviation in the Participating States on behalf of and in collaboration with Participating States.'

In addition, when the governments of the EU Member States[164] notified ICAO about the establishment of EASA, the text of the diplomatic note, coordinated at the EU level, referred to EASA as an 'authorised representative for the fulfilment of governmental obligations as State of design or manufacture, as specified in Part II of Annex 8 to the Chicago Convention.'[165] These notifications were recognised by ICAO, which subsequently conducted two USOAP audits of EASA.[166]

In view of the above, the most obvious conclusion to be drawn with regard to international responsibility of RASOs, or of international organisations of which RASOs are organs, is an analogy with Article 28 of the Chicago Convention. This means that even when a State decides to discharge all or some of its safety related responsibilities through a regional safety body, it has to be aware that, from the Chicago Convention point of view, it has not relieved itself from potential international State responsibility, and the actions of a RASO can be attributed to it.

The non-transferability of legal responsibility in case of an agency relationship is in line with the theory of this legal concept under international law. Sarooshi comments on this issue as follows:

> An important consequence of an agency relationship is that the principal is responsible for its agent's acts that are within the scope of the conferred powers. Accordingly where an organization acts as an agent for certain States then the States concerned are responsible for any unlawful acts committed by the organization in the exercise of conferred powers.[167]

Similarly Amerasinghe observes that:

> It is also clear that where such agency is proved to exist the liability of the members would not really be for the obligations of the organization but a direct liability for their own obligations which have been incurred by the organization acting as their agent ... .[168]

The principle of ultimate State responsibility under the Chicago Convention probably contributes to an overall reluctance of States in establishing RASOs with far reaching regulatory and oversight competences (Level 3 RASOs). Indeed the question of national sovereignty and responsibility has been mentioned in this context by many of the RASO officers interviewed for the purpose of this study. This reluctance to establish an organisation for the actions of which they could be held responsible is something not specific to RASOs, but rather a manifestation of a more general attitude of States towards international organisations. Using the words of Nakatani:

164. In addition to EU Member States, the notification was made also by Norway, Iceland and Switzerland, which are associated with the EU aviation safety system on the basis of separate international agreements and for which EASA also acts as an authorised technical agent.
165. See: Template for EU Member States démarche to ICAO on the transfer of regulatory tasks to EASA, *supra* note 81 in Ch. 4, which states that: 'The ... Government has therefore the pleasure to thereby notify to ICAO and its Contracting States that the European Aviation Safety Agency is now its authorised representative for the fulfilment of its obligation, as State of design or manufacture, as specified in Part II of Annex VIII to the Chicago Convention.'
166. ICAO USOAP report on EASA (2008), *supra* note 100 in Ch. 4, at paragraph 1.1.8.
167. Sarooshi, *supra* note 19 in Ch. 2, pp. 50-51.
168. IIL Yearbook, *supra* note 91 in Ch. 4, at p. 354.

> The reasons why member States resist accepting responsibility for an act of an international organization are twofold. Firstly, within the general context of State responsibility, what States fear most is the loss of their dignity, and this seems to be the main reason why States are reluctant to admit responsibility or even the facts leading to the attribution of responsibility. Secondly, within the particular context of the responsibility of member States, States consider it irrational, or at least unconvincing, the proposition that they should incur responsibility for another entity, even if it has been constituted by their will. Overcoming these selfish concerns does not appear to be easy.[169]

On the other hand, the fact that States remain ultimately responsible under the Chicago Convention also means that they have a stronger incentive to make sure that their RASO is appropriately equipped to discharge the functions and duties the consequences of which may at the end of the day be attributed to them.

From an international law point of view, the non-transferability of safety responsibilities which States have under the Chicago Convention can also be defended using an argument that States should not be allowed to release themselves from international obligations by hiding behind another international legal personality.[170]

To conclude, while the point of departure in international law is that Member States should not be held responsible for wrongful acts committed by international organisations,[171] it is also true that international organisations are governed by the principle of speciality, which was invoked in section §6.02[B], and which may provide for specific rules of attribution and wrongfulness. In this respect, when analysing RASOs it is of fundamental importance to carefully scrutinise the underlying relationship which exists between the organisation and its Member States. This was very aptly underlined by ILC in its commentary to DARIO: 'the diversity of international organizations may affect the application of certain articles, some of which may not apply to certain international organizations in the light of their powers and functions.'[172]

In fact, in the case of an agency relationship between a State and an international organisation, one should apply in the first place the rules concerning the international responsibility of States rather than of international organisations. In this respect, this study very much agrees with Brownlie, who summarised this problem as follows:

> The literature tends to focus upon the existence or not of a distinct legal personality – an international organization – and then to assume that the terms of the constituent instrument are not only relevant but represent a legal regime which third States must accept. The appropriate analysis is to treat the organization (or

169. Kazuhiro Nakatani, 'Responsibility of Member States towards Third Parties for an Internationally Wrongful Act of the Organization', in: Responsibility of international organizations: essays in memory of Sir Ian Brownlie, ed. by Maurizio Ragazzi (2013), p. 301.
170. Dan Sarooshi, 'International Organizations and State Responsibility', in: Responsibility of international organizations: essays in memory of Sir Ian Brownlie, ed. by Maurizio Ragazzi (2013), p. 84; Ian Brownlie, 'The responsibility of States for the acts of international organizations', in: International Responsibility today: Essays in the Memory of Oscar Schachter, ed. by Maurizio Ragazzi (2005), p. 362.
171. Jean d'Aspremont, 'Abuse of the Legal Personality of International Organizations and the Responsibility of Member States', IOLR, (2007), pp. 95-96; UN, 'DARIO commentary (2011)', *supra* note 96 in Ch. 4, at p. 96.
172. UN, 'DARIO commentary (2011)', *supra* note 96 in Ch. 4, at 'General Commentary', p. 3.

> the joint agency of States) simply as a part of the factual elements, which, upon analysis, may lead to the responsibility of the member States, or some of them, to a third State. On this view the applicable legal category is that of State responsibility, and not the law of international organizations.[173]

The above approach will be especially pertinent in the case of organisations such as ECCAA, which, although separate from its Member States from an international law point of view, has been so deeply integrated into the national legal orders of the OECS Member States, that it has, from that internal law perspective, become an organ of these States, as was explained in section §3.06[B][2] of Chapter 3.

Similarly, a clear distinction has to be made between the Level 3 and other RASOs. In the latter case, it is the RASO Member States which continue taking decisions, such as issuing or revoking a certificate, from a legal point of view, although they may be assisted in this process, to a greater or lesser extent, by their RASO.

Finally, the above discussion about ultimate State responsibility under the Chicago Convention should be separated from the question of eventual *parallel* responsibility of a RASO under international law, an issue which is dealt with in section §6.05[D].

[C] Relevance of RASOs Oversight by Its Member States

As the involvement of international organisations in global governance increases so do the calls for their increased accountability for actions. In this sense, the term *accountability* is necessarily broader than responsibility and liability. Leckow and Plith characterise it in the following way:

> Accountability generally refers not only to the political process of ensuring that institutions live up to their promises vis-à-vis its member States and other interested stakeholders, but also to the responsibility to comply with applicable duties and obligations, and to accountability in other senses of the word, including moral accountability.[174]

In the context of this study the question of RASO oversight by its Member States is particularly relevant. ICAO addresses this issue briefly in its RSOO manual, where it is clarified that:

> Although the State may delegate specific safety oversight tasks and functions to an RSOO ..., the State must still retain the minimum capability required to carry out its responsibilities under the Chicago Convention. States must always be able to properly and effectively monitor the safety oversight functions delegated to the RSOO.[175]

The oversight issue, in the context of delegation of ANS provision, is also raised by Van Antwerpen, who attaches important legal consequences to it:

---

173. Brownlie, *supra* note 170, at p. 360.
174. Leckow and Plith, *supra* note 129, at p. 226.
175. ICAO Doc. 9734 Part B, *supra* note 3 in Ch. 1, atparagraph 2.1.8.

> In the event of an act or omission of ... privatised air navigation service provider it turns out that the State has failed to keep the appropriate regulatory oversight or has failed to verify the compliance of the air navigation service provider to rules and regulations imposed by the State, this could trigger the ultimate State responsibility. At the same time, if the State has met its obligations and has not failed to perform audits or regulatory oversight, the act or omission ... should not trigger State responsibility.[176]

Oversight of RASOs is very much linked with the principle of ultimate State responsibility, as States will generally want to exercise a certain degree of control over organisations upon which they confer civil aviation safety related competences. Especially when a RASO is exercising Chicago Convention related safety functions and duties on behalf of its Member States, the latter may feel a particular need to exercise a certain degree of oversight, given States' ultimate responsibility under the Convention. As was pointed out by a former Chairman of the EASA Management Board:

> In the event of an accident in a State's territory, a Minister in that State cannot, for political reasons, simply shrug off regulatory responsibility to EASA. At the very least the Minister would need to demonstrate to his/her public and Parliament that the State has done what it can to monitor the effectiveness of the Agency.[177]

This study agrees that States need to exercise oversight over a RASO they create. However, in this case one should not require the same method of oversight as in respect of a service provider, which should be subject to the same safety requirements regardless of its organisational or corporate structure, and where accordingly the level of oversight should also always be the same.

The level of RASO oversight required from its Member States should not lead to the need to control in detail every aspect of the regional body's actions or to the replication of expertise at national and regional levels, as this would effectively defeat the very purpose of establishing regional safety bodies.

The proper approach should be rather to look at a State and all entities working on its behalf as a system which, taken together, should guarantee the level of safety oversight required by the Chicago Convention and its safety related Annexes. Under this approach, oversight of a RASO could be organised by relying on mechanisms similar to those used by States to control the functioning of national agencies. This includes regular reporting by a RASO on its activities, the setting up of a supervisory or management board, and most importantly the regular and ad hoc auditing of RASO operations, accounts and administrative practices.[178] In this respect a distinction has to be made, between oversight, and direction or operational control.[179]

As to the consequences - from an international law point of view - of a lack of proper oversight over a RASO, this study argues that, in such cases, the eventual RASO

176. Van Antwerpen, *supra* note 52 in Ch. 1, at p. 165.
177. Former Chairman of the EASA Management Board, 'Interview No 12', (2014).
178. For example in the EU, the EASA is subject to regular audits by the European Court of Auditors. See: Regulation (EU) No 216/2008, *supra* note 81 in Ch. 2, Article 60.
179. See in this respect also the commentary to DARIO which explains that from the perspective of the law of international responsibility oversight is in principle not to be identified with either direction or control (UN, 'DARIO commentary (2011)', *supra* note 96 in Ch. 4, at p. 38).

Member States' responsibility is not a question related to the attribution of actions, which stems from the underlying legal relationship between a RASO and its Member States, but rather a matter of the required *standard of conduct*, which has to be assessed on a case by case basis in the light of all the relevant facts and circumstances. By standard of conduct is meant here the overall effectiveness of the safety oversight system of the RASO Member State. This overall effectiveness will also depend on the robustness of the oversight that the Member States exercise over the RASO. For example, it will be more difficult for a State to defend itself if an aviation accident resulted from the fact that it has not notified ICAO of a difference with applicable international safety requirements because 'its' RASO did not have a system for identifying such differences, than in a situation where an accident happened despite all the relevant requirements having being complied with and effectively implemented.

As is the case with engaging international responsibility of a RASO, this study did not identify court cases related to engaging international responsibility of States for the actions of their RASOs. In practice engaging such responsibility could be complicated due to the fact that a RASO acts as an agent representing multiple principals. Which State to engage may not be so obvious, while engaging more than one may not always be practical.

At the same time, liability cases involving questions of aviation safety and oversight responsibilities are usually associated with accidents and resulting damages. Thus, while maintaining ultimate State responsibility is important from the perspective of the improvement of the overall international system of aviation safety, from the perspective of the victims of aviation accidents and their families, the more relevant are questions concerning civil liability of a RASO under domestic law and the duty to compensate damages. These issues are addressed in section §6.06.

[D] Parallel Responsibility of RASOs vis-à-vis Non-Member States

Whilst the principle of ultimate State responsibility under the Chicago Convention answers the question concerning the consequences that the establishment of a RASO may have for its Member States, this principle does not fully explain the question of a possible parallel responsibility of a RASO vis-à-vis the non-Member States.

'Although it may not frequently occur in practice, dual or even multiple attribution of conduct [in international law] cannot be excluded',[180] and the jurisprudence confirms that.[181] In the specific aviation context, the ICAO Council Resolution on non-national aircraft registration which was reviewed under section §6.03[A][1] also suggests that multiple attribution of conduct is possible not only in situations involving States but also an international organisation.

180. *Ibid.*, at p. 16.
181. For an overview of the international case law where multiple attribution took place see: Francesco Messineo, 'Multiple Attribution of Conduct', Research Paper 11 (2012), The Research Project on Shared Responsibility in International Law (SHARES) 2012), available at: www.sharesproject.nl.

Although this study did not identify any case of a State trying to engage international responsibility of a RASO in respect to safety functions envisaged under the Chicago Convention, such possibility should therefore not be completely excluded. What conditions would need to be met, in order for such responsibility to be engaged?

First of all, as was pointed under section §6.05, it is an established principle of international law that the responsibility of an organisation can be engaged only if that organisation is vested with a separate legal personality under international law.[182] Here a distinction has to be made again between, on the one hand, RASOs established in a form of an international organisation and, on the other hand, an organ of an international organisation. With respect to the latter, the potential international responsibility would be engaged not in respect to the RASO but in respect to the international organisation of which it is an organ.

The international legal personality of a RASO or of its mother organisation would be effective vis-à-vis non-Member States only if it has been explicitly or implicitly recognised by such States.[183] Such international recognition 'is implied when a State (or an organization) is admitted as a member, when an agreement is entered into with a State (or an organization), or when the State is invited to a session or a conference.'[184]

With regard to the above, this study found that most of the RASOs or their mother organisations are regularly invited by ICAO to international symposia and conferences. In the case of EASA, the EU has entered into international agreements with third countries and ICAO, under which EASA has been designated as an authorised agent of EU Member States.[185] Some of the RASOs, such as EASA or ECCAA, have been subject to ICAO USOAP audits, which too is a sign of recognition in international relations.[186]

In addition, the present study found that third countries recognise the legal effects that the currently operational Level 3 RASOs, that is EASA, IAC and ECCAA, take on behalf of States. In the case of IAC, third countries readily accept that this RASO acts on behalf of, for example, the Russian Federation in aviation accident investigations.[187] Airlines certified by the ECCAA are able to operate to third countries, meaning that the AOCs and Certificates of Airworthiness issued by this RASO are considered as valid under the Chicago Convention.[188]

182. UN, 'DARIO (2011)', *supra* note 130, Article 2(a).
183. Schermers and Blokker, *supra* note 72 in Ch. 4, at p. 990.
184. *Ibid.*, at p. 1183.
185. These international agreements include BASAs which were addressed in section §4.03[D] of Chapter 4 and the EU-ICAO MoC which was referred to in section §4.04[C][3] of Chapter 4.
186. ICAO USOAP report on EASA (2008), *supra* note 100 in Ch. 4; ICAO USOAP report on OECS (2007), *supra* note 290 in Ch. 3.
187. See for example: Accident Investigation Board Norway, 'Report concerning aviation accident on the Cape Heer heliport, Svalbard, Norway, 30 March 2008 with MIL MI-8MT, RA-06152, operated by SPARK+ AIRLINE LTD.', Report, SL 2013/06, (2013); National Transportation Safety Committee of Indonesia, 'Aircraft Accident Investigation Report, Sukhoi Civil Aircraft Company, Sukhoi RRJ-95B; 97004, Mount Salak, West Java, Republic of Indonesia, 9 May 2012', KNKT.12.05.09.04, (2012); Ministry of Infrastructure Development Tanzania, 'Report on the accident to Ilyushin IL-76TD aircraft registration ER-IBR which occurred on 23 March 2005 in lake Victoria near Mwanza, Tanzania', Civil aircraft accident No. CAV/ACC/3/05.
188. In 2006 the ECCAA has obtained Category 1 under the US FAA IASA programme. This gave to the ECCAA certified airlines the possibility to fly to the US. In 2014 the LIAT international

The case of EASA is quite specific and one could argue that the relationship of international agency that exists between EU, acting through EASA, and its Member States is globally recognised. This is because EASA acts as a 'State of Design' for one of the leading aircraft manufacturers in the world, namely Airbus. Airbus aircraft can be found on registries of many countries around the world.[189] This means that such third country 'States of Registry', readily accept Type Certificates issued by EASA on behalf of EU Member States,[190] and exchange with EASA information which is necessary for ensuring the continuing airworthiness of the aircraft.[191]

The second element which would need to be established before engaging international legal responsibility of a RASO, or of its mother organisation, is a breach of an international legal obligation. In the case of international responsibility vis-à-vis the non-Member States, this means that one would have to demonstrate that a RASO or its mother organisation is effectively bound by the provisions of the Chicago Convention. Given the fact that international organisations cannot be parties to this Convention, the existence of such an obligation would have to be demonstrated through other means.

Sarooshi argues that even in the relationship of an international agency there is a 'general presumption that an organization retains a joint responsibility for any unlawful acts committed',[192] although this study was not able to identify other authorities which explicitly share this view.

Another way of making such a determination would be to argue that some provisions of the Chicago Convention, and more generally the obligation to provide effective safety oversight is an obligation *erga omnes*, as was already demonstrated by Huang.[193] This would mean that RASOs are bound by these obligations, because as was stated by the ICJ:

> International organizations are subjects of international law and, as such, are bound by any obligation incumbent upon them under general rules of international law, under their constitutions or under international agreements to which they are parties. [194]

The above argument is especially relevant in case of RASOs enjoying Level 3 delegations, which are expected to carry out their safety functions in compliance with Chicago Convention and its Annexes. The obligation to respect the Chicago Convention

---

airlines, an ECCAA certified operator incorporated in Antigua and Barbuda was operating scheduled flights to Puerto Rico (US).

189. At the beginning of May 2014 Airbus aircraft were operated by 398 operators coming from all the regions of the world. For a detailed overview see: Airbus, 'Airbus for analysts' http://www.airbus.com/tools/airbusfor/analysts/ [accessed 10 May 2014].
190. For a list of working arrangements between EASA and non-EU countries concerning the validation of EASA Type Certificates see: EASA, 'Working Arrangements' http://easa.europa.eu/document-library/working-arrangements [accessed 6 August 2014].
191. For obligations concerning interactions between 'State of Design' and 'State of Registry' see Annex 8 to the Chicago Convention.
192. Sarooshi, *supra* note 19 in Ch. 2, at p. 51.
193. Huang, *supra* note 29 in Ch. 1, at p. 231.
194. 'Interpretation of the Agreement of 25 March 1951 between WHO and Egypt, Advisory Opinion', in: [1980] ICJ Reports 73, (ICJ,1980), pp. 89-90).

and its Annexes has been for example explicitly stated in the EASA Basic Regulation.[195] Similarly ICAO, when auditing RASOs, takes the Chicago Convention and its Annexes as reference standards, and expects the RASOs, as agents of States, to be compliant with relevant provisions of these instruments.[196]

Finally, in the case of EU, BASAs have been concluded by this international organisation with third countries, such as the US, Canada or Brazil, and where the EU has undertaken to carry out, through EASA, Chicago Convention related safety functions on behalf of its Member States. Under these BASAs bilateral partners of EU expect this regional organisation to carry out the relevant safety functions in compliance with the ICAO SARPs, and thus to be bound by them.[197]

The proposition made in this section, namely the recognition that some of the RASOs or their mother organisations could be bound by the provisions of the Chicago Convention, can of course be controversial. However, this study would not be complete without considering this issue, even if on a preliminary basis. Level 3 RASOs or their mother organisations in particular, have both the legal capacity, being an international legal person, and operational competences such as safety certification, which can be discharged negligently. Outright rejection of the possibility of holding such organisations responsible for acts, which at the end of the day create binding effects under the Chicago Convention, could effectively amount to putting them in a legal vacuum, especially if there is also no mechanism allowing individuals to engage RASOs' non-contractual liability.

The possibility of holding an organisation responsible or liable for its actions generally contributes to this organisation exercising more due diligence, or better duty of care in the performance of its functions. This would be relevant especially in cases where a State has delegated the exercise of all or most of its safety functions to a RASO and has to rely to a very large extent on such an organisation for demonstrating compliance with the Chicago Convention and its Annexes.

At the same time, it is not expected that the question of international responsibility of a RASO would readily arise in front of international courts or tribunals. In the history of the Chicago Convention, there has not been a single case heard by international judicial bodies and related to breach of international obligations directly involving State safety oversight responsibilities.[198] Also, 'as in the case of international claims against States, claims against international organizations can be brought as

195. Regulation (EU) No 216/2008, *supra* note 81 in Ch. 2, at Preamble clause No 7, Article 20(1), and Article 27.
196. ICAO USOAP report on EASA (2008), *supra* note 100 in Ch. 4; ICAO USOAP report on OECS (2007), *supra* note 290 in Ch. 3.
197. See in particular paragraph 3.3.2 of the EU-US BASA, which provides that the EU technical agent 'shall carry out on behalf of the EU Member States the State of Design functions applicable to them under Annex 8 of the Chicago Convention for regulated entities over which it has jurisdiction'.
198. The shooting down of the Malaysian Airlines aircraft, flight MH17, in July 2014 could change that however, if the accident investigation (ongoing at the moment of writing this study) would reveal serious deficiencies in the safety management system of the ANSP which was responsible, on behalf of the Ukrainian State, for taking decisions related to the management of the airspace in which the shooting down took place.

international claims only when the local remedies have been exhausted.'[199] This means bringing the claim first before the competent organ of the organisation or 'before arbitral tribunals, national courts or administrative bodies when the international organization has accepted their competence to examine claims.'[200]

In this respect, the question of civil liability of RASOs, which is the subject matter of the next section, is probably of greater practical relevance.

§6.06 CIVIL LIABILITY OF RASOs FOR NEGLIGENT SAFETY OVERSIGHT UNDER DOMESTIC LAW

[A] Introduction

Liability of regulators and supervisors for non-contractual damages is a topic of recurrent debate in law.[201] As pointed out by Gisen and Bell, this can in part be attributed to the fact that modern societies can increasingly be characterised as service-providing societies, with greater focus on the citizen as a consumer, and the emergence of supervision as a service offered by a State to protect the interests of the general public.[202]

The other reason highlighted in academic writings is the alleged emergence of the *compensation culture*, where victims may be seeking compensation not only from the primary *tortfeasor*, but also from other *deep pockets*, including the State.[203]

Regardless of the policy discussions, the fact is that courts recognise the possibility of holding regulators liable for damages stemming from their negligent actions. An overview of case law from EU Member States shows that such liability can be established in cases involving areas as diverse as: damages caused by police, fire-fighting brigades, unsafe road infrastructure, food safety authorities, motor vehicle inspections, and financial regulation.[204]

The above is also true in respect to aviation safety regulation – although, fortunately, the cases involving liability of aviation safety regulators and supervisors are not numerous. However, the available, aviation related, case law comes mainly from the common law jurisdictions, so it is not certain if the civil law countries would adopt a similar approach.

199. Schermers and Blokker, *supra* note 72 in Ch. 4, at p. 1192.
200. UN, 'DARIO commentary (2011)', *supra* note 96 in Ch. 4, at pp. 72-74.
201. For a good overview see: Mads Andenas, Duncan Fairgrieve, and John Bell, Tort Liability of Public Authorities in Comparative Perspective, (2002); Cherie Booth QC and Dan Squires, The Negligence Liability of Public Authorities, (2006).
202. Ivo Gisen, 'Regulating regulators through liability: the case for applying normal tort rules to supervisors', Utrecht Law Review, 2 (2006), p. 8; John Bell, 'Governmental Liability: some comparative reflections', InDret, 1 (2006), p. 3.
203. Gisen, 'Regulating regulators', *supra* note 202, at p. 13.
204. Cees C. van Dam, 'Aansprakelijkheid van Toezichthouders, Een analyse van de aansprakelijkheidsrisico's voor toezichthouders wegens inadequaat handhavingstoezicht en enige aanbevelingen voor toekomstig beleid', Text primarily in English, (British Institute of International and Comparative Law, 2006), http://www.wodc.nl/images/1189-deel2-volledige-tekst_tcm44-59298.pdf [accessed 7 August 2014].

[B] Non-contractual Liability of Civil Aviation Safety Regulators: Review of Case Law[205]

The analysis of the available case law, which, as underlined above, comes mainly from the common law jurisdictions, allows the conclusion to be reached that generally two conditions need to be demonstrated by a plaintiff in order to establish civil liability involving an aviation safety regulator, that is a breach of a duty of care, and damages resulting from the breach.[206]

In the reviewed cases the courts recognised that aviation safety regulators owe a duty of care to the general public, including individual airline passengers:

- In *Perrett v. Collins*, the claimant was injured as a result of an airworthiness problem which was not detected by an inspector acting on behalf of the UK Civil Aviation Authority. The court found that the defendants owed a duty of care to the claimant:

  > An injured passenger's sole remedy may be against the person who has certified the aircraft to fly. The denial of a duty of care owed by such a person in relation to the safety of the aircraft towards those who may suffer personal injuries, whether as passengers in the aircraft or upon ground, would leave a gap in the law of tort (Lord Justice Hobhouse).[207]

- Similarly in *Swanson v. Canada*, which involved negligent safety oversight and lack of enforcement action in respect of a small airline which suffered an accident involving passenger casualties, the Federal Court of Appeal of Canada stated that:

  > The Aeronautics Act [RSC 1985, c A-2 (Canada)] and [the] Regulations made thereunder if not explicitly imposing a duty of care of the general public, at least do so by implication in that this is the very reason for their existence. The flying public has no protection against avaricious airlines, irresponsible or inadequately trained pilots, and defective aircraft if not [for] the Department of Transport and must rely on it for enforcement of the law and regulations in the interest of public safety.[208]

---

205. For further commentary on some of these cases see: John Korzeniowski, 'Liability of Aviation Regulators: Are the floodgates opening?', ASL, XXV (2000), pp. 31-34.
206. More generally, in the EU case law it was established that when an action for damages against an act of EU institution is brought to the CJEU, the elements that have to be demonstrated are a wrongful or illegal act, damage, and causation. These elements can be considered as general principles of tort liability in EU Member States; see: 'Case C-4/69, Lütticke v. Commission', in: [1971] ECR I-325, (CJEU,1969), (p. 337).
207. 'Perrett v. Collins', in: [1998] 2 Lloyd's LR 255, (p. 259).
208. 'Swanson et al v. The Queen in right of Canada', in: [1991] 80 DLR (4) 741, (Federal Court of Appeal of Canada, (p. 750). For a more general commentary on this case see: Ewa M. Swiecicki, 'Liability of the Canadian Government for the Negligent Enforcement of Aviation Safety Legislation', AASL, XVIII/I (1993), pp. 275-308.

And thereafter:

> Transport Canada's failure to take any meaningful steps to correct the explosive situation which it knew existed at Wapiti amounted to a breach of the duty of care it owed the passengers.[209]

- Finally in another UK case, *Philcox v. The Civil Aviation Authority*, Lord Justice Millet argues as follows:

> It is clear to my mind that the risk which the scheme of the legislation is designed to prevent is the risk that the owner or operator of an aircraft will fly the aircraft even when it is unfit to fly; and that the persons for whose protection the scheme has been established are the passengers, cargo owners and other members of the public likely to be harmed if an unfit aircraft is allowed to fly.[210]

As far as the breach of the duty of care is concerned, the *standard of conduct* required by the courts in the abovementioned cases was negligence:

- In *Perrett v. Collins,* the court found that the duty of care was exercised negligently which resulted in liability for damages:

  Lord Justice Hobhouse stated:

> An inspector exercising reasonable care would not have certified that the aircraft was in an airworthy condition.

  Similarly Lord Justice Bruxton observed that:

> A person who has the misfortune to suffer these consequences (death or injury) should surely be able to look to the organisation that has certified the plane as fit to fly, and that exists in order to enable the plane to fly, if that certification was made negligently.

  Finally Lord Justice Swinton Thomas concluded:

> A member of the public would expect that a person who is appointed to carry out these functions of inspecting aircraft and issuing permits would exercise reasonable care in doing so.[211]

- Similarly, in *Swanson v. Canada,* the court found that an agency charged with the regulation of the safety of commercial airlines was liable for negligently permitting an airline to continue unsafe practices. The agency had issued warnings to the airline in question but failed to take any further enforcement proceedings to require compliance with safety standards. In the words of the court:

209. 'Swanson v. Canada', *supra* note 208, at pp. 756-757.
210. 25 May 1995 (unreported). Quote following 'Perrett v. Collins', at *supra* note 207.
211. 'Perrett v. Collins', *supra* note 207.

> Transport Canada officials negligently performed the job they were hired to do; they did not achieve the reasonable standard of safety inspection, and enforcement which the law requires of professional persons similarly situated. It was not reasonable to accept empty promises to improve where no improvement was forthcoming. It is incomprehensible that a professional inspector of reasonable competence and skill would choose not to intervene in a situation which one of his own senior staff predicted was virtually certain to produce a fatal accident. [212]

A different approach seems to exist in the US, where the FAA may enjoy immunity from claims under the so called discretionary function exception of the Federal Tort Claims Act.[213] Two cases are of relevance here: *United States v. Varig Airlines*, and *United States v. United Scottish Insurance Company,* which were considered jointly by the US Supreme Court.[214] The circumstances of the cases were very similar, and involved aspects related to airworthiness certification of aircraft. In both cases, following appeals, the lower instance courts found that the US government, acting through the FAA, was liable for negligently certifying the design of an aircraft or its modification.

Both of the above cases were ultimately referred to the US Supreme Court which reversed the decisions on the basis of statutory exception which excludes from the scope of the Federal Tort Claims Act:

> Any claim based upon ... the exercise or performance or the failure to exercise or perform a discretionary function or duty on the part of a federal agency or an employee of the Government, whether or not the discretion involved be abused.[215]

The US Supreme Court came to the conclusion that:

> The FAA's implementation of a mechanism for compliance review is plainly discretionary activity of the 'nature and quality' protected by 2680(a). Judicial intervention, through private tort suits, in the FAA's decision to utilize a 'spot-checking' program as the best way to accommodate the goal of air transportation safety and the reality of finite agency resources would require the courts to 'second-guess' the political, social, and economic judgments of an agency exercising its regulatory function.[216]

No other circumstances of the case were analysed by the US Supreme Court.

[C] Review of Case Law: Conclusions

All of the above cases were considered in a domestic, common law context. In addition, in all these cases, both the claimant and the defendant had the same nationality.

212. 'Swanson v. Canada', *supra* note 208, at pp. 756-757.
213. Federal Tort Claims Act, Title 28 of USC, Part IV, paragraph 2680(A).
214. US Supreme Court, *United States v. S.A. Empresa de Viacao Aerea Rio Grandense (Varig Airlines) et al.*, Certiorari to the United States Court of Appeals for the Ninth Circuit, No. 82-1349. Together with No. 82-1350, United States v. United Scottish Insurance Co. et al., also on certiorari to the same court; 467 US 797 (1984), 19 June, 1984.
215. Federal Tort Claims Act, *supra* note 213.
216. US Supreme Court, *supra* note 214, at section IV.

With the exception of the cases of US origin, where the US Supreme Court has excluded FAA responsibility for negligent certification of aircraft airworthiness on the basis of a statutory exemption, all of the other cases recognise the possibility of holding aviation regulators liable for damages.

In particular, the cases cited are unanimous in recognising that the aviation regulators owe a *duty of care* towards the travelling public, and set *negligence* as a threshold beyond which the regulator may be held liable.

[D] Application of Tort Liability Principles to RASOs

There is at present no international instrument which would harmonise the domestic civil liability regimes of States in respect to damage caused through the conduct of civil aviation safety regulatory and oversight tasks. Such instruments exist for example as regards the carriage of passengers and cargo by air,[217] damage caused by aircraft to third parties,[218] or, going beyond aviation, the launching of objects into outer space.[219]

In view of the above, the possibility to engage civil liability of a regional aviation safety body would depend on the provisions of the RASO founding document and relevant national law, and in the first place on the recognition of separate legal personality of such a body under domestic law. Here the situation is slightly clearer than in the case of international legal personality, as this study found that the domestic legal personality is usually explicitly provided for in the RASO founding documents (see Table 6.1 in section §6.05[A] above).

[1] Recognition of RASOs Legal Personality in Domestic Proceedings

In the case of RASOs, that is organisations established on the basis of international agreements or supranational law, in the majority of cases studied, the legal instruments concerned explicitly recognise the domestic legal personality of the organisations including their right to be a party to legal proceedings or to *sue and be sued.*[220] Of course such recognition is granted only for the purpose of domestic proceedings in the territories of the Member States of the organisation and may be conditional upon incorporation of the agreement into the national legal system.[221]

217. 'Convention for the Unification of Certain Rules for International Carriage by Air', Montreal, 28 May 1999.
218. 'Convention on Compensation for Damage Caused by Aircraft to Third Parties', Montreal, 2 May 2009, (not yet in force).
219. 'Outer Space Treaty', *supra* note 111.
220. For EASA see: Regulation (EU) No 216/2008, *supra* note 81 in Ch. 2, Article 28(2); For IAC see: 'IAC Statute', *supra* note 126 in Ch. 3, Article 6; For BAGASOO see: 'BAGASOO Agreement', *supra* note 147 in Ch. 3, Article 2(3); For CASSOA see: CASSOA Protocol, *supra* note 191 in Ch. 3, Article 3(3); For AAMAC see: 'AAMAC Treaty', *supra* note 81 in Ch. 3, Article 7(2); For PASO see: 'PICASST', *supra* note 100 in Ch. 3, Article 4.3; For ECCAA see: 'ECCAA Agreement', *supra* note 268 in Ch. 3, Article 5; For CASSOS see: CASSOS Agreement, *supra* note 168 in Ch. 3, Article V; For EUROCONTROL see Articles 34-35 of: 'EUROCONTROL consolidated Convention (1997)', *supra* note 147.
221. Amerasinghe, *supra* note 128, at p. 70.

Amerasinghe argues that even when the constituent document does not provide for domestic legal personality, Member States of the organisation are under an obligation to grant it based on the principle of good faith.[222] Similarly Blokker and Schermers point out that national courts usually 'see no reason to deny the legal personality of organizations in which their own State participates.'[223] This would mean that even when domestic legal personality of a RASO is not explicitly envisaged under its founding document, it should not prevent Member States from recognising such personality if needed.

As far as third countries are concerned, the recognition of a legal personality of a RASO is not certain but also not entirely excluded. Some States, such as Switzerland, may recognise legal personality of an organisation in its internal legal system on the basis of the fact that the organisation has international legal personality.[224] Others, such as the UK, may recognise the personality of an international organisation of which they are not members if executive organs of their government have had previous dealings with the organisation, that is, already recognised it, or if the organisation has personality in one or more of the foreign States that are its members.[225]

[2] Jurisdictional Immunity of RASOs in Domestic Proceedings

The question of immunity from jurisdiction may also have to be considered. In majority of cases studied, RASO constituent documents contain provisions on privileges and immunities although the scope of these rights varies considerably.

Some of the agreements explicitly provide for almost complete immunity of a RASO from legal proceedings. This is the case for ECCAA and its employees, which are immune from 'legal process with respect to acts performed by them in their official capacity except when such immunity is waived by the [ECCAA].'[226] Other agreements may simply require RASO Member States to accord to the organisation and its personnel privileges and immunities as may be necessary for the fulfilment of their objectives and the exercise of their functions, which is the case for BAGASOO,[227] BAGAIA,[228] and CASSOS.[229]

In the case of a RASO established under the aegis of a REIO, its privileges and immunities may derive from the REIO founding treaty, as in the case for EASA,[230] and CASSOA.[231]

222. *Ibid.*, at p. 76.
223. Schermers and Blokker, *supra* note 72 in Ch. 4, at p. 1023.
224. Amerasinghe, *supra* note 128, at p. 71.
225. *Ibid.*, at p. 75.
226. 'ECCAA Agreement', *supra* note 268 in Ch. 3, Article 25(7).
227. 'BAGASOO Agreement', *supra* note 147 in Ch. 3, Article 7(2).
228. 'BAGAIA Agreement', *supra* note 221 in Ch. 3, Article 15(2).
229. 'CASSOS Agreement', *supra* note 168 in Ch. 3, Article XVI(1).
230. Regulation (EU) No 216/2008, *supra* note 81 in Ch. 2, Article 30.
231. 'CASSOA Protocol', *supra* note 191 in Ch. 3, Article 17.

Finally special protocols may be attached to a RASO founding agreement specifying in detail the immunities and privileges granted, which is the case for AAMAC.[232]

A number of RASO founding documents also envisage conclusion of headquarters or host-State agreements where further privileges and immunities may be granted, as is the case for instance with BAGASOO, BAGAIA, AAMAC, and CASSOS.

Some RASOs, such as IAC or ECCAA, have concluded headquarters agreements, which contain privileges and immunities, although the conclusion of such agreements is not explicitly envisaged in the founding documents of these RASOs.[233]

A review of the recent practice of domestic courts' cases concerning immunity of international organisations, demonstrates that generally courts are not willing to uphold immunity of organisations in absence of a clear treaty provision in this respect.[234]

In addition, at least in Europe, before upholding immunity of an international organisation the courts will normally check if the organisation has provided for an alternative mechanism which ensures an aggravated individual's right to an effective remedy. Where this is not the case, some courts may decide to deny an international organisation the right to immunity if granting it would put its State in breach of the constitution or international law obligations related to human rights.[235]

In view of the above it is important to verify to what extent the RASOs provide individuals with effective means for reviewing and satisfying their eventual claims. The results of this review are presented in the following section.

[3] Tort Liability Provisions in RASOs Founding Documents

As far as tort liability is concerned, only a limited number of RASO founding documents contain any provisions dealing explicitly with this issue. This limited treatment of tort liability in founding documents is a general trend for international organisations.[236] Such provisions were identified in the founding documents of EASA, EUROCONTROL and AAMAC.[237] These three organisations have very similar principles applicable to them:[238]

---

232. 'AAMAC Treaty', *supra* note 81 in Ch. 3, at 'Protocole annexé au Traité instituant les AAMAC'.
233. 'Соглашение между Правительством Российской Федерации и Межгосударственным Авиа-цион ным Комитетом об условиях его пребывания на территории Российской Федерации (Agreement between the Government of the Russian Federation and the Interstate Aviation Committee on the conditions of its stay in the Russian Federation) ', Moscow, 20 October 1995, on file with the author; 'Agreement between the Government of Antigua and Barbuda and the Eastern Caribbean Civil Aviation Authority regarding the Headquarters of the Authority', St. John's, 15 April 2008, on file with the author.
234. Cedric Ryngaert, 'The Immunity of International Organizations Before Domestic Courts: Recent Trends', IOLR, 7 (2010), p. 124.
235. *Ibid.*, pp. 132-144.
236. Klabbers, *supra* note 75 in Ch. 4, at p. 272.
237. In addition the Minsk Agreement, which establishes the IAC, contains provisions on the liability of the States – Contracting Parties to this Agreement ('Minsk Agreement', *supra* note 124 in Ch. 3, Article 16).
238. For EUROCONTROL see: 'EUROCONTROL consolidated Convention (1997)', *supra* note 147, Article 28; For EASA see: Regulation (EU) No 216/2008, *supra* note 81 in Ch. 2, Article 31; For AAMAC see: 'AAMAC Treaty', *supra* note 81 in Ch. 3, Article 8.

(1) The contractual liability is governed by the law applicable to the contract in question.
(2) In the case of non-contractual liability, the organization shall, in accordance with the general principles common to the laws of the Member States, make good any damage caused by its services or by its servants in the performance of their duties (EASA, AAMAC); or, make reparation for damage caused by the negligence of its organs, or of its servants in the scope of their employment, in so far as that damage can be attributed to them (EUROCONTROL).

The case of PASO is also worth mentioning. This organisation only assists its Member States in the performance of safety oversight duties. PASO inspectors, when performing their tasks are treated as inspectors of the Member States concerned (Level 1 delegation). Accordingly, while the PASO founding agreement does not contain liability provisions, it obliges the Member States to 'indemnify inspectors from any pertinent legal suit arising out of the appropriate performance of their duties.'[239]

What is therefore clear from the above analysis is that RASO founding documents do not follow a particular pattern as far as civil liability provisions are concerned. European States seem to accord greater importance to clarity here, but this can be partly attributed to the fact that both EASA and EUROCONTROL have operational and executive functions – that is provision of ANS in the case of EUROCONTROL, and certification of aircraft in case of EASA – the negligent exercise of which may result in damages to the general public. The AAMAC treaty is an exception as far as other parts of the world are concerned, but it was largely inspired by the EASA Basic Regulation.[240]

This study proposes that, from a policy point of view, the treatment of RASOs regarding civil liability should chiefly depend on the type of delegations and competences they have been granted by States. This means that:

- In case of 'Level 1' delegations – authorisation of individual inspectors only – the approach taken by PASO seems to be reasonable. Given that in such cases the regional inspectors act under the control and in the name of the national authority and execute national law, there would be little grounds for holding a RASO liable for their actions. In such cases, indemnification by the Member States of regional inspectors should be sufficient should they be found liable by national courts. 'Level 1' RASOs should therefore require that an indemnification clause is included in the service contracts and ensure that insurance policies of the national authorities for which they work, if used, also cover their inspectors.
- The situation is different with Level 2 delegations – where the performance of technical work is delegated to a RASO – and especially Level 3 delegations – where a regional authority also takes legally binding decisions. In Level 2, but especially in Level 3 delegations, the treatment afforded to RASOs should not

239. 'PICASST', *supra* note 100 in Ch. 3, Article 8(3).
240. A former EASA rulemaking director was advising the AAMAC States on the drafting of the AAMAC Treaty.

be significantly different to the one applicable to national aviation authorities. This is because in both cases the RASO will be conducting – within the scope of delegation – actual tasks of safety oversight, including certifications, inspections, etc.

In the EU, during the discussions on the establishment of EASA, there had also been no doubt about the necessity of a liability regime 'to ensure that EASA, including its staff, would be liable for its own wrongdoings.'[241] The legal experts who studied the various options for the setting up of EASA observed that the need for such a liability regime would be justified on the grounds that EASA would have rulemaking and certification competences.[242]

The possibility of a liability action encourages regulators and supervisors to exercise their operational tasks diligently and with care, meaning that the risk of damage to be caused by the supervised or regulated entities is also reduced. In addition, if a public body has been given regulatory tasks, it should perform them properly and if it fails to do so and this results in damages, there should be a possibility to hold it liable, just as any other person would be held accountable for an improper performance.

The availability of appropriate mechanisms allowing individuals to claim damages from a RASO in case of non-contractual liability becomes particularly important in the case of RASOs which enjoy Level 3 delegations. Given that, to a large extent, such RASOs will be acting as agents of States under the Chicago Convention, a liability mechanism may in practice be the only way to recover damages from a RASO that it may have caused as a result of potentially negligent performance of its regulatory functions.

Where the possibility of holding a RASO liable for negligent oversight is envisaged, or at least not excluded, the regional body can arrange for an insurance policy or other scheme covering such potential liability exposure.[243]

§6.07 ASSESSING THE NEED FOR AN AMENDMENT OF THE CHICAGO CONVENTION

The emergence of RASOs, especially those with Level 3 competences, could also trigger questions as to the eventual need to amend the Chicago Convention in order to clearly enable these organisations to exercise safety related competences in their own name, and thus to take full responsibility, from the international law point of view, for the work they are doing.

241. Report on the Work of the Expert Group on Legal Issues (AER/98/17), *supra* note 20 in Ch. 4, at p. 11.
242. *Ibid.*
243. In the EU the liability exposure of EASA for negligent safety oversight or certification work is entirely covered by the EU budget; see: EASA, 'Opinion of the EASA Management Board on the 2010 Annual Accounts, Annex 1, Non-contractual liabilities', (EASA Management Board Decision 07-2011, 2011).

While this study does not believe that there would be, at present, sufficient interest amongst the ICAO Member States in opening a discussion on this subject, should such a debate be launched in the future, two main possibilities could be further explored.

The first option could be a limited amendment of the Chicago Convention, altering the scope of its current Article 83bis in a way to allow transfer of safety functions not only to other States but also to international organisations.

Another option would be through the inclusion of the so called *REIO clause*, which provides for the possibility of adherence to an international treaty of a REIO, such as the African RECs or the EU.[244]

The consequence of adding a REIO clause to the Chicago Convention would be the recognition by all ICAO Member States of the possibility of transferring certain competences from States to a REIO. This would, de lege, reverse the direction of attribution of conduct from the perspective of the Chicago Convention. Such a situation exists, for example, in the context of World Trade Organisation (WTO), in which the EU participates as a REIO, and where the actions of EU Member States implementing EU law and constituting a breach of WTO obligations are attributed to the EU in the WTO dispute settlement process.[245] At the same time, adding a REIO clause to the Chicago Convention would not cover the RASOs which are established outside of a REIO framework, so this solution also has its shortcomings.

This study recognises of course that the actual need for an amendment of the Chicago Convention, putting aside the political willingness of the States to actually do that, could be a point of moot. On the one hand, the principle of ultimate responsibility for safety oversight may discourage States from establishing 'Level 3' RASOs which 'provide the best dividend in terms of efficiency and the effective use of resources'.[246] On the other hand, States could take less interest in aviation safety, if they were to be allowed to release themselves from ultimate responsibility and *hide* behind a regional body - which is why ICAO puts so much emphasis on individual State responsibility it its manual on RSOOs.[247]

In view of the above - should an amendment to the Chicago Convention be seriously considered - a reasonable compromise to reflect the most far reaching delegations to RASOs would probably be not to release States from responsibility, but rather to clearly establish in the Chicago Convention a principle of *joint and several responsibility* of a RASO/international organisation of which it is an organ and its Member States. There are precedents for using such solutions in international treaties. This is the case for example under the 'Treaty on Principles Governing the Activities of

244. For example by 2011, EU had acceded to over 70 international treaties by virtue of a REIO clause. See: CEPS, 'Upgrading the EU's role as Global Actor: Institutions, Law and the Restructuring of European Diplomacy', (2011), p. 5.
245. Jose Manuel Cortés Martin, 'European Exceptionalism in International Law? The European Union and the System of International Responsibility', in: Responsibility of international organizations: essays in memeory of Sir Ian Brownlie, ed. by Maurizio Ragazzi (2013), pp. 194-195.
246. ICAO Doc. 9734 Part B, *supra* note 3 in Ch. 1, at paragraph 3.1.1.
247. *Ibid.*, at paragraph 4.1.35.

States in the Exploration and Use of Outer Space, including Moon and Other Celestial Bodies'[248] Another solution could be to establish a subsidiary responsibility of the RASO Member States, which is a solution used under Article XI of the 'Operating Agreement on the International Maritime Satellite Organization (INMARSAT)'.[249]

§6.08 GENERAL CONCLUSIONS

The success of the GASON proposed in Chapter 2, measured by more effective and uniform implementation of ICAO SARPs and efficiencies in terms of the use of resources by ICAO and its Member States, will to a large degree depend on whether the RASOs which form GASON's building blocks are appropriately empowered to exercise civil aviation safety functions and duties – either on behalf of their Member States or in RASOs own name. In this respect, the clarity of concepts, limitations, conditions and consequences of attributing and delegating safety functions to RASOs is of fundamental importance for the feasibility of the GASON.

This chapter has therefore, first of all, clarified and systematised the general principles concerning the attribution and delegation of civil aviation safety functions, both in domestic and international law context. Secondly, it has verified to what extent the Chicago Convention and its safety related Annexes establish limitations or conditions concerning the attribution and delegation of such functions. Finally, this chapter has analysed the consequences that the establishment of RASOs can have for States and the regional body itself from the perspective of their international responsibility and liability under domestic law.

In this respect the following conclusions have been reached:

While a State has numerous safety related responsibilities under the Chicago Convention and its Annexes, it does not necessarily have to discharge all these responsibilities through governmental departments. This chapter has identified numerous examples of Chicago Convention related responsibilities being exercised through non-governmental entities, including sub-contractors, not-for-profit associations, approved organisations, individual designees, and even, as in the case of Austria, aviation authorities established in a form of a limited liability company.

In accordance with the *principle of legality*, the competence of a non-governmental entity to exercise civil aviation regulatory or oversight tasks has to be clearly identified, or in other words *attributed* to such entity by law. In addition, given that delegation cannot be presumed, a national civil aviation authority can delegate to other entities the exercise of tasks which have been attributed to it only on the basis of

---

248. See in particular the last sentence of Article VI of the Outer Space Treaty (*supra* note 111), which provides that: 'When activities are carried out in outer space, including the moon and other celestial bodies, by an international organization, responsibility for compliance with this Treaty shall be borne both by the international organization and by the States Parties to the Treaty participating in such organization.'
249. 'Operating Agreement on the International Maritime Satellite Organization (INMARSAT)', London, 3 September 1976, 15 ILM 233.

a clear statutory authorisation. Finally, a review of the Chicago Convention and its safety related Annexes has demonstrated that:

(1) Although there is no consistency in the way the different formulations regarding aviation authorities are used in the Annexes, the vast majority of the ICAO SARPs use broad formulations which refer to a *State* and/or to an *authority* in a generic sense without specifying that it has to be a national authority.
(2) In the rare cases where an ICAO Annex uses the term *national*, the relevant State and ICAO practice demonstrates that this term is actually interpreted as covering also RASO type authorities.
(3) Many of the ICAO Annexes explicitly envisage that a State has an obligation to designate an authority, which is to discharge on its behalf relevant safety related responsibilities, or provide services necessary for international air navigation.

In 2014, there were only two ICAO Annexes, that is No 13 and No 19, which explicitly refer to RASOs, although only Annex 13 actually contains Standards and Recommended Practices in this respect. Analysis of the relevant provisions of these two Annexes revealed that ICAO is still struggling somewhat with accepting that a RASO could completely replace a national aviation authority.

Based on the above, it was concluded that ICAO should ensure that SARPs more clearly reflect that it is perfectly acceptable for a State to discharge its safety related obligations under Annex 13 or any other safety related Annex to the Chicago Convention by relying in part or even entirely on a RASO type body, as long as the State can demonstrate that the relevant SARPs are effectively implemented.

Similar to the domestic law context, from the perspective of international law, the competence of an international organisation to act is governed by the principle of *attribution*, or *speciality*. There is however today 'considerable lack of clarity and consistent usage in the conceptual labels used to describe different types of conferrals by States of powers on international organizations.'[250]

Nevertheless, having reviewed and analysed the provisions of RASO founding documents, relevant ICAO documentation, State and international courts practice, as well as academic writings, this chapter came to the following conclusions:

(1) From the international law point of view, nothing today prevents a State from delegating the exercise of its State safety functions, as envisaged under the Chicago Convention and its Annexes, to a RASO. However, given the fact that *de lege lata*, only States can be parties to the Chicago Convention, such delegation does not relieve a State from *ultimate responsibility* of compliance. Even when States establish Level 3 RASOs, as was proposed under Chapter 5,

250. Sarooshi, *supra* note 19 in Ch. 2, pp. 28-31.

the transfer of responsibility in such cases takes place only *inter se*, not vis-à-vis other ICAO Member States.

(2) Furthermore, three general types of delegations of powers to RASOs were distinguished: agency relationships, delegations proper, and transfers. Although this typology corresponds to the general theory of conferrals of powers on international organisations as proposed by Sarooshi, it was also adapted in order to take into account the specificities of the international aviation law context:

(a) An *agency relationship* occurs, when States use Level 3 delegations in respect to functions for which they are responsible under the Chicago Convention. In such cases a RASO will be exercising such functions on behalf of the State concerned, meaning that it can change its rights and obligations under international law.

(b) *Delegation proper* occurs when States give to a RASO functions which are not created by the Chicago Convention. In such case, we can in fact speak about an attribution of a competence which a RASO will be carrying out in its own name. An example of such a delegation would be the establishment of a regional inspection scheme like the EU standardisation programme which was presented in Chapter 4.

(c) *Transfer of responsibilities* results in releasing a State from an obligation of compliance. Today transfers are envisaged only under Article 83bis of the Chicago Convention. Given the fact that RASOs cannot be parties to the Convention, Article 83bis transfers are in principle possible only between States. This study has identified a potential, but very limited, possibility of a RASO concluding Article 83bis agreements in the case when it would be designated as common mark registering authority under Article 77 of the Chicago Convention dealing with aircraft of international operating agencies.

When it comes to potential responsibility of RASOs under international law, the basic premise stemming from case law of the ICJ and the provisions of DARIO is that such responsibility can be engaged only in respect to organisations which have a recognised separate international legal personality.

This chapter concluded that, as few RASO founding agreements explicitly provide for it, the existence of such a separate legal personality has to be assessed on a case by case basis.

Furthermore, this chapter explained that a distinction has to be made between, on the one hand, RASOs established in a form of an international organisation and, on the other hand, established in a form of an organ of an international organisation. In the latter case, it is not the RASO which is a separate international legal person but its mother organisation.

In the case of RASOs analysed for the purpose of this study, it was found that the majority of them can be considered as having legal personality and thus having their international legal personality potentially engaged. The substance of such responsibility in the first place depends on the underlying relationship which exists between a

RASO and its Member States in accordance with the principle of specialty. Given the fact that RASOs cannot be parties to the Chicago Convention, the main source of their international law obligations are their founding agreements. The obligations stemming from such founding agreements are directed towards RASO Member States.

This chapter demonstrated that, from the perspective of international responsibility for the exercise of functions created by the Chicago Convention, the actions of RASOs would normally be attributed to its Member States. This is because, in such cases, the RASO acts as an agent of States.

This chapter also considered whether the international legal responsibility of a RASO or of its mother organisation, could be engaged by a non-Member State in respect to the provisions of the Chicago Convention. This question is especially relevant in respect to Level 3 RASOs which are expected to carry out their delegated safety functions in compliance with the Convention and its safety related Annexes. While realising that arguing in favour of such responsibility is a controversial issue in view of the fact that international organisations cannot be a party to the Chicago Convention, this study nevertheless came to the conclusion that such possibility should not be excluded *a priori*, especially in the case of organisations which have operational responsibilities, such as aircraft certification, the negligent exercise of which could contribute to accidents.

This chapter argued that, from a legal point of view, responsibility of a RASO or of its mother organisation vis-à-vis third countries could be justified by the fact that some of the safety oversight obligations can be considered as *erga omnes*, as was demonstrated by other studies. This chapter also pointed out that according to some sources a joint and several responsibility of States and international organisation can stem from the relationship of an international agency. In addition, such responsibility could be considered at least in those cases where a RASO or its mother organisation concludes an international agreement with a third country, and which creates an obligation for the regional body to act in accordance with the provisions of the Chicago Convention and its Annexes. This is, for example, the case for the BASAs concluded by the EU with third countries.

Irrespective of the above, this study did not identify any cases heard by international courts or tribunals and related to breach by either a State or a RASO of international safety oversight or regulatory obligations. In practical terms it is therefore more likely that, rather than international responsibility of RASOs being engaged by States, potential victims of aviation accidents would rather try to engage RASOs civil liability for damages. In this respect this study concluded as follows:

(1) There is at present no international instrument which harmonises the domestic civil liability regimes of States in respect to damage caused by negligent conduct of civil aviation safety regulatory and oversight tasks. Accordingly such civil liability would depend primarily on provisions of the RASO founding documents and applicable domestic law.

(2) A limited number, that is three, founding documents of the RASOs studied explicitly provide for the possibility of holding them liable for non-contractual damages. In addition this study has identified case law – albeit entirely from

domestic, common law jurisdictions – where courts confirmed that national aviation regulators owe a duty of care towards the travelling public and set negligence as a threshold beyond which the regulator may be held liable. Similar principles could be applied to RASOs.

(3) The possibility to engage civil liability of a RASO would in the first place depend on the recognition of its separate legal personality under domestic law. This should normally not be a problem as far as the jurisdictions of the RASO Member States are concerned, but could be more difficult in case of non-Member States. The question of jurisdictional immunity in domestic proceedings would also have to be considered. In this respect the study concluded that most of the RASO founding documents studied contain provisions on privileges and immunities, although the scope of the rights granted vary considerably.

(4) It is recommended that the treatment of RASOs, from a civil liability point of view, should chiefly depend on the type of delegations and competences they have been granted by their Member States. The more operational competences have been given to a RASO, the exercise of which can result in damages to third parties, the more stringent the liability regime should be. In this respect, it was advocated that States should promote in the RASO founding agreements clear provisions on their liability, especially in the case of organisations enjoying 'Level 3' delegations.

Overall, this chapter found no evidence that any particular provision or principle of international law would be a serious obstacle for the establishment or functioning of RASOs. It was concluded that States are even able to establish organisations vested with power to issue certificates on their behalf.

From the perspective of the Chicago Convention, and as was pointed above, the main limitation to RASO functioning is the fact that only States can be a party to the Convention. This means that, from the perspective of the Chicago Convention, RASOs can only act as agents of States and the latter cannot be released from their ultimate responsibility for compliance with the requirements of the Convention and its safety related Annexes by establishing a RASO.

In addition, three more specific limitations were identified from the perspective of the Chicago Convention concerning the delegation of State safety functions to a RASO. These limitations are related to the exercise by a RASO of the functions and duties of the 'State of Registry' and 'State of the Operator':

(1) Although a RASO can act as a 'State of Registry' with respect to individual States, meaning registering aircraft on their behalf, such aircraft would still have the nationality of the State on behalf of which they were registered in accordance with Article 17 of the Chicago Convention. There is thus today no possibility for a RASO to register aircraft on a *multinational* basis. The only exception to this rule could be aircraft operated by international operating agencies under Article 77 of the Chicago Convention. To date however there has been only one case of an international operating agency having its aircraft

registered on a non-national basis (Arab Air Cargo), but this scheme involved a number of States acting jointly as a 'State of Registry' rather than delegating registration functions to an international organisation.

(2) Where a RASO exercises on behalf of its Member States the functions and duties of the 'State of the Operator' or 'State of Registry' it will not be able to conclude Article 83bis with third countries in its own name. This stems from the fact that only States can be parties to the Chicago Convention and thus benefit from its Article 83bis.

(3) Where a RASO exercises on behalf of its Member States the functions and duties of the 'State of Registry', while the RASO Member States continue to exercise the functions and duties of the 'State of Operator', agreements concerning the transfer of responsibilities which may be concluded between the RASO and its Member States, may not be recognised by third countries. Similar to point (2) above this limitation results from the fact that RASOs cannot be party to the Chicago Convention.

This chapter also considered the need to amend the Chicago Convention in order to clearly enable RASOs to exercise safety tasks in their own name. While realising that such an amendment is not a realistic prospect for the time being, two suggestions have been put forward for consideration. The first option could be a limited amendment of the Chicago Convention, altering the scope of its current Article 83bis in a way to allow transfer of safety functions not only to other States but also to international organisations. The second option could be to introduce into the Chicago Convention a REIO clause, which provides for the possibility of adherence to an international treaty of a REIO, such as the African RECs or the EU. The latter option would however not cover the RASOs which are established outside of a REIO framework.

This chapter recognised that the actual need to amend the Chicago Convention, putting aside the political willingness of the States to actually do that, could be a point of moot. On the one hand, it was argued, ultimate responsibility for safety oversight discourages States from establishing 'Level 3' RASOs which 'provide the best dividend in terms of efficiency and the effective use of resources'.[251] On the other hand, it was argued, States could take less interest in aviation safety, if they were to be allowed to release themselves from ultimate responsibility and *hide* behind a regional body - which is why ICAO puts so much emphasis on individual State responsibility it its manual on RSOOs.[252]

While not excluding the possibility of amending the Chicago Convention in the long term, this chapter argued that what is needed in the short term is a much clearer policy from ICAO on the role of States in the supervision of RASOs. It was proposed that such a policy could be included in one of the future editions of the ICAO RSOO and RAIO manuals, or the new Annex 19 which, as it applies to safety management in general, has a horizontal application.

251. ICAO Doc. 9734 Part B, *supra* note 3 in Ch. 1, at paragraph 3.1.1.
252. *Ibid.*, at paragraph 4.1.35.

This chapter further advocated that such supervision policy should be based on the principle that States and RASOs working on their behalf must be seen as a system which, taken together, should guarantee the level of safety oversight required by the Chicago Convention. Such oversight policy should not lead to the need to control in detail the actions of a regional body, or create a risk of duplication of expertise at national and regional levels.

CHAPTER 7
Conclusions and Recommendations

There is no real ending. It is just the place where you stop the story.

Frank Herbert (1920-1986)[1]

§7.01 INTRODUCTION

This study has been a first comprehensive attempt to analyse, from the legal and institutional points of view, how regional cooperation and more specifically RASOs can contribute to the improvement of civil aviation safety and the achievement of the objectives of 'uniformity in regulations, standards, procedures, and organization' as formulated in Article 37 of the Chicago Convention.

Aviation safety has traditionally been regulated at the global level by ICAO, while aviation regulations are implemented and enforced at the national level by competent aviation authorities of ICAO Member States. Though this is still largely the case today, the last twelve years have seen the emergence and rapid development of RASOs, which form an intermediate level between ICAO and individual States.

RASOs are not an entirely new concept, as section §5.04[B] of Chapter 5 has explained. However, the increasing reliance on these organisations is a clear demonstration of a growing conviction of the international aviation community, as was demonstrated under section §2.04[C] of Chapter 2, that they can significantly help States in enhancing their safety oversight capabilities in a cost efficient way, and contribute to the achievement of the Chicago Convention objectives of uniformity of regulations, procedures and requirements which are essential for the global aviation industry.

With a view to reaching the primary objective of verifying the extent to which RASOs meet the expectations vested in them by the international aviation community, Chapter 1 formulated seven specific research questions:

1. Frank Herbert was a critically acclaimed American science fiction novelist, author of the famous 'Dune' saga.

(1) What should be the role of RASOs in global governance of civil aviation safety?
(2) Can the optimal RASO model be identified from a legal point of view? If yes, how can it best be defined and structured?
(3) In which domains can RASOs yield maximum safety benefits, and under which legal conditions?
(4) For which States are RASOs most relevant?
(5) What is the expected future evolution of RASO type bodies?
(6) Are there any shortcomings in the current international legal framework that pose an obstacle to further development of RASOs?
(7) What are the international responsibility and civil liability implications resulting from RASOs establishment and functioning?

This final chapter will now draw on the analysis and conclusions reached in the preceding parts of the present study in order to answer these research questions.

§7.02 CONCLUSIONS AND RECOMMENDATIONS WITH REGARD TO SPECIFIC RESEARCH QUESTIONS

(1) What should be the role of RASOs in global governance of civil aviation safety?
This study has demonstrated in Chapter 2 that despite past criticism of ICAO regarding its effectiveness in ensuring the implementation and enforcement of aviation safety standards at the global level, States have consistently managed to improve the level of effective implementation of USAOP protocols.

Chapter 2 also concluded that States with completely deficient safety oversight systems constitute only 0.3% of the worldwide international air traffic, which is a marginal risk to aviation safety. Overall, aviation safety, in particular in commercial air transport, stands at present at a very high level.

Notwithstanding the above, Chapters 1 and 2 have also demonstrated that the current global aviation safety framework, as established by the Chicago Convention, faces a number of important challenges:

(1) The first one is that not all of the States, in particular in Africa, have as yet been able to build safety oversight systems to at least the minimum level of effectiveness required by ICAO, mainly due to lack of financial resources or technical capability. In 2014, 43% of ICAO Member States had below-average level of effective implementation of the eight CEs of safety oversight system as defined by ICAO. The current financially challenging times are equally putting pressure on aviation authorities who traditionally did not have problems with resources, such as in Europe or the United States.
(2) Secondly, aviation safety levels and the levels of effective implementation of the eight CEs of safety oversight vary significantly between States around the world, as well as within ICAO regions. As air traffic continues to grow, there is also a concern that absolute numbers of accidents could increase if the

current improvement rates stagnate. It has been demonstrated in Chapter 1 that two of the three ICAO regions which between 2005 and 2012 experienced the highest rate of traffic growth (Latin America and the Caribbean: 17%; Africa: 20%; Asia: 38%), also demonstrate the lowest level of effective implementation of the eight CEs (Latin America and the Caribbean: 68%; Africa: 44%; Asia: 71%).

(3) Finally in order to further reduce accident rates, which will be necessary in view of the ongoing traffic growth, more sophisticated methods of oversight will be needed, including pro-active and even predictive safety management tools as rightly advocated by GASP. Chapter 1 argued that not all the States individually may be able to deploy such methods in an effective manner.

The current system also suffers, as section §2.02[D] of Chapter 2 has shown, from a *death by audit syndrome*, which stems from redundant regulatory oversight and repetitive certifications of the same aviation activities conducted within jurisdictions of different States. In addition, some jurisdictions of the world, such as the EU or US, have implemented unilateral auditing schemes which to a large extent replicate the objective of ICAO USOAP, namely verification of effective compliance of States with minimum ICAO SARPs. These repetitive certifications and auditing schemes, although necessary, currently represent one of the major inefficiencies of the global aviation safety system, which according to Article 37 of the Chicago Convention, should be based on 'the highest practicable degree of uniformity in regulations, standards, procedures, and organization in relation to aircraft, personnel, airways and auxiliary services.'

Chapter 2 of this study has reached the conclusion that, whilst there are elements which can be further improved, such as more standardisation and uniformity in application of Article 38 on the filing of differences (see section §2.02[B] of Chapter 2), the main challenge for ICAO and the global aviation community in the years to come will be to achieve the required harmonisation of the global regulatory framework and effective implementation of the new proactive and predictive safety management techniques called for by GASP, by continuing to rely exclusively on national safety oversight systems.

Chapter 2 has also concluded that, with ICAO membership standing at 191 States in 2014 and based on the principle of individual State responsibility for safety oversight, it has become unavoidable that the level of implementation of SARPs and eight CEs will be variable across the world. In this respect it was argued that, to effectively standardise this large number of States, ICAO will not be able to continue working as it did in the past with the limited resources available. The recent shift to the USOAP-CMA methodology, which was mentioned in section §2.02[D] of Chapter 2, is a very telling demonstration of that new reality.

Based on the above considerations, Chapter 2 has argued that ICAO needs to find a way which would allow it, in addition to monitoring State safety performance, helping States in addressing the detected deficiencies and enforcing global standards, to also address more decisively the ongoing erosion of the present aviation safety system in terms of redundant regulatory oversight and waste of resources deriving from duplicate certifications. Chapter 2 has proposed that the way forward to achieve these objectives is to build a GASON, with RASO type organisations as its main building blocks.

With respect to the proposed GASON, this study has proposed (see section §2.05 of Chapter 2) that its architecture should be based on ICAO relying on and working closely with a number of strong RASOs, which could ensure harmonised implementation of SARPs and organise enforcement mechanisms. Such a system, it was argued, would not only allow ICAO to be more efficient in its use of limited resources, but would also contribute to a more uniform implementation of SARPs, as instead of a multitude of national regimes the system could ultimately provide for a more limited number of regional schemes which would be easier for ICAO to standardise and monitor. The regional approach would also contribute to harmonisation of actual safety performance through regional safety performance planning, at the RASGs level, in consistent with the globally agreed safety targets.

Based on the above considerations, section §2.05 of Chapter 2 has proposed the following definition of the GASON:

> A worldwide system for the standardisation and monitoring of ICAO Member States' level of effective implementation of eight Critical Elements of State safety oversight, relying on information generated by Regional Aviation Safety Organisations; which are empowered, through international agreements or supranational law, to ensure uniform compliance of their Member States with the Chicago Convention and Standards and Recommended Practices laid down in the Annexes to this Convention.

Having proposed the GASON, this study, in Chapter 3, looked in more detail at the very notion of a RASO and more generally at regional aviation safety cooperation initiatives. It has been noted in this respect (see section §3.04 of Chapter 3) that RASOs are already a positive reality. By mid-2014, over 100 ICAO Member States were members of such organisations, if looked at from the perspective of a broad interpretation of this term as currently followed by ICAO. In addition, a number of ICAO Member States have been considering or are in the course of setting up similar organisations, as was explained under section §5.04[B] of Chapter 5.

The RASO concept has already been reflected in a number of ICAO Assembly Resolutions, and one of them even puts RASOs on equal terms with States (see section §2.04[C] of Chapter 2). References to RASOs are also present in ICAO Annexes 13 and 19 (see section §6.03 of Chapter 6). In addition, ICAO has published two manuals dedicated entirely to RASOs' establishment and functioning (see section §3.04[C] of Chapter 3).

This study has also found in section §3.04[A][1] of Chapter 3 that the recent boom of RASOs has resulted, in particular in Africa, in the establishment of a significant number of such organisations, but unfortunately sometimes with an overlapping membership. Similar duplications exist to a certain extent in Europe where a number of regional aviation organisations, that is EASA, EUROCONTROL and ECAC, continue to function in parallel, as Chapter 4 has demonstrated. While this study did not analyse in detail the consequences of these overlaps and duplications, it was argued that they are likely to result in inefficiencies and should be further studied.

Finally, while arguing that RASOs should be more closely integrated into global governance of aviation safety through the GASON, this study also acknowledged, in section §2.05 of Chapter 2, that this would require a high level of confidence by ICAO in the robustness of the regional systems. This in turn would necessitate strong and appropriately empowered RASOs which at present is rarely the case. This is because, as section §5.02 of Chapter 5 has found, the majority of present RASOs provide mainly advisory and coordination services, without carrying out safety functions with legally binding effects.

Recommendation No 1:
ICAO and its Member States should give consideration to the development of a Global Aviation Safety Oversight Network (GASON). Building a GASON would require appropriately empowered RASOs, which is at present still rarely the case. The GASON should therefore be treated as a long term strategy for integrating RASOs into the global governance for civil aviation safety management.

(2) Can the optimal RASO model be identified from a legal point of view? If yes, how can it best be defined and structured?

Despite RASOs having been a positive reality for many years, there is at present still no definition of RASO agreed at the international level, as section §3.02 of Chapter 3 has explained. The international aviation community recommended in 2011 the development of such a definition, but so far this recommendation has not been implemented. In this respect, as a first step, this study has classified these organisations (see section §3.02 of Chapter 3) into two broad categories, that is RSOOs and RAIOs, depending on whether their function is safety regulation and oversight, or investigation of aviation accidents.

The common denominator which is used today by ICAO and States to define an organisation or form of cooperation as a RSOO or a RAIO is its general objective of strengthening safety oversight/investigation capabilities of States located in the same geographical region rather than a particular institutional or legal setup. This was discussed in section §3.02 of Chapter 3.

Based on the above, this study has concluded, in section §3.03 of Chapter 3, that developing a RASO definition would be advantageous for two main reasons:

(1) Firstly, because the notions of RSOO and RAIO are being increasingly used in ICAO documentation, including Assembly Resolutions and Annexes to the Chicago Convention, such definition would help in ensuring clarity as to who exactly is an addressee of these documents, especially where they give to a RSOO or a RAIO a right to carry out functions or duties so far normally exercised only by States.

(2) Secondly, there is a need for a definition which would promote the most efficient forms of RASOs, and notably those which have the competence to carry out, on behalf of States, safety related functions and duties set out by the Chicago Convention, in a legally binding manner.

The objective of a RASO definition should be therefore, in addition to clarifying the roles of States and RASOs, to promote those forms of RASOs which are able to accept the most advanced forms of delegations. This capability will make RASOs more suitable to constitute strong building blocks of the GASON. In this respect, section §4.03[B] of Chapter 4 has demonstrated that where States delegate to an organisation the carrying out, on their behalf, of civil aviation safety functions with legally binding effects, this requires the organisation to have a separate international legal personality or to be established in a form of an organ of an international legal person.

In view of the above, Chapter 3 has proposed the following definition of a RASO:

> An organisation established by States from the same geographical region, which has legal personality under international law or is established in a form of an organ of an international legal person, and whose principal purpose is the provision of support for the carrying out of safety-related functions and duties set out by the Chicago Convention and its Annexes, and preferably the actual carrying out of some or all of such functions and duties on behalf of its participating States.

This study has also concluded in section §5.04[A] of Chapter 5 that there is no single template that States use when setting up regional aviation safety bodies, and that the organisational and legal frameworks of these organisations are far from being uniform. Nevertheless, for the purpose of this study a typology of regional aviation safety bodies has been proposed, in Chapter 3, which distinguishes between two main categories: (i) pre-RASOs and (ii) RASOs.

While pre-RASOs do not strictly speaking fall within the scope of the proposed RASO definition because of their lack of international legal personality or formal link with an international legal person, they have however been included in the proposed typology for the sake of completeness, and because such pre-RASOs have a tendency to evolve into RASOs proper, as section §5.04[B] of Chapter 5 has demonstrated.

In addition to proposing a RASO typology, this study has also reviewed, analysed and categorised, in section §5.02 of Chapter 5 the various types of delegation arrangements commonly used by States when setting up RASOs and pre-RASOs. In this respect, three levels of delegations have been distinguished from an operational point of view:

(1) *Level 1 (Coordination level):* At the basic level, States may decide to delegate specific competences to individuals not employed by their national civil aviation authorities. Such authorisations then give the underlying authority to inspectors of a regional body to perform audits, inspections and other oversight or investigative work on behalf of the national authority which gave the authorisation.

(2) *Level 2 (Harmonisation level):* The next level, which goes beyond authorisation of individuals only, is the delegation to a RASO/pre-RASO, as an organisation, of the competence to perform specific technical work on behalf of its Member States or member authorities. In other words, this type of delegation means that a regional body will perform the technical findings, such as inspections, tests, examinations, on behalf of all or selected Member

States/aviation authorities, and then submit the results, together with recommendations, for further legal action at the national level(s).

(3) *Level 3 (Unification level):* Finally, States may want to delegate to a regional body both the conduct of the technical work, as well as responsibility for the issuance of the certificate/approval confirming that the applicable requirements have been met. Under this option, efficiencies are potentially most significant, because it effectively results in centralisation of a given safety function at regional level. There is only one technical process and one approval issued at its end. From the perspective of the aviation industry this is a one-stop-shop for obtaining the approvals that they need to provide the services at the market.

While this study did not recommend, *a priori,* any particular level of delegation, as this choice should be based on a thorough assessment of the needs and policies of the States concerned and their aviation industries, Chapter 5 has concluded that Level 3 delegations can offer the following advantages:

- Centralisation of a particular safety function at the regional level, which allows for economies of scale and better pooling of resources.
- Less risk of duplication between the national and regional levels, as in this case the safety function normally ceases to be exercised at the national level.
- From a regulatory point of view, Level 3 delegations offer a fully unified action, be it a single certificate valid throughout the region, or a single rule applicable, in a uniform manner, to all aviation organisations under the jurisdiction of the RASO.

Whilst Level 3 RASOs offer the above advantages which make them very well placed to form effective building blocks of the GASON, this study also found, in Chapter 5, that Level 3 RASOs are still very rare. In mid-2014, there were only four RASOs, that is EASA in the EU, IAC in the CIS, ECCAA in the OECS, and ASSA-AC in Africa which effectively possessed such powers.

One of the reasons behind this still low number of Level 3 RASOs is the presence of, as also identified by ICAO, strong sovereignty issues that impede regional cooperation.[2] In this respect, this study recalled in section §2.02[A] of Chapter 2, that a distinction should be made between the principle of State sovereignty in aviation law, which is indivisible, and the exercise of this sovereignty which can be delegated to other States or international organisations, as is the case for example in the ATM sector with the provision of ANS.

2. Outcomes of 2011 RSOO Symposium (C-WP/13810), *supra* note 4 in Ch. 1, at Paragraph 2.3.1.

Recommendation No 2:
a) *ICAO is invited to consider the definition of RASO proposed in this study as a basis for developing a corresponding definition for inclusion in subsequent editions of its RSOO and RAIO manuals.*
b) *States are invited to take note of the conclusions reached by this study with respect to the different levels of delegations available for RASOs. In particular they are invited to consider the benefits that this study has demonstrated as regards Level 3 delegations.*

(3) In which domains can RASOs yield maximum safety benefits, and under which legal conditions?

Chapter 3 found that the RASOs in existence today have broad mandates and do not specialise in any single domain of aviation safety. RAIOs, which were addressed in section §3.05 of Chapter 3, could be expected to be such specialised RASOs, but so far there is still little experience with RAIO functioning. In practice, until mid-2014 there was only one RAIO, that is IAC, which was fully operational, but it functions within a broader organisational framework of a RASO which also performs other functions (see section §3.04[C][3] of Chapter 3). It was also found in Chapter 3 that some RASOs, such as PASO, CASSOA, or ECCAA in addition to aviation safety deal also with aviation security.

The fact that RASOs have rather general mandates can be considered a good thing from a safety point of view, given the interrelatedness of the different components of the aviation system which makes it difficult to consider one domain in isolation from the others.

In order to assist States in setting up RASOs, based on analysis of case studies of these organisations from around the world, as well as review of practical examples of the different safety functions that these bodies perform, this study proposed, in Chapter 5, a practical 'tool-box' for the setting up of RASOs. Structured around the eight ICAO CEs of safety oversight, this 'tool-box' provides States with a *menu* of potential options from which they could choose, taking into account that, as advocated by ICAO, when setting up RASOs States should focus on those activities that demonstrate a higher impact on regional safety oversight and contribute towards developing an effective aviation safety oversight framework.'[3]

A similar approach to the proposed 'tool-box' method was used in the EU during the initial establishment process of EASA, and when States first created a list of potential functions and tasks, such as rulemaking, certification, standardisation, and considered the implications of the different institutional solutions on each of them.

With respect to the establishment of the GASON, there is a number of safety functions to which States should pay particular attention:

3. ICAO Doc. 9734 Part B, *supra* note 3 in Ch. 1, at Paragraph 2.2.1.

(1) Existence of a harmonised regulatory framework without, in principle, national differences, although, as section §4.04[A][1] of Chapter 4 has demonstrated, this is an ideal objective which in practice may be difficult to achieve even for supranational systems such as the EU.
(2) Existence of a regional mechanism, similar to EU standardisation inspections and other monitoring activities (see sections §4.04[C][1] and §4.04[C][3] of Chapter 4), which would allow a RASO to feed the ICAO USOAP-CMA programme, and thus enable ICAO to rely on a RASO for monitoring its Member States' compliance with the Chicago Convention and relevant SARPs (existence of a harmonised regulatory framework is a pre-requisite to achieve this synergy).

With regard to point (1) above, this study found (see section §5.02 of Chapter 5) that while a RASO may be involved in the development of aviation safety regulations from a technical point of view by preparing drafts thereof, the actual adoption of aviation safety legislation is very unlikely to be given to a RASO. This study did not identify a single RASO which enjoys legislative functions. This demonstrates that States essentially treat RASOs as technical agencies implementing and enforcing the law but not creating it.

Finally, this study found (see section §5.04[E] of Chapter 5) that there may be unintended consequences when transferring the exercise of safety functions from a State to a regional level. This is because, when one or more State safety functions are taken out of the national framework and transferred to the regional level, some essential safety links may be lost. This was demonstrated in section §5.04[E][1] of Chapter 5 by the example of the transfer of 'State of Design' functions in the context of EASA in the EU. For this reason, this study has recommended in section §5.04[E] of Chapter 5 that every RASO should be considered as part of the overall civil aviation safety system of its Member States, and that RASO functions should be fully integrated into that system.

Recommendation No 3:
a) States are invited to use a 'tool-box' approach when setting up RASOs. This method structures the RASO development process along the eight CEs of State safety oversight and assists States in choosing the safety functions and levels of delegations which are best suited to the particular situation of the States in the region, and the needs of their aviation industry.
b) States should treat RASOs as part of their overall civil aviation safety system, and to ensure that RASOs are fully integrated into that system. This helps to avoid breaking essential safety links between the different ICAO requirements when transferring the exercise of a given safety function from a State level to a regional level.

(4) For which States are RASOs most relevant?
The analysis of ICAO documentation, including Assembly Resolutions and RASO manuals which was conducted in section §2.04[C] of Chapter 2 and section §3.02 of Chapter 3, revealed that at present the primary focus of ICAO is on seeing RASOs as tools for assisting States in raising their safety oversight capabilities, in particular by allowing them to pool resources and achieve economies of scale.

While the above is certainly a very valid RASO function, such organisations can equally offer benefits for States which do not face pressing problems with establishing effectively functioning safety oversight systems. This is the case for example in Europe, where States have historically enjoyed a high level of aviation safety, underpinned by effective levels of oversight, but where the primary reason, at least initially, behind the establishment of, first JAA, and subsequently EASA was to achieve regulatory efficiencies for the aeronautical industry as Chapter 4 has demonstrated.

Similarly, with regard to the proposed GASON, as section §2.05 of Chapter 2 highlighted, the main RASO function would be to ensure regulatory harmonisation and standardisation at regional levels, and to allow ICAO, instead of monitoring directly 191 Member States, to rely in this respect on a more limited number of regional systems. This in turn means that any ICAO Member State should be seen as a potential candidate for participating in a RASO-based system. Indeed, this is already largely the case today. This study has found in Chapter 3, that in 2014 over 100 ICAO Member States were members of RASOs, if looked at from the perspective of a broad interpretation of this term as currently followed by ICAO.

The findings of this study however also bring a note of caution with regard to the expectations vested into RASOs by the international aviation community. This stems from the fact that some of the regional initiatives reviewed have experienced or reported difficulties in relation to financing their activities or attracting and recruiting sufficient numbers of qualified technical personnel. For example, the experiences of the AFI-CIS and of ECCAA demonstrate that it may be difficult to recruit or to pool aviation safety inspectors at a regional level, if they are simply not available in sufficient numbers. These difficulties were summarised in section §5.04[C] of Chapter 5.

Similarly, in the vast majority of cases RASOs functioning today do not replace the national aviation authorities but function in parallel to them, as was highlighted in section §5.04[A] of Chapter 5. This suggests that if the additional costs resulting from establishment of a RASO are not offset by efficiencies stemming from its operations or by additional revenues, States may actually be worst off in terms of their overall budgets. Although this issue was not studied in detail, based on examples of financial and resource related difficulties reported by some of the RASOs (see section §5.04[C] of Chapter 5) it was argued that if States cannot reduce their costs, while at the same time will need to contribute to the financing of a RASO, this may actually lead to lack of sustainable funding of the latter and putting in danger its operations. Such a negative scenario materialised in the case of one of the RASOs studied, that is PASO which was addressed in section §3.04[C][2] of Chapter 3.

Overall, whilst different examples of RASOs were reviewed and analysed in the study, two of them merit particular highlighting in these final conclusions:

(1) The first one is the RCAA model, which was presented and discussed in section §3.06 of Chapter 3. In 2014, there was just one example of such an authority actually functioning in practice – the ECCAA. This is a unique organisation which acts as a single aviation authority for all its Member States. While experiencing its own challenges, ECCAA enabled its Member States 'to achieve effective civil aviation safety oversight at a fraction of the cost of establishing their own civil aviation authorities.'[4] This RASO model should be particularly considered by large groupings of small States with limited resources and/or States with low level of aviation activities which are unable to generate revenues big enough to support fully fledged national civil aviation authorities.

(2) The second model worth highlighting in these final conclusions is a supranational RASO, meaning a RASO which evolves within the broader legal and institutional framework of a REIO, and relies on the latter for its functioning. In 2014, there were still very few such organisations. The most notable example of such a RASO is EASA in the EU. Its case study, presented in Chapter 4, has demonstrated that combining the supranational legal competences of a REIO, with the technical capabilities of a RASO can offer substantial benefits. These include the possibility of creating a harmonised, legally binding and directly applicable legal framework, large-scale recognition of certificates and approvals, and possibility of Level 3 delegations which are exercised in a uniform manner in all the RASO Member States.

Recommendation No 4:
a) *Regional groupings of small States with limited resources and/or States with low level of aviation activity which are unable to generate revenues big enough to support fully fledged national civil aviation authorities, are recommended to consider establishing RASOs in the form of a single regional civil aviation authority.*
b) *States which are members of supranational regional integration organisations, similar to the EU, are recommended to set up their RASOs within the legal and institutional framework of such supranational organisations.*

(5) What is the expected future evolution of RASO type bodies?

Although the institutional frameworks and legal basis of RASOs and pre-RASOs are very varied, this study also found in section §5.04[B] of Chapter 5 that there is a strong tendency for these organisations to evolve over time into more formal entities. Section

4. 'Interview No 7', (2014), *supra* note 274 in Ch. 3.

§5.04[B] of Chapter 5 has demonstrated that out of the nine organisations established since 2003, six have already undergone such evolution, while some of the other are considering it in the future.

The key characteristic feature of the above identified RASO/pre-RASO evolution trend is transition into organisations established by international agreements and having a legal personality, if not under international law, then at least under the domestic law of one of the Member States. ICAO also has a general policy of transitioning COSCAPs into RASO type bodies, although this process is still ongoing as was demonstrated in section §3.04[A][1] of Chapter 3.

Section §5.04[B] of Chapter 5 has identified the following typical examples of evolutions: from a technical cooperation project (Pre-RASO Type I) into an international regional safety organisation with legal personality (RASO Type I); or a network of aviation safety authorities (pre-RASO Type II) evolving into an international regional safety organisation with legal personality (RASO Type I). In Europe, a network of aviation safety authorities (pre-RASO Type II) evolved into a supranational aviation safety agency (RASO Type II).

Based on the trend identified above, it can be expected that RASOs/pre-RASOs will continue to evolve in the years to come towards organisations established under international law and having a legal personality separate from its Member States. Section §5.04[B] of Chapter 5 has found that the evolution trend characterises especially young RASOs. Given the fact that a large number of such organisations were established only in the last decade, and that additional RASOs are in the planning, in particular in Africa and Middle East, the expectation of further evolutions can be formulated with a relatively high degree of confidence.

The fact that regional aviation safety bodies have an overall tendency to evolve into organisations with legal personality hopefully means that it is likely in the future that there will be more RASOs vested with delegations of safety functions at Level 3. Such RASOs would further contribute to the development of the GASON as proposed in Chapter 2.

Following on from the above, this study recommends the setting up of regional aviation safety bodies in the form of RASOs, that is organisations established by international agreements or supranational acts which create direct legal effects and enable Level 3 delegations (see section §5.02 of Chapter 5). This legal form, by also providing for legal personality of RASOs under domestic law of its Member States, eliminates the need for establishing additional associations or foundations under private law (see section §3.03 of Chapter 3 and section §5.04[D] of Chapter 5).

Recommendation No 5:
States and ICAO should consistently support the evolution of regional aviation safety bodies, into more institutionalised types of organisations established on the basis of international agreements or supranational law and having international and domestic legal personality.

(6) Are there any shortcomings in the current international legal framework that pose an obstacle to further development of RASOs?

Overall, this study found no evidence that any particular provision or principle of international law is a serious obstacle to the establishment of RASOs. States have even been able to establish organisations vested with power to issue certificates on their behalf, as section §5.02 of Chapter 5 has demonstrated.

From the perspective of the Chicago Convention the main limitation is the fact that only States can be a party to the Convention. This means that, from the perspective of the Chicago Convention, RASOs can act only as agents of States and the latter cannot transfer to a RASO their ultimate responsibility for compliance with requirements of the Convention and its safety related Annexes. This conclusion, which has been reached in Chapter 6 of the study, is further elaborated in a summary related to the research question No 7 below.

In addition, this study has identified three more specific limitations from the perspective of the Chicago Convention concerning the delegation of State safety functions to a RASO. These limitations are related to the exercise by a RASO of the responsibilities and tasks of the 'State of Registry' (see section §6.03[A][1] of Chapter 6), and 'State of the Operator' (see section §6.03[A][2] of Chapter 6):

(1) Although a RASO can act as a 'State of Registry' with respect to individual States, meaning registering aircraft on their behalf, such aircraft would still have the *nationality* of the State on behalf of which they were registered in accordance with Article 17 of the Chicago Convention. It is thus not possible today for a RASO to register aircraft on a *multinational* basis. The only exception to this rule could be aircraft operated by international operating agencies under Article 77 of the Chicago Convention. Until 2014 there has only been one case of an international operating agency having its aircraft registered on a non-national basis (Arab Air Cargo), but this scheme involved a number of States acting jointly as a 'State of Registry' rather than delegating registration functions to an international organisation.

(2) Where a RASO exercises on behalf of its Member States the functions and duties of the 'State of the Operator' or 'State of Registry' it will not be able to conclude Article 83bis with third countries in its own name. This stems from the fact that only States can be parties to the Chicago Convention and thus directly use its Article 83bis.

(3) Where a RASO exercises on behalf of its Member States only the functions and duties of the 'State of Registry', while the RASO Member States continue to exercise the functions and duties of the 'State of Operator', any agreements concerning the transfer of responsibilities which may be concluded between the RASO and its Member States, may not be recognised by third countries. Similar to point (2) above this limitation results from the fact that RASOs cannot be party to the Chicago Convention.

Chapter 6 also explored the need to amend the Chicago Convention in order to clearly enable RASOs which enjoy the most far reaching regulatory powers to exercise them in RASOs own name, and thus to take full responsibility, from international law point of view, for the work they are doing.

While this study argued that at present there is insufficient interest amongst the ICAO Member States in opening a discussion on amending the Chicago Convention, should such a debate be launched in the future, two main possibilities could be further explored: (1) The first option could be a limited amendment of the Chicago Convention, altering the scope of its current Article 83bis in a way to allow transfer of safety functions not only to other States but also to international organisations; (2) Another option would be through the inclusion of the so called *REIO clause*, which provides for the possibility of adherence to an international treaty of a REIO, such as the African RECs or the EU.

The study highlighted that the actual need to amend the Chicago Convention, putting aside the political willingness of the States to actually do that, could be a point of moot. On the one hand, it can be argued that the principle of ultimate State responsibility for safety oversight discourages ICAO Member States from establishing 'Level 3' RASOs which 'provide the best dividend in terms of efficiency and the effective use of resources'.[5] The fact that there are very few Level 3 RASOs can be used as an argument to support such a claim. On the other hand, and this is a point of view this study supports, it can be argued that States would take less interest in aviation safety, if they were to be allowed to release themselves from responsibility and *hide* behind a regional body – which is why ICAO puts so much emphasis on individual State responsibility in its manual on RSOOs.

As far as the safety related Annexes to the Chicago Convention are concerned, a detailed analysis of their provisions conducted in section §6.03 of Chapter 6 has revealed the following:

(1) Although there is no consistency in the way the different formulations regarding aviation authorities are used in the Annexes, the vast majority of the SARPs use broad formulations which refer to a *State* and/or to an *authority* in a more general sense without specifying that it has to be a *national* authority.
(2) In the rare cases where an ICAO Annex uses the term *national*, the relevant State and ICAO practice demonstrates that this term is actually interpreted as covering also RASO type bodies.
(3) Many of the ICAO Annexes explicitly envisage that a State has an obligation to designate an authority, which is to discharge, on its behalf, relevant safety related responsibilities or provision of services necessary for international air navigation.

In 2014, there were only two ICAO Annexes, that is No 13 and No 19, which explicitly refer to RASOs, although only Annex 13 actually contains Standards and Recommended Practices in this respect. Analysis of the relevant provisions of these

5. ICAO Doc. 9734 Part B, *supra* note 3 in Ch. 1, at Paragraph 3.1.1.

two Annexes which was conducted in section §6.03 of Chapter 6 revealed that ICAO is still struggling somewhat with accepting that a RASO could completely replace a national aviation authority. In particular section §6.03 of Chapter 6 found that, although Annex 19 suggests that there may be limitations regarding the safety management functions which may be delegated to a RSOO or a RAIO, that Annex does not offer further guidance in this respect.

Recommendation No 6:
a) *ICAO Annexes should be drafted in a way which recognises that it is perfectly acceptable for a State to discharge its safety related obligations under the Chicago Convention and related Annexes by relying either on a national authority(ies) or, in part or even entirely, on a RASO type body, as long as the State concerned can demonstrate that the relevant SARPs are effectively implemented.*
b) *Should the possibility for an amendment of the Chicago Convention arise in the future, it is recommended that consideration is given to either adjusting its Article 83bis in a way which would allow the transfer of safety functions and duties not only between States but also to international organisations, or incorporating a REIO-type clause into the Convention. It is further recommended not to relieve States from their responsibility for safety regulation and oversight but rather provide for a joint and several responsibility of States and RASOs.*

(7) What are the international responsibility and civil liability implications resulting from RASOs establishment and functioning?
The success of the GASON proposed in Chapter 2, measured by more effective and uniform implementation of ICAO SARPs and efficiencies in terms of the use of resources by ICAO and its Member States, will to a large degree depend on whether the RASOs which form its building blocks are appropriately empowered by its Member States to exercise civil aviation safety responsibilities and functions - either on behalf of these Member States or in RASOs own name.

In order to facilitate successful empowerment of RASOs, section §6.02 of Chapter 6 has first of all clarified and systematised the general principles and concepts concerning the attribution and delegation of civil aviation safety responsibilities and functions both in domestic, and international law context.

Having clarified the concepts and principles, Chapter 6 has, building on the general theory of conferrals of powers on international organisations, reached the following conclusions (see sections §6.02[B] and §6.05 of Chapter 6):

(1) From the international law point of view nothing prevents a State from delegating the exercise of its State safety functions, as envisaged under the Chicago Convention and its Annexes, to a RASO. However, given the fact that only States can be parties to the Chicago Convention, such delegation does not relieve a State from *ultimate responsibility* of compliance. Even when

States establish Level 3 RASOs, the transfer of responsibility in such cases takes place only *inter se*, but not vis-à-vis other ICAO Member States.

(2) Furthermore, three general types of delegations of powers to RASOs can be distinguished, that is agency relationships, delegations proper, and transfers:
   (a) An *agency relationship* occurs when States use Level 3 delegations in respect to functions for which they are responsible under the Chicago Convention. In such cases a RASO will be exercising such a function on behalf of the States concerned, meaning that it can change their rights and obligations under international law.
   (b) *Delegation proper* occurs when States give to a RASO functions which are not created by the Chicago Convention. In such cases States attribute to a RASO a new competence, which the RASO will be carrying out in its own name and for which it will be responsible.
   (c) *Transfer of responsibilities* results in releasing a State from an obligation of compliance. Transfers are at present envisaged only under Article 83bis of the Chicago Convention. Given the fact that RASOs cannot be parties to the Convention, in principle Article 83bis transfers are only possible between States.

When it comes to the potential responsibility of regional aviation safety bodies under international law, section §6.05 of Chapter 6 has concluded that this will depend, in accordance with ICJ case law, whether an organisation has a separate international legal personality. Whether such legal personality exists has to be assessed on a case by case basis, as few RASO founding agreements explicitly provide for it.

Furthermore, this study explained in section §6.05 of Chapter 6 that a distinction has to be made between, on the one hand, RASOs established in a form of an international organisation and, on the other hand, established in a form of an organ of an international organisation. In the latter case, it is not the RASO which is a separate international legal person but its mother organisation.

Section §6.05 of Chapter 6 has found that the majority of current RASOs can be considered as having international legal personality and thus having their international legal responsibility potentially engaged. This conclusion was reached based on considerations such as: whether an organisation is established on the basis of an international agreement, explicit provisions to this end in the RASO founding agreements, or existence of a relationship of an international agency between a RASO and its Member States.

The substance of such responsibility in the first place depends on the underlying relationship which exists between a RASO, or its mother organisation, and its Member States in accordance with the principle of specialty. Given the fact that international organisations cannot be parties to the Chicago Convention, the main source of their international law obligations are their founding agreements. The obligations stemming from such founding agreements are directed towards RASO Member States (see section §6.05 of Chapter 6).

This study also considered, in section §6.05[D] of Chapter 6, whether international responsibility of a RASO or of its mother organisation could be engaged by a non-Member State in respect to the provisions of the Chicago Convention. That question is especially relevant for Level 3 RASOs which are expected to carry out their delegated functions in compliance with the Convention and its Annexes. The present study came to the conclusion that such possibility should not be excluded *a priori*, especially in the case of RASOs which have operational responsibilities, such as aircraft certification, the negligent exercise of which could contribute to accidents. From a legal point of view, such responsibility vis-à-vis third countries could be justified by the fact that some of the safety oversight obligations can be considered as *erga omnes*, as was demonstrated by other studies. This study also pointed out that according to some sources a joint and several responsibility of States and international organisation can stem from the relationship of an international agency. In addition, such responsibility could be considered at least in those cases where a RASO or its mother organisation concludes an international agreement with a third country, and which creates an obligation for the regional safety body to act in accordance with the provisions of the Chicago Convention and its Annexes.

However, the international legal personality of a RASO or of its mother organisation would be effective vis-à-vis non-Member States only if it has been explicitly or implicitly recognised by such third States. In this respect, section §6.05[D] of Chapter 6 has found that most of the RASOs or their mother organisations are regularly invited by ICAO to international symposia and conferences. In the case of EASA, the EU has entered into international agreements with third countries and ICAO, under which EASA has been designated as an authorised agent of EU Member States. Some of the RASOs, such as EASA or ECCAA, have been subject to ICAO USOAP audits, which too is a sign of recognition in international relations.

In addition, this study demonstrated in section §6.05[D] of Chapter 6 that third countries recognise the legal effects that the currently operational Level 3 RASOs, that is EASA, IAC and ECCAA, take on behalf of States. In the case of EASA the relationship of international agency that exists between EU, acting through EASA, and its Member States is even globally recognised. This is because EASA, as was also demonstrated in section §6.05[D] of Chapter 6, acts as a 'State of Design' for one of the leading aircraft manufacturers in the world, namely Airbus. This means that third country 'States of Registry' readily accept Type Certificates issued by EASA on behalf of EU Member States, and exchange with EASA information which is necessary for ensuring the continuing airworthiness of the aircraft under Annex 8 to the Chicago Convention.

Irrespective of the above, this study did not identify any cases heard by international courts or tribunals and related to breach by either a State or a RASO of international safety oversight or regulatory obligations (see section §6.05[D] of Chapter 6). On this basis it was concluded that it is more likely that, rather than the international responsibility of RASOs or their mother organisations being engaged by States, victims of aviation accidents would be trying to engage RASOs civil liability in domestic courts. In this respect, this study concluded as follows:

(1) There is at present no international legal instrument which would harmonise the domestic civil liability regimes of States in respect to damage caused through the conduct of civil aviation safety regulatory and oversight tasks.

Accordingly such civil liability would depend primarily on provisions of the RASO founding documents and applicable domestic law (see section §6.06[D] of Chapter 6).

(2) Only three RASOs founding documents explicitly provide for the possibility of holding RASOs liable for non-contractual civil damages (see section §6.06[D][3] of Chapter 6). In addition this study has identified case law – albeit entirely from domestic, common law jurisdictions – where courts confirmed that national aviation regulators owe a *duty of care* towards the travelling public and set *negligence* as a threshold beyond which the regulator may be held liable. Similar principles could be applied to RASOs (see section §6.06[B] of Chapter 6).

(3) The possibility to engage civil liability of a RASO would in the first case depend on the recognition of its separate legal personality under domestic law. This should normally not be a problem as far as the jurisdictions of the RASO Member States are concerned, but could be more difficult in case of non-Member States. The question of jurisdictional immunity in domestic proceedings would also have to be considered. In this respect the study concluded that most of the RASO founding documents studied contain provisions on privileges and immunities, although the scope of the rights granted vary considerably (see section §6.06[D][2] of Chapter 6).

(4) This study advocates that treatment of RASOs from a liability point of view should chiefly depend on the type of delegations and competences they have been granted by States. The more operational competences were given to a RASO, the exercise of which can result in damages to third parties, the more stringent the liability regime should be (see section §6.06[D][3] of Chapter 6).

Finally, this study has concluded in section §6.07 of Chapter 6, that there is a need for a clear ICAO policy on the role of States in the supervision of RASOs, which could be included in one of the future editions of the ICAO RSOO and RAIO manuals, or the new Annex 19 which, as it applies to safety management in general, has a horizontal application. It was argued that ICAO should in particular offer more guidelines on how such supervision should be organised depending on the level of delegation effectuated. It was recommended that the supervision policy should be based on the principle that States and RASOs working on their behalf are seen by ICAO and its Member States as a system which, taken together, should guarantee the level of safety oversight required by the Chicago Convention.

Recommendation No 7:
a) It is recommended that ICAO develops guidance and/or SARPs on how States should be organising oversight of RASOs. The supervision policy should be based on the principle that States and RASOs working on their behalf are seen by ICAO and its Member States as a single system which, taken together, should guarantee the level of safety oversight required by the Chicago Convention.

b) *States should also promote in the RASO founding agreements clear provisions on RASO civil liability for non-contractual damages, especially in the case of organisations enjoying 'Level 3' delegations.*

§7.03 RECOMMENDATIONS FOR FURTHER RESEARCH

This has been the first comprehensive study of legal and institutional aspects related to RASOs' establishment and functioning, and their role in supporting global aviation safety. As such it necessarily focused, in the first place, on mapping this new area of international cooperation and identifying key elements of RASO functioning which are most essential for enhancing global aviation safety and achievement of ICAO objectives of regulatory harmonisation and standardisation.

The author hopes that this topic, including the findings and recommendations of this particular study, will be subject to further review, analysis and critical discussion. In this respect, the issues meriting further research are related, in particular, to the following questions:

- delegation arrangements, in particular those needed for establishing RCAA;
- international responsibility of RASOs and their Member States;
- domestic civil liability of RASOs for negligent exercise of regulatory and oversight functions;
- sustainability of RASOs, including possibly the development of a methodology for measuring their effectiveness;
- how different RASOs could best cooperate with each other to harmonise their activities and achieve efficiencies within the GASON.

The author would also like to invite practitioners and academics to conduct further, detailed case studies of different RASOs, similar to the case study of EASA in Chapter 4, and to present the resulting conclusions and recommendations.

It would also be worthwhile in several years' time to conduct a follow-up study in order to verify whether the RASO evolution trends which were identified in Chapter 5 will continue.

Appendix: Core Sample of Organisations Selected for the Study

(1) European Aviation Safety Agency (EASA)
(2) European Organisation for the safety of air navigation (EUROCONTROL)
(3) European Network of Civil Aviation Safety Investigation Authorities (EN-CASIA)
(4) Interstate Aviation Committee (IAC)
(5) Banjul Accord Group Aviation Safety Oversight Organisation (BAGASOO)
(6) Banjul Accord Group Accident Investigation Agency (BAGAIA)
(7) East African Community Civil Aviation Safety and Security Oversight Agency (CASSOA)
(8) Civil Aviation Authorities of Africa and Madagascar (AAMAC)
(9) Pacific Aviation Safety Office (PASO)
(10) Eastern Caribbean Civil Aviation Authority (ECCAA)
(11) Caribbean Aviation Safety and Security Oversight System (CASSOS)
(12) Regional Cooperation System on Safety Oversight in Latin America (SRV-SOP)
(13) Central American Aviation Safety Agency (ACSA)
(14) Central African Aviation Safety Oversight Agency (ASSA-AC)

Selected Bibliography

Treaties and Working Arrangements

AFCAC, 'Memorandum of Understanding (MoU) between the African Civil Aviation Commission (AFCAC) and African States for the use of national inspectors under the AFI Cooperative Inspector Scheme', (2013).

'Agreement between the European Community and the Swiss Confederation on Air Transport', 21 June 1999, (OJ L 114, 30.4.2002).

'Agreement between the European Union and the Government of the Federative Republic of Brazil on civil aviation safety', 14 July 2010, (OJ L 273, 19.10.2011).

'Agreement between the Government of Antigua and Barbuda and the Eastern Caribbean Civil Aviation Authority regarding the Headquarters of the Authority', St. John's, 15 April 2008.

'Agreement between the government of the Russian Federation and the Government of the United States of America for the promotion of aviation safety', (Moscow, 1998).

'Agreement between the United States of America and the European Community on cooperation in the regulation of civil aviation safety', 30 June 2008, (OJ L 291, 9.11.2011).

'Agreement establishing the Caribbean Aviation Safety and Security Oversight System', Gros Islet, 9 May 2008.

'Agreement Establishing the Eastern Caribbean Civil Aviation Authority', Grenada, 21 October 2003.

'Agreement for the establishment of the Banjul Accord Group', Banjul, 29 January 2004, ICAO Registration No. 5455.

'Agreement on Civil Aviation and Airspace Utilization ', Minsk, 30 December 1991, ICAO Registration No. 3720.

'Agreement on civil aviation safety between the European Community and Canada', 6 May 2009, (OJ L 153, 17.06.2009).

'Agreement on the European Economic Area', 2 May 1992 (OJ L 1, 3.1.1994).

'Annex on aviation safety to the Memorandum of Cooperation between the European Union and the International Civil Aviation Organization providing a framework for enhanced cooperation', (OJ L 232, 9 September 2011).

'Arrangements concerning the development, the acceptance and the implementation of Joint Aviation Requirements', (Cyprus, 1990).

Aviation Safety Network, 'EASA grounds all Dassault Falcon 7X aircraft pending incident investigation' <http://news.aviation-safety.net/2011/05/26/easa-grounds-all-dassault-falcon-7x-aircraft-pending-incident-investigation/> [accessed 14 June 2014].

'Banjul Accord Group Accident Investigation Agency Agreement', Montreal, 30 June 2009, ICAO Registration No. 5463.

'Banjul Accord Group Aviation Safety Oversight Organisation Agreement', Montreal, 30 June 2009 ICAO Registration No. 5462.

'Common Aviation Area Agreement between the European Union and its Member States and Georgia', 2 December 2010, (OJ L 321, 20.11.2012).

'Common Aviation Area Agreement between the European Union and its Member States and the Republic of Moldova', 26 June 2012, (OJ L 292, 20.10.2012).

'Consolidated version of the EUROCONTROL International Convention Relating to Co-operation for the Safety of Air Navigation of 13 December 1960, as variously amended', Brussels, 27 June 1997, Final Act of the Diplomatic Conference.

'Convention on International Civil Aviation', Chicago, 7.12.1944, 15 UNTS 295.

'Convention relating to Co-operation for the Safety of Air Navigation (EUROCONTROL) with Annexes and Protocols', 13 December 1960, UK Treaty Series No. 39 (1963).

'Convention Relating to International Air Navigation Agreed to by the Allied and Associated Parties', Paris, 13 October 1919, LNTS (1922) No. 297.

'Convention relative a l'Agence pour la Securite de la Navigation Aerienne en Afrique et Madagascar (ASECNA)', Ouagadougou, 28 avril 2010, Official Journal of the Republic of Senegal N° 6641, 28 January 2012.

'Decision No 1/2013 of the Joint European Union/Switzerland Air Transport Committee set up under the Agreement between the European Community and the Swiss Confederation on Air Transport of 2 December 2013 replacing the Annex to the Agreement between the European Community and the Swiss Confederation on Air Transport', 2 December 2013, (OJ L 12, 17.1.2014).

'Decision of the EEA Joint Committee No 179/2004 of 9 December 2004 amending Annex XIII (Transport) to the EEA Agreement', 9 December 2004, (OJ L 133, 26.5.2005).

'Decision of the EU-ICAO Joint Committee of 21 September 2011 on the adoption of an Annex on aviation safety to the Memorandum of Cooperation between the European Union and the International Civil Aviation Organization providing a framework for enhanced cooperation', (OJ L 172, 25.6.2013).

EASA, 'Working Arrangement on Airworthiness between the European Aviation Safety Agency and the InterState Aviation Committee', (St. Petersburg, 2004).

EASA, 'Airworthiness Directives Publishing Tool' <http://ad.easa.europa.eu/> [accessed 02 March 2014].

EU, 'Treaty on the Functioning of the European Union (TFEU)', in: Consolidated Treaties and Charter of Fundamental Rights (2010).

'Letter of agreement for the implementation of the Regional Safety Oversight Cooperation System of Latin America'.

ICAO, 'Annex 1 to the Chicago Convention: Personnel Licensing', (2011).

ICAO, 'Annex 2 to the Chicago Convention: Rules of the Air', (2005).

ICAO, 'Annex 4 to the Chicago Convention: Aeronautical Charts', (2009).

ICAO, 'Annex 6 to the Chicago Convention: Operation of Aircraft, Part I - International Commercial Air Transport with Aeroplanes', (2010).

ICAO, 'Annex 6 to the Chicago Convention: Operation of Aircraft, Part II - International General Aviation with Aeroplanes', (2008).

ICAO, 'Annex 7 to the Chicago Convention: Aircraft Nationality and Registration Marks', (2012).

ICAO, 'Annex 8 to the Chicago Convention: Airworthiness of Aircraft', (2010).

ICAO, 'Annex 10 to the Chicago Convention: Aeronautical Telecommunications, Volume I - Radio Navigation Aids', (2006).

ICAO, 'Annex 11 to the Chicago Convention: Air Traffic Services', (2001).

ICAO, 'Annex 12 to the Chicago Convention: Search and Rescue', (2004).

ICAO, 'Annex 13 to the Chicago Convention: Aircraft Accident and Incident Investigation', (2010).

ICAO, 'Annex 14 to the Chicago Convention: Aerodromes, Volume I - Aerodrome Design and Operations', (2013).

ICAO, 'Annex 18 to the Chicago Convention: The Safe Transport of Dangerous Goods by Air', (2011).

ICAO, 'Annex 19 to the Chicago Convention: Safety Management', (2013).

ICAO, 'Protocol Relating to an Amendment to the Convention on International Civil Aviation (Article 83bis)', ICAO Doc 9318, (1980).

'Memorandum of Cooperation between the European Union and the International Civil Aviation Organization providing a framework for enhanced cooperation', 4 May 2011, (OJ L 232, 9 September 2011).

'Memorandum of Cooperation between the International Civil Aviation Organisation and the European Community regarding security audits/inspections and related matters', 17 September 2008, (OJ L 36, 5.2.2009).

'Memorandum of Understanding between the government of the United States of America and the government of the Russian Federation on cooperation in the field of civil aircraft accident/incident investigation and prevention', 2nd September 1998, 1998 TIAS 12983.

'Memorandum of Understanding between the Latin American Civil Aviation Commission and the International Civil Aviation Organization on the establishment of Regional Safety Oversight Cooperation System of Latin America', (1998).

'Multilateral Agreement between the European Community and its Member States, the Republic of Albania, Bosnia and Herzegovina, the Republic of Bulgaria, the Republic of Croatia, the former Yugoslav Republic of Macedonia, the Republic of Iceland, the Republic of Montenegro, the Kingdom of Norway, Romania, the Republic of Serbia and the United Nations Interim Administration Mission in Kosovo on the establishment of a European Common Aviation Area', 9 June 2006, (OJ L 285, 16.10.2006).

'Multilateral Agreement Relating to Certificates of Airworthiness for Imported Aircraft', Paris, 22 April 1960, ICAO Doc. 8056.

'Operating Agreement on the International Maritime Satellite Organization (INMARSAT)', London, 3 September 1976, 15 ILM 233.

'Pacific Islands Civil Aviation Safety and Security Treaty', Apia, 7 August 2004, ICAO Registration No. 5381.
'Protocol on the establishment of the East African Community Civil Aviation Safety and Security Oversight Agency', signed on 18 April 2007 and approved during the 5th Extraordinary Summit of EAC Heads of State held in Kampala, Uganda on 18th June 2007', <http://www.cassoa.org/index.php/key-documents/cassoa-protocol> [accessed 10 August 2014].
'Revised Treaty of Basseterre establishing the Organisation of Eastern Caribbean States Economic Union', Gros Islet, 18 June 2010.
'Revised Treaty of Chaguaramas Establishing the Caribbean Community including the CARICOM single Market and Economy', The Bahamas, 5 July 2001.
'Statute of the Council for Aviation and Airspace Utilization and the Statute of the Interstate Aviation Committee', 19 February 1992, ICAO Registration No. 3720.
'Traité relative aux Autorités Africaines et Malgache de l'Aviation Civile (AAMAC Treaty)', N'Djaména, 20 January 2012, LOI n°2012 -012, of 29 July 2012, Le Congrès de la Transition et le Conseil Supérieur de la Transition, République de Madagascar.
'Treaty establishing the Organisation of Eastern Caribbean States', Basseterre, 18 June 1981, 1338 UNTS 97.
'Treaty on Principles Governing the Activities of States in the Exploration and Use of Outer Space, including the Moon and other Celestial Bodies', London, Moscow and Washington, 27 January 1967, 610 UNTS 205.
UN, 'Commentary to draft articles on the responsibility of international organizations', Yearbook of the International Law Commission, Volume II, Part 2 (2011).
UN, 'Draft articles on responsibility of States for internationally wrongful acts (DASR)', Yearbook of the International Law Commission, Volume II, Part 2 (2001).
UN, 'Draft articles on the responsibility of international organizations (DARIO)', Yearbook of the International Law Commission, Volume II, Part 2 (2011).
'Vienna Convention on the Law of the Treaties', Vienna, 23 May 1969, 1155 UNTS 33.
'Соглашение между Правительством Российской Федерации и Межгосударственным авиационным комитетом об условиях его пребывания на территории Российской Федерации (Agreement between the Government of the Russian Federation and the InterState Aviation Committee on the conditions of its stay in the Russian Federation) ', Moscow, 20 October 1995.

Court Cases

Court of Justice of the European Union

'Case C-4/69, Lütticke v. Commission', in: [1971] ECR I-325 (CJEU, 1969).
'Case C-6/64, Flaminio Costa v. ENEL', in: [1964] ECR I-585 (CJEU, 1964).
'Case C-9/56 Meroni and Co., Industrie Metallurgiche S.p.A. v. Highly Authority', in: [1957-1958] ECR I-133 (CJEU, 1958).

'Case C-26/62, Van Gend en Loos v. Administratie der Belastingen', in: [1963] ECR I-1 (CJEU, 1963).
'Case C-98/80, Giuseppe Romano v. Institut national d'assurance maladie-invalidité', in: [1981] ECR I-1241 (CJEU, 1981).
'Case C-247/87, Star Fruit Company v. Commission', in: [1989] ECR I-291 (CJEU, 1989).
'Case C-270/12, United Kingdom v. Parliament and Council ', in: not yet published (available on-line) (CJEU, 2014).
'Case C-327/91, French Republic v. Commission', in: [1994] ECR I-03641, (CJEU,1994).
'Case C-366/10, Air Transport Association of America v. Secretary of State for Energy and Climate Change', in: [2011] ECR I-13755 (CJEU, 2011).
'Case T-311/06, FMC Chemical SPRL v. European Food Safety Authority (EFSA)', in: [2008] ECR II-88 (CJEU, 2008).
'Case T-571/93, Lefebvre and Others v. Commission ', in: [1995] ECR II-02379 (CJEU, 1995).
'Joined Cases C-154/04 and C-155/04, The Queen v. Secretary of State for Health and National Assembly for Wales', in: [2005] ECR I-06451 (CJEU, 2005).
'Joint Cases C-6 and C-9/90, Francovich and Bonifaci v. Republic of Italy', in: [1991] ECR I-05375 (CJEU, 1991).
'Opinion 1/76 concerning the draft agreement establishing a European laying-up fund for inland waterway vessels', in: [1977] ECR I-741 (CJEU, 1977).

International Court of Justice and Permanent Court of International Justice

'Case concerning the Factory at Chorzów (Germany v. Poland), Judgement', in: [1928] PCIJ Series A-No 17 (PCIJ, 1928).
'Certain Phosphate Lands in Nauru (Nauru v. Australia), Preliminary Objections', in: [1992] ICJ Reports 240 (ICJ, 1992).
'Corfu Channel, Judgement', in: [1949] ICJ Reports 4 (ICJ, 1949).
'Difference Relating to Immunity from Legal Process of a Special Rapporteur of the Commission on Human Rights, Advisory Opinion', in: [1999] ICJ Reports 62 (ICJ, 1999).
'Interpretation of the Agreement of 25 March 1951 between WHO and Egypt, Advisory Opinion', in: [1980] ICJ Reports 73 (ICJ, 1980).
'Legality of the Threat or Use of Nuclear Weapons, Advisory Opinion', in: [1996] ICJ Reports 66 (ICJ, 1996).
'Military and Paramilitary Activities in and against Nicaragua (Nicaragua v. United States of America)', in: [1986] ICJ Reports 14 (ICJ, 1986).
'Phosphates in Morocco (Italy v. France), Judgement', in: [1938] PCIJ Series A/B-No 74 (PCIJ, 1938).
'Reparation for Injuries Suffered in the Service of the United Nations, Advisory Opinion', in: [1949] ICJ Reports 174 (ICJ, 1949).

'United States Diplomatic and Consular Staff in Tehran (United States of America v. Iran), Judgement', in: [1980] ICJ Reports 3 (ICJ, 1980).

Other Cases

'Rainbow Warrior (New Zealand v. France)', in: [1990] RIAA, Volume XX (New Zealand-France Arbitral Tribunal, 1990).
'Swanson et al v. The Queen in right of Canada', in: [1991] 80 DLR (4) 741 (Federal Court of Appeal of Canada).
'Perrett v. Collins', in: [1998] 2 Lloyd's LR 255.

Books and Monographs

Amerasinghe, Chittharanjan F., 'Principles of the International Law of International Organisations' (2005).
Andenas, Mads, Fairgrieve, Duncan, and Bell, John, 'Tort Liability of Public Authorities in Comparative Perspective' (2002).
Bailey, Stephen H., 'Cases materials and Commentaty on administrative law' (2005).
Blumenkron, Jimena, 'Transparency and the International Civil Aviation Organisation: Implications of increased transparency in safety audit information' (2011).
Boisson de Chazournes, Laurence, 'Les relations entre organisations régionales et organisations universelles', in: L'Académie de droit international de la Haye: Recueil des Cours' (2010).
Booth QC, Cherie, and Squires, Dan, 'The Negligence Liability of Public Authorities' (2006).
Boteva, Meglena, 'A new century and a new attitude towards safety oversight in air transportation', in: Master Thesis (McGill University: Institute of Air and Space Law, 2000).
Boulle, Laurence, 'The Law of Globalization: An Introduction' (2009).
Brown, Lionel N., and Bell, John, 'French Administrative Law' (2003).
Brownlie, Ian, 'The responsibility of States for the acts of international organizations', in: International Responsibility today: Essays in the Memory of Oscar Schachter, ed. by Ragazzi, Maurizio (2005).
Calleja Crespo, Daniel, and Mendes de Leon, Pablo, eds., 'Achieving the Single European Sky: Goals and challenges' (2011).
Cannizzaro, Enzo, Palchetti, Peolo, and Wessel, A. Ramses, eds., 'International law as law of the European Union' (2012).
Cobb, Roger W., and Primo, David M., 'The plane truth: Airline crashes, the media and transportation policy' (2003).
Correia, Vincent, 'La contribution des agences de régulation à l'action extérieure de l'Union européenne', in: L'Europe face au monde, ed. by Grard, Loic (2013).

Cortés Martin, Jose Manuel, 'European Exceptionalism in International Law? The European Union and the System of International Responsibility', in: Responsibility of international organizations: essays in memeory of Sir Ian Brownlie, ed. by Ragazzi, Maurizio (2013).

Craig, Paul, and de Búrca, Gráinne, 'EU Law: Text, Cases, and Materials' (2011).

Crawford, James, 'Brownlie's principles of public international law' (2012).

Crawford, James, 'The International Law Commission's Articles on State Responsibility: Introduction, Text and Commentaries' (2002).

Crawford, James, 'State Responsibility: The General Part' (2013).

De Florio, Filippo, 'Airworthiness, An Introduction to Aircraft Certification: A guide to understanding JAA, EASA and FAA standards' (2006).

Detra, Zachary D., 'The legitimacy of the International Civil Aviation Organization's Universal Safety Oversight Audit Programme', in: Master Thesis (McGill University: Institute of Air and Space Law, 2006).

Diederiks-Verschoor, Isabella H. Ph., 'An Introduction to Air Law' (2006).

Eeckhout, Piet, 'External Relations of the European Union: Legal and Constitutional Foundations' (2004).

Funk, William F., and Seamon, Richard H., 'Administrative Law: Examples and explanations' (2009).

Hawke, Neil, and Parpworth, Neil, 'Introduction to Administrative Law' (1996).

Hofmann, Herwig C.H., Rowe, Gerard C., and Türk, Alexander H., 'Administrative Law and Policy of the European Union' (2011).

Huang, Jiefang, 'Aviation Safety through the Rule of Law: ICAO's mechanism and practices' (2009).

Institute of International Law, 'Yearbook', Volume 66, Part I, Session of Lisbon, (1995).

Klabbers, Jan, 'An Introduction to International Institutional Law' (2009).

Kraus, Theresa L., 'The Federal Aviation Administration: A historical perspective, 1903-2008' (2008).

Kuijper, Jan Pieter, and Paasivirta, Esa, 'EU International Responsibility and its Attribution: From the Inside Looking Out', in: The International Responsibility of the European Union: European and International Perspectives, ed. by Evans, Malcolm and Koutrakos, Panos (2013).

European Group on Tort Law, 'Principles of European Tort Law: text and commentary' (2005).

Leckow, Ross, and Plith, Erik, 'Codification, Progressive Development or Innovation? - Some Reflections on the ILC Articles on the Responsibility of International Organizations', in: Responsibility of international organizations: essays in memory of Sir Ian Brownlie, ed. by Ragazzi, Maurizio (2013).

Lenaerts, Koen, and Verhoeven, Amaryllis, 'Institutional Balance as a Guarantee for Democracy in EU Governance', in: Good Governance in Europe's Integrated Market, ed. by Joerges, Christian and Dehousse, Renaud (2002).

Manuhutu, Frank, 'Article 83bis (Revisited): Transfer of Safety Oversight Responsibilities Seen from a European's Regulator Perspective', in: From Lowlands to High Skies: A multilevel Jurisdictional Approach towards Air Law, ed. by de Leon, Pablo Mendes (2013).

McInally, John, 'EUROCONTROL: History Book', (2010).

Mendes de Leon, Pablo, 'Cabotage in Air Transport Regulation' (1992).

Michaelides-Mateou, Sofia, and Mateou, Andreas, 'Flying in the Face of Criminalization: The Safety Implications of Prosecuting Aviation Professionals for Accidents' (2010).

Milde, Michael, 'International Air Law and ICAO' (2012).

Nakatani, Kazuhiro, 'Responsibility of Member States towards Third Parties for an Internationally Wrongful Act of the Organization', in: Responsibility of international organizations: essays in memory of Sir Ian Brownlie, ed. by Ragazzi, Maurizio (2013).

Nierhaus, Michael, 'Administrative Law', in: Introduction to German Law, ed. by Reimann, Mathias and Zekoll, Joachim (2005).

Ott, Andrea, Vos, Ellen I. L., and Coman-Kund, Florin, 'European Agencies on the Global Scene: EU and International Law Perspectives', in: European Agencies in between Institutions and Member States, ed. by Everson, Michelle, Monda, Cosimo and Vos, Ellen I. L. (2014).

Ragazzi, Maurizio, ed., 'Responsibility of international organizations: essays in memory of Sir Ian Brownlie' (2013).

Ringbom, Henrik, 'The EU maritime safety policy and international law' (2008).

Sarooshi, Dan, 'International Organizations and State Responsibility', in: Responsibility of international organizations: essays in memory of Sir Ian Brownlie, ed. by Ragazzi, Maurizio (2013).

Sarooshi, Dan, 'International organizations and their exercise of sovereign powers' (2005).

Schermers, Henry G., and Blokker, Niels M., 'International Institutional Law' (2011).

Schipke, Alfred, Cebotari, Aliona, and Thacker, Nita, 'The Eastern Caribbean Economic and Currency Union: Macroeconomics and Financial Systems' (2013).

Schlumberger, Charles, 'Open Skies for Africa: Implementing the Yamoussoukro Decision' (2010).

Shaffer, Gregory, and Pollack, Mark A., 'Hard and Soft Law', in: Interdisciplinary Perspectives on International Law and International Relations: The State of the Art, ed. by Dunoff, Jeffrey L. and Pollack, Mark A. (2013).

Spyropoulos, Philippos K., and Fortsakis, Théodore, 'Constitutional Law in Greece' (2009).

Steinberger, Helmut, 'Sovereignty', in: Encyclopedia of Public International Law, ed. by Bernhardt, Rudolf (2000), p. 501.

Van Antwerpen, Niels, 'Cross-Border Provision of Air Navigation Services with Specific Reference to Europe: Safeguarding Transparent Lines of Responsibility and Liability' (2008).

Venzke, Ingo, 'How Interpretation Makes International Law: On Semantic Change and Normative Twists' (2012).

von den Steinen, Erwin, 'National interest and international aviation' (2006).

von Erlach, Burkhart, 'Public law aspects of lease, charter and interchange of aircraft in international operations', in: Master Thesis (McGill University: Institute of Air and Space Law, 1990).

Wassenbergh, Henri A., 'Post-War International Civil Aviation Policy and the Law of the Air' (1962).
Weber, Ludwig, 'International Civil Aviation Organization: An Introduction' (2007).

JOURNAL ARTICLES

Abeyratne, Ruwantissa, 'Ensuring regional safety in air transport', ASL, 35 (2010).
Aras, Aytaç, 'European aviation safety regulatory framework and Turkey: A critical analysis', University of Turkish Aeronautical Association, Faculty of Business Working Papers (2011).
Aviassist, 'Insight into the EU Blacklist', in: Safety Focus: Quarterly Journal on African aviation safety (Aviassist, 2010).
Bell, John, 'Governmental Liability: some comparative reflections', InDret, 1 (2006).
Bradley, Curtis A., and Kelley, Judith G., 'The concept of international delegation', Law and Contemporary Problems, 71 (2008).
Broderick, Anthony J., and Loos, James, 'Government Aviation Safety Oversight: trust but verify ', JALC, 67 (2002).
Cariou, Pierre, Mejia, Maximo Q. Jr., and Wolff, Francois-Charles, 'On the effectiveness of port State control inspections', Transportation Research Part E (2008).
d'Aspremont, Jean, 'Abuse of the Legal Personality of International Organizations and the Responsibility of Member States', IOLR (2007).
Dempsey, Paul S., 'Blacklisting: Banning the unfit from the heavens', AASL, XXXII (2007).
Dempsey, Paul S., 'Compliance and enforcement in international law: achieving global uniformity in aviation safety', North Carolina Journal of International Law and Commercial Regulation, 30 (2004).
Dempsey, Paul S., 'Independence of Aviation Safety Investigation Authorities: Keeping the Foxes from the Henhouse', JALC, 75 (2010).
El - Hussainy, Khairy, 'Registration and Nationality of Aircraft operated by International Agencies in Law and Practice', Air Law, X (1985).
Freer, Duane W., 'Regionalism is asserted: ICAN's global prospects fade (1926 to 1943)', ICAO Bulletin, Special Series 4 (1986).
Gisen, Ivo, 'Regulating regulators through liability: the case for applying normal tort rules to supervisors', Utrecht Law Review, 2 (2006).
Guillaume, Gilbert, 'ICAO at the beginning of the 21st century ', ASL, 33 (2008).
Hoffmeister, Frank, 'Litigating against the European Union and its Member States - Who responds under the ILC's Draft Articles on International Responsibility of International Organizations?', EJIL, 21 (2010).
Hofmann, Herwig C.H., and Morini, Alessandro, 'The Pluralisation of EU Executive - Constitutional Aspects of "Agencification"', ELR, 37 (2012).
ICAO, 'Journal', 1 (2012).
Jennison, Michael, 'The Future of Aviation Safety Regulation: New US-EU Agreement Harmonizes and Consolidates the Transatlantic Regime, but What is the Potential for Genuine Regulatory Reform', ASL, 38 (2013).

Jennison, Michael, 'Regional safety oversight bodies deliver economies of scale and greater uniformity', ICAO Journal, 61 (2006).

Kasprzyk, Piotr, 'Legal Ramifications of the Investigations of the 2010 Polish President's Aircraft Accident', ASL, 36 (2011).

Korzeniowski, John, 'Liability of Aviation Regulators: Are the floodgates opening?', ASL, XXV (2000).

Manuhutu, Frank, 'Aviation Safety Regulation in Europe: Towards a European Aviation Safety Authority', ASL, 25 (2000).

McDorman, Ted L., 'Regional port State control agreements: some issues of international law', OCLJ, 5 (2000).

Melanie, Fink, 'Frontex Working Arrangements: Legitimacy and Human Rights Concerns Regarding 'Technical Relationships'', Utrecht Journal of International and European Law, 28 (2012).

Mendes de Leon, Pablo, 'The Relationship between Eurocontrol and the EC: Living Apart Together', IOLR, 4 (2008).

Messineo, Francesco, 'Multiple Attribution of Conduct', in: The Research Project on Shared Responsibility in International Law (SHARES) (2012).

Milde, Michael, 'Aviation Safety Oversight: Audits and the Law', AASL, XXVI (2001).

Milde, Michael, 'Nationality and registration of aircraft operated by Joint Air Transport Operating Organizations or International Operating Agencies', AASL, X (1985).

Onidi, Olivier, 'A critical perspective on ICAO', ASL, 33 (2008).

Ott, Andrea, 'EU regulatory agencies in EU external relations: Trapped in a legal minefield between European and International Law', European Foreign Affairs Review, 13 (2008).

Özçayır, Oya Z., 'The use of port State control in maritime industry and the application of the Paris MoU', OCLJ, 14 (2009).

Pierre, Jon, and Peters, Guy B., 'From a club to a bureaucracy: JAA, EASA, and European aviation regulation', JEPP, 16 (2009).

Ratajczyk, Mikołaj 'Regional Safety Oversight Organisations: an overview', The Aviation and Space Journal, X (2011).

Reitzfeld, Alan D., and Mpande, Cheryl S., 'EU Regulation on Banning of Airlines for Safety Concerns', ASL, 33 (2008).

Ryngaert, Cedric, 'The Immunity of International Organizations Before Domestic Courts: Recent Trends', IOLR, 7 (2010).

Schlumberger, Charles, and Vijayakumar, Shruti, 'Regional Safety Oversight Organisation: Service provider or more? The case of the Pacific Aviation Safety Office', AASL, XXXIX (2014).

Schusterschitz, Gregor, 'European Agencies as Subjects of International Law', IOLR, 1 (2004).

Sereni, Angelo P., 'Agency in International Law', American Journal of International Law, 34 (1940).

Sulocki, Thaddée, and Cartier, Axelle, 'Continuing Airworthiness in the framework of the transition from the Joint Aviation Authorities to the European Aviation Safety Agency', ASL, 28 (2003).

Swiecicki, Ewa M., 'Liability of the Canadian Government for the Negligent Enforcement of Aviation Safety Legislation', AASL, XVIII/I (1993).

Vos, Ellen I. L., 'Reforming the European Commission: What Role to Play for EU Agencies?', CMLR, 37 (2000).

Zayko, Sergey V., 'Russia's Interstate Aviation Committee', ISASI Forum, 46 (2013).

INTERVIEWS

Former President of the ICAO Air Navigation Commission, 'Interview No 1', (2013).

Official of the European Maritime Safety Agency, 'Interview No 2', (2012).

Official of the Swiss Civil Aviation Authority, 'Interview No 3', (2014).

Official of the European Aviation Safety Agency, 'Interview No 4', (2014).

Former official of the European Maritime Safety Agency, 'Interview No 5', (2014).

Official of the Banjul Accord Group Aviation Safety Oversight Organization, 'Interview No 6', (2014).

Official of the Eastern Caribbean Civil Aviation Authority, 'Interview No 7', (2014).

Official of the Regional System on Safety Oversight in Latin America, 'Interview No 8', (2014).

Official of the European Commission, 'Interview No 9', (2014).

Official of the Banjul Accord Group Accident Investigation Agency, 'Interview No 10', (2014).

Former Rulemaking Director of the European Aviation Safety Agency, 'Interview No 11', (2014).

Former Chairman of the European Aviation Safety Agency Management Board, 'Interview No 12', (2014).

Official of the Caribbean Aviation Safety and Security Oversight System, 'Interview No 13', (2014).

LEGISLATION

CEMAC, 'Regulation No 06/12-UEAC-204-CM-23, portant organisation et fonctionnement de l'Agence de Supervision de la Sècurité Aérienne en Afrique Centrale (ASSA-AC)', (2012).

'Civil Aviation Act', Laws of Grenada, Act No. 12 of 2004, amended by Act No. 18 of 2006.

'Civil Aviation Regulations', Laws of Grenada, SRO 12 of 2005.

'Code of Federal Regulations', <http://www.gpo.gov/fdsys/pkg/CFR-2014-title14-vol1/pdf/CFR-2014-title14-vol1.pdf> [Accessed 29 March 2014].

EASA, 'Notice of Proposed Amendment relating to rules on third country operators for commercial air transport', (NPA No 2011-05).

EC, 'Proposal for a Regulation of the European Parliament and of the Council amending Regulation (EC) No 216/2008 in the field of aerodromes, air traffic management and air navigation services', (COM(2013) 409 final).

EC, 'Proposal for a Regulation of the European Parliament and of the Council on establishing common rules in the field of civil aviation and creating a European Aviation Safety Agency', (COM(2000) 595 final).

EU, 'Commission implementing Regulation (EU) No 659/2013 of 10 July 2013 amending Regulation (EC) No 474/2006 establishing the Community list of air carriers which are subject to an operating ban within the Community', (OJ L 190, 11.7.2013).

EU, 'Commission Implementing Regulation (EU) No 923/2012 of 26 September 2012 laying down the common rules of the air and operational provisions regarding services and procedures in air navigation and amending Implementing Regulation (EU) No 1035/2011 and Regulations (EC) No 1265/2007, (EC) No 1794/2006, (EC) No 730/2006, (EC) No 1033/2006 and (EU) No 255/2010', (OJ L 281, 13.10.2012).

EU, 'Commission Regulation (EC) No 1962/2006 of 21 December 2006 in application of Article 37 of the Act of Accession of Bulgaria to the European Union', (OJ L 408, 30.12.2006).

EU, 'Commission Regulation (EU) No 646/2012 of 16 July 2012 laying down detailed rules on fines and periodic penalty payments pursuant to Regulation (EC) No 216/2008 of the European Parliament and of the Council', (OJ L 187, 17.7.2012).

EU, 'Commission Regulation (EU) No 748/2012 of 3 August 2012 laying down implementing rules for the airworthiness and environmental certification of aircraft and related products, parts and appliances, as well as for the certification of design and production organisations', (OJ L 224, 21.8.2012).

EU, 'Commission Regulation (EU) No 1332/2011 of 16 December 2011 laying down common airspace usage requirements and operating procedures for airborne collision avoidance', (OJ L 336, 20.12.2011).

EU, 'Regulation (EC) No 1049/2001 of the European Parliament and of the Council of 30 May 2001 regarding public access to European Parliament, Council and Commission documents', (OJ L 145, 31.5.2001).

EU, 'Regulation (EC) No 1108/2009 of the European Parliament and of the Council of 21 October 2009 amending Regulation (EC) No 216/2008 in the field of aerodromes, air traffic management and air navigation services and repealing Directive 2006/23/EC', (OJ L 309, 24.11.2009).

EU, 'Regulation (EC) No 1592/2002 of 15 July 2002 on common rules in the field of civil aviation and establishing a European Aviation Safety Agency', (OJ L 240, 7.9.2002).

EU, 'Regulation (EC) No 2111/2005 of the European Parliament and of the Council of 14 December 2005 on the establishment of a Community list of air carriers subject to an operating ban within the Community and on informing air transport passengers of the identity of the operating air carrier, and repealing Article 9 of Directive 2004/36/EC', (OJ L 344, 27.12.2005).

EU, 'Regulation (EU) No 216/2008 of 20 February 2008 on common rules in the field of civil aviation and establishing a European Aviation Safety Agency, and repealing Council Directive 91/670/EEC, Regulation (EC) No 1592/2002 and Directive 2004/36/EC', (OJ L 79, 19.3.2008).

EU, 'Regulation (EU) No 628/2013 of 28 June 2013 on working methods of the European Aviation Safety Agency for conducting standardisation inspections and for monitoring the application of the rules of Regulation (EC) No 216/2008 of the European Parliament and of the Council and repealing Commission Regulation (EC) No 736/2006', (OJ L 179, 29.06.2013).

EU, 'Regulation (EU) No 996/2010 of the European Parliament and of the Council of 20 October 2010 on the investigation and prevention of accidents and incidents in civil aviation and repealing Directive 94/56/EC', (OJ L 295, 12.11.2010).

EU, 'Regulation No 376/2014 of the European Parliament and of the Council of 3 April 2014 on the reporting, analysis and follow-up of occurrences in civil aviation, amending Regulation (EU) No 996/2010 of the European Parliament and of the Council and repealing Directive 2003/42/EC of the European Parliament and of the Council and Commission Regulations (EC) No 1321/2007 and (EC) No 1330/2007', (OJ L 122, 24.4.2014).

'Eastern Caribbean Civil Aviation Authority Agreement Act', Laws of Grenada, Act No. 11 of 2004.

IAC, ' АВИАЦИОННЫЕ ПРАВИЛА (Aviation Regulations)' <http://www.mak.ru/russian/russian.html> [Accessed 10 August 2014].

Le Congrès de la Transition et le Conseil Supérieur de la Transition, République de Madagascar, 'LOI n°2012-012: Autorisant la ratification du Traité relatif aux Autorités Africaines et Malgache de l'Aviation Civile signé à N'Djaména le 20 janvier 2012, Exposé des motifs', (2012).

ICAO Assembly Resolutions

ICAO, 'Assembly Resolution A10-5: Relationship of ICAO with the European Civil Aviation Conference', (10th ICAO Assembly, 1956).

ICAO, 'Assembly Resolution A27-17: Relationship between ICAO and Regional Civil Aviation Bodies', (27th ICAO Assembly, 1989).

ICAO, 'Assembly Resolution A29-3: Global Rule Harmonization', (29th ICAO Assembly, 1992).

ICAO, 'Assembly Resolution A32-11: Establishment of an ICAO universal safety oversight audit programme', (32nd ICAO Assembly, 1998).

ICAO, 'Assembly Resolution A33-9: Resolving Deficiencies and Encouraging Quality Assurance', Assembly Resolution A33-9, (33rd ICAO Assembly, 2001).

ICAO, 'Assembly Resolution A33-11: A global design code for aircraft', (33rd ICAO Assembly, 2001).

ICAO, 'Assembly Resolution A35-7: Unified strategy to resolve safety related deficiencies', (35th ICAO Assembly, 2004).

ICAO, 'Assembly Resolution A36-5: International Financial Facility for Aviation Safety (IFFAS)', (36th ICAO Assembly, 2007).

ICAO, 'Assembly Resolution A36-6: State Recognition of the Air Operator Certificate of Foreign Operators and Surveillance of their Operations', (36th ICAO Assembly, 2007).

ICAO, 'Assembly Resolution A37-1: Principles for a code of conduct on the sharing and use of safety information', (37th ICAO Assembly, 2010).

ICAO, 'Assembly Resolution A37-5: The Universal Safety Oversight Audit Programme (USOAP) continuous monitoring approach', (37th ICAO Assembly, 2010).

ICAO, 'Assembly Resolution A37-8: Regional cooperation and assistance to resolve safety-related deficiencies', (37th ICAO Assembly, 2010).

ICAO, 'Assembly Resolution A37-21: Cooperation with regional organizations and regional civil aviation bodies', (37th ICAO Assembly, 2010).

ICAO, 'Assembly Resolution A38-2: ICAO global planning for safety and air navigation', (38th ICAO Assembly 2013).

ICAO, 'Assembly Resolution A38-5: Regional cooperation and assistance to resolve safety deficiencies, establishing priorities and setting measurable targets', (38th ICAO Assembly, 2013).

ICAO, 'Assembly Resolution A38-7: Comprehensive Regional Implementation Plan for Aviation Safety in Africa', (38th ICAO Assembly, 2013).

ICAO, 'Assembly Resolution A38-11: Formulation and implementation of Standards and Recommended Practices (SARPs) and Procedures for Air Navigation Services (PANS) and notification of differences', (38th ICAO Assembly, 2013).

ICAO, 'Assembly Resolution A38-12: Consolidated Statement of continuing ICAO policies and associated practices related specifically to air navigation', (38th ICAO Assembly, 2013).

ICAO, 'Assemby Resolution A36-1: Comprehensive Regional Implementation Plan for Aviation Safety in Africa', (36th ICAO Assembly, 2007).

Conference Proceedings

'2013 EASA/FAA International Aviation Safety Conference', <http://easa.europa.eu/newsroom-and-events/events/easa-faa-international-aviation-safety-conference-2013> [Accessed 5 August 2014].

ACAC/ICAO, 'Seminar/Workshop on Regional Safety Oversight Programmes', (Rabat, Morocco, 2012).

AFCAC, 'AFI Cooperative Inspectorate Scheme (AFI-CIS)', in: Africa-Indian Ocean (AFI) Aviation Safety Symposium (Dakar: 2014).

United States of America, 'Improving international cooperation in certification and validation of products and parts', in: ICAO High Level Safety Conference (Montréal: 2010).

UAE General Civil Aviation Authority, 'Regional Accident Investigation Organization', in: ACAC/ICAO Seminar/Workshop on Regional Safety Oversight Programmes (Rabat, Morocco: 2012).

Banal, Francesco, former EASA Quality and Standardisation Director, 'EASA Standardisation', in: Aircraft Engineers International Conference (Belgrade 2006).

Belai, Haile, 'Air Transport Safety: Africa', in: Symposium on Regional Aviation Safety Agencies (Livingstone, Zambia: 2009).

Benjamin, Raymond, 'Closing remarks, Final Report of the Conference', in: ICAO High Level Safety Conference (Montreal: 2010).

'Canadian Revised Preliminary Draft of an International Air Convention', in: International Civil Aviation Conference (Chicago, USA: 1944).

CASSOA, 'Regional cooperation for the enhancement of safety oversight: obstacles and lessons learnt', in: ACAC/ICAO Seminar/Workshop on Regional Safety Oversight Programmes, (Rabat, Morocco, 2012).

Ceubah, Guelpina 'Autorités Africaines et Malgaches de l'Aviation Civile', in: Symposium on Regional Aviation Safety Agencies (Livingstone, Zambia: 2009).

Cheston, Mary, 'U.S. Perspective on Bilateral Safety Agreements: where we've been and where we're going', in: Europe/U.S. International Aviation Safety Conference.

Cormier, Len, 'Cooperative Arrangements Under ICAO Modalities - Safety', in: ICAO Symposium on Regional Safety Oversight Organizations (Montréal, Canada: 2011).

EASA, 'Aviation Safety Agreement between the United States and the European Community'2011) <www.faa.gov/aircraft/repair/media/EASA_US_roadshows.pdf,> [Accessed 5 August 2014].

EASA, 'The EASA system as an integral part of the EU (Aviation) legal system', in: EASA International Cooperation Forum Legal Workshop (Brussels, 12-14 October 2009).

'EC-ICAO Symposium on Regional Organisations', (Montréal, Canada: 2008).

Graham, Nancy, 'Briefing on the State of global aviation safety', in: ICAO High Level Safety Conference (Montréal, Canada: 2010).

IAC, 'The Role of a Regional International Civil Aviation Organization in Ensuring Flight Safety', in: Directors General of Civil Aviation Conference on Global Strategy for Aviation Safety (Montréal, Canada: 2006).

ICAO, 'COSCAPs in Five Regions ', in: World Bank/ICAO Air Transport Development Forum (Kuala Lumpur: 2008).

ICAO, 'Improving ICAO Transparency Policy: Sharing and Using Information in a Transparent, Consistent and Fair Manner', in: ICAO High Level Safety Conference (Montréal: 2010).

ICAO, 'Mutual Recognition', in: Directors General of Civil Aviation Conference on Global Strategy for Aviation Safety (Montréal, Canada: 2006).

ICAO, 'Recognition and validation of approvals and certificates issued by other States', in: ICAO High Level Safety Conference (Montréal: 2010).

ICAO, 'Symposium on Regional Safety Oversight Organisations' 2011) <http://www.icao.int/Meetings/RSOOSYMPO/Pages/default.aspx> [Accessed 6 August 2014.

ICAO/AFCAC/EASA, 'Symposium on regional civil aviation agencies', (Livingstone, Zambia: 2009).

Jallow, Mam Sait, 'Progress on key activities of the comprehensive regional implementation plan for aviation safety in africa (AFI PLAN)', in: AFI Ministerial briefing (Montréal: 2013).

Jennison, Michael, 'Is the RSOO a success story?', in: ICAO Symposium on Regional Safety Oversight Organisations (Montréal, Canada: 2011).

Konate, Gaoussou, 'Air Safety Situation in Africa, Current Problems: need for innovation', in: Symposium on Regional Aviation Safety Agencies (Livingstone, Zambia: 2009).

LACAC, 'Cost-effectiveness of the safety oversight cooperation system (SRVSOP)', ATConf/6-WP/58, (6th ICAO Worldwide Air Transport Conference, 2013).

LACAC, 'Recognition and validation of approvals and certifications within the Latin American safety oversight regional system', HLSC 2010-WP/65, (ICAO High Level Safety Conference, 2010).

'Main conclusions and follow-up to the Symposium', in: Symposium on Regional Aviation Safety Agencies (Livingstone, Zambia: 2009).

Ratajczyk, Mikołaj, 'Features and Evolution of Regional Safety Oversight Organisations: Comparative Analysis', in: ICAO Symposium on Regional Safety Oversight Organizations (Montréal: 2011).

Singapore, 'Recognition and validation of foreign AMO approvals', in: ICAO High Level Safety Conference (Montréal: 2010).

Tuala, Seiuli A.W., 'Establishment of a funding mechanism to ensure the sustainability of an RSOO', in: ICAO Symposium on Regional Safety Oversight Organizations (Montréal, Canada: 2011).

Tuala, Seiuli A.W., 'Regional cooperation for the enhancement of safety oversight', in: ICAO Symposium on Regional Safety Oversight Organizations (Montréal, Canada: 2011).

Wilson-Hunter, Cornelia, 'Remarks', in: ICAO Symposium on Regional Aviation Safety Organisations (2011).

EU and EASA Documents

European Network of Civil Aviation Safety Investigation Authorities (ENCASIA), '2014 Work Programme', (2014).

European Network of Civil Aviation Safety Investigation Authorities (ENCASIA), 'Annual Report', (2013).

Horváth & Partners Management Consultants on behalf of the EASA management board, 'Evaluation on the Implementation of EU Regulation 1592/2002: Final Report ', EASA evaluation prepared on the basis of Article 51 of Regulation (EC) 1592/2002, (2007).

Pricewaterhouse Coopers on behalf of the European Parliament's Committee on Budgets, 'The impact on the EU and national budgets of EU agencies: case studies, PricewaterhouseCoopers study prepared for the European Parliament's Committee on Budgets', (2012).

Ramboll-Euréval-Matrix on behalf of the European Commission, 'Evaluation of the EU decentralised agencies: Final Report - Volume III, Agency level findings', (2009).

EASA, '10th Anniversary Chronicle', (2013).

EASA, 'Annual General Reports for the years 2010-2013' <http://easa.europa.eu/newsroom-and-events/general-publications> [Accessed 28 July 2014].

EASA, 'Annual Safety Review', (2013).

EASA, 'Article 62 Panel Evalutation: final report', (2013).

EASA, 'Business Plan 2014-2018', EASA Management Board Decision Nr 12-2013, (2013).

EASA, 'General Principles Related to the Certification procedures to be applied by the Agency for the issuing of certificates for products, parts, and appliances (Product Certification Procedures) ', (Decision of the EASA Management Board No 07-2004, and amended by Decision No 12-2007).

EASA, 'Guidelines for the allocation of certification tasks to National Aviation Authorities and Qualified Entities', (Decision of the EASA Management Board No 01-2011).

EASA, 'Information Note: Agreement between the United States of America and the European Union on cooperation in the regulation of civil aviation safety' <http://easa.europa.eu/document-library/bilateral-agreements/eu-usa> [Accessed 5 August 2014].

EASA, 'Revised 4-year Rulemaking Programme 2014-2017', Annex I to EASA Executive Director's Decision No 2013/029/R, (2013).

EASA, 'Safety Assessment of Foreign Aircraft (EC SAFA Programme)' <http://easa.europa.eu/easa-and-you/aviation-domain/commercial-aviation/safety-assessment-foreign-aircraft-ec-safa-programme> [Accessed 5 August 2014].

EC, 'Commission Working Document: In view of the discussions within the Council on the creation of the European Aviation Safety Authority in the Community framework', COM (2000) 144 final, (Brussels, 2000).

EC, 'Communication from the Commission to the European Parliament and the Council: European Agencies: The Way Forward', COM (2008) 135 final.

EC, 'Communication from the Commission to the European Parliament, the Council, the European Economic and Social Committee and the Committee of the Regions: Accelerating the implementation of the Single European Sky', (COM (2013) 408 final, 2013).

EC, 'Communication from the Commission: Governance and incentive mechanisms for the deployment of SESAR, the Single European Sky's technological pillar', COM(2011) 923 final, (Brussels, 2011).

EC, 'Decentralised agencies: 2012 Overhaul (analitical fiches)' <http://europa.eu/agencies/documents/fiche_3_sent_to_ep_cons_2010-12-15_en.pdf> [Accessed 9 January 2014].

EC, 'Draft Interinstitutional Agreement on the operating framework for the European regulatory agencies', COM (2005) 59 final.

EC, 'The EC SAFA Programme: Past, Present and Future' <http://ec.europa.eu/transport/modes/air/safety/doc/2009_12_04_info_fiche_safa_programme.pdf> [Accessed 5 August 2014].

EC, 'The EU's External Aviation Policy: Addressing Future Challenges, Communication from the Commission to the European Parliament, the Council, the European

Economic and Social Committee and the Committee of the Regions', COM(2012) 556, (Brussels, 2012).

EC, 'European Governance: A White Paper', (COM (2001) 428 final).

EC, 'European Union SAFA Program', COM (2012) 91 final.

EC, 'Impact Assessment accompanying the proposal of the European Commission for a Regulation of the European Parliament and of the Council on investigation and prevention of accidents and incidents in civil aviation', COM(2009) 611 final, (Brussels, 2009).

EC, 'Information Note: Handling of notifications in the context of the flexibility provisions under Articles 14(1), 14(4) and 14(6) of EU Regulation No 216/2008', (meeting of the EASA committee No 3/2013).

EC, 'A new response to a changing Neighbourhood: Joint Communication by the High Representative of The Union For Foreign Affairs And Security Policy and the European Commission', COM (2011) 303, (Brussels, 2011).

EC, 'Participation of European third countries in the work of the European Aviation Safety Agency, Commission Staff Working Paper', SEC(2002) 1090, (Brussels, 2002).

EC, 'Roadmap for a policy initiative on aviation safety and a possible revision of Regulation (EC) No 216/2008 on common rules in the field of civil aviation and establishing a European Aviation Safety Agency', (2014).

EC, 'Template for EU Member States démarche to ICAO on the transfer of regulatory tasks to EASA', (EU Council archives, Brussels, 14 November 2003).

EU, 'European Organisation Responsible for Civil Aviation Safety: Report on the Work of the Expert Group on Legal Issues', Working Party on Aviation of 19 February 1998, Working Document AER/98/17, (EU Council archives, Brussels, 1998).

EU, 'Joint Statement of the European Parliament, the Council of the EU and the European Commission on decentralised agencies', (2012), <http://ec.europa.eu/commission_2010-2014/sefcovic/documents/120719_agencies_joint_statement_en.pdf> [accessed 9 January 2014].

EU, 'Recommandation de décision du Conseil autorisant la Commission à engage des négociations en vue de la création d'une organisation européenne pour la sécurité de l'aviation civile', SEC(96) 2152 final, (EU Council archives, Brussels, 1996).

Kinnock, Neil, Member of the European Commission responsible for Transport, 'Meeting the global challenge: the outlook for civil aviation in the EU', SPEECH/98/1, (Forum Europe, Brussels, 1998).

'Report of the High Level Group for the Future European Aviation Regulatory Framework: A framework for driving performance improvement', (2007).

Verhaugen, Günter, Vice-President of the European Commission responsible for Enterprise and Industry, 'The role of the Aviation Safety Agency from an industry point of view', SPEECH/04/536, (Speech at the occasion of the inauguration of EASA in Cologne, 2004).

ICAO Documents

AFCAC, 'Establishment of Regional Safety Oversight Organizations in Africa', A37-WP/166, (37th ICAO Assembly, 2010).

AFCAC, 'Progress report on the implementation of AFI Cooperative Inspectorate Scheme (AFI-CIS)', A38-WP/214, (38th ICAO Assembly, 2013).

Akatue, Emmanuel 'Institutionalization of the Banjul Accord Group Safety Oversight Organization', RASG-AFI/1 - IP/7, (First meeting of the Africa - Indian Ocean Regional Aviation Safety Group, RASG-AFI/1, 2012).

BAGASOO, 'Framework of the Banjul Accord Group Aviation Safety Oversight Organization (BAGASOO) and The Banjul Accord Group Accident Investigation Agency (BAGAIA)', C-WP/13396, (187th session of the ICAO Council, 2009).

Brazil, on behalf of the Member States of the Latin American Civil Aviation Commission, 'The role of regional cooperation in Latin America', A38-WP/231, (38th ICAO Assembly, 2013).

CASSOA, 'Safety Initiatives and Regional Organizations in the AFI Region', RASG-AFI/1 - IP/8, (First meeting of the Africa Indian Ocean Regional Aviation Safety Group, 2012).

CASSOS, 'Caribbean Aviation Safety and Security Oversight System (CASSOS) - Report of activities and progress since the 37th General Assembly', A38-WP/328, (38th ICAO Assembly, 2013).

IAC, 'Regional Organizations in Accident and Incident Investigations', AIG/08-WP/22, (ICAO Accident Investigation and Prevention (AIG) Divisional Meeting, 2008).

ICAO, 'Annual Report to Council on Regional Offices' activities during 2012 and Work Programmes for 2013', C-WP/13919, (2013).

ICAO, 'Annual Reports of the Council (2009-2013)'.

ICAO, 'Comprehensive Regional Implementation Plan for Aviation Safety in Africa, 12th meeting of the steering committee: report', AFI SC/2013/12, (2013).

ICAO, 'Cooperation with Regional Organizations and Regional Civil Aviation Bodies', C-WP/13885, (197th session of the ICAO Council, 2012).

ICAO, 'Cooperation with Regional Organizations and Regional Civil Aviation Bodies', A38-WP/9, (38th ICAO Assembly, 2013).

ICAO, 'Cooperation with Regional Organizations and Regional Civil Aviation Bodies', A37-WP/28, (37th ICAO Assembly, 2010).

ICAO, 'Directives to Regional Air Navigation Meetings and Rules of Procedure for their Conduct', ICAO Doc. 8144-AN/874, (1991).

ICAO, 'Encouraging the improvement of safety oversight in States with significant safety concerns (SSCs): Summary of decisions', C-DEC 195/6, (195th session of the ICAO Council, 2012).

ICAO, 'Evolution of the ICAO Universal Safety Oversight Audit Programme (USOAP) beyond 2010', C-WP/13356, (187th session of the ICAO Council).

ICAO, 'Final Report on the ICAO Coordinated Validation Mission in the Organization of Eastern Caribbean States', (2013).

ICAO, 'Final Report on the safety oversight audit of the civil aviation system of the European Aviation Safety Agency', (2008).

ICAO, 'Final Report on the safety oversight audit of the civil aviation system of the Federal Republic of Germany', (2005), <http://cfapp.icao.int/fsix/AuditReps/CSAfinal/Germany_CSA_%20Final_Report.pdf> [accessed 21 July 2014].

ICAO, 'Final report on the safety oversight audit of the civil aviation system of the Kingdom of Norway', (2006).

ICAO, 'Final report on the safety oversight audit of the civil aviation system of the Organization of Eastern Caribbean States (Antigua and Barbuda; Grenada; St. Kitts and Nevis; Saint Lucia; and Saint Vincent and the Grenadines)', (2007).

ICAO, 'Final review of proposed amendment to Annex 13 relating to independence of accident and incident investigations', AN-WP/8803, (Air Navigation Commission, 2013).

ICAO, 'Formulation and implementation of Standards and Recommended Practices (SARPS) and Procedures for Air Navigation Services (PANS) and notification of differences', A38-WP/48, (38th ICAO Assembly, 2013).

ICAO, 'Global Aviation Safety Plan', Doc. 10004, (2013).

ICAO, 'Guidance on the Implementation of Article 83 bis of the Convention on International Civil Aviation', Circular 295, (2003).

ICAO, 'ICAO plans of action for States under the review of the MARB', AFI Plan-SC/2013/11-DP/02, (11th AFI Plan Steering Committee, 2013).

ICAO, 'Infractions of the Convention on International Civil Aviation', C-WP/11186, (185th session of the ICAO Council, 1999).

ICAO, 'Known Issues and Difficulties', in: 1st Meeting of Filing of Differences Task Force (Montreal, Canada: 2011).

ICAO, 'Manual of Procedures for Operations Inspection, Certification and Continued Surveillance', Doc. 8335, (2010).

ICAO, 'Manual on Regional Accident and Incident Investigation Organization', Doc. 9946, (2011).

ICAO, 'Notification and publication of differences: Report to Council by the President of the Air Navigation Commission', C-WP/12412, (177th session of the ICAO Council, 2006).

ICAO, 'Notification and publication of differences: Summary of Decisions', C-DEC 177/14, (177th session of the ICAO Council, 2006).

ICAO, 'Outcomes of the Symposium on Regional Safety Oversight Organisations', Oral report by the ICAO Secretary General, (194th session of the ICAO Council, 2011).

ICAO, 'Outlook for Air Transport to the Year 2025', Circular 313, AT/134, (2007).

ICAO, 'Policy and Guidance Material on the Economic Regulation of International Air Transport', ICAO Doc. 9587, (2008).

ICAO, 'Policy and Principles on the Use of the Electronic Filing of Differences (EFOD) System', C-WP/13803, (195th session of the ICAO Council, 2012).

ICAO, 'Progress in Africa – report on the Comprehensive Regional Implementation Plan for Aviation Safety in Africa (AFI PLAN)', A38-WP/67, (38th ICAO Assembly, 2013).

ICAO, 'Progress Report on Comprehensive Study on Known Issues in Respect of the Notification and Publication of Differences', C-WP/13954, (198th session of the ICAO Council, 2013).

ICAO, 'Progress report on the implementation of the electronic filing of differences (EFOD) system ', C-WP/13803, (195th session of the ICAO Council, 2012).

ICAO, 'Proposed Terms of Reference of the Secretariat/Council Group on Regional Bodies: Summary of Decisions', C-DEC 186/2, (186th session of the ICAO Council, 2009).

ICAO, 'Regional Performance Dashboards' <http://www.icao.int/safety/Pages/Regional-Targets.aspx> [Accessed 4 August 2014].

ICAO, 'Relationship of ICAO with regional civil aviation bodies', A21-WP/35, (21st ICAO Assembly, 1974).

ICAO, 'Report of ANC — Establishment of Regional Aviation Safety Groups (RASGs): Summary of Decisions', C-Dec 190/4, (190th session of the ICAO Council 2010).

ICAO, 'Report of ARRB - Report of the Audit Results Review Board (ARRB): Summary of Decisions', C-DEC 191/2, (191st session of the ICAO Council, 2010).

ICAO, 'Report of the Secretariat/Council Group on Regional Bodies', C-WP/13404, (188th session of the ICAO Council, 2009).

ICAO, 'Report of the Secretariat/Council Group on Regional Bodies: Summary of Decisions', C-Dec 188/3, (2009).

ICAO, 'Resolution on Nationality and Registration of Aircraft Operated by International Operating Agencies', (Reproduced in ICAO Doc. 9587 'Policy and Guidance Material on the Economic Regulation of International Air Transport').

ICAO, 'Review of the outcomes of the Symposium on Regional Safety Oversight Organizations', C-WP/13810, (195th session of the ICAO Council, 2011).

ICAO, 'RSOOs and COSCAPs' (2014), <http://www.icao.int/safety/Implementation/Lists/COSCAP_RSOO/AllItems.aspx> [Accessed 14 March 2014].

ICAO, 'Safety Audit Information' <http://www.icao.int/safety/Pages/USOAP-Results.aspx> [Accessed 14 March 2014].

ICAO, 'Safety Management Manual ', Doc. 9859, (2013).

ICAO, 'Safety Oversight Manual, Part A: The Establishment and Management of a State's Safety Oversight System', Doc. 9734, Part A, (2006).

ICAO, 'Safety Oversight Manual, Part B: The Establishment and Management of a Regional Safety Oversight Organization', Doc. 9734, (2011).

ICAO, 'Safety Report', (2014).

ICAO, 'Second meeting of the Regional Aviation Safety Group for Africa and the Indian Ocean region (RASG-AFI/2):Update on the AFI Plan and Other Safety Initiatives', RASG-AFI/2 - WP/13, (2013).

ICAO, 'Significant Safety Concerns (SSCs) - A mechanism for the sharing of SSCs with the public: Summary of decisions', C-DEC 197/4, (197th session of the ICAO Council, 2012).

ICAO, 'State letter concerning the adoption of Amendment 16 to Annex 6, Part III, Attachement D: Note on the notification of differences', AN 11/32.3.8-11/46, (2011).

ICAO, 'State of Global Aviation Safety', (2013).

ICAO, 'Universal Safety Oversight Audit Programme - Continuous Monitoring Approach (USOAP CMA)', A38-WP/50, (38th ICAO Assembly, 2013).

ICAO, 'Universal Safety Oversight Audit Programme Continuous Monitoring Manual', Doc. 9735, (2011).

El Salvador, 'Establishment of a central american accident and incident investigation organization', A38-WP/232, (38th ICAO Assembly, 2013).

OTHER SOURCES

The Aviation & Allied Business Journal (12.10.2012), 'BAGASOO: Future Regional Safety Pivot', Interview with Mr Emmanuel Akatue, Executive Director of the BAGASOO' <http://www.aviationbusinessjournal.aero/2012/10/12/bagasoo-future-regional-safety-pivot.aspx> [Accessed 23 July 2014].

AFCAC, 'Report on progress made in the areas of Safety, Security, Implementation of Yamoussoukro Decision and Environment: Progress Report on the Implementation of AFI-CIS', WP/3, (22nd AFCAC Plenary Session, 2013).

Allianz, 'Safety and Shipping 1912-2012: From Titanic to Costa Concordia', (2012).

BAGASOO, 'Revised Brochure' <http://www.bagasoo.org/en/images/docs/downloads/bagasoo_brochure_revised.pdf> [Accessed 10 August 2014].

Asian Development Bank, 'Institutional Strengthening for Aviation Regulation' <http://www.adb.org/projects/43429-012/details> [Accessed 10 August 2014].

World Bank, 'Pacific Aviation Safety Office Reform Project', Report No: PAD532, (2013).

World Bank, 'Pacific Aviation Safety Office Reform, project No. P145057' <http://www.worldbank.org/projects/P145057/pacific-aviation-investment-program?lang=en> [Accessed 14 August 2014].

CANSO, 'Guide to Separation of Service Provision and Regulation', (2011).

CASSOA, 'Revised Strategic Plan 2010/11–2014/15', <http://www.cassoa.org/index.php/key-documents/strategic-plan> [accessed 10 August 2014].

CEMAC, 'Reunion des ministres des transports des etats membres de la cemac et sao tome et principe - communique final' <http://www.cemac.int/communique-presse/reunion-des-ministres-des-transports-des-etats-membres-de-la-cemac-et-sao-tome-et> [Accessed 7 August 2014].

CEPS, 'Upgrading the EU's role as Global Actor: Institutions, Law and the Restructuring of European Diplomacy', (2011).

COSCAP-SA, 'Model bilateral agreement between COSCAP South Asia and States for obtaining Services of Technical Experts from COSCAP South Asia to perform Safety Oversight functions'2009) <http://www.coscapsa.org/Manuals/ifapmanual.pdf> [Accessed 6 August 2014].

ECAC, 'Code of Conduct on co-operation in the field of civil aviation accident/incident investigation' <https://www.ecac-ceac.org//publications_events_news/ecac_documents/codes_of_conduct> [Accessed 7 August 2014].

ECAC, 'Report on 'JAA activities'', DGCA/86, (ECAC archives, Paris, 1992).

ECAC, 'Report on JAA activities, presented by the Chairman of JAA Committee', (ECAC DGCA/16, ECAC archives in Paris, 1994).

ECAC, 'Roadmap for JAA', (2005).

EUROCONTROL, 'Challenges of Growth 2013: Task 4: European Air Traffic in 2013', (2013).

EUROCONTROL, 'Who we are' <https://www.eurocontrol.int/articles/who-we-are> [accessed 3 March 2014].

FAA, 'Bilateral agreements: purpose' <http://www.faa.gov/aircraft/air_cert/international/bilateral_agreements/purpose/> [Accessed 5 August 2014].

FAA, 'Generic Steps for Obtaining a Bilateral Aviation Safety Agreement' <http://www.faa.gov/aircraft/air_cert/international/bilateral_agreements/media/BASAProcess.pdf> [Accessed 5 August 2014].

GAO, US, 'FAA Needs to Strengthen the Management of Its Designee Programs', GAO-05-40, (2004).

Aviation Working Group, 'Economic impact assessment and select recommendations: dissimilar technical regulatory requirements impacting cross border transfer of aircraft', (2011), p. 2.

ICAO, 'Cooperative Development of Operational Safety and Continuing Airworthiness Programme - South Asia (COSCAP-SA) Phase III' <http://www.coscapsa.org/maindocuments.php> [Accessed 6 August 2014].

NLR Air Transport Safety Institute, 'Safety Oversight Comparative Analysis Study', NLR-CR-2009-260, (2010).

Radio New Zealand International, 'Pacific Aviation Safety Office in financial strife' <http://www.radionz.co.nz/international/pacific-news/205665/pacific-aviation-safety-office-in-financial-strife> [Accessed 22 March 2014].

JAA, 'FUJA II Working Group: Final Report (2008)' <www.jaa.nl/fuja/fuja_report.html> [Accessed 28 March 2014].

Murray, Kimball, Bartsch, Ron, and Foon, Max, 'Legal and Technical Review Report for the Pacific Aviation Safety Office', (AvLaw Aviation Consultants, 2007).

Murray, Kim, and Murray, Michael, 'Technical Assistance Consultant's Report, Regional: Institutional Strengthening for Aviation Regulation', Asian Development Bank, Project No 43429, (2014), www.adb.org/projects/documents/institutional-strengthening-aviation-regulation-tacr [accessed 14 October 2014].

OECS, 'Eastern Caribbean Civil Aviation Authority' <http://www.oecs.org/about-the-oecs/institutions/eastern-caribbean-civil-aviation-authority-eccaa> [Accessed 8 August 2014].

PASO, 'Regional approach to aviation through harmonised regulatory application in the south west pacific', Working Paper WP/23, (First Meeting of the Regional Aviation Safety Group - Asia and Pacific Regions - RASG-APAC/1, 2011).

Congressional Research Service, 'International Law and Agreements: Their Effect Upon U.S. Law', RL32528, (2010).

van Dam, Cees C., 'Aansprakelijkheid van Toezichthouders, Een analyse van de aansprakelijkheidsrisico's voor toezichthouders wegens inadequaat handhavingstoezicht en enige aanbevelingen voor toekomstig beleid', (British Institute of International and Comparative Law, 2006), <http://www.wodc.nl/images/1189-deel2-volledige-tekst_tcm44-59298.pdf> [accessed 7 August 2014].

Index

J

V

W

AVIATION LAW AND POLICY SERIES

1. Erwin von den Steinen, *National Interest and International Aviation* (ISBN 90-411-2455-1).
2. Ludwig Weber, *International Civil Aviation Organisation: An Introduction* (ISBN 978-90-411-2622-1).
3. Niels van Antwerpen, *Cross-Border Provision of Air Navigation Services with Specific Reference to Europe: Safeguarding Transparent Lines of Responsibility and Liability* (ISBN 978-90-411-2688-7).
4. Brian F. Havel, *Beyond Open Skies: A New Regime for International Aviation* (ISBN 978-90-411-2389-3).
5. Jiefang Huang, *Aviation Safety through the Rule of Law: ICAO's Mechanisms and Practices* (ISBN 978-90-411-3115-7).
6. Marian Hoeks, *Multimodal Transport Law: The Law Applicable to the Multimodal Contract for the Carriage of Goods* (ISBN 978-90-411-3246-8).
7. George N. Tompkins, Jr., *Liability Rules Applicable to International Air Transportation as Developed by the Courts in the United States: From Warsaw 1929 to Montreal 1999* (ISBN 978-90-411-2646-7).
8. Daniel Calleja Crespo and Pablo Mendes de Leon (eds), *Achieving the Single European Sky: Goals and Challenges* (ISBN 978-90-411-3730-2).
9. Donal Patrick Hanley, *Aircraft Operating Leasing: A Legal and Practical Analysis in the Context of Public and Private International Air Law* (ISBN 978-90-411-4045-6).
10. Mikołaj Ratajczyk, *Regional Aviation Safety Organisations: Enhancing Air Transport Safety through Regional Cooperation* (ISBN 978-90-411-5861-1).